T0389281

Partition of India

The Partition of British India in 1947 set in motion events that have had far-reaching consequences in South Asia – wars, military tensions, secessionist movements and militancy/terrorism. This book looks at key events in 1947 and explores the aftermath of the Partition and its continued impact in the present-day understanding of nationhood and identity. It also examines the diverse and fractured narratives that framed popular memory and understanding of history in the region.

The volume includes discussions on the manner in which regions such as the Punjab, Sindh, Kashmir, Bengal, Uttar Pradesh (Lucknow) and North-East India were influenced. It deals with issues such as communal politics, class conflict, religion, peasant nationalism, decolonization, migration, displacement, riots, the state of refugees, women and minorities, as well as the political relationship between India, Pakistan and Bangladesh.

Drawing on major flashpoints in contemporary South Asian history along with representations from literature, art and popular culture, this book will interest scholars of modern Indian history, Partition studies, colonial history, postcolonial studies, international relations, politics, sociology, literature and South Asian studies.

Amit Ranjan is Visiting Research Fellow at the Institute of South Asia Studies (ISAS), National University of Singapore (NUS), Singapore.

Partition of India

Postcolonial Legacies

Edited by Amit Ranjan

LONDON AND NEW YORK

First published 2019
by Routledge
2 Park Square, Milton Park, Abingdon, Oxon OX14 4RN

and by Routledge
52 Vanderbilt Avenue, New York, NY 10017

Routledge is an imprint of the Taylor & Francis Group, an informa business

British Library Cataloguing-in-Publication Data
A catalogue record for this book is available from the British Library

Library of Congress Cataloging-in-Publication Data
A catalog record for this book has been requested

ISBN: 978-1-138-08003-4 (hbk)
ISBN: 978-0-429-42295-9 (ebk)

Typeset in Sabon
by Apex CoVantage, LLC

Contents

Illustrations

Figures

Tables

Contributors

Ishtiaq Ahmed is Professor Emeritus of Political Science at Stockholm University and Visiting Professor at Government College University, Lahore, Pakistan. His publications include *The Punjab Bloodied, Partitioned and Cleansed: Unravelling the 1947 Tragedy through Secret British Reports and First-Person Accounts* (2011), *Karachi* (2012) and *Pakistan: The Garrison State, Origins, Evolution, Consequences (1947–2011)* (2013). His research interests are political Islam, ethnicity and nationalism, human, minority and group rights and Partition studies.

Nizam Rahim Baloch is a researcher and writer. He has worked with Free Press Unlimited's project for Makran region. His articles on politics, governance, culture and the Balochistan issue are published in *PakVoices* and *Balochistan Voices*. The latter is the leading online newspaper of Balochistan. He belongs to the Panjgur District, a western district of the Balochistan province of Pakistan. He received his Master's in Political Science from Government College University, Lahore and his M.Phil in Political Science from the University of the Punjab, Lahore.

Rituparna Bhattacharyya is Editor-in-Chief of the open access journal *Space and Culture, India*, and a volunteer at the UK registered charity Alliance for Community Capacity Building in North East India.

Nandita Bhavnani is the author of *Sindhnamah* (2018), *The Making of Exile: Sindhi Hindus and the partition of India* (2014) and *I Will & I Can: The Story of Jai Hind College* (2011). She has been engaged in extensive research on Sindhi history and culture since 1997, and is based in Mumbai, India.

Pallavi Deka teaches political science at Handique Girls' College, Assam, India. Her research interests include human migration, ethnicity, North East India and South Asia.

Binayak Dutta is a faculty member in the Department of History, North Eastern Hill University, India. His publications include *Religion in Politics: Eastern India (1905–1947)* (2009) and *The History of Judiciary in Assam* (co-authored with Bhupen Sarmah, 2013). His research interests include the partition of India and Assam, immigration and law-making in Assam and other related themes of legal and historical interest.

Subhasri Ghosh is Assistant Professor of History at Asutosh College, West Bengal, India. She has published widely in various journals.

Taj Hashmi is a Fellow of the Royal Asiatic Society, London, UK. He is a retired professor of history, Asian studies, and security studies. He has taught at various universities in Australia, Bangladesh, Canada, Singapore, and the United States of America. His publications include *Global Jihad and America: The Hundred-Year War beyond Iraq and Afghanistan* (2014), *Women and Islam in Bangladesh: Beyond Subjection and Tyranny* (2000), *Islam, Muslims and the Modern State* (co-edited with Hussin Mutalib, 1994), *Pakistan as a Peasant Utopia: The Communalization of Class Politics in East Bengal, 1920–1947* (1992) and *Colonial Bengal* (1985).

Mehru Jaffer is a journalist and author based in Lucknow, India. She is the author of *The Book of Muhammad* (2013), *The Book of Muinuddin Chisti* (2006) and *The Book of Nizamuddin Aulia* (2012).

Altaf Khan was a senior Visiting Fulbright faculty (post doctorate) at the Centre for International Studies, Ohio University, USA in 2008–09. He was a Glidden Visiting Professor in Spring 2018 at the Centre for International Journalism, Scripps School of Journalism, Ohio University, USA. He has taught at the Department of Journalism and Mass Communication at University of Peshawar from 1990 to 2018. At present he is a professor at Formen Christian College University, Lahore. His books include *Indo-Pak Press; An Unpopular View* (1998), *News Media and Journalism in Pakistan* (2003), and *Reporting the*

Frontier: Media and Media Capacity Building in North Western Pakistan (2011).

Kalathmika Natarajan is a PhD Fellow at the University of Copenhagen, Denmark. Her doctoral work explores the postcolonial India-Britain diplomatic relationship (1947–1962) as a negotiation of entangled identities, multiple claims to citizenship and racialised limits to mobility shaped by Empire.

Sajad Padder teaches in the Department of Political Science at the University of Kashmir, India.

Punam Pandey is a PhD graduate from the University of Delhi (DU). Before joining the University of Free State, she was an Assistant Professor at DU. Punam is a Research Associate with the Institute for Reconciliation and Social Justice (IRSJ), University of the Free State, Bloemfontein, South Africa. Her book, *India Bangladesh Domestic Politics: The Ganges River Issue* was published in 2016. She broadly works on issues of South Asia with a special focus on India and Bangladesh. She has written extensively on water politics from the perspective of international relations. Some of her publications can be accessed in refereed journals such as *Asian Survey*, *India Quarterly: A Journal of International Affairs* and *South Asian Survey* among others. Her current research project at the IRSJ is on the issues of memory contestation where she researches the Liberation movement in the competitive politics of Bangladesh.

Roshni Sharma is an assistant professor at BMS College of Law, Bengaluru. Prior to this, she worked as an assistant professor at Ramaiah College of Law, Bengaluru. Her chapter in this volume is a part of her M.Phil. Dissertation on Partition Literature and Refugee Woman submitted to University of Delhi. Currently, she is pursuing her doctoral degree from Jain University, Bengaluru. She has been awarded a gold medal from Panjab University, Chandigarh, for ranking first in the Master's degree in Political Science. Her research interests include women issues especially in understanding the way literature is written by and on women. Her previous work includes 'Image of Refugee Women in Post Partition Literature' in *Arts and Education International Academic Journal.*

Farhan Hanif Siddiqi is an associate professor in the School of Politics and International Relations at the Quaid-i-Azam University,

Islamabad, Pakistan. He is the author of *The Politics of Ethnicity in Pakistan: The Baloch, Sindhi and Mohajir Ethnic Movements* (2012). His research has appeared in various journals, including *African and Asian Studies*, *Nationalities Papers*, *Asian Ethnicity* and *Asian Affairs: An American Review*. His research interests include nationalism and ethnicity, theories of international relations, conflict resolution and security dynamics in South Asia and the Middle East.

Farooq Sulehria is an assistant professor at Beaconhouse National University (BNU) Lahore. Earlier, he was Senior Teaching Fellow at SOAS University of London. He is author of *Media Imperialism in India and Pakistan* (Routledge).

Preface

The spectre of the Partition of British India in 1947 still haunts and influences political relationships between India, Pakistan and Bangladesh; Partition and debates around it have also knitted some forms of relationships among the different groups and between the individuals living across or within the sovereign borders of the respective countries. It was this thinking which has taken the shape of an edited book. This idea germinated in my mind during the winter of 2016 at New Delhi. To get a second opinion, I sent a message expressing my desire to have an edited book on the theme to Farooq Sulehria, Prakash Kumar Ray and Kumar Dhananjay, and subsequently to Professor Ishtiaq Ahmed. All of them agreed it was a good idea and have since then extended their support for this book in various ways. Afterwards I started writing emails to many prospective contributors and shared my views with them. I am grateful to all the contributors who supported this project and never let me feel that I could not edit a book on such a complicated issue. Their support helped me to move ahead with this project without fear of being wrong. I am thankful to Shoma Choudhury of Routledge, India, for her faith in me. The editor also acknowledges the editor of *South Asia: Journal of South Asian Studies* and the publisher, Routledge, for granting permission to re-publish Nandita Bhavnani's paper 'Unwanted Refugees: Sindhi Hindus in India and Muhajirs in Sindh' in this edited book.

Amit Ranjan
Singapore, 2018

Abbreviations

AFSPA	Armed Forces Special Powers Act
AIDCL	All India Depressed Class League
AIML	All India Muslim League
BAKSAL	Bangladesh Krishak Sramik Awami League
CBMs	Confidence Building Measures
CPEC	China Pakistan Economic Corridor
CPI	Communist Party of India
DMK	Dravida Munnetra Kazhagam
GB	Gilgit-Baltistan
HeI	Hefazat-e-Islam
ICT	International Crime Tribunal
INA	Indian National Army
INC	Indian National Congress
JI	Jamaat-e-Islami
JKLF	Jammu & Kashmir Liberation Front
JKSLF	Jammu & Kashmir Student Liberation Front
KP	Khyber Pakhtunkhwa
KPP	Krishak Proja Party
LEP	Look East Policy
LoC	Line of Control
MC	Muslim Conference
MHS	Mutually Hurting Stalemate
NAP	National Awami Party
NC	National Conference
NEFA	North East Frontier Agency
NNC	Naga National Council
NSCN	National Socialist Council of Nagaland
NWFP	North West Frontier Province

PPP	Pakistan People's Party
RSS	Rashtriya Swamsevak Sangh
SCF	Scheduled Castes Federation
UN	United Nations
UP	United Province/Uttar Pradesh

Glossary

Abba Father
Ashraf Upper class Muslims
Bangal Inhabitants from East Bengal (Bangladesh)
Bhadraloke Upper class and upper caste Hindu professional class from Bengal
Bharat Mata Mother India
Bobo Grandmother
Chai Tea
Dar-ul-Awam Lower House of People
Dar-ul-Uma Upper House of Legislature
Hari Landless peasants
Islamiat Islamic religious studies
Janab Mister
Jagir Property
Jotedar Wealthy peasants
Mahajan Moneylender
Muhajirs Muslim refugees who migrated from India to Pakistan
Pani Water
Salam Salute
Shahi Jirga Highest Council of Tribal people
Shuddist Purification
Srihatta Old name of Sylhet; presently in Bangladesh
Tebhaga One-third
Ulema Muslim clerics
Ummah Muslim community
Zamindari Landlordism

Introduction

Even after seventy-one years, the partition of India in 1947 influences the relationships between the South Asian nuclear neighbours – India and Pakistan – and greatly influences the social behaviour between majority and minority community members against each other's respective countries. Bangladesh was also a part of British India in 1947. In 1947, East Bengal separated from West Bengal in the name of religion and became a part of Pakistan. Soon after the birth of Pakistan, Bengalis from the East Pakistan realised that religion is not the *only* force which can bind people together. An individual wears multiple identities and religion is one of them. As early as in 1948, the demand for recognising Bengali too as a national language of Pakistan started in East Pakistan. The Bengali speaking population of the country was furious over what it saw as imposing Urdu on them. In 1952 during one of the protest marches a few protestors were killed. Later, in 1955 Bengali was recognised as a national language of Pakistan. However, many other differences between the Bengali and non-Bengali population remained. All such eventually led to the liberation of East Pakistan in 1971. The immediate cause for the liberation of Bangladesh was the denial of an opportunity for the leader of Awami League (AL), Sheikh Mujibur Rahman, to become the prime minister of Pakistan even though his party had won the majority number of seats in the parliamentary elections of 1970. Hence the myth of having a religion-based state shattered in 1971. However, religion remains a crucial factor. Even today, it is the basis of differences and discrimination, as well as cause for communal violence, in India, Pakistan and Bangladesh.

In the seventy-one years of partition, India and Pakistan have fought three full wars (1947–1948, 1965 and 1971), engaged in one limited war in the Kargil sector in 1999, been at the brink of war three times (1987, 2002 and 2008), and spent most of the rest of the time in tension. A glimpse of their day-to-day relationship can be viewed during the flag retreat ceremony at Wagah, a town straddling the border between India (Punjab) and Pakistan (Punjab). This ceremony at Wagah started in 1959. Describing the ceremony at Wagah, Jisha Menon in *The Performance of Nationalism: India, Pakistan, and the Memory of Partition* writes that the 'border ceremonies inadvertently reflect popular Partition discourse that casts the event as an image of twins, violently separated at birth by the nation's founding fathers.'[1] It also reflects the jingoism of each evening's attempt by both sides to prove superiority over the other. This is said to be a 'normal' situation between India and Pakistan. Unlike its relationship with Pakistan, India's relationship with Bangladesh is cordial because of India's assistance in its liberation in 1971.

Beyond the border, the Partition's impact is, to an extent, palpable in the inter-community relationships, mainly between Hindu and Muslims in India, Pakistan and Bangladesh. Unlike, Pakistan, the Indian constituent assembly formulated a secular constitution for India where all forms of differences and discriminations based on groups or individuals are not accepted. Constitutionally, in secular India, the State maintains a 'principled distance'[2] from the religion. Hence, some members from the minority communities have occupied the highest office of the land, and many from those communities have held important positions in State institutions. By contrast, soon after its birth, Pakistan turned into an Islamic State, where minorities have not been able to share political rights and status on an equal footing with the Muslim majority. Articles 41(2) and 91(3) of Pakistan's Constitution, for example, reserve the offices of the president and prime minister only for Muslims,[3] although there are no such constitutional restrictions and prohibitions on the members of non-Muslim communities occupying other public offices. Originally, in 1972, Bangladesh adopted secular principles in its constitution. However, after the assassination of Sheikh Mujibur Rahman in 1975, the political situation in the country changed. In a quick succession, Khondaker Mostaq Ahmad (15 August 1975–6 November 1975) was appointed as the president of the country. He was succeeded by Justice Abu Sadat Mohammad Sayam (November 1975–April 1977). In April 1977, General Ziaur Rahman (1977–1981) became the head of the state. During his term in power, General Rahman faced three coup attempts and several rebellions organised by both political right and centre-left forces.[4] To overcome their challenges, General Rahman attempted to appease the religious groups. He enacted the Political Party Regulation Act to clear the way for Bangladesh Jamat-e-Islami and other like-minded groups to participate in the political activities of the country. To facilitate the agenda, a series of amendments were made in the Constitution to change the nature of the Bangladeshi state. The word 'secularism' was deleted from the Preamble and Article 8 of the Constitution. A sentence, 'absolute trust and faith in the Almighty Allah' should be 'the basis of all actions,' was inserted through the Second Proclamation Order Number 1 in 1977. The words 'Bismillah-ar-Rahman-ar-Rahim' (in the name of Allah, the Beneficent, the Merciful) were also inserted above the Preamble to the Constitution.[5]

In the 1980s, General HM Earshad's government introduced Islamiat (Islamic religious studies) in the constitution as a mandatory subject for students from grades three to ten. In 2010, the Supreme Court of Bangladesh reinstated the principle of secularism. However, confusion persists after the 15th amendment to the constitution was passed in 2015 which reincorporated and restored secularism in Bangladesh's constitution without disturbing the words 'Bismillah-ar-Rahman-ar-Rahim' above the Preamble.

Different from the constitution, a large section of the Indian society could not embrace the secular spirit and retained colonial debates about conversion, cow slaughter and music before mosques which still dominate social discourse. Communal tensions on such issues have been highlighted frequently by the Indian and foreign media, notably, since 2014, when the Hindu right wing political party Bhartiya Janta Party (BJP)-led National Democratic Alliance (NDA) under Narendra Modi formed the union government. Prior to becoming prime minister, Modi was the chief minister of the Indian state of Gujarat. Under his rule in 2002, the state witnessed serious communal riots in which a large number of innocents lost their lives. Allegations were brought against those who headed important public institutions for the systematic and planned execution of the riots.[6] It was not a new format of communal riots – in the past, similar patterns had been followed by the members of other political groups, for example, in the anti-Sikh riots of 1984.[7]

With Modi at the helm, some of the self-proclaimed saviours of the Hindutva have made an attempt to transform themselves from a fringe group into main advocates of the Hinduism. Lynching or violence used to take place in the name of cow protection, even before 2014.[8] However, such violence was less frequent than what has transpired since Modi took over as the prime minister of India. The first case in recent years was the lynching of Mohammad Aklakh in his village Dadri in Uttar Pradesh in 2015 by a mob due to the mere suspicion that his family possessed and consumed beef.[9] Since then, other such cases have come to light, despite Modi's (repeated) warnings against mob attacks on cattle traders and dairy farmers.[10] In June 2017, he stated that, 'killing people in the name of protecting cows is unacceptable.'[11] Characterising those engaged in cow protection activities, the Indian Prime Minister had earlier said, 'I get so angry at those who are into the *Gau-Rakshak* (cow protector) business. A *Gau-Bhakt* (cow devotee) is different, *Gau-Seva* (cow protection) is different. I have seen that some people are into crimes all night and wear the garb of *Gau Rakshaks* in the day. . . . 70–80% will be those who indulge in anti-social activities and try to hide their sins by pretending to be *Gau Rakshaks*. If they are true protectors, they should realise that most cows die because of plastic, not slaughter. They should stop cows from eating plastic.'[12]

Notably, India exports around 19 per cent of the total beef consumed in the world. Within India, there are caste based and regional differences over the status of cows. Both the slaughter and consumption of beef are, primarily, associated with Muslims, though even a number of the Hindu Dalits are engaged in the leather industry and have been beaten up for skinning dead cows.[13] According to the last consumer expenditure survey by the National Sample Survey Office, conducted in 2011–2012, as published in an Indian daily, *The Mint*, out of 80 million Indians who consume beef or buffalo meat, around 12.5 million were Hindus.[14] Caste wise, more than 70 per cent of the beef-eating population is from Schedule Caste/Schedule Tribe, 21 per cent is from the Other Backward Class and only 7 per cent belongs to the upper castes.[15] The number of Muslim beef consumers is 63.4 million. It is about 40 per cent of the total population in India.[16] In the Indian constitution, Article 48 in Chapter IV in the Directive Principles of State Policy calls on the Indian state to take certain measures to protect cows in India. Using this provision, most of the Indian states have enacted anti-cow slaughtering acts.

Conversions and re-conversions catalyse tensions between the two communities in both India and Pakistan. Due to religious beliefs,[17] in India, there are a negligible number of cases of conversions of members of the minority religious communities in Hinduism. One such recent case occurred in December 2014, when re-conversions (*ghar wapsi*) of Muslims were carried out in Agra in Uttar Pradesh. A family of four brothers, their wives and children – 17 members in total – converted back to Islam a few weeks after the *ghar wapsi* ceremony. Although it was alleged that the re-conversion was carried out by prominent Hindu groups, the priest who performed the ceremony denied having any links with groups such as Rashtriya Swamsevak Sangh or Bajrang Dal.[18]

In Pakistan abduction, illegal confinement and then conversion of Hindu girls is a serious social issue. This is especially so in upper and northern Sindh. One such case was that of Rinkle Kumari, who was abducted in 2012 and forced to marry her abductor, Abdul Haq (aka Mian Mithu), then a Pakistan People's Party parliamentarian (he was subsequently denied a ticket in the next election). Rinkle's family fought the case in court. However, the Supreme Court favoured the abductor by sending Rinkle with him. This despite the fact that at one point during the hearing, Rinkle expressed her will to go with her parents.[19] In June 2017, another case, that of Ravita Meghwar, came to light. In court, Ravita's father, Satram Das Meghwar, said that his daughter was illegally married to Syed Nawaz Ali Shah. Satram Meghwar alleged that Syed Nawaz Ali Shah kidnapped her from her village near Nagarparkar Town (Sindh) on 6 June.[20] To check the growing number of such cases, in 2016, the Sindh assembly had passed the Criminal Law (Protection of Minorities) Act 2015 to protect the rights of minorities. However, its effectiveness has yet to be tested.

Not only Hindu minorities but also Qaidani Ahmadis, who were declared non-Muslims in 1974, have since then faced social discrimination and violence against them. In the past, and even at present the Sunnis blame the Ahmadis, and especially their leader Zafarullah Khan, for the loss of territory like Ferozepur and Gurdaspur to India.[21] Other religious groups like Christians, a few Sikhs in Punjab and Khyber Pakhtunkhwa (KP) of Pakistan also face violence from radical groups. As the violence against the community is on the rise a large number of the Sikh population from KP have migrated to other parts of Pakistan, and some have even crossed into the Indian side of the border.[22]

Over the years, instead of cementing communal trust, to an extent the two communities have fallen apart and ghettoised religiously and socially. This is because of many global and local issues like the rise of terrorism, where a particular community is branded as a supporter, sympathiser or one who is responsible for carrying out all terrorist activities around the world. This development has increased the trust deficit in recent years in India between the Hindus and the Muslims. This trust deficit in India is probably best exemplified by the incident involving the famous film actress Shabana Azmi, who, in 2008, claimed that she was denied a flat in Mumbai because she is a Muslim.[23] Later, a few other film actors like Saif Ali Khan and Emran Hasmi were reported to have faced similar ordeals while buying flats in Mumbai.[24]

In Pakistan, with the radicalisation of society, there has been an increase of violence against minorities. In many cases Hindus have been physically attacked or have feared being attacked by neighbours. To protect themselves, many members of the Hindu community from Sindh province in Pakistan have crossed over to the Indian side of the border.[25] Contemporarily, little efforts have been made to make present-day Pakistan a communally 'inclusive' state. In 2015, then-Prime Minister Nawaz Sharif attended the Hindu *Diwali* (festival of light) in Sindh. In his address to the community members, he said, 'Every community living here whether Hindu, Muslim or Parsi, everyone belongs to me and I belong to them. I am prime minister of all communities.'[26] Again, in March 2017, he also attended the *Holi* (festival of colours) in Sindh.[27] However, it is difficult to deduce what impact these overtures would have on inter-communal relations in the country. However, based on past and current states of affairs, there does not appear to have been much of an impact.

In Bangladesh too, the rise of Islamists have made minorities vulnerable. There have been many instances where minority groups affiliated with Hinduism and other religions and sects were attacked by the Islamists. Even the supposedly secular have not shied away from taking advantage of minority communities in Bangladesh. The 1992–1993 Babri mosque demolition by Hindu radicals followed by communal riots in India had their impact on Bangladesh too. The Hindus were attacked by the Islamists.[28] Besides attacks on people, attacks on Hindu and Buddhist temples have also occurred frequently. For example, in 2012 in the Ramu area of Cox's Bazar, a large crowd including many supporters of three major political groups – Awami League (AL), the Bangladesh Nationalist Party (BNP) and Bangladesh Jamaat-e-Islami (BJI) – attacked 12 Buddhist pagodas and more than 50 houses.[29] More serious than the attacks on and ransacking of temples, however, have been occupations of temple lands by influential individuals. Sometimes to garner votes, the political class of the country accepts it. BNP leader Nazrul Islam, during an interaction with Hindu devotees at Dhakeshwari Temple, said that most of the land of the temple had been occupied by influential people, and he called upon the government to take steps to recover it. He stated, 'I've come to know from the Sarbojonin Puja Committee president that 14 bigahs of land out of 20 of the temple have been grabbed.'[30]

Research by Professor Abu Barakat of Dhaka University has shown that as of 1997, through various versions of the Enemy Property Act, 53 per cent of the land owned by Hindus has been forcibly taken over, most of it between 1972 and 1980. This has affected four out of every ten Hindu households. The largest beneficiaries of these illegally dispossessed lands were those affiliated with the 'secular' party, AL, followed by BNP and BJI.[31] In Bangladesh, this land-grabbing and discrimination against Hindu minorities is quite common, especially in rural areas. During my visit to Dhaka in 2015, a Hindu professor informed me that in areas where the Islamic outfits are strong, occupation of land belonging to the Hindu minorities is a 'normal' issue. Even the police do not do anything to stop it, no matter who is in power. The professor also informed me that once upon a time in many posh areas of Dhaka, Hindus owned property but now one hardly finds any property in those areas belonging to a Hindu individual. Most of their property has been occupied through various legal and illegal means by the individuals belonging to the majority religious community. This, he said, is a post-1971 development.

In all the three countries – India, Pakistan and Bangladesh – the impact of Partition is still visible in matters of the state (in Pakistan and Bangladesh) and in social relationships because of the way the dreadful event has been narrated. Narratives of Partition have constructed an image of people belonging to different religions based on each narrator's experience during Partition or in its aftermath. Therefore it is important to understand those narratives, those constructions, within the historiography of Partition.

Narrating the partition

As there are a million stories related to the partition of British India in 1947, there are as many ways to interpret and narrate the events. Some of those stories have been documented and published by the protagonists themselves, while a large number of people have left their stories to be told by others. In the latter cases, many narrators have tried to take on the character of the protagonist but have rarely done them justice. Moreover, despite a plethora of literature on the subject of Partition, women and Dalits are notably absent from most of it. Hence, most of the emotionally charged stories related to Partition – those expressing hatred towards the other, calling for vengeance, desiring a sense of belonging, yearning for a lost 'home,' and searching for a new identity – are political, sociological and psychological expression of the dominant social groups. It is their narration of Partition that has been accepted as the official version in India, Bangladesh and Pakistan. The non-dominant groups have their own stories and interpretations, which in many cases are different from the official one, but they have been ignored by most of the scholars and official historians of Partition.

In recent years, attempts have been made to uncover some of the alternative narratives of Partition, focusing mainly on women and the subaltern group. In many cases, even official historians accept that women's bodies turned into a space that people from other religious groups, and in some cases even those from their own groups, wished to violate, while the relatives of those women wished to secure those bodies from getting 'polluted', even at the cost of 'honour' killings. It was the issue of the '(im) purity' of their bodies which made many abducted women choose to remain with their violators instead of reuniting with their families. Urvashi Butalia's *The Other Side of Silence*[32] and Ritu Menon and Kamla Bhasin's work *Border and Boundaries: Women in India's Partition*[33] have brought to light many stories related to women. Others have also unearthed some of the stories about the experiences of women during Partition. Due to the emergence of such works, the writings of Krishna Sobti, Saadat Hasan Manto and others are being revisited time and again by Partition historiographers. But a large number of such stories have been buried under the weight of patriarchy and smothered because of a lack of available social and political space. Those which became public remains secondary, insignificant,[34] and they often reflect only what is accepted by the patriarchy or by their 'own' people. Women, like subalterns, cannot speak[35] their minds freely; they have been given representation in Partition texts by some of the scholars.

Another group that remains underrepresented in the history of Partition is the Dalit, members of which occupy similar social positions across the religions of South Asia. After the rise of Islam and Christianity in India, many Dalits converted to these religions in search of better treatment, but even these 'egalitarian' religions failed to treat them as equals. Butalia in *The Other Side of Silence* and a few others, including Ramnarayan Rawat, in his research works has discussed the Dalit stories of Partition, but many of the mainstream literature is either silent on the matter. Even the work of Bhima Rao Ambedkar on Partition attained more prominence only after the rise of Dalit consciousness in the 1980s in India. Due to their economic positions, many did not cross immediately to the other side of the border in 1947, but both rumours and actual occurrences of communal riots in following years eventually forced some of them to join their religious community across the border. Dalits were also stopped by the AIML leaderships because their evacuation affected the essential services such as sweeping in some of the Pakistani cities. It is estimated that there were about 200,000 Hindu Dalits living in Sindh at the time of partition. Once some of them began to migrate the members of Rashtra Seva Dal (an organisation set up by Sane Guruji) and the Muslim National Guard were obliged to sweep the Sukkur city.[36] To control the situation, the Sind Public Safety Ordinance was amended to give power to the government to prohibit washermen and sweepers – primarly Dalits – from leaving the cities without written permission from the District Magistrate. Police were posted around the Dalit colonies to stop their departure.[37] To indicate their identity, they were asked to wear a badge on their arm. Even those Dalits who were not sweepers or cleaners were forced into the service.[38] They were allowed to freely migrate to India by the beginning of 1948 when the AIML leadership started giving consideration to an idea of 'importing' around 10,000 Muslim sweepers from Bihar to replace the Hindu Dalits[39]. However, those who migrated were not welcomed in India; they faced caste-based discriminations against them from the caste Hindus.[40]

In 2013, thanks to my journalist friend Sehyr Mirza, I met a few Hindu Dalit members in Lahore and asked them about this Jinnah's ploy to keep them in Pakistan. An elderly man I encountered said his family did not cross over to the Indian side of the border during Partition because his father had told them that Lahore was their home and questioned why they should have to move to an alien land. This territorial identity caused his family to remain in Lahore. When I asked whether there were economic reasons for leaving, or whether it had to do with not having relatives in India, as this could have made their lives a bit difficult, he informed me that his father was economically better off in Lahore and that they did have relatives in India. But at that time they had experienced no violence from their Muslim neighbours. The situation became different afterwards, however, and his family and community members in Pakistan have faced many forms of violence particularly since the 1990s.

Relatedly, there are interpretations of individuals' behaviours during partition-related violence and the stories of the survivors. This differs from one individual to another. Everyone who crossed the border from Punjab or Bengal has their story; some of these stories are sad, while others end humanely.[41] Ritwik Ghatak's Bengali movies, such as *Meghe Dhaka Tara* (1960), *Komal Gandhar* (1961), and *Subarnrekha* (1965) are stories of migrants from the East to the West due to the partition of Bengal. Not only the survivors have their stories but also those who carried out violence and attacks and committed rapes have their own interpretations and explanations for engaging in such acts. Some have justified them, though a few have admitted that they were propelled by feelings for their community, by the powerful or influential people of their areas who incited them to violence, and by the violence they witnessed or heard about perpetrated by the 'other' community against their own. A small number of people from the latter group have been remorseful about their behaviour. A few of such stories have been recounted by Ishtiaq Ahmed in *The Punjab Bloodied, Partitioned and Cleansed*.[42] Personal accounts still dominate partition-related memories and shape the behaviour of the generation of Partition survivors towards the 'other' community. I myself have heard both forms of this experience, which has shaped both the social interactions of individuals with those from the 'other' community and their feelings about the 'other' country.

Lahore Music House, a shop in Daryaganj in New Delhi is run by two Sikh brothers.[43] The elder brother was six years old when India was partitioned. The family had been settled in Lahore where his father owned a medicine shop. He said that as the violence spread in Lahore his family packed a few necessary things and left the city. They went to Jammu, and from there they went to Amritsar before finally settling down in Delhi. He also shared memories of his childhood days, his home and the cityscape. The army was already divided along religious lines, he said, and there was no reason to trust the police because of their spreading inter-community hatred. When I asked whether he had visited Lahore after Partition, he said that he had not but his younger brother, who was there, had visited Pakistan as a part of a Sikh *jathas* (group of pilgrims) to Nankana Sahib in the 1980s. His younger brother said that during his visit he went to Shahdara as well as to Lahore. In Lahore, he visited the medicine shop once owned by his father. The person in charge of the shop, after learning about him and his past, took him to his ancestral home. There he met an old woman who was its post-Partition owner. She showed him the place where his father used to store medicines. Some of them were still there because the old lady could not clean them up. When asked why they changed the family business from medicine to musical instruments, the elder brother said that their father had been a music lover.

Unlike the Lahore Music House owners, Sardar Avtar Singh Datta had a different story and feeling about Partition. I met Datta in Kamla Market in New Delhi in January 2014. At the time of Partition, he was about 12 years old. His family used to live in Mohalla Mojala at Moni Road in Lahore. His ancestral village's name was Ghania Shikhan, which was in Lyallpur district. His grandfather, Sardar Bhadur Amar Singh, was a landlord who had been granted lands in a canal colony by the British commissioner of Punjab Province. At the time of Partition his family was in Lahore. When I asked about the nature of the relationship his family had with the neighbours, he said, 'There were Muslims in my neighbourhood. They were gentle people and never created any sort of problem for my family even during those awful days. It was the people from other parts of the city who created problems in my area.' About inter-community tensions, he said that things speedily changed after a bomb blast occurred in his locality in the beginning of August 1947. A few days after the blast, his house was set on fire. This forced his family to leave the city and migrate to India. For a few days his family stayed in a police station at Qila Gujjar Singh, where one of his relatives, who was in the police force, was posted. Datta lost his father in partition-related riots. After facing problems and spending months in refugee camps in the Punjab, he and his brothers arrived in New Delhi on 1 January 1948.

One issue that haunts many people is that of 'honour' killings carried out during Partition. Datta told me that 15 of the female members from a joint family on his maternal uncle's side were either killed by the male members of the house or they 'willingly' committed suicide. The name of his maternal uncle's village was

Kotla Arbali Gaon, which was in the Gujrat district of Pakistan. The killing happened after rumours or confirmed news that their village had been attacked by the Muslims had reached them. When I asked him if he now feels that the killing of female family members had been wrong and barbaric, he said it had not because of the time and situation in question. Finally, when I asked whether or not he had visited Pakistan after 1947, he replied that he had not. He said that he had a fading memory of his Muslim neighbours and that none of his relatives now live in Pakistan.

One's relationship to an ancestral land is the dominant marker of an individual's identity – even if one has never even lived there. A sense of 'belonging' to a particular territory is always dominant in one's subconscious. In 2013 when I visited Lahore for the first time to attend a Trust for History, Art and Architecture of Pakistan (THAAP) conference, I was introduced to a professor from the University of Gujrat by Usha Gandhi and Rajmohan Gandhi. He was born in pre-Partition India in Ara district of Bihar, migrated with his parents to East Pakistan (present-day Bangladesh) during Partition, completed his education at the University of Dhaka and re-migrated to West Pakistan in 1971. In 1947, the professor's religion was his identity; in 1971, he said he identified himself as a Muslim who spoke Urdu – yet Ara clearly remained in his subconscious memory during our conversation.[44]

Demographic factors taken into consideration by Sir Cyril Radcliffe, head of Boundary Commissions, bracketed many other communities either as Hindu or Muslim, which was not the case. On this William van Schendel writes:[45] 'In view of categories that informed the decisions of the Boundary Commission, the post-Partition nations had little option but to legitimate themselves in terms of the Muslim/non-Muslim dichotomy. Dominant political interpretations, however, narrowed this down to the categories of Muslims and Hindus and these were treated as overarching, unproblematic and antagonistic. As a result, history writing shaded easily into patterns of thought that were dualistic and left little room for other players in the historical drama of the region.' For example, Garo Hills/Khasi and Jaintia Hills (now in Meghalaya in India) stretch was Christian-dominated[46] but partitioned for geographical reasons. Hence individuals from communities other than those of Hindus, Sikhs and Muslims too bear the trauma of Partition. From the day I met the Parsi sisters at Lahore in 2013, I wanted to write their story which is a distinct example of inhumane times we are still living in. However, their ordeal due to the

India–Pakistan relationship has been excellently presented by Anam Zakaria in her work *The Footprints of Partition.*[47]

It is not always the self or the group that constructs one's identity; it is sometimes the 'others' who do so. Through identifying a group the dominant members of a majority community construct the identity of the 'others' and draw differences between various groups.[48] In India today, those who immigrated from Pakistan during or after Partition are still looked at and considered as 'refugees,' despite their enormous contribution to the country. They are still not fully 'accepted' as a part of the land they adopted in or after 1947. In Pakistan, *Muhajirs* (Muslim refugees) are still regarded as outsiders despite the fact that it was their ancestors who launched the Pakistan movement in British India. The ethnic violence against them is often unleashed by the Punjabi dominated managers of the Pakistan state. In Bangladesh, the debate between Bengali and non-Bengali speakers is still active. It led to the liberation of East Bengal in 1971 and is at present one of the most significant reasons for existing group violence in Bangladesh. Hence, both self-identification and the construction of identity by others have kept the issues related to Partition alive.

This book is not about the interpretations of Partition-related stories or pre- and post-Partition identity, yet these subjects are essential to discuss within the scope of any Partition-related work because they regulate the history and historiography of Partition, which is why I have briefly talked about them and their complexities in this introduction. Almost all of the contributions to this book in one way or another at least touch upon these issues.

About this book

This book is an attempt to reexamine the partition of India after 71 years. This is an important undertaking because the inter-state relationships between India, Pakistan and Bangladesh, as well as communal relationships among the religious and sectarian groups living within and across the territorial boundaries of these countries, are still being guided by the spectre of Partition. In this book, contributors have made an attempt to give their own narratives of the partition of India.

This book is divided into four parts. The first chapter is an individual's attempt to explain why Partition occurred and, hence, it does not fall into any particular section of the volume. The reason for Partition that is argued in this chapter is one of many in debates over the causes of Partition; so some scholars may not agree with the arguments made in this chapter. The other 16 essays are divided into four parts.

Before introducing the chapters, it is important to note that the contributors are from different countries of South Asia, and some of them are citizens of countries outside the regions they describe and have used terms to refer to topics related to those regions according to their respective beliefs. As an editor, I have not compelled any of them to use a unified set of terms or phrases when discussing controversial issues or conflictual phrases or terms.

Impact of Partition in provinces and princely states

Professor Ishtiaq Ahmed seeks to demonstrate how and why the partition of the Punjab in 1947 bore the brunt of the violence that claimed 70–80 per cent of all fatalities and for the large number of people who were forced to flee for their lives across the border laid down by the Radcliffe Award of 13–17 August 1947. The ethnic cleansing it entailed is a unique feature of the partition of the Punjab. Farhan Siddiqi discusses the communal politics, class conflicts and competing nationalism in Sindh. It was at the first Sindh Provincial Muslim League Conference in Karachi in 1938 where Jinnah and All-India Muslim League leaders expressed the need for a separate homeland for Muslims. Since then, Sindh has witnessed forms of social and political developments on the issue of a separate homeland for Indian Muslims. Taj Hashmi's chapter is an attempt to see the second partition of Bengal from below. Binayak Dutta writes that while 'there is little doubt over Partition of India causing extreme violence, displacement and agony, very little space has been given to the study of the suffering during Partition and after in Eastern India, till recent times.' Dutta's chapter in this volume tries to fulfil that gap. The next chapter on North-East India in general is by Rituparna Bhattacharyya, who shows how the spectre of Partition and its legacy continues to haunt diverse groups of people from that region. Altaf Khan has explored the legacy of the Khudai kidmatgaar movement and effects of Partition in Khyber Pakhtunkhwa (earlier known as the North-West Frontier Province). Nizam Rahim Baloch unfolds the story of Balochistan and links it to post-Partition developments in the erstwhile princely state.

Displacements and migrants

Partition created a situation where a large number of people migrated to an unknown territory. The identities of those migrants still hovered around them and often became a cause for tensions. They were the linking thread to Partition, which had constructed their identities. Hence the partition of India cannot be studied without looking into the issues of displacement and migration. Nandita Bhavnani discusses the situation in Sindh, and Subhasri Ghosh's chapter focusses on Bengal. Nandita explains the increasingly vitiated communal atmosphere in Sindh from 3 June 1947, when Partition was announced, until December 1947. The chapter then dwells on two significant episodes of violence that took place in Sindh: the anti-Hindu pogrom in Hyderabad on 17 December 1947 and the anti-Sikh and -Hindu pogrom in Karachi on 6 January 1948. It was after these two pogroms that there was a massive exodus of Hindus and Sikhs from Sindh, which continued for months. Ghosh's chapter attempts to explore somewhat 'sporadic localised' riots in Calcutta and its twin city across the river – Howrah – in February and March of 1950. Culling information from archival documents, personal memoirs, newspaper reports and government records, the chapter foregrounds the broad implication lurking behind this communal violence and contextualises the issue within the larger framework of the rehabilitation policy of the West Bengal government, which was saddled with an unending stream of refugees from East Bengal after independence.

Personal history, interpretations and (re)presentation

Departing from typical conventions of academic research, Farooq Sulehria's and Mehru Jaffer's chapters discuss their respective personal histories. Sulheria's paper on Jammu and Kashmir is a mix of family history (as his grandfather immigrated from Jammu), personal experience (as he was an activist for the cause of Kashmiris) and academic scholarship (because of his current profession). Jaffer's chapter is a collection of personal stories of ordinary people from in and around Lucknow that reflect only a fraction of the millions of other ordinary lives scarred by Partition. Most of the information gathered, as she writes, comes from long conversations with ordinary family members and friends. In his chapter,

Altaf Khan discusses the legacy of Khan Abul Ghaffar Khan in the Khyber Pakhtunkhwa.

Kalathmika Natarajan's chapter presents a visual interpretation of Partition through Tamil cinema. Natarajan discusses Tamil cinema's response to Partition as a means of understanding the ways in which the southern state of Tamil Nadu negotiated the centrality of Partition in the making of Indian identity. Roshni Sharma's chapter addresses the (re)presentation of women in popular literature about partition of Bengal. Her chapter also illustrates how extraordinary determination and grit would combine with an exceptionally strong survival instinct to endure the disaster that women faced through no fault of their own. Sharma focusses on two texts: *Epar Ganga, Opar Ganga*, which deals with women's sexuality as a domain of exploitation, oppression and violence, and *Swarlipi*, which sees women's sexuality as a realm of exploration, agency and autonomy.

India–Pakistan–Bangladesh

Partition-related memories constructed through interpretations and (re)presentations dominate interpersonal and inter-state relationships between India, Pakistan and Bangladesh. These constructions are kept alive by the leaders of these three states to secure their respective power interests. However, interpersonal relationships vary because of their varying images of the 'other.' Sajad Padder's chapter is an analysis of India–Pakistan relationships. He reveals that even after 70 years of their existence as independent nations, both countries have failed to resolve the main bilateral contentious issues. Punam Pandey discuses India–Bangladesh relations in light of the trials of perpetrators of violence during 1971's liberation war under the International Crime Tribunal. This chapter explores India's relationship with Bangladesh as well as, to an extent, with Pakistan. Pallavi Deka has traced the relationship between Pakistan and Bangladesh. She argues that Pakistan's stance on Bangladesh was dominated by two approaches. The first and more dominant approach was to rely on conspiracy theories and blame everything on India, denying Bangladesh agency. The other approach was a hesitant, liberal one, which acknowledged the problem yet stopped short of doing what was needed. Even after 1971 the two countries had gone through many ups and downs in their bilateral relationships because of the spectre of war-related atrocities, which are interpreted differently by different actors.

To the best of my knowledge, all chapters, except where otherwise indicated, are original and were written specifically for publication in this book. Where versions of chapters have been previously published, it has been noted. All contributors are responsible for their respective words, phrases, views and arguments expressed in this volume. They are also responsible for the facts, quotations and citations used in their respective chapters. One may not necessarily agree with the arguments made within the pages of this book, but, still, they are important to know. It is in this spirit and under the ideals of academic freedom that this volume was conceived. Thanks to my contributors who also share these ideals, despite having had second thoughts or disagreements about one or more of the chapters. The aim of this volume is to present a set of arguments because, as expressed above, the reasons for Partition and the events related to it have many dimensions and interpretations. Therefore, the chapters do not reflect a single argument or a hypothesis but, rather, seek to understand those dimensions and interpretations.

Notes

1 Menon, Jisha (2013) *The Performance of Nationalism: India, Pakistan, and the Memory of Partition*. New Delhi: Cambridge University Press, p. 49.
2 See Bhargava, Rajeev (2002) 'India's Secular Constitution,' in *India's Living Constitution: Ideas, Practices, Controversies* ed. Zoya Hasan, E. Sridharan and R. Sudarshan. New Delhi: Permanent Black, pp. 105–133.
3 The Constitution of the Islamic Republic of Pakistan. Retrieved from http://na.gov.pk/uploads/documents/1333523681_951.pdf. Accessed on 12 June 2017.
4 Riaz, Ali (2016) *Bangladesh: A Political History since Independence*. London: I B Tauris & Co Ltd.
5 Majumder, Shantanu (2016) 'Secularism and anti-Secularism,' in *Routledge Handbook of Contemporary Bangladesh* ed. Riaz Ali & Mohammad Sajjadur Rahman. Oxon & New York: Routledge, pp. 40–51.
6 Setalvad, Teesta (2017) *Foot Soldier of the Constitution: A Memoir*. New Delhi: Leftword Publications; Ayyub, Rana (2016) *Gujrat Files: Anatomy of a Cover Up*. Published by Rana Ayyub.
7 See Suri, Sanjay (2015) *1984: The Anti-Sikh Violence and After*. Noida: Harper Collins.
8 Many political commentators blame the Bharatiya Janata Party-led National Democratic Alliance government, which came to power in 2014, for the beginning of such brutalities in India. What has happened after 2014 is that the fringe elements have surfaced and have been trying to occupy the "mainstream" public space, mainly in North India.

9 Saran, Bedanti and Sanjoy Dey 'Man Accused of Carrying Beef Beaten to Death by 100-Strong Mob in Jharkhand,' *The Hindustan Times*. Retrieved from www.hindustantimes.com/india-news/jharkhand-man-accused-of-carrying-beef-beaten-to-death/story-3fuowiHpgloxAbERlouZ4M.html. Accessed on 12 July 2017.
10 Ibid.
11 Ibid.
12 "PM Modi Hits Out At Cow Vigilantes, Says 'Gau Rakshak Business Makes Me Angry,'" *NDTV* 7 August 2016. Retrieved from www.ndtv.com/india-news/pm-modi-hits-out-at-cow-vigilantes-says-most-cows-die-after-eating-plastic-1441079. Accessed on 16 July 2017.
13 Kateshia, Gopal B. (20 July 2016) 'Gujarat: 7 of Dalit Family Beaten Up for Skinning Dead Cow,' *The Indian Express*. Retrieved from http://indianexpress.com/article/india/india-news-india/gujarat-7-of-dalit-family-beaten-up-for-skinning-dead-cow-2910054/.
14 Kishore, Roshan (20 October 2015) 'Who Are the Beef Eaters in India?,' *The Livemint*. Retrieved from www.livemint.com/Politics/RhPVLUFmclIDWRIiSoTC7N/Who-are-the-beef-eaters-in-India.html. Accessed on 21 October 2015. Also see '*The Myth of the Holy Cow*' by Professor DN Jha. This can be considered one of the essential texts on the religious side of the cow.
15 Ibid.
16 Ibid.
17 The practice of *Shuddhikaran* (purification) was started by Dayanand Sarswati to convert people into the Hindu religion, but it is less practiced in present times. Today, Hindu groups mainly appeal to Hindu couples to have more children.
18 Mishral, Isha (1 May 2015) 'After "Ghar Wapsi," Now Re-Conversion to Islam,' *Times of India*. Retrieved from http://timesofindia.indiatimes.com/city/agra/After-ghar-wapsi-now-reconversiontoIslam/articleshow/47124941.cms. Accessed on 12 January 2016.
19 Veengas (14 January 2017) 'Bring Back Our Girls: Pakistan Hindus Struggle against Forced Conversion,' *The Wire*. Retrieved from https://thewire.in/99522/pakistan-minorities-girls/. Accessed on 15 July 2017.
20 '"Forced Conversion": Police Told to Produce Ravita in Sindh High Court on June 22.' Retrieved from www.dawn.com/news/1340717.
21 Qasmi, Ali Usman (2015) *The Ahmadis and the Politics of Religious Exclusion in Pakistan*. Delhi: Anthem Press.
22 Malik, Mehreen Zahra (2018, 12 June) 'With killings on the rise, Sikhs in Pakistan's Peshawar weigh exit'. TRT World. https://www.trtworld.com/magazine/ with-killings-on-the-rise-sikhs-in-pakistan-s-peshawar-weigh-exit-1 8160. Accessed on 15 September 2018.
23 'Indian Democracy Unfair to Muslims: Shabana Azmi,' *Times of India*, 17 August 2008. Retrieved from http://timesofindia.indiatimes.com/india/Indian-democracy-unfair-to-Muslims-Shabana-Azmi/articleshow/3371893.cms. Accessed on 11 July 2016. Tehsin, Arefa (2 June 2012) 'No Muslims Please!,' *The Hindu*. Retrieved from www.thehindu.com/features/magazine/no-muslims-please/article3482963.ece. Accessed on 11 July 2016.

24 Ibid.
25 '"Partition Is Not Over": Pakistani Hindus Fleeing Persecution Find Little Refuge in India,' *The Dawn*, 31 July 2017. Retrieved from www.dawn.com/news/1348748. Accessed on 31 July 2017.
26 Ghori, Habib Khan (12 November 2015) 'PM Vows to Protect Rights of All Religious Communities,' *The Dawn*. Retrieved from www.dawn.com/news/1219105. Accessed on 2 August 2017.
27 www.samaa.tv/pakistan/2017/03/pm-to-attend-holi-festival-of-colours-in-karachi/.
28 See Nasreen, Tasleema (1997) *Shame: A Novel*. MI: Promotheous Books.
29 Chatterjee, Garga (15 October 2012) 'The Dangerous Slide of Bangladesh,' *DNA*. Retrieved from www.dnaindia.com/analysis/column-the-dangerous-slide-of-bangladesh-1752464. Accessed on 15 November 2015.
30 'BNP Deadly against Communalism: Nazrul Islam,' *Bangladesh Today*, 23 October 2015. Retrieved from www.bdchronicle.com/detail/news/32/24439. Accessed on 15 November 2015. Accessed on 17 June 2017.
31 Chatterjee, Garga (15 October 2012) 'The Dangerous Slide of Bangladesh,' *DNA*. Retrieved from www.dnaindia.com/analysis/column-the-dangerous-slide-of-bangladesh-1752464. Accessed on 15 November 2015.
32 Butalia, Urvashi (2014) *The Other Side of Silence: Voices from the partition of India*. New Delhi: Penguin Books.
33 Menon, Ritu and Kamla Bhasin (1998) *Border and Boundaries: Women in India's Partition*. New Delhi: Kali for Women.
34 Chawla, Devika (2014) *Home Uprooted: Oral Histories of India's Partition*. New York: Fordham University Press.
35 See Spivak, Gyatri 'Can the Subaltern Speak?' Retrieved from http://postcolonial.net/@/DigitalLibrary/_entries/40/file-pdf.pdf. Accessed on 10 February 2014.
36 Bhavnani, Nandita (2014) *The Making of Exile: Sindhi Hindus and the partition of India*. Chennai: Tranquebar Press, 89.
37 Ibid.
38 Ibid.
39 Ibid.
40 Ibid.
41 See Kaur, Ravinder (2007) *Since 1947: Partition Narratives among Punjabi Migrants of Delhi*. New Delhi: Oxford University Press.
42 Ahmed, Ishtiaq (2014) *The Punjab Bloodied, Partitioned and Cleansed: Unravelling the 1947 Tragedy through Secret British Reports and First-Person Accounts*. Karachi: Oxford University Press.
43 For more on the Lahore Music House, See Ranjan, Amit (10 December 2014) 'Lahore Music House,' *Daily Times*. Retrieved from www.dailytimes.com.pk/opinion/10-Dec-2014/lahore-music-house. Accessed on 10 December 2014. For second story see Ranjan, Amit (24 January 2014) 'An Hour with History,' *Daily Times*. Retrieved from http://dailytimes.com.pk/opinion/23-Jan-14/an-hour-with-history. Accessed on 24 January 2014.

44 See Ranjan, Amit (10 July 2015) *The Friday Times*. Retrieved from www.thefridaytimes.com/tft/which-way-home/. Accessed on 10 July 2015.
45 Schendel, Willem van (2005) *The Bengal Borderland: Beyond State and Nation in South Asia*. London: Anthem South Asian Studies, pp. 46–47.
46 Partition Proceedings Volume VI, Reports of the Members and Awards of the Chairman of the Boundary Commissions (1950) Superintendent, Government Printing West Bengal Government Press, Alipore; Schendel, Willem van (2005) *The Bengal Borderland: Beyond State and Nation in South Asia*. London: Anthem South Asian Studies.
47 Zakaria, Anam (2015) *The Footprints of Partition: Narratives of Four Generations of Pakistanis and Indians*. New Delhi: Harper and Collins, pp. 56–71.
48 Bhabha, Homi K. (1994) *The Location of Culture*. Oxon: Routledge.

Chapter 1

Partition of India

A reaction against 'differences'?

Amit Ranjan

The partition of India in 1947 is one of the most intriguing subjects in the history of modern South Asia. Scholars have presented many narratives, interpretations, examinations and analyses to discuss and examine the reasons for Partition, yet every such study has not 'absolutely' convinced those who have worked or are currently working on the issue. The available literature on the partition of India can be categorized based on Partition historiography, which looks into its history from various dimensions, including high politics, provincial politics and subaltern politics.[1] One of the works on high politics is *The Sole Spokesman: Jinnah, The Muslim League and the demand for Pakistan* by Ayesha Jalal. Jalal has basically argued that Mohammad Ali Jinnah used Pakistan as a means to achieve equal social and political status for the Indian Muslims.[2] A more recent publication reflecting the role of provinces in the Partition is *Creating a New Medina: State Power, Islam, and the Quest for Pakistan in Late Colonial North India* by Venkat Dhulipala. Dhulipala's argument is that the demand for Pakistan was, mainly, raised in 1930s in the Muslim minority United Province (UP) (present Indian state of Uttar Pradesh).[3] He has brought religion back into the partition debate. Many other works focusing on high politics and the provinces, published between and prior to these two texts, populate the list of Partition literature. Contrary to them, most of the subaltern scholars have focussed on social, political and economic structures and related tensions in colonial society.

Success in high politics was impossible without the support of those living at the margins and who faced all forms of discrimination due to 'differences.' Some of those 'differences' were constructed and then communalised to make political benefits out of them. More than the power elites, it was the Muslim middle class intelligentsia that significantly highlighted, and in certain cases successfully constructed, the 'differences' between the Hindus and Muslims. However, some of the writings, practices and activities by the Hindu religious groups proved support to such constructions. Hence, it is this Muslim middle class that spearheaded the political movement for Pakistan. But a few members of the Muslim middle class and some of their leaders did not accept the arguments of proponents of a separate land for Indian Muslims. They also pointed out 'differences' within the Muslim community, where everyone is supposed to be equal. This has been well examined in a few past writings, and in recent times Ali Usman Qasmi and Megan Eaton Robb's edited *Muslims against the Muslim League* sheds light on it.[4]

'Differences': religious, social and economic

Demographically, according to the last census of British India in 1941, the country had a population of 389 million, comprising 255 million Hindus (including the members of Schedule Castes), 92 million Muslims, 6.3 million Christians, 5.6 million Sikhs and a number of other communities. There were Muslim majority areas (in the north-east and the north-west) and Hindu majority areas, but no part of India was exclusively inhabited by any one community,[5] except in some areas where the communities used to live in separate localities.

Religiously, for the majority of Hindus, Islam remains an outsider's religion despite having centuries of interaction and cultural assimilation between people following Hinduism and Islam in India. As a religion, Islam was born in the present-day Middle East and then spread throughout the subcontinent in many ways and for different reasons. The first connection between South Asia and Islam was made through trade and commerce. Arab traders came first, and their religion followed. Trade brought them to India's southern sea coasts and the coasts of Sri Lanka, where small Muslim communities were established at least by the early eighth century. These traders played key economic roles and were patronised by non-Muslim kings, like the Zamorin of Calicut (Kozhikode) who welcomed diverse merchant communities.[6] In many kingdoms Arab and Jewish merchants not only sojourned on the Arabian Sea littoral of the subcontinent, but some were even granted special protection to practise their faiths and were relieved of taxation.[7]

Afterwards, once connected through land, when the situation in the Arab peninsula worsened and a race began to spread Islam by the power of the sword, the subcontinent could not remain aloof.[8] Repeated attacks on the subcontinent were made by Central Asians and Arab invaders. History textbooks at the graduate level in Pakistan consider the ideological foundation of Pakistan to have formed with the attack of Mohammad bin Qasim in around AD 711.[9] In reality, bin Qasim's conquest had been taken for granted at the time and in no sense turned into a watershed moment in the subcontinent's history. Instead, it was the Turko-Afghans invaders who began to establish settled kingdoms in the northern heartlands of the subcontinent in the early thirteenth century by contract and inaugurated an era of continuous Muslim rule in the region.[10] Hence, Muslim rule in India began with advancements made by Turko-Afghan rulers and ended when the British took charge of Delhi after crushing the rebellion of 1857.[11]

With the establishment of Muslim rule in the subcontinent, some people converted to Islam because of its egalitarian principles. In certain places, it was the religion of victors, imposed upon the vanquished, while some converted to Islam to gain political patronage from the local Muslim rulers. There were also regional variations.[12] In the south and the east, Muslim rule was relatively benign and inclusivist. In Hyderabad-Deccan and Bengal, Muslim rulers presided over vast Hindu populations and conversion was extensive and peaceful. However, some regions experienced the militant and exclusivist side of Islam where Hindu temples like those in Multan and Somnath[13] were attacked and Hindus were killed, their property looted and their women raped by the invaders.[14]

Despite closer interactions among individuals, a few real differences between the two religions remained because of their respective religious rituals. But a few significant differences were constructed, primarily by the Hindu and Muslim revival groups. The British supported such constructions and exploited the 'differences' to maintain their imperial rule in India. Most of such constructions glorified their respective religion's past and focused on achieving a better future. G.D. Khosla writes that

> in the desire to recapture self-esteem, Indian minds harked back to ancient Hindu and Muslim cultures. The Hindu minds sought solace in the memory of the Golden Age of Hindu imperialism and the Vedas. . . . The Hindu mind, in trying to rehablitate its lost pride, sought an escape in glorifying its ancient achivements towards which the Muslims had made no contribution, and Hindu revivalism, therefore, took a religious and

> communal form. By a similar psychological process, the Muslims took recourse to the glory of the Prophet, the Khilafat and the Muslim conquest of the countries around Mediterranean.[15]

The Muslim elites chose divisive rather than composite symbols to represent themselves because, as Paul Brass writes, they 'did not recognise a common destiny with the Hindus, because they saw themselves in danger of losing their privileges as a dominant community.'[16] The myth versus reality of the Muslim backwardness in North India, especially in UP is at the core of the debate between Francis Robinson and Paul Brass as well as among many other scholars. Communal tones were also used to degrade people from other communities at that time. Imagining the character of Muslims, analysing Saratchandra Chattopadhya's *Bartman Hindu-Muslim Samasya*, Joya Chatterji writes,

> it is their [Muslims] basic lack of "culture" that, Saratchandra argues, accounts for brutality, barbarism and fanaticism of Muslims. These are the age-old universal and unchanging attributes of the Muslim community, as much as in evidence among the first Ghaznavite conquerors, who "were not satisfied merely with looting-they destroyed temples, they demolished idols, they raped women", as any present-day Bengali Muslims. . . .[17]

On the basis of religion, Sir Syed Ahmad Khan determined that Hindus and Muslims were two different nations. Later, the All India Muslim League (AIML) accepted this as a basis for their demand for Pakistan. At the Lahore session of 1940 where Pakistan resolution was passed by the AIML, Mohammad Ali Jinnah in his presidential address insisted that both Hindus and Muslims were two different people belonging to different nations and had irreconcilable aspirations that could not be fulfilled by living together. Along similar lines, Vinayak Damodar Savarkar, founder of the Hindu Mahasabha, accepted Hindus from across the regions of India as a part of a nation while, he found, Muslims identifying themselves with the outside world. [18] These two versions of nationalism were accepted not only by the Hindu and Muslim communal groups but also by a number of members from the INC.[19]

Based on religious identity, differences were constructed and promoted in other spheres. It was popularised that Hindus and Muslims had different dietary habits, spoke different languages, admired different heroes, etc. For example, in July 1933 the All Bengal Urdu Association declared, 'Bengali is a Hinduised and Sanskritised language,' and so 'in the interests of the Muslims themselves it is necessary that they should try to have one language which cannot but be Urdu.'[20] On the other hand, the Hindu groups since the decline of Mughal power were trying to replace Urdu with Hindi. They claimed Hindi as a language of Hindus while labelling Urdu a foreign language spoken by the Muslims.[21] This constituted the negation of theoretical and practical aspects of language, which has nothing to do with religion as such. It was the cultural aspects of language that led to the tension between East and West Pakistan beginning in 1948 and that eventually contributed to the liberation of Bangladesh in 1971.[22]

Although some attempts were made to settle the differences between the two religious groups, they failed. As Bhim Rao Ambedkar writes:

> Just as attempts were made to bring about unity on political questions, attempts were also made to bring about unity on social and religious questions such as:- 1. Cow slaughter[23] 2. Music before Mosque and 3. Conversions. The first attempt in this direction was made in 1923 when the Indian National Pact was proposed. It failed. At that time Mahatma Gandhi was in jail. He was released from jail on the 5th February 1924. Stunned by the destruction of his work for Hindu-Moslem unity, he decided to go on a twenty one days fast, holding himself morally responsible for the murderous riots that had taken place between Hindus and Muslims. Advantage was taken of the fast to gather leading Indians of all communities at a Unity Conference, which was attended also by the Metropolitan of Calcutta. The Conference held prolonged sittings from 26th September to October 2nd 1924. This Unity Conference did not produce peace between the two communities. It only produced a lull in the rioting which had become the order of the day. Between 1925 and 1926, rioting was renewed with an intensity and malignity unknown before.[24]

In 1923 C.R. Das proposed an inter-community pact whose terms were as follows:[25]

1 The number of members of the two communities would be decided by their respective strength in Bengal's population

and the two communities would vote separately to elect their members.

2 The Muslims would have 60 per cent and the Hindus 40 per cent of the seats in local self-government institutions.
3 Fifty-five per cent of government appointments must be filled by Muslims, but 80 per cent of the vacancies would be filled by them until the overall percentage of 35 per cent reached.
4 Music near mosques, usually a standard excuse for Hindu-Muslim riots, was to be banned.
5 Killing of cows for religious purposes of *Bakr-id*, a standard pretext for starting communal violence, was to be permitted and nobody was allowed to object it.

The INC in its Kakinada session of 1923 rejected it.

Any form of religious reconciliation failed because, as Ambedkar writes:

> The Muslim ideology has undergone a complete revolution. . . . The Hindus say that the British policy of divide and rule is the real cause of this failure and of this ideological revolution . . . the policy of divide and rule . . . cannot succeed unless there are elements which make division possible, and further, if the policy succeeds for such a long time, it means that the elements which divide are more or less permanent and irreconcilable and are not transitory or superficial. Jinnah, who represents this ideological transformation, can never be suspected of being a tool in the hands of the British even by the worst of his enemies. He may be too self-opinionated, an egotist without the mask and has perhaps a degree of arrogance which is not compensated by any extraordinary intellect or equipment. . . . The real explanation of this failure of Hindu-Moslem Unity lies in their failure to realize that stands between the Hindus and Muslims is not to be attributed to material causes. It is spiritual in its character. It is formed by causes which take their origin in historical, religious, cultural and social antipathy, of which political antipathy is only a reflection.[26]

There were also class differences. In most parts of British India, the economic position of the individual was based on their religious and caste identity. The upper caste Hindus and Muslims were also economically dominant groups, while the lower caste Hindus and the converts from the lower castes to Islam were peasants who were being exploited by the two elite classes from different religions. In Bengal, the British policy of allocating lands benefitted a large number of Hindu *bhadraloke* (upper middle class in Bengal), who thus, mostly turned into big landlords living lavish lives by exploiting their Muslim peasants.[27] There were also Muslim landowners in certain districts of northern and central Bengal.[28] Likewise, in Punjab, moneylenders, who were important to the rural economy, were either Hindus or Sikhs. Large-scale modern firms and companies were owned by Hindus or Sikhs. The canal lands were distributed among all three religious groups. Muslims and Sikhs were predominantly in the landowning class, except in Eastern Punjab where Jat Hindus dominated.[29]

The Pakistan movement was born not in Muslim majority provinces of Bengal and Punjab but, rather, in provinces like UP where only about 14 per cent of the population followed Islam. The demand for a separate homeland for Indian Muslims was raised by the Muslim power elites of UP whose social status and economic dominance were on the relative decline under the British rule. This decline, Paul Brass argues, was a myth erected by the Muslim politicians and power elites to which Francis Robinson disagrees.[30] There was a general decline in the number of Muslims in the government jobs because a large section of Muslims still relied on madrassas (Islamic religious schools), and they were reluctant to accept the British education system[31] which was a must for getting into government jobs. In terms of land occupancy there was also a considerable decline in the status of the Muslims in UP. From the settlement reports of 1868–1891 to 1892–1915 Lance Brennan finds out that the Muslims share of land was reduced in about two-third districts of UP. The reduction of land share varied from 38 per cent in Sultanpur to 1 per cent in the Barabanki districts of the province. On the other hand they had improved their land share in Pratapgarh district by 24 per cent. However, on average the share of land by the community declined an average of 3 per cent per district.[32]

Treatment due to 'differences'

Religiously constructed social differences regulate communal interactions between the groups. Such interactions also have a class basis. Although the Hindu and Muslim elites, at least in public, used to interact with each other on equal terms, most of the Hindus hesitated to eat at Muslim homes and shied away from offering Muslims food at their own homes. This pattern of discrimination was clearly visible when there were also class and caste differences.

Informing the discrimination of the time, well-known Bengali poet Siraji wrote in 1917 about how from their childhood the children of Muslim peasants were taught by the Hindu teachers that they were descendants of the low castes and of untouchable Hindu castes.[33] Social discrimination was at such a high degree that all cooked food was thrown away as unclean if a Muslim entered the room, and the Muslim tenants were seated only on the separate *piris* (low wooden seats) whenever they visited their landlord's place.[34] Urvashi Butalia, talking about the treatment of one community member by another, writes:

> Bir Bahadur Singh, one of the people I interviewed told me what he thought of the way Hindus and Sikhs treated Muslims: Such good relations we had that if there was any function that we had, then we used to call Musalmaans to our homes, they would eat in our houses, but we would not eat in theirs and this is a bad thing, which I realise now. If they would come to our houses we would have two utensils in one corner of the house, and we would tell them, pick these up and eat in them; they would then wash them and keep them aside and this was such terrible thing. This was the reason Pakistan was created. . . . A [Muslim] guest comes to our house and we say to him, bring those utensils and wash them, and if my mother or sister have to give him food, they will more or less throw the roti from such a distance, fearing that they may touch the dish and become polluted. . . . We don't have such low dealings with our lower castes as Hindus and Sikhs did with Musalmaans.[35]

Devika Chawla talks about Veeranji, one of her respondents, who told her that it was the Hindus who never ate in their homes, as they did. They ate and drank in ours.[36] Indian writer Krishna Sobti in an interview with Alok Bhalla agreed that in Punjab the conflict was between the peasants and zamindars which turned into a religious conflict. She said that:

> If a poor Muslim student wanted a seat in a medical college, he couldn't get one. That was also true of engineering colleges . . . the children of poor Hindus could go to school. There was a

> reason for it. The Hindu is "civilized" – the *sala* is hardworking and doesn't waste money. . . . In the village, however, they (Muslims) were never allowed to enter the kitchen of Hindu households. No one minded this till *politics* started playing it up as an example of Hindu arrogance. . . . Dhabas used separate plates and glasses for Hindus and Muslims. However the same dhabas served food to both communities.[37]

About his own experiences, Sheikh Mujibur Rahman, the founding father of Bangladesh in 1971, writes that the 'local Hindus held my own family in high esteem. And yet when I went to visit some of my Hindu friends they wouldn't invite me into their houses because their families feared I would pollute them.'[38] Mentioning one incident he further writes:

> I had a friend called Noni Kumar Das. We used to study together and he lived close by. He used to spend the whole day with us and would secretly eat with us. One day I went to his house. He took me to a room inside their house and made me sit there. He used to stay with his uncle. His aunt used to treat me affectionately. After I returned, Noni came to my house close to tears. I asked 'Noni what is the matter?' Noni said, 'Don't come to my house any more. After you left my aunt scolded me a lot for bringing you inside the house. She had the whole floor cleaned with water afterwards and forced me to wash everything.'[39]

This was, as Mujib mentions, not the case with his many other Hindu friends; he used to visit their homes. But this sort of behaviour certainly caused Bengali Muslims to resent the Hindus for their religious prejudices against the Muslims.[40]

These religion based differences were such that even at secular spaces like railway stations, Hindu and Muslim water carriers were used by the members of their respective religious communities. *Hindu Pani* (water) and *Muslim Pani* or *Hindu and Muslim chai* (tea) were visible at railway stations and other places too.[41]

Reactions against 'differences' and treatments

The social discrimination meted out by one group against the other and economic inequality were reasons for non-inclusive anti-colonial movements in India. The anti-colonial movement was led by the then dominant group whose members were from the upper caste and upper or middle class, and most of them had been educated in Europe. Hence the marginal groups could not identify themselves with that political leadership and on certain issues opposed them. About the *Swadeshi* movement, which started in Bengal and spread to other parts of India, Sumit Sarkar writes: 'despite much talk about the need for mass awakening, the Swadeshi movement of 1905–1908 seldom got beyond the confines of Hindu upper caste bhadralok groups – students, journalists, teachers, doctors and lawyers who very often had a link with rentier interests in land in the form of zamindari and intermediate tenure holding.'[42] In 1905, when Bengal was divided, 20,000 people, mainly Muslim peasants, gathered to offer thanksgiving prayers to God for saving them from 'Hindu oppression.'[43] During the anti-Bengal division movement itself, communal violence occurred in Mymensingh in 1906–1907. The root of the violence was class based animosity between the landlords and the exploited peasants. Most of the landlords were the Hindus, while peasants were Muslims. One of the causes of the communal tension was the rise in food prices in 1906–1907 which had profited the landlords while cursing the large number of already poverty stricken Muslim peasants. This had caused clashes between the two classes at many places – one of them was at Iswarganj in 1906. The Hindu-Muslim press and the community leaders further fomented tensions between the community members by provoking their members and using politically harsh tones against the members of the other community.[44]

Politically, Nawab of Dhaka Salimullah Khan, under whose patronage the Muslim League was formed in 1906, extended his support to the All India division of Bengal in 1905. At a conference in 1907, responding to criticism of the division by Rash Behari Ghosh, Salimullah Khan said:[45]

> The partition has given a new life to the people in the Eastern Province. They are feeling a refreshing sense and a relief from the thraldom of . . . (clauses omitted) Calcutta. They find their rights more quickly recognised and their existence and importance more adequately appreciated than they could as a mere appendage, as heretofore, of Western Bengal. They find that if . . . some 100 deputy magistrates and a like number of sub deputies, *Munsiffs* and sub-registrars have had to be appointed, these appointments went to the children of the soil,

> Hindus and Mohammadens. In fact the people feel neglected in Eastern Bengal. The people have got what Ireland has so strenuously been fighting for, I mean home-rule and not rule from Calcutta . . . so far, therefore, the cry of nationalism in danger is false and unfounded cry; for what is really in danger is not nationalism, but spirit of exclusivism and privilege of monopoly.'

Also, the AIML adopted a resolution in support of the partition of Bengal. The AIML Resolution Number IV of 1906 states: 'Resolved that this meeting in view of the clear interest of the Musalmans of Eastern Bengal, considers that the partition is sure to prove beneficial to the Mohameddan community which constitutes the vast majority of that Province and that all such methods of agitation as boycotting should be strongly condemned and discouraged.'[46]

For Mushirul Hasan, until 1937 the League was a paper organisation.[47] The branch in Bombay, Jinnah's home ground, could only boast of 71 members in 1927. The 1929 session was adjourned because of lack of a quorum. When Iqbal spoke at Allahabad in 1930, the meeting failed to muster the required quorum of 75 members. INC's decision in the summer of 1937 not to include Muslim League members in its government in UP created a space for the League's revival[48] 'and offered Jinnah a chance to establish his hold in a province that had spurned his initial overtures.'[49] In the later part of 1937 in provinces like Bihar, there were instances where Congressmen left the party to join the AIML. One of the Muslim leaders of INC from Bihar, Sayid Muhammad Ismail, in his letter to Dr Rajendra Prasad wrote that 'the burning question facing all patriotic Indians was "how to remove the differences between the Hindus and Muslims, both [the] intelligentsia and masses".'[50] After the formation of their party's governments in many provinces the congress ministries were accused of 'Hinduizing social space'[51] which was politically exploited by the League leadership.

The political rise of the League was also reflected in social churning through which the Muslim community was passing through. At the social level, Sabyasachi Bhattacharyya shows that by 1920s, with an emergence of Muslim middle class intelligentsia in Bengal, there was a strong reaction against the social behaviour of the Hindu *bhadraloke* in everyday life, and this was about private domain:[52] The rising Muslim intelligentsia began to assert their '*Bengali* Muslim' identity on the one hand in their interface with Hindus and, on the other, with the pan-Islamist sentiments that spread in the course of the *khilafat* movement. In their behaviour the emphasis was on purification and consolidation of Islam in India in the 1920s.[53] It was a response to a new religious consciousness that figured in the discourse of Khilafat, on the one hand, and on the other, it was a reaction against activities of the Arya Samaj and the *Shuddist* (purification and re-conversion to Hinduism) movement that they started Islamise themselves and their co-religionists. For example, they started objecting to Gandhi *topi* worn by Muslims or the use of *Sree* in the name of Muslims instead of *janab*. Both were considered anti-Islam.[54]

During that phase, not only Muslim intelligentsia but also revivalists spread their influences in many areas. Noakhali and Tippera of Bengal province had been affected by the Fairaizi movement.[55] Local religious leaders kept the banner of Islam flying in the eyes and imaginations of the Muslim peasantry. Maktabs and Madarsahs, religious debates and *mehfils* all served to heighten the sense of Islamic identity.[56] Although the Faraizi movement is often related with the rise of religious radicalism among the peasants in Noakhali and Tippera, it was primarily a peasant movement against the landlords. It gained a religious tone only after the Muslim revivalists managed to infiltrate the organisation.[57] However, in many places, despite the role of the revivalists, the decision of the peasants to rebel against their exploitative landlords was their own. On the position of peasants in his study from Awadh, Gyanendra Pandey finds out that it was an abstract question of whom the Congress might choose as ally, and then educate and train for political action. There the peasants had already taken the lead in the political process.[58]

Like Fairaizi, the Moplah revolt in 1921 in Kerala was mainly the rise of a class against its oppressor instead of a religious confrontation. Most of the Moplah peasants were Muslim converts mainly from Tiyya, Cheruman and Mukkuvan castes. Many of them had been agrestic slaves. Even after their conversion to Islam many of them experienced physical violence from the upper caste Hindus for not following the Hindu customs.[59] Although the movement was suppressed in the 1920s, the demand for Moplhistan was in the air for a while in the 1940s.

As most of the peasants, especially in Bengal, were Muslims, they suffered during the Bengal famine of the 1940s the worst. Mainly in the 1940s, AIML succeeded in mobilising those peasants along communal lines, impelling them to recognise that their economic condition was related to their religious belongingness. The propaganda was supported by the religion-based class structure existing in most of the towns and rural areas of Bengal and many parts of British India. To accomplish economic transformation in such a society, the League made electoral promises to abolish the *zamindari* system in Pakistan, give 'land to the tiller' and introduce other socialist policies. Those slogans worked in favour of the League candidates, although the INC too had such socialist programmes[60] in its manifesto. As a result, in the 1946 elections, the Muslim League won 439 of the 494 seats reserved for Muslims in the provincial assemblies. It captured 75 per cent of the total Muslim vote in comparison to the 4 per cent it had secured in 1937.[61]

Questions about Dalits

Pertinently, if real and constructed 'differences' and discriminations led to the partition of India in 1947, a question arises about why other groups, especially Dalits, did not demand a separate land – socially, Dalits are still the most oppressed group in India and Pakistan. It is beyond the scope of this chapter. But a few arguments can be made.

First, during British rule in India, many parts of the country witnessed movements for social, political and economic upliftment for the Dalits. BR Ambedkar made demands, such as a separate electorate system,[62] to improve the position of the untouchables in India. In South India, EV Ramaswamy 'Periyar' led movements against the upper caste and North Indian domination over South India. These movements tried to present their version of nationalism and nation, which was different from those of the INC and the AIML.[63] However, despite all such social movements, a majority of the Dalits considered themselves a part of either Hinduism or Islam. They could not imagine themselves as a different group. In 1946 a number of Hindu Dalits identified themselves with the religion and provided electoral support to the INC. Later, in 1947 some of them also participated in the anti-Muslim riots.[64] Even before 1947, clashes between Hindu Dalits and Muslims had occurred in Bengal.[65]

During the partition-related riots, many of them faced violence, rapes and more because of their religious identity. In certain cases their Dalit identity superseded their belongingness to a particular religion. Even during the riots, rapes and plunders, their bodies remained 'impure' and untouchable for most of the upper caste Hindus or Muslim male perpetrators of physical violence. In an interview with Urvashi Butalia, Maya Rani, who was 16 years old in 1947, said, 'There was no danger for us. Because we are Harijans. Whether it had become Pakistan or Hindustan, it made no difference to us.'[66] However Ramnarayan Rawat speculated that the Dalit woman may escaped because of formal alliance between the Scheduled Castes Federation (SCF) and the AIML in Punjab, the former had supported the demand for Pakistan.[67] This was not the case at all places. In Sindh molestation of Dalit women by Muhajirs were reported at that time. This caused exodus of many Dalits from Pakistan to India.[68]

Second, unlike the Dalits, the Indian Muslims, because of their past as rulers of India, raised a protest about their political decline and bleak future in 'Hindu India.' Most of the glories the of Dalits' past had been suppressed. For example at Koregaon Bhima near Pune in the Indian state of Maharashtra in 1818 the British forces which included the Mahars defeated the powerful army of Peshwa Baji Rao II. This has found popular space only after the rise of Dalit leaders and movements in India.

Third, the Muslim middle class managed to construct an imagination and successfully sell the idea that they were 'different' from the Hindus. With the help of their social groups and political organisations, the Muslim power elite succeeded in communalising those 'differences.' This was not the case with the Dalits. Most of them chose their country on the basis of religion, political position of their organisation and, in certain cases, because of their economic position.[69] However, there was a short-lived demand for *Achhutistan* (land of untouchables) which emphasised their distinct identity from the Hindus, Muslims and Sikhs. The demand was raised in 1946 by the All India Achhutistan movement founded by Beah Lall.

Finally, although Dalits had social and political organisations in colonial India, none of them were as popular or as politically and socially effective as AIML was among the Indian Muslims. To secure the interests of their members, most of the Dalit organisations extended their political support to one of the other groups. For example the SCF chose to support AIML, while the All India Depressed Class League (AIDCL) was considered closer to the Hindu groups. The SCF had a formal alliance with the Muslim League in Bengal, UP and Punjab. In Punjab the SCF supported the

League's movement against Premiere of Punjab Sikander Hyat Khan and the establishment of Pakistan.[70] However, its leader, Jogendra Nath Mandal[71] had lent his support to Undivided Bengal. He said:[72]

> if Bengal is partitioned Schedule Castes will suffer the most. The caste Hindus of East Bengal are wealthy and many have salaried jobs. They will have little difficulty in moving from east to west Bengal. Poor scheduled caste peasants, fishermen and artisans will have to remain in east Bengal where the proportion of Hindus will decline and they will be at the mercy of the majority Muslim community.

Later, the SCF members casted their votes along with the AIML in the referendum of Sylhet.

Active mainly in Punjab where Dalits constituted 6.9 per cent of the total population, the AIDCL demanded representation in the Boundary Commission but was denied. Allegedly, this group was politically closer to the Hindu organisations in Punjab. In June 1947, after the Partition plan was announced, HJ Khandekar, president of the AIDCL, sent a representative to Mountbatten asking for adequate representation of the 'Depressed Classes' in the Boundary Commission.[73] In this regard, in May 1947 a resolution was passed by the AIDCL which stated:[74]

1 Depressed Classes of the Bengal and Punjab will be greatly affected by the division of these two provinces and it is feared that there will be forcible conversions of the Depressed Classes in the Muslim Predominating Provinces and to stop this, it is vitally necessary that the boundary commission to be formed under the H.M.G.'s (His Majesty Government's) Plan, must include representatives of the Depressed Classes.
2 The Committee appeals to the Congress, Hindu and Sikh leaders to give accurate representation to the Depressed Classes in the regional ministries, to be formed in the province in the near future.
3 The Committee views with great concern the growing activities of the Muslim, Christian and Sikh missionaries for the conversion of the Depressed Classes to their respective faiths with a view to increasing their number solely for political purpose. These activities, if not checked in time, will not only reduce Depressed Classes to a non-entity but will also affect Hindu Society in general and will create fresh political problems and complications in every province.

Conclusion

As discussed, there were 'differences' between the Hindus and the Muslims in colonial India, which to an extent were also reasons for discrimination between the two religious groups. Some differences were real while others were constructed to serve the social and political demands of the Muslim power elites.

With the rise of the Muslim middle class, these 'differences' were challenged. A majority of the educated Muslim middle class asserted their demands and raised their voices against the oppression of lower class Muslims. At a later stage, this class created and disseminated an imagined community, a separate homeland for Muslims where justice would be done for everyone. For example, in UP students from Aligarh Muslim University were leading campaigners of the Pakistan movement in 1940s.[75] To help their cause, even some of the Hindu groups depicted the Muslims as foreigners in India. Eventually, India was partitioned due to the intersection of historical reasons with immediate conflicts between the Hindus and the Muslims.

Notes

1 See Talbot, Ian and Gurharpal Singh (2009) *The partition of India*. New Delhi: Cambridge University Press, pp. 7–24.
2 See Jalal, Ayesha (1994) *The Sole Spokesman: Jinnah, The Muslim League and the Demand for Pakistan*. Cambridge: Cambridge University Press.
3 Dhulipala, Venkat (2015) *Creating a New Medina: State Power, Islam, and the Quest for Pakistan in Late Colonial North India*. New Delhi: Cambridge University Press.
4 Qasmi, Usman Ali and Megan Eaton Robb (2017) *Muslims against the Muslim League: Critiques of the Idea of Pakistan*. Cambridge: Cambridge University Press.
5 Khosla, GD (2012) 'The Parting of the Ways.' In Roy, Kaushik (Ed.), *Partition of India: Why 1947?* New Delhi: Oxford University Press, pp. 1–34.
6 Barbara D. Metcalf (2009) 'A Historical Overview of Islam in South Asia.' In Metcalf, Barbara D. (Ed.), *Islam in South Asia: In Practice*. Ranikhet: Permanent Black, pp. 1–39.
7 Stein, Burton (1998) *A History of India*. New Delhi: Oxford University Press, p. 134.
8 See Sardar, Ziauddin (2014) *Mecca: The Sacred City*. New Delhi: Bloomsbury.
9 Gill, Sadiq A. (2010) *A Text Book of Pakistan Studies for BA, BSc, B.Com., Professional Degrees & Competitive Exams*. Lahore: Publishers Emporium.

10 See Sardar, Ziauddin (2014) *Mecca: The Sacred City*. New Delhi: Bloomsbury.
11 The rebellion is also known as the Sepoy Mutiny or first war for Indian independence. In this war most of the princely states participated because of the 'doctrine of lapse' introduced by the Lord Dalhousie in 1856. The sepoys or soldiers participated because of social, religious and economic reasons.
12 Cohen, Stephen P. (2005) *The Idea of Pakistan*. New Delhi: Oxford University Press.
13 Destruction and looting of temples was common during ancient and mediaeval India because of the wealth these religious places used to accumulate. Even Hindu kings attacked temples like Somnath for such reasons. See Thapar, Romila (2008) *Somnath: The Many Voices of A History*. New Delhi: Penguin Books.
14 Cohen, Stephen P. (2005) *The Idea of Pakistan*. New Delhi: Oxford University Press.
15 Khosla, GD (2012) 'The Parting of the Ways.' In Roy, Kaushik (Ed.), *Partition of India: Why 1947?* New Delhi: Oxford University Press, pp. 1–34.
16 As mentioned in Robinson, Francis (2012) 'Islam and Muslim Separatism.' In Roy, Kaushik (Ed.), *Partition of India: Why 1947?* New Delhi: Oxford University Press, pp. 85–115.
17 Cited in Chaterji, Joya (1994) *Bengal Divided: Hindu Communalism and Partition, 1932–1947*. Cambridge: Cambridge University Press, p. 174.
18 Savarkar, Vir Damodar (1949) *Hindu Rashtra Darshan*. Bombay: V.V. Bambardekar Press, p. 102.
19 Moore, R.J. (2001) 'Jinnah and the Pakistan Demand.' In Hasan, Mushirul (Ed.), *India's Partition: Process, Strategy and Mobilization*. New Delhi: Oxford University Press, pp. 160–198.
20 Cited in Talbot, Ian and Gurharpal Singh (2009) *The partition of India*. New Delhi: Cambridge University Press, p. 52.
21 See Rai, Alok (2000). *Hindi Nationalism: Tracts for the Times*. Hyderabad: Orient Longman.
22 See Fazal, Tanveer (2016) 'Religion and Language in the Formation of Nationhood in Pakistan and Bangladesh.' In Bandyopadhyay, Sekhar (Ed.), *Decolonisation and Politics of Transition in South Asia*. Hydrabad: Orient Black Swan, pp. 324–347.
23 This is still a dominant issue in India in 2017. In many of the Indian states under the Rashtriya Swamsevak Sangh backed Bhartiya Janta Party government, cases have been registered against the groups engaged in the killing of people they perceived to be engaged in cow-slaughtering or whose acts support such acts. The debate is also ongoing over whether one can consume beef or not. In Directive Principles of State Policy of the Indian constitution there is a provision against cow-slaughtering. In some of the Indian states this is a legally banned profession.
24 Ambedkar, Bhim Rao (1945) (second edition) *Pakistan or Partition of India*. Bombay: Thacker and Company Limited, pp. 304–305.
25 Cited in Sengupta, Nitish (2007) *Bengal Divided: The Unmaking of a Nation (1905–1971)*. New Delhi: Penguin Books, pp. 124–125.

26 Ambedkar, Bhim Rao (1945) (second edition) *Pakistan or Partition of India*. Bombay: Thacker and Company Limited, p. 322–324.
27 Iqbal, Iftekhar (2011) *The Bengal Delta: Ecology, State and Social Change, 1840–1943*. New York: Palgrave Macmillan, p. 98.
28 Chatterjee, Partha (2001) 'Bengal Politics and the Muslim Masses, 1920–47.' In Hasan, Mushirul (Ed.), *India's Partition: Process, Strategy and Mobilization*. New Delhi: Oxford University Press, pp. 259–278.
29 Ahmed, Ishtiaq (2011) *The Punjab Bloodied Partition and Cleansed: Unravelling the 1947 Tragedy through Secret British Reports and First Person Accounts*. New Delhi: Rupa, p. 34.
30 For debate between Paul Brass and Francis Robinson See Brass, Paul (1974) *Language, Religion and Politics in North India*. Cambridge: Cambridge University Press; Robinson, Francis (2000) *Islam and Muslim History in South Asia*. New Delhi: Oxford University Press.
31 Robinson, Francis (2000) *Islam and Muslim History in South Asia*. New Delhi: Oxford University Press, p. 167.
32 Brennan, Lance (2001) 'The Illusion of Security: The Background to Muslim Separatism in the United Provinces.' In Hasan, Mushirul (Ed.), *India's Partition: Process, Strategy and Mobilization*. New Delhi: Oxford University Press, pp. 323–360.
33 Cited in Bhattacharya, Sabyasachi (2014) *The Defining Moments in Bengal, 1920–1947*. New Delhi: Oxford University Press.
34 Sengupta, Nitish (2007) *Bengal Divided: The Unmaking of a Nation (1905–1971)*. New Delhi: Penguin Books, p. 150.
35 Butalia, Urvashi (2014) *The Other Side of Silence: Voices from the partition of India*. New Delhi: Penguin Books, pp. 39–40.
36 Chawla, Devika (2014) *Home Uprooted: Oral Histories of India's Partition*. New York: Fordham University Press, p. 172.
37 Bhalla, Alok (2006) *Partition Dialogues: Memories of a Lost Home*. New Delhi: Oxford University Press, pp. 147–148.
38 Rahman, Sheikh Mujibur (2012) *The Unfinished Memoirs*. New Delhi: Penguin Books, p. 24.
39 Ibid.
40 Ibid.
41 See Khan, Yasmin (2007) *The Great Partition: The Making of India and Pakistan*. New Delhi: Penguin Books; Bhalla, Alok (2006) *Partition Dialogues: Memories of a Lost Home*. New Delhi: Oxford University Press, pp. 147–148.
42 Sarkar, Sumit (1984) 'The Conditions and Nature of Subaltern Militancy: Bengal from Swadeshi to Non-Co-Operation, c. 1905–1922.' In Guha, Ranajit (Ed.), *Subaltern Studies III: Writings on South Asian History and Society*. New Delhi: Oxford University Press, pp. 271–321.
43 Iqbal, Iftekhar (2011) *The Bengal Delta: Ecology, State and Social Change, 1840–1943*. New York: Palgrave Macmillan, p. 98.
44 Das, Suranjan (1991) *Communal Riots in Bengal 1905–1947*. New Delhi: Oxford University Press.
45 Saxena, Vinod Kumar (1987) *The Partition of Bengal 1905–1911: Select Documents*. New Delhi: Kanishka Publishers, p. 115.
46 Ibid., p. 157.

47 Cited in Hasan, Mushirul (2002) *Islam in the Subcontinent: Muslim in Plural Society*. New Delhi: Manohar.
48 *See* Azad, Maulana Abul Kalam (2003) *India Wins Freedom*. Hyderabad: Orients Blackswan.
49 Hasan, Mushirul (2002) *Islam in the Subcontinent: Muslim in Plural Society*. New Delhi: Manohar.
50 Cited in Ghosh, Papiya (2010) *Muhajirs and the Nation: Bihar in 1940s*. London, New York, Delhi: Routledge, p. 2.
51 See Robinson, Francis (2000) *Islam and Muslim History in South Asia*. New Delhi: Oxford University Press.
52 Bhattacharya, Sabyasachi (2014) *The Defining Moments in Bengal, 1920–1947*. New Delhi: Oxford University Press.
53 Ibid.
54 Ibid.
55 The Faraizi Movement was founded in 1818 by Haji Shariatullah to give up un-Islamic practices and act upon their duties as Muslims. This became very popular among the tenants of east Bengal. It was very popular in Dhaka, Faridpur, Barisal, Mymensingh and Comila. Started as a peasant movement it distracted from its agenda after the death of its leader Noa Miyan in 1884. It further lost its influence when one faction joined the AIML in 1906.
56 Bose, Sugata (1986) *Agrarian Bengal: Economic, Social Structure and Politics, 1919–1947*. Cambridge: Cambridge University Press.
57 See Iqbal, Iftekhar (2011) *The Bengal Delta: Ecology, State and Social Change, 1840–1943*. New York: Palgrave Macmillan.
58 Pandey, Gyanendra (1982) ‘Peasants Revolt and Indian Nationalism: The Peasent Movement in Awadh, 1919–1922.’ In Guha, Ranajit (Ed.), *Subaltern Studies I*. Oxford: Oxford University Press, pp. 182 of 143–197.
59 Verghese, Ajay (2016) *The Colonial Origins of Ethnic Violence in India*. Stanford: Stanford University Press, p. 119; Sathar, KK Muhammad Abdul (2012) *Mappila Leader in Exile: A Political Biography of Syed Fazal Tangal*. Calicut: Other Books.
60 On the INC’s position on zamindari system, See Nehru, Jawaharlal (2004) *The Discovery of India*. Gurgaon: Penguin Books, pp. 407–408.
61 Talbot, Ian and Gurharpal Singh (2009) *The partition of India*. New Delhi: Cambridge University Press, p. 36.
62 The separate electorate for the depressed classes outlined under Ramsay Mcdonald’s ‘Communal Award’ was replaced by special concessions like reserved seats in regional legislative councils and the central council under the Poona Pact of 1932 between Gandhi and Ambedkar. The aim of the pact was to encourage the depressed classes to remain Hindu instead of defining themselves as a different group.
63 Raghavan, Srinath (2016) *India’s War: The Making of Modern South Asia*. New Delhi: Penguin Books.
64 Chatterji, Joya (1994) *Bengal Divided: Hindu Communalism and Partition, 1932–1947*. Cambridge: Cambridge University Press.
65 Ibid & see Sarkar, Sumit (1984) ‘The Conditions and Nature of Subaltern Militancy: Bengal from Swadeshi to Non-Co-operation, c. 1905–22.’ In Guha, Ranajit (Ed.), *Subaltern Studies III: Writings on South Asian History ad Society*. New Delhi: Oxford University Press, pp. 271–321.

66 Butalia, Urvashi (2014) *The Other Side of Silence: Voices from the partition of India*. New Delhi: Penguin Books, p. 313.
67 Rawat, Ramnarayan S. (2001) 'Partition Politics and Acchut Identity: A Study of Scheduled Castes Federation and Identity Politics.' In Kaul, Suvir (Ed.), *The Partitions Memory: The Afterlife of the Division of India*. Ranikhet: Permanent Black, pp. 111–139
68 Bhavnani, Nandita (2014) *The Making of Exile: Sindhi Hindus and the partition of India*. Chennai: Tranquebar Press, p. 91.
69 Many Dalits because of their economic position could not afford to displace themselves.
70 Rawat, Ramnarayan S. (2001) 'Partition Politics and Acchut Identity: A Study of Scheduled Castes Federation and Identity Politics.' In Kaul, Suvir (Ed.), *The Partitions Memory: The Afterlife of the Division of India*. Ranikhet: Permanent Black, pp. 111–139.
71 After the partition of India Jogendra Nath Mandal became the first law minister of Pakistan. After the death of Jinnah in 1948, Mandal found that the Pakistani state turned anti-Hindu and anti-minorities under the leadership of Liaqat Ali Khan. He returned to India in 1950 with some of his supporters and became an Indian citizen.
72 Partha Chaterjee (2012) 'The Second Partition of Bengal.' In Roy, Kaushik (Ed.), *Partition of India: Why 1947?* New Delhi: Oxford University Press, pp. 146–163.
73 Butalia, Urvashi (2014) *The Other Side of Silence: Voices from the partition of India*. New Delhi: Penguin Books, p. 316.
74 Ibid.
75 See Hasan, Mushirul (2012) 'The Local Roots of the Pakistan Movement: The Aligarh Muslim University.' In Roy, Kaushik (Ed.), *Partition of India: Why 1947?* New Delhi: Oxford University Press, pp. 116–145.

Part I

Impact of partition in the provinces and princely states

Chapter 2

The 1947 partition of Punjab

Ishtiaq Ahmed

Every day at dusk, during the flag-lowering ceremony at the Wagah-Attari International Border between India and Pakistan, situated between Lahore on the Pakistani side and Amritsar on the Indian side, large crowds congregate on both sides to watch the spectacle of Indian and Pakistani soldiers symbolically sealing the border by ramming the iron gates with a fierce bang to indicate that an impassable barrier exists between the two countries and between their peoples. The spectators nervously clap, shout slogans and make other gesticulations to express their 'patriotism.' Since mid-August 1947, the Punjabis on both sides have hardly ever met. Pakistanis can almost never visit the Indian East Punjab, and similarly, Indians are practically barred from visiting West Punjab. Before Partition, some people daily caught the early bus or train from either of these cities, did their job or business in the other and returned. The distance between the two cities is 30 miles, or 48 kilometres. They were closely integrated economically and were expanding towards one another and were expected to merge in the future. All that was interrupted and arrested irreversibly when the Punjab was partitioned in 1947 and the Radcliffe Award drew a line between Lahore and Amritsar that became the international border between India and Pakistan.

Ideas of partitioning India

Ideas to partition India to separate Hindus (majority) and Muslims (minority of 25 per cent but concentrated in the northwestern and northeastern zones of the Indian subcontinent) go back to the late nineteenth century. Both Hindu and Muslim versions of it had been set forth on the basis that the interests of these two groups were irreconcilable.[1] In the early 1930s, two Muslim Punjabis advanced the idea of a separate Muslim state in northwestern India. The theory underlying such a demand came to be known as the two-nation theory. The poet-thinker Allama Iqbal presented the idea of such a Muslim state in his presidential address at the annual session of the Muslim League at Allahabad. He was not, however, thinking of complete separation from the rest of India at that stage.[2] In 1933, some Muslim students at Cambridge University led by Chowdhary Rahmat Ali published a pamphlet, *Now or Never*, in which a demand to create a separate Muslim state was given a name: PAKISTAN representing the Muslim majority provinces (Punjab, Afghania, Kashmir, Sindh and Baluchistan) of northwestern India by Chowdhary Rahmat Ali.[3]

Ideas of partitioning Punjab

The Punjab was a region which throughout history saw the movement of people entering the Indian subcontinent from the northwestern mountain passes. Islam arrived in the tenth century along with Muslim armies, which paved the way for the Sufi Orders originating in the Middle East and Central Asia to establish their presence in the Punjab. Many tribes converted to Islam. Among Hindus, the Gorakhnathi yogis and later the Bhaktis represented also peaceful reform movements. The founding of Sikhism as a brotherhood by Guru Nanak in the fifteenth century added further pluralism to the Punjabi cultural scene. The first four Sikh Gurus were men of peace, but from the time of the fifth, Guru Arjun, tension and conflict had emerged between him and his disciples and the Mughal emperors based in Agra. At the popular level syncretism due to the fusion of Islamic, Hindu and Sikh ideas became the way of life of the people although orthodox and puritan forms of religion also existed. The Sikhs under Ranjit Singh emerged as the ruling community in the Punjab at the beginning of the nineteenth century. The Sikh Kingdom lasted until 1849, when the British annexed the Punjab after a combination of wars and intrigue.[4]

The British Punjab Province included both the directly administered areas and the princely states which were under British paramountcy through treaty. From 1911 onwards, the directly administered Punjab comprised five large administrative divisions: Ambala, Jallandhar, Lahore, Multan and Rawalpindi. Each division included five to six districts. There were altogether 29 districts in the British-administered Punjab. According to the 1941 census, Muslims formed 53.2 per cent of the total population of the Punjab Province, which included the princely states. Hindus were 29.1 per cent, and Sikhs, 14.9 per cent of the population. In the British-administered districts, Muslims formed 57.7 per cent of the population. The Hindus made up 26.5 per cent, and Sikhs were 13.2 per cent of the British-administered Punjab population.[5]

The Punjab fared very favourably under British rule. They laid down a canal system in the semi-desert areas of Western Punjab, which converted them into the granary of India. Punjabi Muslims, Hindus and Sikhs selected carefully based on the so-called Martial Races Theory and enlisted in large numbers in the British Indian Army. During World Wars I and II, Punjabis were overrepresented in the army. They saw action in the Middle East, Africa, Europe and Southeast Asia.[6]

Ideas of partitioning the Punjab also had existed for a long time. Thus, the Arya Samaj leader Lala Lajpat Rai wrote several articles in the *Tribune* of Lahore in November-December 1924 in which he said: ‘My suggestion is a that the Punjab should be partitioned into two provinces, the Western Punjab with large Muslim majority to be [a] Muslim-governed province; the Eastern Punjab with a large Hindu-Sikh majority to be [a] non-Muslim-governed province.’[7] He also suggested that Muslim provinces be established in the North West Frontier Province (NWFP), Sindh and East Bengal. Some prominent Punjabi Muslims were in favour of the predominantly Hindu majority and Hindi-speaking Ambala division in the east being separated from rest of the province. Iqbal had supported such an idea. Other notable Muslims who supported this idea in different forms included Nawab Sir Mohammad Shahn awaz Khan.[8] The British, too, were thinking of solving the problem of communal tension by separating the Ambala division from the Punjab and thus making the Muslim community predominant in the Punjab. Such suggestions were resented not only by Hindus, whose numbers in the Punjab would decrease drastically if such a scheme were to be adopted, but also by the Sikhs. Already at the Indian Round Table Conference held in London in 1930–1931 Sikh delegates tried to confront the idea of making Punjab a conclusively Muslim majority province by the following argument:

> If the Muslims refuse to accept in this province, where they are in a slight majority in population anything but their present

> demand of reserved majority, we ask for a territorial rearrangement which would take from the Punjab and Multan divisions (excluding Montgomery and Lyallpur districts). These divisions are overwhelmingly Muslim as well as racially akin to the North West Frontier Province. These . . . can either form a separate province or be amalgamated with the North West Frontier Province.[9]

In the Punjab tangle, the aspirations of the Sikhs need to be taken note of in particular because, as the third major community of the Punjab, and one with complete identification with the Punjab as their religious and cultural homeland but with majority in no district of the Punjab, the position of their leaders on the shape of the Punjab mattered. They had a very large presence in the British Indian army and were therefore an important community in the province. Although in the 1920s a bitter conflict broke out between Hindus and Sikhs when some Arya Samaj leaders described the Sikhs as merely a Hindu sect and the Sikhs responded by asserting that they were not Hindus in 1935, the Sikhs clashed with the Muslims over the custody of a shrine in Lahore, known as the Masjid-Gurdwara Shaheedganj. Thereafter, events unfolded in such a manner that the Hindus and Sikhs closed ranks against the Punjabi Muslims.[10]

An important feature of the evolution of political parties during the colonial period was the emergence of the Indian National Congress (founded 1885). Its main leaders were leaders Gandhi and Nehru and the All-India Muslim League (founded 1906) which had Mohammad Ali Jinnah as the supreme leader. These two main parties represented conflicting versions of nationalism. The Congress claimed to be a secular party of all Indians, while the Muslim League was a party exclusively of Muslims. There were strong regional parties in different parts of India as well. However, until the second half of the 1930s, neither the Congress nor the Muslim League had a strong presence in the Punjab.

The Punjab Unionist Party and communal harmony

The Punjab Unionist Party, founded in 1923, dominated the politics of pre-partition Punjab until the election of 1946. Its founder, Sir Fazl-i-Hussain (who died in 1936), had established the basis of communal harmony, but one that preserved the interests of the

Muslim and Hindu landowning and agricultural classes vis-à-vis urban Hindus. The Sikhs were not part of it[11] but were allied to it during the elections through the Khalsa National Party of Sir Sunder Sikh Majithia. From 1909 onwards, Indian Muslims, including Punjabi Muslims, voted separately for a reserved number of seats. The 1935 Act introduced wholly elected ministries in the provinces, though the governor, who was always British, continued to enjoy overriding executive powers. The right to vote had been gradually expanding after 1909, but even in 1937, when the elections were held, the franchise was limited to around ten per cent of the Indian population. Sir Sikandar Hayat Khan succeeded Sir Fazl as the leader of the Unionist Party. He was elected the first premier of Punjab province. He despised the Congress Party's anti-British radical nationalism. The Congress leader Jawaharlal Nehru had threatened to carry out land reforms to abolish landlordism and that was unacceptable to the Unionist Party. Therefore, Sir Sikander entered into the so-called Jinnah-Sikandar Pact of 1937 by which Muslim members of the Unionist Party in the Punjab legislature agreed to become members of the Muslim League and thus strengthen the hands of the central Muslim League on the national level. On the other hand, the Unionist Party was to continue freely to decide its political priorities in the Punjab.[12]

The Lahore resolution of 23 March 1940

Although the idea that the Muslim League should demand a separate state had been floated by Iqbal in 1930, it was taken up in earnest in 1938, when several resolutions were proposed and discussed in favour of creating separate Muslim states. But at that time India was still very much a part of the British Empire. On 23 March 1940, a resolution was moved publicly at the annual session of the Muslim League in Lahore. It was a grand manifestation of Muslim resolve to assert that they were a separate nation and therefore entitled to separate statehood. Delegates attended it from all parts of India. The resolution stated:

> Resolved that it is the considered view of this session of the All-India Muslim League that no constitutional plan would be workable in this country or acceptable to Muslims unless it is designed on the following principle, viz., that geographically contiguous units are demarcated into regions which should be

> grouped to constitute 'independent states' in which the constituted units shall be autonomous and sovereign.[13]

Subsequent research clearly shows that the Lahore resolution was a turning point in the destiny of the Punjab, as well as of India. The Punjabi Hindus and Sikhs reacted with great alarm to the idea of a separate Muslim state. It was dubbed the 'Pakistan Resolution' by Hindu and Sikh newspapers. In any event, after the 23 March 1940 Lahore Resolution, the focus of Muslim politics shifted decisively from the Muslim minority provinces to the Muslim majority provinces of northwestern India. Punjab Governor Sir Henry Craik observed in a long telegram of 1 April 1940 to Viceroy Linlithgow: 'Muslim opinion is now, outwardly at least, in favour of the partition of India. Only a very courageous Muslim leader would now come forward openly to oppose or even criticise it.'[14]

The Punjab became the key province in the struggle for a separate Muslim state. Not surprisingly the community that perceived the creation of such a state as clashing with its deepest interests in the province was that of the Sikhs. Unlike Hindus and Muslims, who were to be found all over India, the Sikhs were essentially a Punjab-based community. Their leaders began to clamour that a majoritarian tyranny of Muslims would be established in Pakistan. They therefore demanded that if India was partitioned on a religious basis then the Punjab should also be partitioned on a similar basis so that the non-Muslim-majority areas would be given either to India or to a Sikh state. They continued agitating throughout 1940 and 1941, and when Sir Stafford Cripps came with his mission in early 1942 to find out if a constitutional formula could be found that would keep India united, they presented a memorandum to him on 31 March in which they complained that Sikh interests would be sacrificed if the British government conceded to the creation of Pakistan. They wrote, 'We shall resist, however, by all possible means the separation of the Punjab from the All-India Union. We shall never permit our motherland to be at the mercy of those who disown it.'[15]

The Khizr ministry

Sir Sikander died suddenly on 26 December 1942. It created a major political crisis. His successor Sir Khizr Hayat Khan Tiwana was, like his predecessor, opposed to the division of India on religious grounds, and especially to suggestions about partitioning Punjab on such a basis. He was a firm believer in the benefit of continued British rule. However, he lacked the political skills of Sikandar and faced leadership challenges from within the Unionist Party.[16] Moreover, Khizr clashed with Jinnah in 1943 and 1944 when the latter, in contravention of the 1937 Jinnah-Sikandar Pact, tried to expand his direct influence in the Punjab. Khizr offered considerable resistance to Jinnah's increasingly communal rhetoric and demand for a separate Pakistan. But challenges from within to his leadership, launched by Sir Sikandar's son, Sardar Shaukat Hayat, in 1943, and later defections of other powerful landowners greatly weakened Khizr's position.[17] As the moment of British departure came nearer, the landlords shifted their support to the Muslim League, since they did not want to live in a united India ruled by Congress because that party had declared the abolition of the *zamindari* system as a priority reform when it came to power.

On the other hand, the Muslim League presented the idea of Pakistan as a panacea for all economic and social problems afflicting Muslims. As early as 1944, the Punjab Governor Sir Bertrand Glancy noticed that such a trend was gaining pace in the Punjab. In a secret report dated 26 October 1944, he remarked:

> I would lay very great emphasis on a point that I endeavoured to make recently at Delhi – and that is the intense danger in the crude Pakistan theory. The more one considers this theory, the more fantastic – and the more ruinous to Muslims and all other interests – does it appear. No one can deny the possibility of political unrest after the end of the war, but I can think of no more alarming menace to peace, so far as the Punjab is concerned, then the pursuit of the Pakistan doctrine. Any serious attempt to carry out into effect this idea in the Punjab with its bare Muslim majority and its highly virile elements of non-Muslims means that we shall be heading directly towards communal disturbances of the first magnitude. Hence I maintain that we should do our utmost to expose the fallacies involved by any such doctrine: we should try to wean Muslim opinion into acceptance of equal or adequate representation at the Centre, while endeavouring to persuade Hindus that they should be prepared to pay this premium for unity and security.[18]

Elections

In July 1945, Winston Churchill was defeated in the British general elections, and a Labour government headed by Clement Attlee came to power. Attlee announced elections for India in early 1946. A general feeling prevailed that Great Britain could not hold on to India anymore because World War II had shattered its economy and industrial and military might. An election campaign began in which the Muslim League demanded a mandate from Muslim voters for a separate Pakistan while the Congress stood for a united India. The Muslim League in its election campaign resorted to Islamist slogans such as '*Pakistan ka Nara/Matlab kya? La Illaha Illillah*' ('the meaning of Pakistan is that there is no god but Allah'). It made extravagant promises that the creation of Pakistan would bring to an end the tyranny of the horrible caste system as well as the stranglehold of Hindu and Sikh moneylender.[19] Muslim voters were told that voting for the Muslim League was voting for the Holy Prophet and for those who would not vote for it their nikah (marriage) would be annulled and they would be refused an Islamic burial. Governor Glancy continued to warn the Viceroy that such a campaign would generate bad blood between the Muslims, on the one hand, and Hindus and Sikhs, on the other. The governor reported several times that the Sikhs would resist being included in Pakistan by all means. In a report dated 2 February 1946, only days before the elections, Glancy wrote to Viceroy Wavell:

> The ML (Muslim League) orators are becoming increasingly fanatical in their speeches. *Maulvis* and *Pirs* and students travel all round the Province and preach that those who fail to vote for the League candidates will cease to be Muslims; their marriages will no longer be valid and they will be entirely excommunicated . . . It is not easy to foresee what the results of the elections will be. But there seems little doubt the Muslim League, thanks to the ruthless methods by which they have pursued their campaign of 'Islam in danger,' will considerably increase the number of their seats and unionist representatives will correspondingly decline.[20]

The Muslim League tactics proved spectacularly successful. In the Punjab, it won 73 seats out of 86 reserved for Muslims. The Congress won 50 general seats and the Sikhs won 23 reserved Sikh seats. The inter-communal Punjab Unionist Party was reduced to a rump of merely 18 seats. The Punjabi electorate had voted clearly along communal lines. Elsewhere too, the Muslim League swept the polls, capturing 440 reserved Muslim seats out of the total of 495 for the whole of India. The Congress won a clear majority of general seats: it won 905 seats out of a total of 1585, including 324 without a contest.[21] Thus, both the Muslim League's stand for Pakistan and the Congress' stand in favour of a united India had been vindicated by the voters.

British response to the election results

The British government sent a high-powered mission consisting of three ministers of the British cabinet to India to probe the possibility of a rapprochement between the Muslim League and Congress. It found that both sides were intransigent on their basic positions on the future of India: Congress envisioned a united India with a strong centre, and the Muslim League wanted a separate Pakistan. Therefore, on 16 May 1946, a Cabinet Mission Plan was announced. While it rejected the idea of Pakistan as unviable it recommended a loose federation consisting of three groups of provinces: A (Hindu majority), B (Muslim majority in the north-west) and C (Muslim majority in the north-east). The powers of the centre were limited to defence, foreign affairs and communications and the right to raise taxes only for these three functions. The Sikh leaders raised strong objections to being placed in Group B. At any rate, the Muslim League reluctantly accepted the plan, but the Congress leadership rejected it objecting that it would create a powerless and ineffective centre which no independent and sovereign state could accept.[22] The Sikh leader Master Tara Singh sent a letter dated 25 May 1946 to Secretary of State for India Pethick-Lawrence in which he wrote:

> The Sikhs have been entirely thrown at the mercy of the Muslims. Group B comprises the Punjab, the N.W.F. Province, Sind and Baluchistan. . . . The Cabinet Mission recognises 'the very genuine and acute anxiety of the Muslims lest they should find themselves subjected to a perpetual Hindu majority rule.' But is there no 'genuine and acute anxiety' among the Sikhs lest they should find themselves subjected to a perpetual Muslim majority rule? If the British Government is not aware of the Sikh feelings, the Sikhs will have to resort to some measures in

order to convince everybody of the Sikh anxiety, in case they are subjected to a perpetual Muslim domination.[23]

Escalation of communal violence

After a rash remark by Jawaharlal Nehru in a press conference on 10 July 1946 that Congress would enter the constituent assembly (which had been setup for a united India) free of all agreements and choose its policies freely, things began to take a tragic turn. Jinnah gave a call for direct action, which on 16 August 1946 took on an ugly form in Calcutta where a holiday had been announced by the provincial government headed by the Muslim League party. Evidence suggests that trouble started first when Muslim hoodlums attacked Hindu locals, but Hindu retaliation was swift and terrible. Several thousand people were killed. The Bengal Muslim League and Bengal Congress leaderships were involved in fomenting those riots. Several thousand Hindus and Muslims perished in mob attacks and counter attacks.[24] Thereafter things began to grow out of control. Violence spread to Noakhali in Bengal and then to Bihar where several thousand Muslims were butchered. The next was western UP; then, Hazara district in NWFP. Finally, in March 1947, communal riots shook four cities of Punjab – Lahore, Amritsar, Multan and Rawalpindi.[25]

A bloody March 1947 in the Punjab

The election in Punjab had not returned any clear majority. The Muslim League was undoubtedly the party with the most seats in the Punjab Legislative Assembly. Its numbers had risen from 73 to 75 as some Unionists crossed the floor to join. Yet it was short by ten seats to form the government. On the other hand, while the Unionist Party had been routed because most of its members had decamped and joined the Muslim League, the Congress and Sikhs were determined not to let the Muslim League form the government. Finally, a coalition government comprising the Unionist Party, the Punjab Congress and the Panthic Parties was formed with Khizr Tiwana as premier. The Muslim League felt deprived of the chance to form the government but it could not produce evidence that it enjoyed a majority in the Punjab Assembly. It started direct action against the Khizr ministry on 24 January 1947. It gathered momentum quickly because the Muslim League had successfully convinced the Muslims that it had been wrongly deprived of the right to form the government. Each day not only did Muslim League cadres come out to protest but many ordinary members of the public also joined the agitation. The jails were filled with such agitators. Governor Jenkins noted that the agitation was likely to accentuate the Sikh demand to partition the Punjab. He observed:

> It is quite impossible for one community to rule the Punjab with its present boundaries. Long-term alternatives are therefore reversion to Unionist principles with Muslim domination or partition which would create intolerable minor(ity) problems. Effect of agitation is to force second alternative on non-Muslims and to impair very seriously long-term prospects of Muslim League and Muslims generally. Muslim League are in fact wantonly throwing away certainty of Muslim leadership in a United Punjab for uncertain advantages of a partition which Sikhs will gradually now demand. But nobody has the brains to understand this.[26]

Negotiations between Khizr and the Muslim League finally resulted in the end of the agitation on 26 February. However, on 20 February 1947, the British Government had announced that it would transfer power to Indians by June 1948. Premier Khizr, who was a staunch supporter of continued British rule, lost heart. He therefore resigned on 2 March 1947, precipitating an acute political crisis. On 3 March, Master Tara Singh famously flashed his *kirpan* (sword) outside the Punjab Assembly calling for the destruction of the Pakistan idea. That evening, Hindu and Sikh leaders gathered in Purani Anarkali, in Lahore, and made even more extremist speeches.[27]

The next day, Hindu-Sikh protestors and Muslims clashed in Lahore. That evening, Sikhs and Muslim clashed in Amritsar. On 5 March, violence spread to Multan and Rawalpindi. The same day, Governor Jenkins imposed governor's rule. (Punjab remained under governor's rule until power was transferred to Indian and Pakistan Punjab administrations on 15 August 1947.) In Multan, the fight was uneven from the first day. There were very few Sikhs and the Hindu minority was also heavily outnumbered. Almost all casualties were Hindus and a few Sikhs.[28]

In Rawalpindi, Hindu-Sikhs and Muslims clashed on 5 March. In the evening of 6 March Muslim mobs numbering in the thousands headed towards Sikh villages in Rawalpindi, Attock and Jhelum districts. Until 13 March, government troops were not sent to establish law and order. In the meantime, a slaughter of Sikhs had taken place. The reason was that the Sikhs, not Hindus, were the richest community in the Rawalpindi division. According to British sources, some two thousand people were killed in the carnage in the three rural districts: almost all non-Muslims. The Sikhs claimed seven thousand dead. Government reports showed that Muslim ex-service persons had taken part in the planned attacks. The Muslim League leaders, Jinnah and others did not issue any condemnation of those atrocities. An exodus of thousands of Sikhs from Rawalpindi to the eastern districts and the Sikh princely states took place, where they narrated their woes and the nucleus of a revenge movement was setup.[29]

Meanwhile, since at least 1945, the main Sikh communal party, the Akali Dal, had been trying to convince Sikh rulers of princely states in the eastern regions of the Punjab to try establishing a Sikh State. They had even earlier begun campaigning for greater adherence to the Sikh religion and rituals among the ruling families and nobility. Thus after 1945 loyal Muslim and Hindu ministers and higher officers serving in the Sikh states began to be replaced by Sikhs.[30] The argument was that if India could be partitioned into two nations based on religion, then why could it not partition into three for the Sikh nation as well? To achieve that, a compact Sikh majority was needed and that could be achieved only by expelling nearly six million Muslims from East Punjab. However, at that point in time in 1947 making the bid for a Sikh state was too early; it emerged in the 1980s as the Khalistan movement.

Towards partition

In any event, by May 1947 it dawned upon the Muslim League leader, Jinnah, that the Sikhs were not going to join Pakistan. For a while he argued that Punjabi Hindus, Muslims and Sikhs shared a common culture and identity.[31] However, it contradicted his basic stance that Hindus (and by that token the Sikhs as well) were separate nations who did not share any national character. Therefore, now claiming that they were all Punjabis proved to be a weak argument which was rejected both by the Sikh and Congress leaders as well as the British. Meanwhile, Khizr Tiwana met Mountbatten and proposed that the Punjab could be a free dominion besides India and Pakistan. He strongly objected to the partition of the Punjab and warned it would result in unprecedented violence because no division of the province would satisfy all the communities.[32]

On the other hand, Viceroy Mountbatten brokered talks between Jinnah and the Sikhs during May 14–16 with a view to keeping the Punjab united. Jinnah offered very generous terms. Hardit Singh Malik who acted as spokesperson of the Sikhs reported the following concluding remarks:

> This put us in an awkward position. We were determined not to accept Pakistan under any circumstances and here was a Muslim leader offering us everything. What to do?
>
> Then I had an inspiration and I said, 'Mr Jinnah, you are being very generous. But, supposing, God forbid, you are no longer there when the time comes to implement your promises?'
>
> His reply was astounding . . . He said, 'My friend, my word in Pakistan will be like the world of God. No one will go back on it.'
>
> There was nothing to be said after this and the meeting ended.[33]

Meanwhile, communal violence intensified in the Punjab, mainly in the Muslim majority urban areas. The Punjab governor Sir Evan Jenkins warned in several reports to Mountbatten that a bloodbath was inevitable in the Punjab unless all communities accepted the partition as well as the division of territories.

On 3 June 1947, the British government announced the Partition Plan. It brought forward the transfer of power date to India and Pakistan to mid-August 1947 from June 1948. On 23 June, the Punjab Assembly voted in favour of partitioning Punjab. Until then, most of the communal violence had taken place in the Muslim majority western Punjab, but from July onwards organised Sikh gangs began to menace Muslims in the eastern districts. The Sikhs were better armed and often carried out their raids on horseback. However, it was not until the second week of August that large-scale movement of Muslims from eastern districts towards western districts began to take place.[34]

The next official stage in the partition of the Punjab was the deliberations of the Punjab Boundary Commission. The deliberations, which were conducted before a bench of four judges, two nominated by the Muslim League, one by the Congress and one by the Sikhs, did not result in an agreement on how to divide the

Punjab. Consequently, it was the chair of the Boundary Commission Sir Cyril Radcliffe who gave an award that all sides had to accept. All sides complained that it was not fair. However, Radcliffe had upheld the Muslim League point of view with some deviations: it gave the cities of Lahore, Sialkot, Gujranwala and the birthplace of Guru Nanak to Pakistan as well as the canal colonies of Lyallpur (now Faisalabad) and Montgomery (now Sahiwal) to Pakistan on the basis that these were Muslim majority areas. The Congress and Sikhs had claimed them on the basis of greater property ownership and land revenue paid to the state. Only when it came to the district of Gurdaspur, which had a slight Muslim majority, did the award give three of its four *tahsils* (revenue units) to India. The reason was that otherwise the city of Amritsar, which had a Hindu-Sikh majority, would have been surrounded on three sides out of four by Pakistani territory. With the three tahsils given to India, Amritsar was protected from the northern side as well. In Pakistan, it was alleged that it was a conspiracy because a dirt road in Pathankot Tahsil of the district connected India to the princely state of Jammu and Kashmir. It was later to become the bone of contention between India and Pakistan leading to three military confrontations.[35]

Steep escalation in communal violence

Although the Punjab had been disturbed after the March 1940 violence, and Jenkins had noted that some signs of government functionaries sided with their co-religionists were noted by and large while he was in charge of the Punjab affairs, he kept the casualties quite low. He gave a figure of five thousand two hundred dead by early August. It was most likely a low estimate and the fatalities could be twice that number. However, once power was transferred to the Indian and Pakistani administrations in the two Punjabs, and once the Radcliffe Award was made public on 17 August, all hell broke loose as millions of Hindus, Muslims and Sikhs were on the wrong side of the border that the Radcliffe Award had laid down. Jenkins had been warning that an impending communal war was going to break out if the partition of the Punjab and its division of territories was not accepted by all the three communities. He had wanted thousands of British troops to monitor a peaceful transfer of power to the Indian and Pakistani administrations, which would takeover if the Punjab was partitioned, but he was told that such troops were not available. A ragtag Punjab Boundary Force headed by some British officers was instituted, but it was woefully weak because of a lack of troops and effective firepower.[36]

Now two partisan administrations had come to power, and the minorities were left to the mercy of marauding gangs constituted by nexuses of ex-service persons, the criminal underworld, police and magistrates and politicians of local, mid-level stature. Together they preyed upon hapless men, women and children. The collapse of the British colonial order created the notorious Hobbesian state of nature but one in which instead of the state disintegrating completely it became an accomplice, through commission or omission or both, of unprecedented violence against minorities. The Sikhs had a plan to expel Muslims from the East Punjab and they carried it out with brute efficiency. They even had access to automatic firearms such as machine guns and ex-service persons fought on their side as well. Robin Jeffrey points out that the villain of the piece who led the attacks on the Muslims was a former Lieutenant Colonel of the Indian National Army, which had been formed by the Japanese from the Indian soldiers of the British forces they had captured during the war in Southeast Asia.[37] Although Hindus and Sikhs had been under attack since at least March 1947 in western Punjab and local Muslim League leaders were involved in the raids, a grand plan to expel Hindus and Sikhs did not exist, but once Muslim refugees started pouring in from East Punjab in the hundreds and thousands, the Pakistan Government also was complicit in forcing Hindus and Sikhs to leave the Pakistani West Punjab.

At the end of the day, between five hundred thousand and eight hundred thousand Hindu, Muslim and Sikh Punjabis lost their lives. Although the first large-scale planned carnage was carried out in the Muslim majority Rawalpindi district in March 1947, by the end of 1947 more Muslims had been killed in East Punjab than had Hindus and Sikhs counted together in West Punjab. Moreover, ten million Punjabis had been driven away from their ancestral homes. The first case of ethnic cleansing after World War II thus took place in the Punjab as East Punjab was emptied of all Muslims and West Punjab, of Hindus and Sikhs.[38]

Conclusion

The partition of the Punjab took place as part of an overall 'agreement' brokered by the British Government between the main India-level political parties – the Indian National Congress, the All-India

Muslim League and the Sikhs of the Punjab – to partition India as well as the Punjab and Bengal. Thus, had there been no Partition of India, there would be no partition of the Punjab either. But from this one cannot conclude that if India were partitioned, so must the Punjab. The external contest and situation was necessary, but it was not sufficient in itself to lead to the partition of the Punjab. Had the Hindu, Muslim and Sikh communities – or rather their leaders – agreed to keep their province united, it could have been given to Pakistan or to India or, as was suggested by Sir Khizr Tiwana, made into a third dominion alongside India and Pakistan. However, communal violence, which broke out in March 1947, created bad blood among Muslims on the one hand and Hindus and Sikhs on the other. The Sikhs decided to join hands with Muslims, one reason for which was that after the March 1947 attacks on their villages in the Rawalpindi division, their leaders were no longer willing to remain in Pakistan.

After such negotiations broke down and violence escalated, the chances of the province remaining united decreased. After the 3 June 1947 partition plan was announced and the Punjab assembly voted for partition, the fate of a united Punjab was sealed. That so many Hindus, Muslims and Sikhs were killed depended on the fact that on all sides, especially that of the Sikhs, preparations existed to expel by force people of the 'enemy community.' Ex-service persons were available, as were soldiers of the princely states, criminal gangs and partisan state functionaries. The two administrations that came to power in the Indian East Punjab and the Pakistani West Punjab tacitly agreed to the expulsion of unwanted minorities. They let the violence complete the process of ethnic cleansing.

Notes

1 Ahmed, Ishtiaq (2014) *The Punjab Bloodied, Partitioned and Cleansed: Unravelling the 1947 Tragedy through Secret British Reports and First-Person Accounts*, Karachi: Oxford University Press, pp. 52–53.
2 Pirzada, Syed Sharifuddin (ed.) (1970) *Foundations of Pakistan: All-India Muslim League Documents, 1906–1947*, Vol. 2, Karachi: National Publishing House Ltd, p. 159.
3 Aziz, K.K. (ed.) (1978) *The Complete Works of Rahmat Ali*, Islamabad: National Commission on Historical and Cultural Research, p. 1–10.
4 Ahmed, Ishtiaq (2014) *The Punjab Bloodied, Partitioned and Cleansed: Unravelling the 1947 Tragedy through Secret British Reports and First-Person Accounts*, Karachi: Oxford University Press, pp. 21–26.

5 Ibid., p. 57.

6 Ibid., pp. 26–28.

7 Aziz, Khursheed Kamal (1995) *History of Partition of India*, Vol. 1–4, New Delhi: Atlantic Publishers and Distributors, p. 145.

8 Singh, Kirpal (1989) *The Partition of the Punjab*, Patiala: Publication Bureau Punjabi University, p. 12.

9 Quoted in Ibid., pp. 11–12.

10 Ahmed, Ishtiaq (2014) *The Punjab Bloodied, Partitioned and Cleansed: Unravelling the 1947 Tragedy through Secret British Reports and First-Person Accounts*, Karachi: Oxford University Press, pp. 31–32.

11 Oren, Stephen (1974) 'The Sikhs, Congress, and the Unionists in British Punjab, 1937–1945,' *Modern Asian Studies*, Vol. 8, No. 3, Cambridge: Cambridge University Press, p. 397 & Ali, Ikram (1970) *History of the Punjab (1799–1947)*, New Delhi: Low Price Publications, pp. 425–481.

12 Carter, Lionel (ed.) (2004) *Punjab Politics 1936–1939: The Start of Provincial Autonomy: Governors' Fortnightly Reports and other Key Documents*, New Delhi: Manohar, pp. 142–147.

13 Allana, Gulam. (ed.) (1977) *Pakistan Movement: Historic Documents*, Lahore: Islamic Book Service, pp. 226–227.

14 Carter, Lionel (ed.) (2005) *Punjab Politics 1940–1943, Strains of War, Governors' Fortnightly Reports and other Key Documents*, New Delhi: Mahohar, pp. 108–109.

15 Mansergh, N. and Lumby, W.W.R. (eds.) (1970) *The Transfer of Power*, January–April 1942, Vol. 1, London: Her Majesty's Stationery Office, pp. 582–588.

16 Talbot, Ian (1996) *Khizr Tiwana: The Punjab Unionist Party and the partition of India*, Richmond, Surrey: Curzon.

17 Ibid., pp. 113–124.

18 Carter, Lionel (ed.) (2006) *Punjab Politics 1 January 1944–3 March 1947Governors' Fortnightly Reports and other Key Documents*, New Delhi: Mahohar, pp. 106–107.

19 Ahmed, Ishtiaq (2014) *The Punjab Bloodied, Partitioned and Cleansed: Unravelling the 1947 Tragedy through Secret British Reports and First-Person Accounts*, Karachi: Oxford University Press, p. 84.

20 Carter, Lionel (ed.) (2006) *Punjab Politics 1 January 1944–3 March 1947Governors' Fortnightly Reports and other Key Documents*, New Delhi: Mahohar, p. 171.

21 Allana, Gulam (ed.) (1977) *Pakistan Movement: Historic Documents*, Lahore: Islamic Book Service, p. 396.

22 Ahmed, Ishtiaq (2014) *The Punjab Bloodied, Partitioned and Cleansed: Unravelling the 1947 Tragedy through Secret British Reports and First-Person Accounts*, Karachi: Oxford University Press, pp. 77–78.

23 Mansergh, N. and Moon, P. (eds.) (1977) *The Transfer of Power, 23 March–29 June 1946*, Vol. 7, London: Her Majesty's Stationery Office, pp. 696–697.

24 Ahmed, Ishtiaq (2014) *The Punjab Bloodied, Partitioned and Cleansed: Unravelling the 1947 Tragedy through Secret British Reports and First-Person Accounts*, Karachi: Oxford University Press, pp. 78–79.

25 Ibid., pp. 79–93.

26 Carter, Lionel (ed.) (2006) *Punjab Politics 1 January 1944–3 March 1947Governors' Fortnightly Reports and other Key Documents*, New Delhi: Mahohar, p. 343.
27 Ahmed, Ishtiaq (2014) *The Punjab Bloodied, Partitioned and Cleansed: Unravelling the 1947 Tragedy through Secret British Reports and First-Person Accounts*, Karachi: Oxford University Press, pp. 107–132.
28 Ibid., pp. 158–164.
29 Ibid., pp. 178–192.
30 Coupland, Ian (2002) 'The Master and the Maharajas: The Sikh Princes and the East Punjab Massacres of 1947,' *Modern Asian Studies*, Vol. 36, No. 3, Cambridge: Cambridge University Press, pp. 675–677.
31 Mansergh, Nicholas and Moon, Penderel (eds.) (1981) *The Transfer of Power 1942–47, Vol. X: The Mounbatten Viceroyalty, Formulation of a Plan, 22 March–30 May 1947*, London: Her Majesty's Stationery Office, p. 543.
32 Ahmed, Ishtiaq (2014) *The Punjab Bloodied, Partitioned and Cleansed: Unravelling the 1947 Tragedy through Secret British Reports and First-Person Accounts*, Karachi: Oxford University Press, pp. 204–205.
33 Singh, Kirpal (ed.) (1991) *Select Documents on Partition of Punjab-1947: Indian and Pakistan, Punjab, Haryana and Himachal, India and Punjab-Pakistan*, New Delhi: National Book Shop, pp. 86–87.
34 Carter, Lionel (ed.) (2007) *Punjab Politics, 1 June–14 August 1947, Tragedy, Governors' Fortnightly Reports and other Key Documents*, New Delhi: Manohar, pp. 226–234.
35 Ahmed, Ishtiaq (1999) 'The 1947 Partition of Punjab: Arguments Put Forth before the Punjab Boundary Commission by the Parties Involved,' in Talbot, Ian and Singh, Gurharpal (eds.), *Region and Partition: Bengal, Punjab and the Partition of the Subcontinent*, Karachi: Oxford University Press, pp. 116–164.
36 Ahmed, Ishtiaq (2014) *The Punjab Bloodied, Partitioned and Cleansed: Unravelling the 1947 Tragedy through Secret British Reports and First-Person Accounts*, Karachi: Oxford University Press, pp. 251–253.
37 Jeffrey, Robin (1974) 'The Punjab Boundary Force and the Problem of Order, August 1947,' *Modern Asian Studies*, Vol. 8, No. 4, Cambridge: Cambridge University Press, pp. 50–57.
38 Ahmed, Ishtiaq (2014) *The Punjab Bloodied, Partitioned and Cleansed: Unravelling the 1947 Tragedy through Secret British Reports and First-Person Accounts*, Karachi: Oxford University Press, pp. 540–543.

Chapter 3

Peregrination of Sindh's march towards Pakistan

Communal politics, class conflict and competing nationalisms

Farhan Hanif Siddiqi

After the announcement of the 3 June 1947 Partition Plan, the Sindh Legislative Assembly was the first in the Muslim majority areas of British India to vote for joining the Pakistan Constituent Assembly. It was at the first Sindh Provincial Muslim League Conference in Karachi in 1938 that Jinnah and All-India Muslim League (AIML) leaders expressed the need for a separate homeland for the Muslims. After the passage of the Lahore Resolution in March 1940, it was again the Sindh Assembly that became the first provincial legislature to endorse the AIML's claim for separate states for the Muslims of the Indian subcontinent.

While Sindh's contribution in the making of the Pakistani state is seminal in light of stated developments, Sindh itself was marred by an internal struggle, which manifested itself in myriad realms. First, a predominantly agricultural society, Sindh's politics was dominated by powerful landlords giving rise in the 1930s to a class movement of the *Hari* (landless peasant farmers). Second, the local politics of the powerful landed elite was marred by an excruciating intra-elite conflict typified by personality, as opposed to ideological contestations. Sindh's politics in the 1930s and 1940s is an increasingly frustrating and exasperating story of personal rivalries and conflicts in which one group of politicians attempts to outdo another. Third, the intensification of communal politics as a consequence of the polarisation of Muslims and Hindus in the sociopolitical and socio-economic realms resulted in the origin of a narrative where Muslim nationalism takes shape specially after the Masjid Manzilgah incident in Sukkur. Finally, politics in Sindh before Pakistan's creation is also tainted with a conflict over competing nationalisms. An incipient rise of Sindhi nationalism along with a Pakistani nationalism amongst Sindh's political elite is strongly evident.

While it was Pakistani nationalism that triumphed, the discourse of Sindhi nationalism, whereby a competing conception of how a future Pakistani polity should be framed, is also present.

Sindh's sociopolitical space

Sindh was conquered by the British, owing to the latter's imperial interests, in 1843. This conquest came as the Anglo-Russian geostrategic rivalry took shape and the British subdued the Khanate of Kalat in neighbouring Balochistan. The conquest of Sindh presented an administrative dilemma, for unlike Balochistan where the Khanate could be instrumentalised for strategic purposes, the defeat of the Talpur Dynasty did not evoke any such consideration owing to the fact that the Talpurs themselves were rulers primarily in name rather than authority. The Sindh formula then coalesced around joining Sindh with the Bombay presidency, which ultimately gave way to a rise in Sindh's sociopolitical consciousness.

Sindh, since the advent of British colonial rule, was a predominantly agricultural society, and the urban spirit of commerce, trade and business was limited mainly to the town of Shikarpur. Shikarpur in northern Sindh became the middle path of a trade nexus involving Balochistan and Afghanistan. It was the safe passage of the trade route between Balochistan and Afghanistan through the Bolan Pass that brought the British into Balochistan. British rule in Sindh, while bringing administrative efficiency, also led to the development of the Karachi Port. This development had unintended social and economic benefits, for it brought with it the mercantile classes, which were primarily non-Muslims, including, in the main, Hindus and Parsis.

The entrenchment of the mercantile class in urban Sindh contrasted with the socio-economic conditions in rural Sindh, where the British cultivated a class of landlords. On 20 May 1843, Napier, the conqueror of Sindh issued a proclamation, 'In God's name, you Baloch Sardars are required to present yourselves before the Governor, and make your *salams* to him, and your *jagirs* and other property will be confirmed to you by the British Government, and no diminution will take place in your rank.'[1] It has to be stated here that the landlords, predominantly Muslim, were also at the mercy of the moneylenders, predominantly Hindus. Thus, the dynamic of Hindu-Muslim conflict in the 1930s and 1940s had to do with two different interdependent (religious) groups in two separate economic niches standing in a competitive relationship intensified by the growing demand for Pakistan in the Muslim minority provinces of the British Empire. Hence, Sindh has to be placed not only in its specific socio-economic setting but also in the larger British Indian politics in order to estimate the dynamics of how and why Sindh became indispensable to the Pakistan nation state project.

Sindh and the development of communalism

Sindh's foray into mainstream Indian politics came at the height of the Khilafat and the Non-Cooperation Movement from 1919 to 1922. Though the Khilafat Movement involved essentially a religious question pertaining to Muslims and Islamic identity, it also coalesced at the same time with Gandhi's non-cooperation movement to produce a distinctly cohesive anti-colonial resistance to British imperialism in India. The Khilafat Movement turned out to be a nursery for latter-day Sindhi politicians who proved phenomenal in the 1940s when Sindh voted to join Pakistan. These politicians included Sir Abdullah Haroon, Shaikh Abdul Majid Sindhi and G.M. Syed amongst others.

Sindh's real test of politics came with the movement of its separation from Bombay. It is interesting to note that a prominent Sindhi Hindu, Harchandrai Vishindas Bharwani, initially made the demand for Sindh's separation from Bombay at the Congress' annual session in Karachi in 1913.[2] The demand based its claim on the grounds of Sindh's distinctive cultural and geographical character as well as a need to disentangle the Sindh province from the powerful financial interests in Bombay.[3] The Sindhi Hindus had come to occupy important positions in Sindh specially after the British conquered the province in 1843. When the British took over, the Hindus did not hold any land, but in a century of their rule, the Hindus came to acquire about 40 per cent of the land, while another 20 per cent was believed to have been mortgaged to them.[4] The Hindus took to the entrepreneurial business and financial profession more earnestly as compared to the Muslims. The latter concentrated mainly in the rural areas, both as landlords and serfs, lacked the urban commercial spirit as a new age of capitalist transformation dawned on Sindh under the British.[5]

The demand for Sindh's separation from Bombay remained dormant for a time until it was revived again in the 1920s, this time by the Muslim elite. Their concerns were based on the fact that

Hindus exercised influence and control in the administrative affairs of the province as well as in the countryside. Thus, as a result, an informal organisation, the Sindh Azad Conference, was formed to bring together the landed aristocracy and the emergent Muslim middle classes, the two groups who felt their positions to be most fragile.[6] These new Sindhi politics not only brought the landed aristocracy and the Muslim middle classes onto a single platform but also shaped the basis of a regional, largely Muslim, Sindhi identity. The advocates of Sindh's separation 'continued the old arguments of Sindh's cultural discreteness and the unjust Bombay connection, but they also evolved new arguments to counter the thrusts of the Hindus.'[7]

While a Sindhi *Muslim* identity was being shaped in contradistinction to Sindhi *Hindu* identity, the latter also found expression in the shape of the Hindu Maha Sabha. In its Jubbulpore Session, the Maha Sabha passed a resolution that 'Sindh shall not be separated because it was a Muslim demand.'[8] At this time, communal riots broke out in Larkana with the Muslims protesting the forced conversion of their faith by the Hindus.[9] The Muslim leadership concluded that the British and Hindus were acting in collusion to protect their own interests, at the expense of Sindh's Muslims.[10] While the Sabha's world view was shaped by a distinct Hindu consciousness as was that of Sindhi Muslims by a rising Islamic consciousness, the Congress supported the separation along with the AIML.[11] The Sindhi Muslims were ultimately successful and Sindh's separation from Bombay took place in April 1936.

Party politics in Sindh and the 1937 elections

The Government of India Act promulgated in 1935 provided for provincial autonomy and new elections were announced. This galvanised the Sindhi political elite and the race for political power ensued between the Sindhis themselves. It is interesting to note that though the movement for Sindh's separation from Bombay sparked off communal sentiments, this was not immediately the case as new political parties took shape. Furthermore, it was not communalism in essence as much as Sindh's rural landscape that privileged the Hindu *banias* (moneylenders) over the decadent and incompetent landlord. While sentiments against the Hindu *banias* were manifest, Sindhi politics took an incessantly non-communal orientation under the aegis of the Sindh United Party. However, rural indebtedness still remained a theme as expressed in the manifestoes of major parties contesting the 1937 elections. Moreover, the issue of rural indebtedness and the feeling of usurpation of the Hindu *bania* found most urgent expression when the Muslim League began its sociopolitical mobilisation as the sole voice of the Muslims of British India.

The first party to make its presence felt was the Sindh Azad Party, which had its roots in the Sindh Azad Conference and was established in September 1935 after a joint meeting of the Sindh Hari Association, Karachi Khilafat Committee and the Sindh branch of the Jamiyyat al-ulama-i-Hind.[12] Shaikh Abdul Majid Sindhi was elected as the provisional leader and the party programme included such items as retrenchment of administrative expenditure in Sindh, revision of the land revenue system, equitable distribution of water for cultivation, the improvement of the economic position of peasants and landlords, the protection of agriculturalists from moneylenders and medical relief and primary education in rural areas.[13]

Out of Sindh's disparate political elite, the Sindh United Party emerged as a front runner for the 1937 elections, with Abdullah Haroon and Shah Nawaz Bhutto as leading figures. Other notables included Ghulam Hussain Hidayatullah, M.A. Khuhro, Allah Bux Soomro, Hatim Alavi, Miran Mohammad Shah and G.M. Syed.[14] The party professed a non-communal ideology aiming to foster understanding between Hindus and Muslims as well as the economic uplift of the province. The Sindh United Party modelled itself along similar lines as the Unionist Party in neighbouring Punjab.

The 1937 election results revealed the dominance of the rural elite of large landholders, clan leaders and religious saints. They secured 27 of the 34 Muslim seats.[15] The elections were held under the principle of separate electorates and weightage for minority community representation.[16] This meant that although the Muslims constituted around 75 per cent of the population of Sindh, their representation in the Sindh Assembly was reduced to around 56 per cent (34 out of a total 60 seats). In addition, the demographic balance meant that in every urban area except Karachi, the Hindus predominated, and in the rural areas the Muslims far outnumbered the Hindus.[17] The results indicated the majority triumph of the Sindh United Party, which won 21 out of the 34 seats allocated for Muslims. However, the party suffered two grave setbacks. Both Shah Nawaz Bhutto and Abdullah Haroon, who had laid the foundations of the Sindh

United Party, were defeated by Shaikh Abdul Majid Sindhi (in Larkana) and Khan Sahib Allah Bakhsh Gabol (in Karachi).[18]

The rise of the Sindh Muslim League and the drive towards Pakistan

In the 1937 elections, the Muslim League failed to secure popular electoral support and representation in the Assembly. It could only secure 4.6 per cent votes; one or, at the most, two Muslim League candidates who were elected soon deserted the Muslim League.[19]

Jinnah, realising the gravity of the Muslim League's position in a Muslim majority province, began a process of reorganising the party by eliciting the support of influential Muslim leaders. As a result, the first Sindh Provincial Muslim League Conference was held at Karachi in October 1938, and at this meeting, the League expressed the need for a separate homeland for the Muslims. The 1938 Muslim League resolution was clearly a precursor to the historic Lahore Resolution of 1940, which firmly established Pakistan as the League's ultimate goal.[20] Consequently, with political manoeuvrings within the provincial assembly, the Muslim League Assembly Party was formed with Sir Hidayatullah as leader and Mir Bandeh Ali as the deputy leader.[21] Sir Abdullah Haroon, on the other hand, became the president of the Sindh Muslim League.[22] The League's strategy of attracting influential Sindhis as party members was indeed successful. The next stage for the League was to build mass support, and the Masjid Manzilgah issue provided the perfect opportunity in this regard.

Masjid Manzilgah was the name popularly given to a complex of buildings on the banks of the Indus at Sukkur dating from the time of the Mughal Emperor Akbar, consisting of a *serai* (inn) and a mosque, reputedly built by Syed Masoom Shah, Governor of Sindh during Akbar's reign.[23] The issue was important because a few years earlier Hindus had built their temple directly opposite the Manzilgah buildings and it had become a much avowed pilgrimage place for them. The issue was raised in the 1920s by Muslims and also in 1936, when the separation struggle for the province was taking place. However, the issue gained prominence when the Muslim League championed the Manzilgah cause, mainly to increase its popular support amongst the Sindhi Muslims.[24] In early 1939 the Sukkur district Muslim League passed a resolution asking the Provincial Muslim League to take up the question of Manzilgah with the government.[25] The

League popularised the issue with the help of the *pirs*,[26] in particular members of the Rashdi and Sirhindi families. The political outcome of the issue was the collapse of the pro-Congress Allah Bakhsh ministry and its replacement by one led by Mir Bandeh Ali Talpur, which included a number of 'Muslim Leaguers' such as M.A. Khuhro, G.M. Syed and Shaikh Abdul Majid Sindhi.[27]

The Sindh Muslim League went from strength to strength after the Masjid Manzilgah incident. It established a full-fledged League Ministry in Sindh in October 1942 with Ghulam Hussain Hidayatullah as premier. The League Ministry was responsible for framing the 3 March 1943 resolution in the Sindh Assembly, which demanded Pakistan for the Muslims of the Indian subcontinent. The resolution echoed the Lahore Resolution passed in March 1940 by asserting that 'Muslims of India are a separate nation possessing religion, philosophy, social customs, literature, traditions, political and economic theories of their own quite different from those of the Hindus.'[28]

The person responsible for moving the resolution forward, G.M. Syed, was the person who had laid the foundations of a distinct Sindhi ethnonationalism in the post-1947 era.[29] The same Syed, it should be mentioned, so overcome with communal feelings, had asserted in a Muslim League session in Karachi in March 1941 that the Hindus were *banias* and Jews and that the salvation of Muslims lay in the Pakistan theory.[30] His colleague, M.H. Gazdar, went so far as to say that if the Hindus 'continued to create dissensions amongst Muslims, they would be turned out of Sindh like the Jews from Germany.'[31]

Syed repented later in the postcolonial years when he saw Sindh being overwhelmed under the weight of the Pakistan project. As the Pakistan idea evolved into a centralised polity denying rights and privileges to Sindhis, Syed's Sindhi nationalism peaked into a separatist ideal called Sindhu Desh. While elaborating on Sindhu Desh, Syed admitted that he was swept away in the wave of what he termed as 'religious prejudice' to the point that the Sufi traditions of peace, love and harmony were forgotten.[32] Also, while equating the Hindus with Jews at the high tide of Muslim nationalism, his later view of Hindus was one of remorse as hundreds of thousands of Hindus who were 'educated, experts in trade, engineers, and with Sufi tendencies were forced to leave Sindh.'[33]

Besides the communal streak, it seems plausible to argue looking at the resolution that though Syed demanded Pakistan, his conception of Pakistan was in consonance with the Lahore Resolution of 1940, which demanded separate *states* for the Muslim majority areas of the Indian subcontinent.[34] Syed explained in 1946 that he supported the idea of Pakistan; however, there was only one difference between his standpoint and that of the Muslim League. He was for complete autonomy for the Muslim majority provinces.[35]

Sindhi proto-nationalism in the 1940s

It is interesting to note that during the period 1940–1947, a distinct Sindhi ethnonationalism had also started to take shape in which increasing apprehension was expressed about the state of Sindh in a future Pakistan. Thus, as much as anger was directed against the Hindu community for taking up administrative jobs and the rural Hindu *bania*, a section of Sindhi leaders had come to resent the Punjabis. This resentment was borne out of the increasing acquisition of the agricultural land of Sindh by the Punjabis, a process which has been unfolding since the 1890s.[36] The phenomenon received considerable attention and controversy when, in 1932, the Sukkur Barrage irrigation scheme, the largest of its kind in the world, brought seven million additional acres in Sindh under cultivation.[37] This increased the number of Punjabi 'settlers' in Sindh aided by their erstwhile British masters, who saw Punjabis as skilled and industrious cultivators, while Sindhi *zamindars* and *haris* were considered lazy.[38]

It was possibly with such developments in mind that Allah Bux Soomro quipped to G.M. Syed in 1940:

> You still think that the creation of Pakistan will solve all problems facing Sindh? This is wrong and far removed from facts. You will get to know that our real difficulties will begin after Pakistan has come into being. . . . At present, the Hindu trader and moneylender's plunder is worrying you but later you will have to face the Punjab bureaucracy and soldiery and the mind of UP.[39]

The Sindh Legislative Assembly became an active forum in the 1940s where politicians vigorously played out the distinction between Sindhis and non-Sindhis. The debate revolved around the question of 'Who is a Sindhi?' especially when it came to taking up employment in the province. For some of the politicians involved in these debates, the suggestion of a qualifying criterion of three years' residence in Sindh was not sufficient; instead, they insisted on a prospective employee being someone 'who is born and resides in Sindh.'[40] Regarding the spectre of Punjabi domination, Sayed Noor Muhammad Shah, a Muslim League member of the Sindh Legislative Assembly stated the following on the floor of the Assembly on 13 March 1947:

> The Musalman members of this Honourable House would be astounded to hear that when the Punjabi Musalmans manage to buy our lands here, they at once start even demolishing the humble huts of the Sindhi Musalmans. Not only that, but even the mosques and graves of the Sindhi Musalmans do not escape their attention. For this they even look for the support of the police. They have such land grabbing instincts that in their vicinity the Sindhi Musalmans cannot find even an inch of land for burying their dead.[41]

The sentiment relating to Punjabi domination as well as the independence of Sindh as a political and economic entity was given full expression by Mohammed Ibrahim Joyo. He wrote a political treatise titled *Save Sindh, Save The Continent* in June 1947 and gave intellectual expression to the fast emerging Sindhi nationalism. In the preface to his treatise, he prophesises along the same lines as Allah Bux Soomro:

> Whether in the proposed set-up for Pakistan or in that for Hindustan we, more than four and a half millions in all, are promised to be treated merely as so many individuals with our collective homogeneity and corporate existence as a people absolutely unrecognised. That would mean that, in either case, we stand to be completely overwhelmed by numbers; and, as the matters seems shaping themselves at present, our scanty economic resources and the key positions in our governmental machinery are, virtually, going to be made a monopoly of others.[42]

Conclusion

Sindh's proto-nationalism gained increased salience in the immediate aftermath of the postcolonial era where the fear of the domination of the Hindu *bania* was now replaced with that of Punjabi domination. As the Pakistani state embarked on its centralisation drive, the non-dominant ethnic groups faced isolation, driving G.M. Syed, once the president of the Sindh Muslim League and ardent supporter of the Pakistan project, to lay emphasis on outright secession. In 1972, Syed argued for and laid the basis of a new ethnopolitical party, Jeay Sindh Mahaz, which advocated a separate state for Sindhis, to be called Sindhu Desh.

Also, Sindhi marginalisation intensified further with the better educated and urban Muslim refugees (*Mohajirs*) arriving from India. In more ways than one, the predicament of the Sindhis being overpowered by others politically, socially and economically continued well into the postcolonial era inviting brutal ethnic conflict between the Mohajirs and Sindhis in the 1980s, as the former organised themselves into their own ethnopolitical party, the Mohajir Qaumi Movement (MQM).

Notes

1 Lari, Suhail Zaheer (1994) *A History of Sindh*. Karachi: Oxford University Press, p. 172.
2 Malkani, Kewalram Ratanmal (1984) *The Sindh Story*. New Delhi: Allied Publishers, p. 95.
3 Ansari, Sarah (1991) 'Political Legacies of Pre-1947 Sind,' in D.A. Low (ed.), *The Political Inheritance of Pakistan*. London: Macmillan, p. 186.
4 Malkani, *op. cit.*, p. 154.
5 Ibid.
6 Ansari, *op. cit.*, p. 186.
7 Jones, Allen Keith (2002) *Politics in Sindh, 1907–1940: Muslim Identity and the Demand for Pakistan*. Oxford: Oxford University Press, p. 25.
8 Pirzada, Din Ali (1995) *Growth of Muslim Nationalism in Sindh: Parting of Ways to Pakistan*. Karachi: Mehran Publishers, p. 50.
9 Among the converts were the Sheikhs of Larkana, who followed a curious mixture of Hindu and Islamic practices. The Sheikhs conversion to Hinduism had started as early as 1905 by the Sukkur unit of the Arya Samaj. Quoted in Kothari, Rita (2006) 'RSS in Sindh: 1942–1948,' *Economic and Political Weekly*, Vol. 41, No. 27/28 (Jul. 8–21), p. 3009.
10 Jones, *op. cit.*, p. 19.
11 Pirzada, *op. cit.*, p. 49.
12 Jones, *op. cit.*, p. 39.
13 Ibid., pp. 39–40.
14 Personal rivalry between Bhutto and Hidayatullah tended to tear the Sindh United Party apart. After Miran Shah was nominated Deputy Leader, Hidayatullah resigned, quit the party and formed his own Sindh Muslim Political Party. This intra-ethnic elite conflict over personal issues and power has characterised Sindh profoundly and is evidenced

both in the colonial and postcolonial phases of Sindhi politics. Allen Keith Jones, *op. cit.*, p. 54.

15 Pirzada, *op. cit.*, p. 70.
16 Jones, *op. cit.*, p. 64.
17 Ibid., p. 67.
18 Ibid., pp. 74–75.
19 Soomro, Muhammad Qasim (1989) *Muslim Politics in Sindh (1938–1947)*. Hyderabad: Sindh University Press, p. 43.
20 Jones, *op. cit.*, p. 118.
21 Soomro, *op. cit.*, p. 49.
22 Abdullah Haroon was a prominent *Memon* sugar merchant of Karachi. Jones, *op. cit.*, p. 75.
23 Khuhro, Hamida (1998) 'Masjid Manzilgah, 1939–40: Test Case for Hindu-Muslim Relations in Sind,' *Modern Asian Studies*, Vol. 32, No. 1 (Feb.), p. 51.
24 It must be mentioned that Sindh during this time was led by the Allah Bakhsh Soomro ministry, which relied on the support of the Congress and Sindhi Hindus. In order to break the shackles of the Congress and Hindus in Sindh, the Muslim League found it convenient to raise the issue in order to mobilise itself in the province. Furthermore, middle class Muslims and rural landlords supported the Muslim League as they came to detest Hindus who were the predominant economic stakeholders in the province.
25 Ibid., p. 54.
26 In Sindh, *pirs* are religious figures with large landholdings and having an important stake in the religious as well as the political life of the province.
27 Sarah, *op. cit.*, pp. 180–181.
28 Soomro *op. cit.*, p. 141.
29 Syed was elected as president of Sindh Provincial Muslim League in June 1943. In 1945, cracks began to appear in the Muslim League in Sindh after the nomination of candidates for the provincial elections. Syed criticised the then Premier Hidayatullah and his Ministry for nominating feudals and unqualified candidates. This stand was not accepted by Jinnah, as Syed's own candidates were feudals as well. Syed was later expelled from the Muslim League and formed his own Progressive Muslim League in 1946. Korejo, Muhammad Soaleh (2000) *G.M. Syed: An Analysis of His Political Perspectives*. Karachi: Oxford University Press, pp. 12–24.
30 Ahmad, Riaz (2008) *The Sindh Muslim League, 1940–1947: Secret Police Abstracts*. Islamabad: National Institute of Historical and Cultural Research, p. 25.
31 Ibid.
32 Syed, Ghulam Murtaza (1991) *Sindhu Desh: A Study in Its Identity through the Ages*. Karachi: G.M. Syed Academy, p. 88.
33 Ibid., p. 88.
34 Syed, Ghulam Murtaza. *The Case of Sindh: G.M. Syed's Deposition in Court*. The text of the Resolution, Syed's speech and the interesting

debate in the Assembly can be found in Appendix III. Retrieved from www.gmsyed.org/case/The%20Case%20of%20Sindh.pdf.

35 Ibid.

36 Ansari, *op. cit.*, p. 188.

37 Jones, *op. cit.*, p. xvi.

38 Ansari, *op. cit.*, p. 188. The same stereotype was used by the newly arriving Mohajirs to distance themselves from the Sindhis in the post-1947 era.

39 Syed, *op. cit.*

40 Ansari, *op. cit.*, p. 187.

41 Quoted in Joyo, Ibrahim (1947) *Save Sindh, Save the Continent: From Feudal Lords, Capitalists and Their Communalisms*. Hyderabad: Creative Communications, p. 28.

42 Ibid., p. 15.

Chapter 4

Peasant nationalism, elite conflict, and the second partition of Bengal, 1918–1947

Taj Hashmi

For its adherents, the concept of Pakistan – literally a 'land of the pure' – like socialism, was a one-size-fits-all solution to all of their mundane problems. While some supporters of the Two-Nation Theory believed Pakistan would restore their dignity, power and the lost glory of the Mughal Empire, others believed that Pakistan would revive the Early Pious Caliphate of the seventh century, or even the State of Medina, established by Prophet Muhammad in 622 CE.[1] However, the overwhelming majority of Bengali Muslims, who were among the most passionate supporters of Jinnah's Two-Nation Theory in the 1940s, believed that Pakistan would end the tyranny of the overpowering Hindu triumvirate of *Zamindar-Bhadralok-Mahajan* (landlords, professional classes and moneylenders). Since the bulk of Bengali Muslims were peasants and agricultural labourers, to them Pakistan would also ensure 'land to the tiller' (a popular communist slogan in the 1940s). East Bengali Muslims believed Pakistan would be 'A Land of Eternal Eid' (celebration)[2] or a 'peasant utopia,' in the sense Eric Wolf has used the expression.[3] However, peasant masses at the grassroots did not create the leadership, let alone formulate the political ideology or philosophy, to translate the Two-Nation Theory into reality. Contrary to the subaltern historiography, the story of the metamorphosis of East Bengal into the eastern wing of Pakistan is almost all about the successful manipulation of peasant consciousness by non-peasant elite leaders from outside, who successfully hegemonised the so-called 'autonomous domain' of mass consciousness with cultural hegemony and 'false consciousness' to support and work for the movement for Pakistan. Although Pakistan was a 'peasant utopia' for Bengali Muslim peasants, the struggle for Pakistan in Bengal was both vertical and horizontal, between Muslim masses and Hindu elites, and between the weaker Muslim and well-entrenched and powerful Hindu elites, respectively. The bulk of the beneficiaries of the Permanent Settlement – high caste Bengali Hindus – not only emerged as the neo-feudal aristocrats in the countryside, but they also emerged as the English-educated professionals or *bhadraloke*, and swelled the ranks of nouveau riche classes in urban and rural areas of Bengal. They were too rich and advanced for the bulk of Bengali Muslims, who were poor, madrasa-educated/illiterate sections of the population, mostly engaged in agriculture and the dying textile industry in East Bengal. In sum, the Muslim triumvirate of *Ashraf-Ulama-Jotedar* (aristocrats, clerics and rich peasants-cum-petty-landlords) provided the leadership, and the Muslim subalterns followed them blindly.[4] It is altogether a different story as to how the same classes of ordinary Bengali Muslims who had fought for Pakistan were soon crestfallen and played a decisive role in the creation of Bangladesh, which virtually amounted to the dismemberment of Pakistan in its more populous eastern wing, in 1971.[5]

Although Pakistan became 'inevitable' only in the late 1940s, we cannot consider the preceding decades as the prehistory of the Partition. Class and communal conflicts between Hindu and Muslim Bengalis predated the period under review. Since the Partition was the culmination of communalism, there was an incorrect assumption that, once partitioned along communal lines, Bengal would be free from all communal conflicts. In South Asian history, politics and culture, 'communalism' denotes and connotes something very different than it does elsewhere. What Wilfred Cantwell Smith elucidated in his seminal essay on communalism in 1943 still seems to be one of the best explanations of the phenomenon in South Asia:

> Communalism in India may be defined as that ideology which has emphasised as the social, political, and economic unit the group of adherents of each religion, and has emphasised the distinction, even the antagonism, between such groups; the words "adherent" and "religion" being taken in the most nominal sense . . . *the phenomenon called "communalism" has developed into something for which "nationalism" now seems a better name.*[6]
>
> (Emphasis the author's)

In view of the above definition of communalism, Bengali Muslims' quest for a separate identity and nationhood during the 1920s and 1940s cannot be just ignored as communalism. While Jawaharlal

Nehru believed that 'honest communalism is fear; false communalism is political reaction,' he preferred to use 'nationalism' rather than 'communalism' to denote a majority community's quest for a separatist identity or homeland.[7] By the same token, one cannot just dismiss Bengali Muslims' (who were in the majority in the province of Bengal) quest for a separate Muslim homeland as 'communalism.' As nations are 'imagined communities,' not something very natural,[8] 'communalism' like nationalism is something that 'needs only to be well started, and then it thrives of itself.'[9] Thus, there was no inevitability about the rise of a distinct communal or national identity among Bengali Muslims. Their quest for equal opportunities and dignity vis-à-vis Hindu elites and professionals played the decisive role in the Partition of 1947. We need to understand this phenomenon to explain why apparently homogeneous and even syncretistic Bengali Muslims and Hindus could not live as citizens of independent India. By the mid-1940s, both Bengali Muslims and Hindus had decided which side of the fence they would choose as their homeland. Contrary to some popular myths, Hindu Bengalis played a decisive role in the second partition of Bengal in 1947.[10] Now, one wonders if the transformation of Muslim majority East Bengal into a province of Pakistan in 1947 signalled the triumph of East Bengali peasant nationalism. As for the bulk of Bengali Muslims, their national aspiration was almost all about eliminating the overpowering influence of Hindu landlords, moneylenders and professional classes.

Contrary to the historiography of communal conflicts in colonial Bengal[11] these were not only Hindu–Muslim elite conflicts but also class conflicts between rich and powerful Hindus and poor and marginalised Muslims of East Bengal. It is important that class struggle goes beyond the domain of economic differences based merely on the 'production relations' of people in a given society in the Marxian parlance. Class struggle is also about the struggle against political subjugation, social marginalisation, and the culture that legitimises the collective or individual humiliation of groups of under-privileged people for the benefit of the rich and powerful. Now, one may raise the question of whether East Bengali Muslim peasants and underdogs set aside their class differences with rich and powerful Muslim elites and accepted them as their friends, guides and protectors only because to them religious or communal solidarity was more important than class struggle or solidarity with non-Muslim subaltern classes on class lines. The answer lies in the broad definition of 'class,' which transcends the boundaries of economics and the ubiquitous production relations. As Nirad C. Chaudhuri[12] (1951) and Bengali Muslim politicians and writer Abul Mansur Ahmed (1970),[13] among other Bengali Hindu and Muslim writers, have spelled out in their autobiographies, up until the Partition of 1947, Bengali Hindus – irrespective of their class and profession – treated their Muslim neighbours as livestock, and sometimes even as untouchables. This demands a broader, if not new, definition of 'class' to understand why the overwhelming majority of East Bengali Muslims favoured Jinnah, not Gandhi, and Pakistan, not united India, as their leader and destiny, respectively. In view of the transformation of the so-called syncretistic Bengali Muslims – whose attire, food habits and popular culture at the grassroots were not that different from their Hindu neighbours and superordinate classes – into ardent supporters of the Partition, it appears that for them Pakistan appeared to be something more than a pragmatic move for economic well-being and political freedom. Hindus and Muslims in Bengal were collectively responsible for the Partition, which was a direct byproduct of mutual hate and prejudice, broadly known as communalism in South Asia. We may agree with W.C. Smith, who writes that: 'Psychologically, it [communalism] is like a habit-forming drug which, so long as it is administered, is needed in ever-increasing doses.'[14]

Soon after the end of World War I, the British government introduced further administrative measures, which it had started in 1905 with the Partition of Bengal, apparently to uplift the socio-economic conditions of the backward Muslim community in East Bengal. In hindsight, one may appraise these measures as divisive colonial methods to drive a wedge between the Hindu and Muslim communities. And the Partition is the glaring example of how successful the British manoeuvring was in this regard. The colonial administration used law-enforcers and even armed forces to contain and crush the growing surge of the Indian nationalist movement under Gandhi. The British also introduced certain constitutional/reformist measures to India, apparently in the name of granting self-governing institutions to Indians. One, however, discovers the real motive behind these reforms: to neutralise the nationalist movement by widening the gulf between the Hindu and Muslim communities. The British wanted to convince Muslims and other marginalised sections of India that not the agitating nationalist leaders but the colonial administration was their real well-wisher. The widening of the franchise, and the introduction of self-governing Union Boards at the grassroots level, may be mentioned in this regard. While the widening of the franchise down to the well-to-do peasants in Bengal (overwhelmingly Muslim) in 1919[15] and the Khilafat Non-Cooperation Movement in 1920–1922 were important milestones towards politicisation of East Bengali Muslims, they also further communalised the Hindu–Muslim class conflicts. While Muslim leaders who organised the extra-territorial Khilafat Movement – in solidarity with the Ottoman Caliph against the Allies, including Britain – believed in Pan-Islamism, Gandhi and other nationalist leaders supported the romantic Khilafat Movement with a view to bringing Muslim masses into the mainstream of the nationalist movement.[16] India during 1918 and 1947 was witnessing the dynamics of the interplay between the conflicting Indian (mainly Hindu) and Indian Muslim nationalisms vis-à-vis the dynamics of the British divide-and-rule policy.

One British government report in 1918 reveals the long-term impact of the various legislative measures on the psyche of the Indian masses:

> Our rule gave them security from the violence of robbers and the exactions of landlords, regulated by amounts of revenue of rent that they had to pay, and assured to both proprietor and cultivator – in the latter case by the device of the occupancy right – a safe title in their lands. . . . As for the idea of self-government, it is simply a planet that has not yet risen above their horizon. . . . Hitherto, they have regarded the official as their representative in the councils of Government; and now we have to tear up that faith by the roots, to teach them that in future they must bring their trouble to the notice of an elected representative – further, that they have the power to compel his attention. . . . Eventually it will dawn upon him . . . that because he has a vote he has the means of protecting himself. . . . It will occur to him eventually that if landlords are oppressive and usurers grasping and subordinate officials corrupt he has at his command better weapon than the lathi or the hatchet with which to redress his wrongs.[17]

The Montague–Chelmsford Reforms – which take their name from Edwin Montague, the Secretary of State for India, and Lord Chelmsford, the Viceroy of India – were all about the gradual introduction of self-governing institutions to India, as outlined in the Montagu-Chelmsford Report prepared in 1918. It was the basis of the Government of India Act 1919. These reforms granted the maximum concessions the British were prepared to make at that time. The Reforms increased the number of voters in Bengal, from nine thousand to one and a half million, of whom there was a large number of well-to-do Muslim peasants. The number of 'rural seats' – practically, Muslim seats – also went up in the Bengal Legislative Council to 33, which alarmed Hindu *zamindars* and *bhadraloke* (professional classes).[18] These measures along with certain legislative and administrative reforms adversely hit the vested interests of Hindu elites and middle classes, who had been the main promoters of anti-British nationalist and extremist movements (which were often terroristic by nature) in Bengal. Although, at the end of the day, these measures failed to bring the nationalist movement to an end, the subtle pro-Muslim bias and divisive nature of the acts emboldened anti-Hindu communal forces in Bengal, which by 1947 made the communal partition of the province inevitable.

In East Bengal society, which was thoroughly polarised on communal-cum-class lines, what the *Zamindar-Bhadraloke-Mahajan* triumvirate was for Hindus in general, the rival *Ashraf-Ulama-Jotedar* triumvirate was for the bulk of the Muslims. They provided leadership, protection and employment for Hindus, and Muslims, respectively. Muslim *ashraf* or aristocrats – many of whom were Urdu-speaking natives or settlers from northwestern India – employed Muslim clerics, or *ulama*, to preach the dogmas of Islamic supremacy, Muslim separatism and the benefits of remaining loyal to the British Raj. The process of promoting loyalism among Bengali (and Indian) Muslims, which started in the 1870s, culminated in rabid anti-Hindu communalism in Hindu *zamindar-* and *mahajan*-dominated districts and subdivisions in East Bengal during and soon after the Swadeshi Movement of 1905–1911. The anti-partition of Bengal (1905–1911) agitation, the Swadeshi Movement, was essentially a Hindu nationalist-cum-revivalist movement in Bengal. Due to Muslim support for the Partition, which created a Muslim majority province of East Bengal and Assam, the gulf between the Hindus and Muslims was further widened, and the bitter relationship between the two communities reached its climax after the British Government annulled the Partition – which the Government had earlier considered a 'settled fact' – in 1911, due to the intensity of the Swadeshi Movement.[19] Muslim leaders singled out Hindus mainly responsible for the annulment. However, some Muslim leaders were also disillusioned with the so-called pro-Muslim bias of the British government, and as mentioned earlier, later joined hands with Hindu nationalists to organise the anti-British Khilafat Non-Cooperation Movement in 1920.[20]

The Muslim *Ashraf-Ulama-Jotedar* triumvirate in East Bengal made further inroads into the Muslim masses and communalised them before their politicisation process began. This was possible because, being far less numerous and weaker than their Hindu counterparts, Muslim landed and professional elites had conflicting class and communal interests with the Hindu *Zamindar-Bhadraloke-Mahajan* triumvirate. In other words, Hindu elites and professional classes were the common enemies of Bengali Muslim lower and upper classes. While *zamindars* were parasitical and rapacious – and some Hindu *zamindars* were communal to the extreme, and would not allow cow-slaughtering by Muslims in their estates – *mahajans* were as ruthless and extortionist as Shylock in *The Merchant of Venice*. *Mahajans*' rates of interest were extremely exorbitant. Many borrowers lost their properties in servicing their debts, and many could not repay their debts in their lifetime. What an East Bengali peasant in 1929 told a government official in this regard partially reflects the state of indebtedness among Bengali peasants: 'My father, Sir, was born in debt, grew up in debt and died in debt. I have inherited my father's debt and my son will inherit mine.'[21]

Unlike the caste- and *varna*-ridden Bengali Hindus, Bengali Muslims – irrespective of their classes – were inter-related through blood and matrimonial ties. Thanks to the manipulation of the Muslim elite, lower class Muslims in East Bengal were fast deluded into believing in the undifferentiated Muslim monolith, juxtaposed against its Hindu counterpart. Despite its ebbs and flows, the colonial administration's divisive 'pro-Muslim' measures played significant roles in the promotion of Muslim separatism in Bengal. These measures resulted in the communal Partition of Bengal, in the name of administrative exigencies, which separated Muslim majority East Bengal from Hindu majority West Bengal in 1905; the establishment of the All-India Muslim League in 1906; the creation of Separate Electorates for Muslims and other minority communities in India in 1909; drastic pro-tenant legislative measures during 1928 and 1938, which ensured occupancy rights to the tenants and curtailed the power of *zamindars* from 1914 onward; the enactment of the Bengal Rural Primary Education Act 1930, which mostly benefitted poor Muslim families; and the introduction of the Debt-Settlement Boards in 1935 for the benefit of debt-ridden peasants, which may be mentioned in this regard. Despite bitter Hindu

Bengali opposition, in 1921, the colonial administration established a university at Dacca (Dhaka) in Muslim majority East Bengal. The university was a landmark in the history of twentieth-century century East Bengal. It created a Bengali Muslim middle class, which subsequently played a leading role in the Pakistan Movement. Afterwards, the Hindu and Muslim communities in Bengal emerged as two amorphous monoliths, as if they had no common homeland, language, heritage and culture to live as citizens of undivided India.

The marginalised and ambitious Muslim elites, who could not compete with their more advanced Hindu counterparts, started politicising sections of the peasant communities to fight for their rights and opportunities through legislative measures. In doing so, Muslim elites and members of the budding middle classes and *ulama* (Muslim clerics) – who were both Bengali- and Urdu-speaking *ashraf* (aristocrats) from landed and professional classes – championed the cause of the Muslim hoi polloi, setting aside their class differences. Consequently, Bengali Muslim peasants believed that Muslim *zamindars* were benign, not as rapacious as their Hindu counterparts. This diffusion of intra-Muslim class conflict during the period under review, albeit delusional, played the decisive role in the creation of Pakistan in East Bengal. Muslims believed Muslim elites were not only benign and less exploitative but were also their friends, guides and protectors. Due to the constant harping on this theme by Muslim politicians and clerics, Bengali Muslims started believing that Muslims could not exploit fellow Muslims because they belonged to the brotherhood of Muslim *ummah*; they believed that, irrespective of the class differences among the Muslims, Hindus were the common enemies of all sections of the Muslim community.[22]

In short, religious differences between the Hindus and Muslims, discriminations and maltreatment of Muslims by Hindu upper classes and conflicting class interests of upper (Hindu) and lower (Muslim) elites played the decisive roles in the emergence of Pakistan in East Bengal.[23] Not a historian but a British Government Report first revealed that rich peasants'/petty landlords' (overwhelmingly Muslim) aspirations to become *bhadraloke* had been the dominant theme in the politics of small towns and rural areas in East Bengal.[24]

In fact, *jotedars, talukdars, tarafdars, chowdhuries, bhuiyans, haoladars* and other overwhelmingly Muslim intermediary classes of rich tenants and petty landlords between the *zamindars* and poor peasants were the mainstay of the Pakistan Movement in East Bengal. As mentioned before, during 1920 and 1947, due to several government measures there was a noticeable rise in the level of political consciousness among well-to-do peasants. Thanks to government measures, while the *zamindars'* power was waning, the hopes and aspirations of *jotedars* and upper-middle class peasants were growing. Another government report reveals that the prosperity of the rich and upper-middle class peasants 'awakened them to a sense of their inferiority.'[25] So, it is not always Frantz Fanon's 'wretched of the earth' or hopeless people in absolute poverty who make history; people far from poverty with growing hopes and expectations are instrumental in staging revolutions or bringing about changes in socio-economic and political systems. Although the twentieth century was the century of 'peasant revolutions'[26] and 'peasant nationalisms,'[27] the peasants in East Bengal were not the 'makers and breakers of revolutions.'[28]

As Chalmers Johnson[29] has used the phrase 'peasant nationalism' in elucidating the Chinese peasant uprising of 1937–1945, we may use it to explain East Bengali Muslim peasants' role in the creation of Pakistan. Johnson pinpoints why the Chinese Communist Party succeeded in mobilising peasant support against the Japanese invaders in China, arguing that it was 'because . . . the population became receptive to one particular type of political appeal . . . [which] offered to meet the *needs of the people* [italics mine].' We know, contextually, that the Chinese and East Bengali peasant uprisings were different. While the Chinese Communist Party created a 'people's army' of predominantly peasant soldiers to fight the Japanese invaders, the Muslim League in East Bengal mobilised Muslim peasant support to fight the Hindu landed, professional and business (mainly moneylending) elites with constitutional methods and legislative measures. As cited earlier, a British Parliamentary Report in 1918 observed that because the Indian peasant had a vote, he knew he had the means of protecting himself from oppressive landlords and moneylenders; he had at his command a 'better weapon than the lathi or the hatchet with which to redress his wrongs.'[30] It seems both the Chinese Communist Party and Bengal Muslim League understood the '*needs of the people*' and mobilised their respective followers accordingly. While the ruthless nature of the Japanese occupation army convinced Mao Zedong that 'power emerges out of the barrel of the gun,' thanks to the concerted efforts by colonial rulers and Muslim leaders in Bengal, the franchised sections of the peasantry knew their votes were better weapons than their 'lathi or the hatchet' to redress their wrongs.

Although East Bengali peasants did not play a decisive role in the Partition of 1947, unlike the absolutely poor and landless peasants in staging the Communist Revolution in China – where landlessness and brutal oppression of landlords turned landless peasants into stubborn revolutionaries – yet an appraisal of the Pakistan Movement in East Bengal remains incomplete without a discussion of the land system that prevailed in Bengal during the British colonial period. The Permanent Settlement of 1793 – which according to Marx, was 'a caricature of English landed property on a large scale'[31] – led to the mass expropriation and impoverishment of the actual cultivators and was the mother of all problems in colonial and postcolonial Bengal, culturally, economically, politically, socially and psychologically. In short, the Permanent Settlement introduced a land system in Bengal that fixed the landlords' revenue liability to the government on a permanent basis – no future legislation or executive action could undo the settlement – while the *zamindars* were at liberty to raise their tenants' rent and could demand illegal exactions or *abwab* from them when they needed extra cash for religious festivals, weddings in the family or for buying horses and elephants for *zamindars*' personal use. In short, the Permanent Settlement in Bengal introduced quasi-feudal relationships between landlords and tenants. As investing money in buying *zamindari* estates was much more lucrative than running businesses, or textile factories – by the late eighteenth century, Bengal's famous muslin and textile industry as a whole suffered an irreparable loss due to uneven competition with the British textile industry – by the early nineteenth century, Bengal was almost completely deindustrialised.

The Permanent Settlement created a new class of landlords by turning erstwhile revenue collectors or *zamindars* into 'proprietors' or landlords in the British sense of the expression. Traders, moneylenders and well-to-do people from professional classes (mostly attorneys of lower and higher courts) – overwhelmingly Hindu – became the new landlords. Hitherto, private ownership of land, and landlordism, as they existed in Britain and elsewhere in Europe, were unknown under the Mughals and Nawabs of Bengal. The so-called rule of property[32] in Bengal had a long-lasting, catastrophic impact on the economy and social fabric of the sub-region. The neo-feudal production relations in rural Bengal nurtured feudal culture and values, which are still well-entrenched in Bengali culture. *Zamindars* and their employees treated their tenants as servants and menials (Interview, Saha). *Zamindars* did not allow their tenants to wear shoes in their estates (wearing shoes was a prerogative of the elites and gentlemen) or ride horses or elephants or construct brick-built houses on their land. The *zaminadri* system in Bengal became the symbol of Hindu domination and Muslim humiliation in general. The new land system created uneven competitions between landed elites and agricultural classes. Not only were the *zamindars* but also the bulk of the trading and professional elites (almost exclusively high caste Hindu Bengalis and Marwari Jain and Hindu moneylenders and traders) the main beneficiaries of the land system. The system widened the class and communal divide between Bengali Hindus and Muslims to such an extent that by the early twentieth century all the ingredients of the Great Divide had already been there, in rural and urban Bengal.

The British volte-face on the Permanent Settlement, most visible in their support for the various tenancy legislations in Bengal, adversely affected the *zamindars'* interests. By 1938, the *zamindari* system had ended its heyday and had lost its legitimacy among people, so much so that by the 1930s even Muslim *zamindars* publicly went against their own class interests and demanded the abolition of the *zaminadri* system. They were more interested in protecting their long-term communal interests than they were in protecting their class interests inherent in the not-so-viable and unpopular *zamindari* system. Running a *zamindari* was no longer the most lucrative business in Bengal. By the 1930s not only Muslim aristocrats but also members of the budding middle classes emerging out of *jotedar* (petty landlords and rich peasants) families also championed the cause of *zamindari*-abolition across Bengal. Top leaders of the 'aristocratic' Muslim League, and the main political platform of Muslim peasants and tenants in Bengal, the Krishak Proja Party (KPP) under Fazlul Huq (Chief Minister of Bengal, 1937–1943), were in the forefront of the anti-*zamindar* campaign. Soon after the Provincial Legislature Elections in 1937, Huq and his followers formally joined the Muslim League. Interestingly, the Communist Party of India (CPI), mostly led by high caste/upper class Hindu Bengalis (some of who came from *zamindar* families, and/or were beneficiaries of the system) hardly ever demanded the abolition of the *zamindari* system. The CPI championed the cause of either factory and railway workers or landless agricultural workers and sharecroppers in Bengal, from the inception of the party in the 1920s until the Partition in 1947.[33]

Unlike northwestern India, the Pakistan movement in East Bengal was more socio-economic than ideological by nature. The *zamindars* were not predominant in every East Bengal district. While petty landlords or *jotedars* were dominant in Rangpur and Dinajpur districts, Muslim middle-class peasants were dominant in Noakhali and Tippera (Comilla) districts. We need to understand these variations and differentiations to understand the background of the Partition at the macro and micro levels across East Bengal. We know the demands for the abolition of the *zamindari* and *mahajani* (usurious moneylending) systems, and the introduction of free primary schools in the rural areas (mainly for the benefit of the Muslim masses) paved the way for the Partition due to the bitter opposition against these demands by Bengali Hindu elites and middle classes. We also need to know that: a) while in the Muslim *jotedar*-dominated northern districts, sections of the peasantry (landless sharecroppers which consisted overwhelmingly of non-Muslim Santal and Garo tribesmen) supported the communist-inspired *Te-Bhaga* Movement on class-lines, demanding nearly two-thirds of the harvest (instead of the traditional one half) for the sharecroppers from the *jotedars*; and that b) in the Comilla and Noakhali districts, where self-sufficient and independent Muslim middle peasants (not *zamindars* and *jotedars*) had been the most dominant classes of people, the Congress Party-led nationalist movement had substantial support among sections of the Muslim community. The Muslim League, which championed the cause of Pakistan, made a breakthrough in these districts only after most of the 'secular nationalist' Muslim leaders shifted allegiance to the Muslim League after KPP's Huq and his associates had joined the Muslim League.[34] It is noteworthy that the Muslim League and the KPP were more radical than the Congress and CPI vis-à-vis the abolition of the *zamindari* system.

Not only did the Muslim elites and the budding professional classes want the communal Partition, but Bengali Muslim masses also wanted the same thing, partially due to the influence of their Muslim patrons, and partially due to their economic exploitation and social marginalisation by Hindu *zamindars, mahajans* and *bhadraloke* classes. Contrary to popular belief, millions of Muslim sharecroppers/landless peasants did not join the CPI-led class-based *Te-Bhaga* movement (1946 and 1947). The non-peasant, high caste, and middle class Hindu communist leaders – who also had the stigma of promoting a 'godless' ideology – were not Muslim masses' ideal leaders.[35] While strong patronage of Muslim *jotedars* and the sanctity of private ownership of land among these peasants dissuaded them from supporting the radical communist ideology, non-Muslim tribesmen, mainly Garos, Hajongs and Santals, who were the mainstay of the *Te-Bhaga* movement, accepted communist leadership. Firstly, the tribal support for communal ownership of land resonated well with the communist programme of expropriation of the landlord classes. Secondly, thanks to the non-existent factionalism among the tribes, which made vertical mobilisation of tribesmen through their chiefs easier, millions of Garos, Hajongs and Santals swelled the ranks of the communists who wanted '*Te-Bhaga* today, Land tomorrow.' Moni Singh (1901–1990), one of the most prominent communist peasant leaders in Bengal, shared his views with me about the failure of the class based *Te-Bhaga* and *Tanka* movements by sharecroppers in Bengal. He himself had led the famous *Tanka* movement of Hajong (tribesmen) sharecroppers in the 1930s and 1940s in northern Mymensingh district at Haluaghat, Susang Durgapur, and adjoining villages at the foot of the Garo Hills. He attributed the main cause of the failure of the *Tebhaga* movement among Muslim sharecroppers to the vitriolic communal propaganda by local Muslim League leaders. Ghiyasuddin Pathan, a prominent Muslim League leader of Mymensingh, is said to have successfully dissuaded Muslim sharecroppers from the *Te-Bhaga* (literally for two-thirds of the crop for sharecroppers) movement, by promising them *Chou-Bhaga* (all of the crop), as he assured them that Pakistan would ensure land-to-the-tiller by kicking all Hindu landlords out of Pakistan.[36]

Appraising the dynamics of the 'Politics of Partition' in Bengal makes us understand that the multiple streams of movements on class and communal lines at the grassroots were actually microcosmic by nature, reflecting the broad stream of Muslim separatism in the subcontinent. The undercurrent of the movement for Pakistan in Bengal represented two other streams, hitherto ignored by historians: a) Bengali Muslims' quest for an independent 'Eastern Pakistan,' crystallised by the All-India Muslim League's Lahore Resolution in March 1940; and b) East Bengali Muslim peasants' aspirations for freedom from the exacting *zamindari* and moneylending systems, which resembled what Chalmers Johnson called 'peasant nationalism' with regard to the Chinese Revolution of 1949.[37] In a way, for Bengali Muslim peasants, Pakistan was a utopia, the culmination of their aspirations for political and economic freedom.

As in China, non-peasant outsiders led Bengali Muslim peasants in their freedom struggle. However, unlike in China, Bengali Muslim peasant leaders belonging to the Muslim *Ashraf-Ulama-Jotedar* triumvirate had a certain hidden agenda. They wanted to replace the Hindu *Zamindar-Bhadraloke-Mahajan* triumvirate by installing themselves to dominant positions in 'Muslim Pakistan' with Muslim grassroots support. It was possible because the Hindu triumvirate was also the common enemy of East Bengali Muslim peasants. We know peasants are not the 'makers and breakers of revolutions,' and, being 'representatives of the unchanging remnants of the past, totally dependent on their masters,' as 'rural idiots' and a 'sack of potatoes,'[38] they are totally incapable of leading themselves against landlords and other exploiting classes. East Bengal peasants were not that different in this regard. Thanks to the rise of a Bengali Muslim middle class, emerging mainly out of the upper peasantry in East Bengal ('East Pakistan' from 1956 to 1971) during 1947 and 1971 – which would not have been possible without the Partition – children and grandchildren of peasants who had supported the creation of Pakistan under non-peasant elite leaders in 1947 played a decisive role in carving out another 'peasant utopia' through another freedom struggle in 1971, this time in the name of Bengali nationalism.

In sum, there was nothing really surprising about the second partition of Bengal in 1947. It was not a partition on communal lines in the narrow sense of the expression. Nothing could be more preposterous than suggesting that a 'homogeneous' province was divided into two only because of colonialism, elite manipulation and the promotion of religion. The convergence of East Bengali Muslim and peasant identities played a very important, if not decisive, role in the Partition. We would fail to fathom the depth of the chasm between Muslim and Hindu Bengalis unless we accept that their respective religions and their strong sense of belonging to their faiths remoulded their identities not long after the British occupation of India. Again, historically Bengalis from East Bengal or Bangladesh have had multiple differences with Bengalis from West Bengal or Paschim Banga (since 2011) and Tripura in terms of culture, dialect, lifestyle and even dietary habits. Ancient and mediaeval Bengal (up until the Mughal conquest in the sixteenth century) was never one undifferentiated landmass with a homogeneous population under one single administration.

Finally, the political use of religion by Gandhi and others – before, during and after the Khilafat Movement – further exacerbated the colonial divide-and-rule policy by widening the gulf between Hindus and Muslims across the subcontinent. We know the so-called Two-Nation Theory predates Jinnah's Lahore speech of March 1940. It is a distortion of history that only Muslims, not Hindus, thought in terms of dividing the subcontinent into Hindu and Muslim states. Many prominent Bengali Hindus – from Bankim Chatterjee to Sarat Chatterjee – always considered Indian Muslims as descendants of alien invaders and favoured their expulsion from India.[39] Even Rabindra Nath Tagore – widely 'worshipped' by millions of Bangladeshi Muslims as a 'non-communal humanist' – in one of his poems glorified Shivaji, who has been an icon of Hindu supremacists for the last two hundred years. It is an incontrovertible fact that it was not Jinnah but rather Nehru who torpedoed the Cabinet Mission Plan in 1946.[40] Bengali Hindu writer and retired ICS officer Annada Shankar Ray (1904–2002) told me how Bengali Hindu leaders, intellectuals and common people in the 1940s had become rabid supporters of the Partition. So much so that, many of them despised Gandhi for his opposition to the Partition. 'Can't we get someone to kill this Evil Gandhi?' they wondered.[41]

To conclude, by the 1940s, Bengal had already been divided on communal-cum-class lines between Hindus and Muslims; Jinnah and Pakistan just formalised it. Sheikh Mujibur Rahman, who later became the Father of the Nation of Bangladesh, revealed how he himself and tens of thousands of young Bengali Muslims by 1946 admired Jinnah and Suhrawardy (and preferred them to Fazlul Huq) for championing the cause of Pakistan.[42] In short, for the overwhelming majority of Bengali Muslims, irrespective of class and occupation, Pakistan was their only way out from the domineering, and grossly discriminatory and humiliating treatment of Hindu landed, professional and business elites towards them. By August 1946 – after Nehru had rejected the Cabinet Mission Plan, which could have preempted the Partition – Bengali Muslims and their Hindu neighbours were quickly becoming estranged from one another. Many of them would not hesitate to kill the other only because they belonged to two different faiths. In sum, for the average Bengali Muslim by the 1940s, Pakistan signified much more than a separate homeland for Muslims. It was their promised land to restore the lost glory of the Caliphate and the Mughal Empire, 'a land of eternal Eid' and, last but not least, a 'peasant utopia.'

Notes

1 Dhulipala, Venkat (2016) *Creating a New Medina: State Power, Islam, and the Quest for Pakistan in Late Colonial North India*, Cambridge University Press, Cambridge.
2 Kamal, Ahmed (1989) "'A Land of Eternal Eid': Independence, People, and Politics in East Bengal," *Dhaka University Studies*, Part A, Vol. 46, No. 1; Kamal, Ahmed (2009) *State against the Nation: The Decline of the Muslim League in Pre-Independence Bangladesh, 1947–54*, The University Press Limited, Dhaka.
3 Wolf, Eric (1968) *Peasant Wars of the Twentieth Century*, Oklahoma University Press, Norman, Oklahoma, pp. 290–292; Hashmi, Taj I. (1992) *Pakistan as a Peasant Utopia: The Communalization of Class Politics in East Bengal, 1920–1947*, Westview Press, Boulder, p. 254.
4 Hashmi, Taj I. (1992) *Pakistan as a Peasant Utopia: The Communalization of Class Politics in East Bengal, 1920–1947*, Westview Press, Boulder, Chapters 2, 5.
5 Badruddin, Umar (2004) *The Emergence of Bangladesh: Class Struggle in East Pakistan (1947–1958)*, Oxford University Press, Oxford, Chapter 5; Kamal, Ahmed (2009) *State against the Nation: The Decline of the Muslim League in Pre-Independence Bangladesh, 1947–54*, The University Press Limited, Dhaka, Chapter 8.
6 Smith, Wilfred Cantwell (1969) *Modern Islam in India: A Social Analysis*, Sh. Muhammad Ashraf, Lahore, pp. 187–232.
7 Gopal, S. (1988) "Nehru and Minorities", *Mainstream Weekly*, November 12.
8 Anderson, Benedict (2016) *Imagined Communities: Reflections on the Origin and Spread of Nationalism*, Verso, London.
9 Smith, Wilfred Cantwell (1969) *Modern Islam in India: A Social Analysis*, Sh. Muhammad Ashraf, Lahore, p. 221.
10 Chatterjee, Joya (1994) *Bengal Divided: Hindu Communalism and Partition, 1932–1947*, Cambridge University Press, Cambridge. Author interviewed Annada Shankar Ray (1904–2002), Calcutta, 15 January 1983.
11 Broomfield, John H. (1968) *Elite Conflict in a Plural Society: Twentieth-Century Bengal*, University of California Press, Berkeley; MacPherson, D. (1926) *Final Report on the Survey and Settlement Operations in the Districts of Pabna and Bogra, 1920 to 1929*, Government of Bengal Press, Calcutta 1930 Report, Calcutta.
12 Chaudhuri, Nirad C. (2001) *Autobiography of an Unknown Indian*, Review Books Classic, New York.
13 Ahmed, Abul Mansur (1970) *Fifty Years of Politics as I Witnessed It* (in Bengali), Nowrose, Dacca.
14 Smith, Wilfred Cantwell (1969) *Modern Islam in India: A Social Analysis*, Sh. Muhammad Ashraf, Lahore, p. 206.
15 Government of Bengal (1919) *Report of the Franchise Committee and the Committee on Division of Franchise*, GOB Press, Calcutta, pp. 383–390.
16 Hashmi, Taj I. (1992) *Pakistan as a Peasant Utopia: The Communalization of Class Politics in East Bengal, 1920–1947*, Westview Press, Boulder, Chapter 3.

17 British Parliamentary Papers, BPP, Cd9101, 1918, pp. 113, 120–121.
18 Hashmi, Taj I. (1992) *Pakistan as a Peasant Utopia: The Communalization of Class Politics in East Bengal, 1920–1947*, Westview Press, Boulder, Chapter 2.
19 Sarkar, Sumit (1977) *The Swadeshi Movement in Bengal: 1903–1908*, People's Publishing House, New Delhi, passim.
20 Hashmi, Taj I. (1992) *Pakistan as a Peasant Utopia: The Communalization of Class Politics in East Bengal, 1920–1947*, Westview Press, Boulder, Chapter 3.
21 Mahalanobis, P.C. et al. (1946) "A Sample Survey of After-Effects of the Bengal Famine of 1943," *Advance Report from Sankhya: The Indian Journal of Statistics*, Part 4, Vol. 7, p. 374.
22 Hashmi, Taj I. (1992) *Pakistan as a Peasant Utopia: The Communalization of Class Politics in East Bengal, 1920–1947*, Westview Press, Boulder, pp. 83–118.
23 Chatterjee, Joya (1994) *Bengal Divided: Hindu Communalism and Partition, 1932–1947*, Cambridge University Press, Cambridge; Broomfield, John H. (1968) *Elite Conflict in a Plural Society: Twentieth-Century Bengal*, University of California Press, Berkeley; McPherson, Kenneth (1974) *The Muslim Microcosm: Calcutta, 1918 to 1935*, Franz Steiner, Heidelberg.
24 Sachse, F.A. (1917) *District Gazetteer, Mymensingh*, GOB, Calcutta, pp. 39 and 43.
25 MacPherson, D. (1926) *Final Report on the Survey and Settlement Operations in the Districts of Pabna and Bogra, 1920 to 1929*, Government of Bengal Press, Calcutta 1930 Report, Calcutta, p. 73.
26 Wolf, Eric (1968) *Peasant Wars of the Twentieth Century*, Oklahoma University Press, Norman, Oklahoma. Migdal, Joel S. (1974) *Peasants, Politics, and Revolution Pressures toward Political and Social Change in the Third World*, Princeton University Press, Princeton, NJ, p. 226.
27 Johnson, Chalmers A. (1962) *Peasant Nationalism and Communist Power: The Emergence of Revolutionary China 1937–1945*, Stanford University Press, Redwood city, CA.
28 Stokes, Eric (1978) *The Peasant and the Raj: Studies in Agrarian Society and Peasant Rebellion in Colonial India*, Cambridge University Press, Cambridge, p. 266.
29 Johnson, Chalmers A. (1962) *Peasant Nationalism and Communist Power: The Emergence of Revolutionary China 1937–1945*, Stanford University Press, Redwood City, CA, p. 7.
30 British Parliamentary Papers, BPP, Cd9101, 1918, and Cd812, 1920, pp. 113, 120–121.
31 Marx, Karl (1993 edition) *Capital: A Critique of Political Economy*, Volume 3, Penguin Books, London, pp. 392–93.
32 Guha, Ranajit (1983) *Elementary Aspects of Peasant Insurgency in Colonial India*, Oxford University Press, Oxford.
33 Hashmi, Taj I. (1992) *Pakistan as a Peasant Utopia: The Communalization of Class Politics in East Bengal, 1920–1947*, Westview Press, Boulder, Chapter 7.
34 Ibid.

35 Author interviewed Dr. Sunil Sen (1920–), He actively took part in the *Te-Bhaga* Movement in northern Bengal; Calcutta 1 May, 1983.
36 Author interviewed Moni Singh (1901–1990), Dhaka, 20 October 1982.
37 Johnson, Chalmers A. (1962) *Peasant Nationalism and Communist Power: The Emergence of Revolutionary China 1937–1945*, Stanford University Press, Redwood City, CA.
38 Marx, Karl (1978) *The Eighteenth Brumaire of Louis Bonaparte*, Foreign Languages Press, Peking (first published in 1852), Chapter 7.
39 Chatterjee, Joya (1994) *Bengal divided: Hindu Communalism and Partition, 1932–1947*, Cambridge University Press, Cambridge.
40 Azad, Maulana Abul Kalam (1988) *India Wins Freedom: The Complete Version*, Orient Longman, New Delhi, pp. 157–166.
41 Author interviewed Annada Shankar Ray (1904–2002), Calcutta, 15 January1983.
42 Rahman, Sheikh Mujibur (2012) *Incomplete Autobiography* (in Bengali), The University Press Limited, Dhaka, pp. 34–54.

Chapter 5

Recovering a forgotten partition

Decolonisation, displacement and memories of home and uprooting in postcolonial Assam

Binayak Dutta

'I began to realize that partition was not, even in my family, a closed chapter of history.'[1] This assertion by Urvashi Butalia in a different context is probably more relevant today to understand the story of Partition as a living process in North-East India, where the emergence of Partition scholarship on North-East India has been a recent development, especially with the recovery of the Sylhet referendum story.[2] Here, Partition was not a simple realignment of cartographic contours but an intensely political event that metamorphosed the life of the people who fell on the 'wrong' side of the boundaries, as location determined socialisations and articulations of culture and politics. Historians from and of this region have only recently entered this campaign to counter the statist historical project on independence and partitions. By shifting towards the use of innovative historical strategies in the reconstruction of narratives, recent attempts have been made to overcome the hiatus between the national and the popular and between history and memory, which had only widened over the years. Conceptually, most of the Partition narratives suffer from their inability to distinguish between the Partition as a process and the politics that arose in its wake. Though the latter is an outcome of the former, the two are not the same. While engaging with both these dimensions, this chapter attempts to locate Partition politics and mobilisation in this region under study. It is important to assert that North-East India as an imagined political category is not homogenous in its encounter with partition. This chapter negotiates between the multi-vocality of the story of partition in North-East India by locating some sites of India's northeastern Partition experiences and by highlighting some of the important issues arising out the politics of Partition on these sites. Therefore, experiences from Assam, Tripura and the Khasi hills form the core of the narrative.

The partition of Assam

When the partition proposals came in May–June 1947, it was decided that if Bengal was to be partitioned, a referendum would be organised under the aegis of the central government to decide whether Sylhet, which was a predominantly Bengali speaking district of south Assam was to remain in Assam or merge with East Bengal.[3] This pronouncement not only brought Assam as yet another colonial province into the vortex of partition politics, it also brought into the partition discourse communities of the hills and plains of North-East India, who otherwise had no stake in the declaration on the proposed partition of the Indian subcontinent. Sylhet was a part of the province of Assam from 1874 until the Partition of 1947, except for a brief period when Assam itself was made a part of a larger province called Eastern Bengal and Assam between 1905 and 1911. Therefore, when agreement came on the decision to partition the Indian subcontinent, the colonial state, the Assam Pradesh Congress and the Muslim League agreed that, contrary to the Muslim League's demand for incorporating the whole province of Assam as a part of Eastern Pakistan, only the Muslim majority district of Sylhet in Assam would be put up for a referendum to decide whether it should be amalgamated with East Pakistan or retained in India. Extant records inform us that the Assam Provincial Congress Committee and the Assamese leaders were eager to transfer the predominantly Bengali speaking district from Assam[4] due to existing ethnic antagonism between the Assamese elites and the Bengal elites of Assam.

When the referendum campaign commenced, while the Assamese Congress leaders remained indifferent, the local Congress leaders, the Communists and Jamiat-ul-ulama-i-Hind and the Muslim League and the Jamiat-i-Islami, jumped into the campaign. It was this battle that decided Sylhet's fate after 14 August 1947. While the first group led by the district congress was in favour of retaining Sylhet within Assam and in India, the Muslim League was in favour of detaching Sylhet from Assam. Both sides were allotted symbols that represented their position before the voters, as they cast their vote in the referendum. While the Pro-Partitionists, that is, those who favoured Sylhet joining Pakistan, were allotted the 'AXE,' those who opposed partition were given the symbol of the 'HUT.' The Muslim League leadership represented by Abdul Matin Choudhury was originally keen to have the 'crescent moon' as their symbol. This demand was resented by the nationalist Muslims as it 'nourished a communal feeling.'[5] Aggressive campaigns accompanied by rhetorical slogans were constructed around these symbols. Rhetoric and slogans of either side rent the air as the days of the referendum drew close. Contrary to most official narratives, the Referendum Campaign had vigorous cultural dimensions reflected in songs, poems and slogans mired in their unique sense of history, culture and even geography.[6] There was little doubt that by 1947, the Pakistan Movement had become predominantly communal, with religion playing an important part in the campaign. As Muslim League leaders arrived in Sylhet from Bengal, they were determined to espouse and establish the case for Pakistan at their campaigns.

Despite being the last, it was not an even battle; the contest was keen and the battle lines were clearly drawn. But there was little doubt in the minds of people on the field, including colonial official, that the Muslim League had an upper hand in this battle.[7] While the Congress-Communist-Jamiyati volunteers spared no effort at getting their message across to the voters of the referendum, their message was lost in the hustle and bustle of the campaign on most occasions.[8] Despite the efforts of the Congress and the anti partition campaigners, the referendum resulted in the victory of the pro partition group led by the Muslim League mired in an enormous amount of violence and intimidation. Though the official report tried to downplay the level of intimidation, there was no denying it. The report noted that 'No doubt some non-violent intimidation by League Muslims had begun but not to the extent claimed by the Hindus.'[9] While the extent of the violence and intimidation in the Sylhet Referendum became a bone of contention for the contending parties, the results of the referendum came to be notified by the colonial government as the viceroy telegraphed the report of the referendum commissioner to the government in London. Firing was resorted to and it caused the death of one League volunteer and the injury of three of the Leaguers and initiated violent retaliation on the Congress workers of the area.[10] The armed intervention to control the riotous crowd let loose a reign of terror at Sylhet and became the metamorphic moment of Sylhet partition.[11] When the result of the referendum was made public, it came to light that a majority of the votes were in favour of amalgamation with East Pakistan. Sylhet was put on the dissection table of the Boundary Commission. Both the sides in the contest were apprehensive about the Bengal Boundary Commission. Many Congress leaders both at Assam and central leadership felt that the Bengal Commission would not to justice to the cause of Assam – relations between the Bengalis and the Assamese elite being extremely antagonistic in Assam. Nehru raised this apprehension with the Viceroy Lord Mountbatten and demanded that a separate Boundary Commission be constituted for Sylhet.[12] The viceroy, on his part, dismissed these apprehensions and rejected the Congress's demand due to a paucity of time.[13] Therefore in the post-referendum situation, the Sylhet question was placed before the Bengal Boundary Commission with the contending sides making detailed presentations. On 14 August, Sylhet, except for three and a half thanas,[14] became a part of East Pakistan. What remained became part of the Cachar district of the composite state of Assam in postcolonial India.

The partition of Tripura

The partition of Tripura, unlike that of Assam, was unique as it was a princely state. Comprising of hills and plains, Tripura presents partition historians with an unprecedented situation. Contrary to claims made in most standard texts, the princely state of Tripura was also partitioned as the lands held by the maharaja in the plains of East Bengal were taken away from his control with the creation of East Pakistan. The Tripura kings had been the rulers of both the hills and some areas in the plains of eastern Bengal since the fifteenth century, especially Comilla and parts of the Sylhet, Noakhali and Chittagong districts. These plains areas came under the sway of colonial control in 1761 after an operation led by Lieutenant Mathews on behalf of the Chittagong Council. 'Marriot the collector was sent from the Chittagong Council on the 15th of March to settle and receive the revenues of Tripura . . . the paying part of Tripura lay on plains and was known as Chakla Roshnabad,'[15] a total area of 555 square miles. A reference to the plains is significant in the context of partition as the hills of Tripura became the home for a multitude of people who migrated from their homes in East Bengal since the eve of partition until the 1970s.

Tripura was an important part of the politics of decolonisation in the Indian subcontinent. When the cabinet mission discussed the fate of the princely states on decolonisation, Tripura, as a part of the Chamber of Princes, was also a signatory to the resolution stating that 'the princely states shared the general desire in the country for the immediate attainment by India of her full stature and will make every possible contribution towards the settlement of Indian constitutional problem.'[16] Tripura therefore decided to join and participate in the deliberations of the constituent assembly. Accordingly Shri G.S. Guha, who was a minister in the Tripura government, was nominated to the constitent assembly. The Maharaja of Tripura was also clear about Tripura joining the Indian union.[17] He had already indicated his decision to the government of India about his decision.

In a letter written to G.S. Guha, Dewan B.K. Sen, advisor to the Ruler of Tripura, dated 22 April 1947, one can see the copy of the format of the Instrument of Accession that was sent to the government of the princely state of Tripura for the purpose of a signature by the government of India. But despite all the political arrangements being relatively certain on the eve of partition, the political situation became extremely fragile with the death of Maharaja Bir Bikram Kishore Manikya on 17 May 1947. His son was then still a minor and therefore a Council of Regency was formed with Maharani Kanchan Prava Devi as president and Satyavrata Mukherjee as the chief minister. The proposals for decolonisation had by then almost been finalised and then-Viceroy Lord Mountbatten proceeded to London to give the final shape to the decolonisation plans. The final declaration about decolonisation was made on 3 June 1947, announcing that the Indian subcontinent would be divided into the two dominions of India and Pakistan and the princely states of India would be given an option to join either of the dominions. A boundary commission was also constituted, with Sir Cyril Radcliffe as the chairman, to demarcate the boundary between India and East Bengal, subsequently forming the core of East Pakistan. Though the maharani, as the president of the Regency Council, signed the Instrument of Accession to the Indian Union on 13 August 1947,[18] the award of the boundary commission formalised the process of Partition and accordingly the estates of Chakla Roshnabad, which belonged to the Maharaja of Tripura as a zamindari, came to be located within East Pakistan. Thus with the partition of India, princely Tripura, along with Punjab, Bengal and Assam, also experienced the process of Partition, and the people living in the princely state of Tripura were also exposed to the vicissitudes of post-Partition politics. Confident about the wisdom of the rulers, the Hindu subjects of Chakla Roshnabad did not submit any memorandum to the Radcliffe Commission for inclusion of the zamindari into the post-Partition Tripura though they had been an inalienable part of the territorial possessions of the king of Tripura long before the onset of colonial rule. The silence of the maharani and the silence of the Hindu subjects of the area emboldened the Muslim riots of the zamindari to assert their claims for including the areas of Chakla Roshnabad into Pakistan and keeping it as such. With the creation of East Pakistan, these subjects led to a fast growing movement in support of the merger of Chakla Roshnabad with Pakistan. Though the maharani, declared that the princely state of Tripura had acceded to the Indian Union according to the wishes of the late Maharaja and called upon the people of Chakla Roshnabad to celebrate the 'historic occasion,' a few members of the royal family who harboured designs on the throne, began to organise agitations for the merger of Tripura with East Pakistan.[19] These members of the royal family had a close relationship with the leaders of the Anjuman Islamia, which was an ally of the Muslim League. A wave of propaganda was carried on in the areas of Chakla Roshnabad by the Anjuman and the Muslim League National Guard which had a field day in those areas as a result of the patronage it enjoyed from the government of East Pakistan. Intelligence reports observed that 'the Muslim League National Guards in East Bengal are carrying on open propaganda that Tripura State belongs to East Pakistan and that preparations are being made to invade Tripura.'[20] Similar reports were also received from ground-based officers of the Tripura government, informing the government about meetings and mobilisation campaigns and resolutions in favour of the merger of Tripura with Pakistan and about the threats by the Muslim League supporting riots to withhold payment of rent if their request of Tripura's merger with Pakistan was not acceded to: 'it is that the Muslim National Guards from East Bengal, Tippera district, have started an agitation against accession of Tripura State to the Indian Union and they may well have raids. Tripura is very feeble and the Raj family is itself divided. . . . '[21] But despite these movements, which continued in some areas of eastern Pakistan, the Instrument of Accession signed on 13 August 1947 was only reinforced by the support extended to Tripura by the government of India to overcome the political crisis that arose in the administration during between 1947 and 1949. The signature of the maharani on the merger agreement on 9 September 1949 sealed all doubts about Tripura's fate as part of the Indian union and ensured the transfer of administration from the regency council to the Indian government. Tripura was made a chief commissioner's province and Chakla Roshnabad became 'the absolute private property'[22] of the Tripura royal family. With the formation of East Pakistan, Chakla Roshnabad was lost on the transfer of power to East Pakistan despite the protests by the Hindu subjects and the subordinate zamindars,[23] completing the partition of Tripura as well.

Some other Partition stories of North-East India

Beyond the narratives of the immediacy of Partition politics, when Partition finally took place, it affected politics and the lives of the people in Assam in many ways. It physically separated North-East India from the rest of the country, except for a small passage of 22 kilometres commonly known as the chicken neck. Assam lost 4,769 square miles of territory and a population of 2,825,282 persons. But the loss of territory was not as significant as the loss of paddy fields, lime, cement industries and the tea gardens of Sylhet.[24] The adverse impact of the transfer of the Sylhet district to East Pakistan was noted in the census report of 1951, which observed that, 'the far reaching effects of this loss will continue to be felt by Assam as well as India for many years to come.'[25] Partition disrupted the natural channels of riverine communication, rail and road networks that linked the hill areas of colonial Assam through the Surma valley. One of the scholars crisply noted that

> Assam's rail link with the rest of the country was snapped following partition. It was only in January, 1950 that the rail link was restored by a metre-gauge line through the narrow chicken neck corridor of north Bengal. The disruption of the rail link had a very adverse effect on Assam's economy. Partition also resulted in the loss of Chittagong port which was a major outlet for Assam tea.[26]

Partition of Assam and the loss of Sylhet[27] made Assam a landlocked province, as its outlet to the sea since 1904[28] through the port of Chittagong became a part of East Pakistan.

Partition of colonial Assam in 1947 also adversely affected the social and economic lives of the various tribal communities residing within colonial Assam. The traditional links connecting the Khasis and Jaintias with Sylhet, on the one hand, and the link connecting the Garos with Mymensingh, on the other hand, were disrupted. These tribes were settled not only in the hill districts of Assam but also in the plains of Sylhet and Mymensingh. With the stroke of a pen these people were internally split into Indians and Pakistanis, depending on their residence. The traditional inter-community linkages in the area were so strong that these hill tribes 'for ages depended on their trade with the plains. . . .'[29] A centuries-old and prosperous border-trade-based economy was killed with the closing of the borders and the erection of check-posts.[30] In the pre-Partition scenario, the plains of Sylhet used to be the main produce market of the hills and foothills of the Khasi-Jaintia lands. As a result of the partition of Sylhet, a border of about 150 miles in length was created across the Khasi-Jaintia hills. The new state of East Pakistan partitioned the lands inhabited by the Khasi, Jaintia and Garo as its boundary came to be demarcated 'from boundary pillar no 1071 located at the tri-junction of Rangpur district of Bangladesh, west Garo Hills district of Meghalaya and Goalpara district of Assam and ends at the boundary pillar no 1338 at the tri-junction of Sylhet district of Bangladesh, Jaintia Hills district and Cachar district of Assam.'[31] Partition and the amalgamation of Sylhet with East Pakistan caused 'a virtual economic blockade of the Khasi hills.'[32] The movement of goods was initially discouraged and subsequently stopped from moving between the Khasi-Jaintia hills and East Pakistan. While the Khasi-Jaintia people of the hills found themselves cut off from their kinsmen in the plains, they were also reduced to penury without a market for their agricultural produce and mineral resources. Trade, which amounted to more than three crores of rupees annually in the pre-partition days, came to a standstill, which resulted in the tribal communities residing at the borders between the Khasi Hills and Sylhet being brought to the brink of starvation.[33] The affected in the Khasi Hills district amounted to about 80,000 people and about 16,000 households. This resulted in large-scale migration of people from these border areas to new settlements selected for their relocation in the Ri-Bhoi region of present-day Meghalaya.[34]

Partition's greatest impact was certainly the migration of populations from one region to another, both within a country and across newly created international borders, and the resulting demographic transformations. Partition changed the way politics came to be perceived not only in Assam but also throughout North-East India. As interprovincial borders of the colonial era became international boundaries, perceptions about population migration also changed. Interprovincial migration, which was easy and mostly unrestricted, became restricted by the legal regimes governing international population movement. Though there was no restriction on the migration of people from East Pakistan to Assam in the initial years after independence, gradually the provincial governments and the government of India began to discourage the migration of people from East Pakistan to India by 1950. Partition introduced the 'foreigners' dimension into politics in North-East India with the creation of the passport system in 1952.

Partition's post-script in North-East India

As the situation became critical, the initial trickle of people wanting to migrate to India from East Pakistan became a flood by 1950 because the political atmosphere in East Pakistan had become increasingly hostile to the minority communities. The census report for Assam, Manipur and Tripura in 1951 observed that:

> the recent influx of Hindu refugees from Pakistan constitutes the biggest migration stream into Assam during the last decade. Following the Noakhali Riots in October 1946, and the partition of India, there has been an almost steady and continuous exodus of the Hindus of Pakistan into Assam and Tripura. According to a census taken in July 1949, there were 24,600 families of displaced persons in Assam or approximately 114,500 persons.[35]

The migration situation was aggravated further as riots broke out in various other parts of East Pakistan in 1949 and 1950.[36] The census report of 1951 observed that:

> Soon after the 1949 Refugee Census occurred the incidences of Soneswar and Habiganj, the oppression of the Hajongs in Northern Mymensingh and the atrocities committed on the Santhals in Rajshahi, in East Dinajpur, etc. Then came the gruesome incidents over large areas of East Pakistan in February-March 1950, especially Dacca. These led to the inevitable result, viz, the desertion by hundreds and thousands of Hindus in East Pakistan of their hearths and homes to seek shelter in the neighboring districts of West Bengal and Assam whichever was nearer.[37]

The number of displaced reached almost half a million people by April, 1950. A large number of the displaced preferred to settle down in Assam. The census of 1951 revealed that as many as 274,455 people were settled in Assam, predominantly in the plains. While 259,946 people settled in plains areas, only 14,509 people moved into the hill areas.[38] The political situation in East Pakistan only contributed to the inflow of more Hindu refugees into Assam. Compared to 273,000 refugees in the census of 1951, the number of refugees in the 1961 census was 628,000. The influx of refugees contributed to social tensions in Assam. Assamese elites feared for their economic, political and cultural lives. The situation became more critical by 1961.[39] The culturally conscious Assamese middle class, who initially welcomed these immigrants, subsequently began to be wary of them, as these immigrants became vote-banks of the ruling party.[40] The birth of Bangladesh on the partition of Pakistan in 1971 made the situation worse. It added the 'Bangladeshi' dimension to the 'foreigners' imbroglio. The Assam anti-foreigner agitations were launched in 1978 and came to a close with the signing of the Assam Accord in 1985. Despite the signing of the accord, the threat of immigrants from across the borders never dissipated from the Assamese popular imagination, fear of which took the form of anti-foreigner demonstrations from time to time.

In Tripura, the partition of Tripura and the loss of Chakla Roshnabad only contributed to aggravation of a social and political crisis. One of the pioneering scholars, Tripur Chandra Sen, in *Tripura in Transition*, pointed out that '[h]ad the zamindary been included in the State of Tripura, the refugee problem would not have been so acute and injurious to the people of this country.'[41] This was similar to the situation in Assam, where the loss of Sylhet deprived the Brahmaputra Valley of a buffer zone for absorbing the partition displaced people from East Pakistan and exposed the Brahmaputra valley to refugee inflow. Partition also exposed Tripura to an enormous inflow of refugees. As a relatively peaceful state contiguous to East Pakistan and as an area that had welcomed the settlement of Bengalis from East Bengal under the patronage of the Maharajas, Tripura was perceived as a safe haven for the displaced Bengali Hindus from the various districts of East Pakistan after Partition, as east Pakistan witnessed a spike in communal violence, especially after 1950. Most of the displaced hailed from those areas that formed the zamindari of the maharaja. In 1950–1951, the number of refugees who migrated to Tripura was as high as 184,000. With violent anti-minority movements breaking out in East Pakistan, the second surge of refugee inflow was in 1964–1965, when census data recorded as many as 100,340 migrants coming in. Gayatri Bhattacharyya very aptly summed up the post-partition scenario when she recorded that:

> [b]efore the partition the progress of settlement of the Bengalees was slow and steady. But after partition especially from 1951 there was a sudden spurt in immigration of the minority community of East Pakistan, now Bangladesh. At times the inflow of displaced persons slowed down but following communal troubles in East Pakistan and introduction of the passport system it again quickened. . . . Today the displaced persons far outnumber the Tribal population.[42]

In lieu of a conclusion

Despite the passage of seven decades since the transfer of power, Partition continues to affect the lives of the people in North-East India. Over the years, the unresolved boundary question in North-East India and the continuous acrimony over the legality of migration across the created state-nation boundaries has drawn attention to the assertion that partition is not an event but a process that is far from its closure. Though the impact of the Partition of 1947 persists throughout the land and in the lives of the peoples of India, there have been few attempts to understand its effects on politics and on the lives of the people of North-East India. It is most likely that official apathy and antagonism, aggravated by violations and violence that Bengali Hindus have faced in the Brahmaputra Valley since 1947, have led Bengali Hindus to adopt denial of the Partition experience as a survival technique. However, it is sad that political expediency and short-term strategies often contributed to 'memocide' and resulted in the loss of thousands of testimonies, through the death of witness/participants of the Sylhet referendum or due to age-related loss of memory. Though some attempts have been made engage academically with stories of Partition in recent years, these have been far from adequate and lack a comprehensive character. We can only conclude by emphasising that the Partition story in North-East India is a complex one that resists the possibility of a definitive conclusion. Here, 'partition is a living history . . . yet to be recovered but which we are still only beginning to remember.'[43]

Notes

1 Butalia, Urvashi (1998) *The Other Side of Silence Voices from the partition of India*, New Delhi: Viking.
2 Dasgupta, Anindita (2008) 'Remembering Sylhet: A Forgotten Story of India's 1947 Partition' *Economic and Political Weekly*, Vol. 43, Issue No. 31, Mumbai: Sameeksha Trust, 02 Aug, pp. 18–22. Also see Bhattacharjee, Nabanipa (2009) 'Unburdening Partition: The "Arrival" of Sylhet' *Economic and Political Weekly*, Vol. 44, Issue No. 04, Mumbai: Sameeksha Trust, 24 Jan, pp. 77–79; Dutta, Binayak (2012) 'Recovering Sylhet' *Himal South Asian, Kathmandu, the Southasia Trust*, 22 Nov.
3 Chakrabarty, Bidyut (2004) *The Partition of Bengal and Assam*, London: RoutledgeCurzon, p. 177.
4 Gopinath Bordoloi, the leader of Assam Provincial Congress Committee candidly pointed out in his meeting with Lord Wavell as early as 1946 that 'Assam would be quite prepared to hand over Sylhet to Eastern Bengal.' In Penderal Moon (1973) *Wavell the Viceroy's Journal*, London: Oxford University Press, p. 233.
5 Governor of Assam's Report to the Viceroy dated 28th June, 1947, Mountbatten Papers, acc no. 5123 National Archives of India New Delhi (herein after NAI).
6 Dutta, Binayak (2014) 'Event, Memory, Lore: Anecdotal History of Partition in Assam' *The NEHU Journal*, Vol. 12, No. 2, Shillong: North Eastern Hill University, pp. 61–76.
7 Annexure C to Referendum Commissioner's report on the Sylhet Referendum in Private Secretary to the Viceroy Papers acc. No. 3471, NAI.
8 Hardy, Peter (1972) *The Muslims of British India*, Cambridge: Cambridge University Press, p. 245 argues that despite building up a viable critique of the Pakistan proposal, the Jamiat ul Ulama i Hind failed to transmit their nuanced arguments to the masses.
9 Annexure C, Referendum Commissioner's Report, Ibid.
10 Political History of Assam, File No. 169, Assam State Archives, Guwahati. (Herein after ASA).
11 See this incident in Binayak Dutta, 'Event, Memory, Lore: Anecdotal History of Partition in Assam' *The NEHU Journal*, Vol. 12, No. 2, Shillong: North Eastern Hill University, pp. 61–76.
12 Mansergh, Nicholas (1983) *Transfer of Power Vol XII*, London: H M Stationary Office, pp. 167–168.
13 Ibid., p. 168.
14 *Thana* means a police outpost. In administrative parlance it is often understood as the administrative area under an outpost.
15 Roy Choudhury, Nalini Ranjan (1983) *Tripura through the Ages*, New Delhi: Sterling Publishers, p. 37–38.
16 Chakravarti, Mahadev (2007) 'Documentation of the Process of Integration of Princely Tripura with the Indian Union' in Sajal Nag, Tejimala Gurung and Abhijit Choudhury (eds.), *Making of the Indian Union*, New Delhi: Akansha Publishing House, p. 316.
17 Nag, Sajal, Tejimala Gurung and Abhijit Choudhury (eds.) (2007) *Making of the Indian Union*, New Delhi: Akansha Publishing House, p. 317.

18 De, Sibopada (2005) *Illegal Migrations and the North East*, New Delhi: Anamika Publishers and Distributors, p. 106.
19 Nag, Sajal, Tejimala Gurung and Abhijit Choudhury (eds.) (2007) *Making of the Indian Union*, New Delhi: Akansha Publishing House, p. 316.
20 Chakravarti, Mahadev (2007) 'Documentation of the Process of Integration of Princely Tripura with the Indian Union' in S. Nag, T. Gurung and A. Choudhury (eds.), *Making of the Indian Union*, New Delhi: Akansha Publishing House, p. 319.
21 De, R.K. (2007) 'Merger and Princely Tripura's Political Transition: 1947–1949' in S. Nag, T. Gurung and A. Choudhury (eds.), *Making of the Indian Union*, New Delhi: Akansha Publishing House, p. 348.
22 Chakravarti, M. (2007) 'Documentation of the Process of Integration of Princely Tripura with the Indian Union' in S. Nag, T. Gurung and A. Choudhury (eds.), *Making of the Indian Union*, New Delhi: Akansha Publishing House, p. 321.
23 De, R.K. (2007) 'Merger and Princely Tripura's Political Transition: 1947–1949' in S. Nag, T. Gurung and A. Choudhury (eds.), *Making of the Indian Union*, New Delhi: Akansha Publishing House, p. 351.
24 Census of India, 1951, Vol. 12, Part I-A, pp. 2–3.
25 Ibid., p. 3.
26 Misra, Udayon (2000) *The Periphery Strikes Back*, Shimla: IIAS, p. 148, ft.nt. no.2.
27 Almost the entire district of Sylhet was transferred to East Pakistan except an area of 709 square miles and a population of 291,320 persons in the three thanas of Bararpur, Ratabari, Patharkandi and a part of the Karimganj thana, which was joined with the district of Cachar and formed a new subdivision. See the Census of India, 1951, Vol. 12, Part I-A, p. 2.
28 In 1904, a rail link linking Dibrugarh with Chittagong was set up to carry the bulk of the tea trade from Assam. See Udayon Misra (2000) *The Periphery Strikes Back*, Shimla: Indian Institute of Advanced Studies, p. 115.
29 Ibid., p. 115.
30 Ibid., pp. 115–116 and 149 ft.nt.3.
31 Statement of the then Chief Minister of Meghalaya Donkupar Roy in the Assembly in (2008, May 6) Oneindia News, www.oneindia.com/2008/05/06/border-fencing-with-bangladesh-in-meghalaya-sector-stalled-1210068341.html accessed on 03.05.017.
32 Rustomji, Nari K. (1973) *Enchanted Frontiers*, Calcutta: Oxford University Press, p. 110–111.
33 Snaitang, O.L. (1997) *Memoirs of Life and Political Writings of the Hon'ble Rev. J.J.M. Nichols Roy*, Vol. 1, Shillong: Shrolenson Marbaniang, p. 170.
34 Ibid., p. 175.
35 Census of India, 1951, Vol. 12, Part I-A, pp. 356–357.
36 Dutta, Binayak (2014) 'Event, Memory, Lore: Anecdotal History of Partition in Assam' *The NEHU Journal*, Vol. 12, No. 2, Shillong: North Eastern Hill University, pp. 61–76.
37 Census of India, 1951, Vol. 12, Part I-A, pp. 356–357.

38 Ibid.
39 Census of India 1961, Vol. 3, Assam Part I-A, p. 204.
40 Barooah, Nirode K. (2010) *Gopinath Bordoloi, 'The Assam Problem' and Nehru's Centre*, Guwahati: Bhabani Print and Publications, p. 393.
41 Sen, Tripur Chandra (1970) *Tripura in Transition*, Agartala: Times Press, p. 7.
42 Bhattacharyya, Gayatri (1988) *Refugee Rehabilitation and its Impact on Tripura's Economy*, New Delhi: Omsons Publication, p. 5.
43 Dutta, Binayak (2012) 'Recovering Sylhet' *Himal South Asian, Kathmandu, the Southasia Trust*, 22 Nov.

Chapter 6

Did India's Partition lead to the segregation of North-East India?

Rituparna Bhattacharyya

My driving instructor hails originally from Sylhet, Bangladesh (erstwhile East Pakistan), who had migrated to the United Kingdom in 1962, almost a decade before Bangladesh gained independence. I address him as Salim (name changed) Dada (elder brother). Historically, Sylhet, known as *Srihatta* was a part of Bengal Presidency, which was then excavated out and joined as a part of then colonial Assam in 1874 until 1947 when it was amalgamated with erstwhile East Pakistan for being a Muslim majority district.[1] I am an Indian-born British citizen originally hailing from Assam. In the midst of his driving instructions, Salim Dada would narrate the memories of his childhood days – the way he grew up in Sylhet listening to the radio – the news broadcast in Assamese language, Bihu songs and songs sung by the emergent and young late (Dr) Bhupen Hazarika, drama, attending Hindu marriages, etc. Indeed, we two are connected to each other by a sense of shared identity. Both of us are conscious that we originally belong to Assam (though Sylhet is now separated by political boundaries) but connected to India (particularly Assam) by rice culture, *hilsa* (fish belonging to the herring family *Clupeidae*), tea gardens, music, art, literature, marriage, and many other things. This chapter, however, is not about the predicaments of Bengalis of Sylhet either pre- or post-Partition. Rather, in keeping in line with the scope of the book, which is about the 70 years of partition and postcolonial legacies, the chapter asks whether the country's 1947 Partition segregated North-East India from the mainstream. In trying to analyse the question, the chapter discusses the problem of illegal immigration from Bangladesh and the various forms of turbulence linked to identity politics that the region continues to witness since pre-independence.

Notwithstanding, Salim Dada's narrative signals that the notions of identity and belonging are indeed very dense with varied metaphors and spatial contexts,[2] and at times are difficult to comprehend. However, it is clear that the legacy of the 1947 Partition continues to haunt Salim Dada through the fond memories he carries of his childhood days. Seemingly, the spectre of 1947 Partition narratives and its legacy continue to beleaguer various groups of people across the nation-state including the North-East Indians.[3] This chapter aims to understand the narratives of continued 'unrest' within the region even after seven decades of independence. For this, the analysis of the chapter is built on the notions of 'identity' and 'belonging.' It begins with a brief review of the notions of 'identity' and 'belonging,' followed by a description of the geospatial location of the northeastern region. Following this, the complex peopling process of North-East India is mapped. In the final sections, I discuss the insurgencies in the region with special reference to the Naga unrest and the discriminations that North-East Indians face in mainstream India.

Identity and belonging

The notions of 'identity' and 'belonging' are very complex and remain highly contested. Often both notions are used interchangeably, albeit the contours of these two notions are multidimensional, fluid and remain highly intertwined with various connotations (place, space, ethnicity, religion, language, nationality, caste, class, community and gender)[4] and might differ from individual to individual. In North-East India, these two notions are understood via the simple catchphrase: *Jati, Mati and Bheti* – nationality, land and the hearth[5] – referring deeply to one's clan, home and homeland.

Pile and Thrift[6] (1995) argue that the 'identity' notion refers to the location of 'self' with respect to 'others.' In 2016, in the BBC's prestigious Reith Lectures, the philosopher Kwame Anthony Appiah revisited the 4Cs – culture, colour, country and creed – under the framework of *Mistaken Identities* to explain how one's identity is powerfully shaped and socially invented by these 4Cs, which, however, could be misleading at times, as the contours of our identities are fluid, multiple and ever-evolving.[7]

Yuval-Davis[8] (page 199) explains the notion of belonging:

> People can 'belong' in many different ways and to many different objects of attachments. These can vary from a particular person to the whole of humanity, in a concrete or abstract way belonging can be an act of self-identification or identification

> by others, in a stable, contested or transient way. Even in its most stable 'primordial' forms, however, belonging is always a dynamic process, not a reified fixity, which is only a naturalized construction of a particular hegemonic form of power relations.

In the context of the argument of Yuval-Davis, Salim Dada's sense of belonging and identity can, perhaps, be attributed to an act of self-identification, although it could be contested by many. Yuval-Davis[9] further constructs the belonging notion into three forms – *social location*, which refers to an individual or group's place crisscrossing class, caste, ethnicity, gender, age and sexuality; *identifications and emotional attachments* based on people's identities emanating from the 'stories that people tell themselves and others about who they are (and who they are not, [as is the case of Salim Dada])'[10](202) and *ethical and political values* where an individual's or a group's attachments and identities could be valued and even judged.

In 1984, Michel De Certeau in his most popular book, *The Practice of Everyday Life*,[11] described the notion of belonging 'as the everyday practice of a particular space gained through the attachment, emotions, and sentiments of an individual's daily activities' (page 313).[12] Bhattacharyya, in a slightly different context, posits that the public spaces of India suffer from a 'culture of misogyny' and lack a 'sense of belonging' stemming from patriarchal power relations buttressing gendered inequalities.[13] This chapter shows that the people from North-East India suffer from a sense of dis(belonging) in different parts of mainstream India[14] where they face varied forms of exploitation.

Much of the crises that North-East India has been witnessing pertains to territorial 'belonging' based on ethnocentrism[15] and the competition for scarce economic resources apace with the culture of the illegal immigration mainly from Bangladesh, threatening the ethnic way of life.[16] Over time, as argued by Yuval-Davis, this form of territorial belonging has been highly politicised and has given rise to 'identity politics.'[17] The following example demonstrates the notion of territorial belonging. Suppose, one buys an aquarium containing five fishes, but after a period of time, one of the fish dies. Now, if one replaces the perished fish with a new one and closely observes the behaviour of the other four fishes in the aquarium, one can easily notice that the older fishes of the aquarium fail to embrace the new fish. This example demonstrates that their space of belonging, their territory, now needs to be shared with an alien fish. Similarly, in his bestselling novel, *Life of Pi*, Yann Martel[18] describes the notion of territorial belonging in Chapter 13 (page 43) through the following words:

> [I]f you fall into a Lion's pit, the reason the lion would tear you to pieces is not because it's hungry – be assured, zoo animals are amply fed – or because it's bloodthirsty, but because you've invaded its territory.

In the case of humans, this issue of territorial belonging compounded by identity politics turns out to be far more complex. In the 70 years of India's independence, the form of identity politics, on the one hand, has made North-East India a hotbed for militancy;[19] on the other hand, scholars argue that the 2015 assembly elections of Assam that led to the win of the Bharatiya Janata Party-led alliance over the Congress-led alliance (that had ruled for 15 years) resulted from 'identity politics.'[20] However, further research is required to make a nuanced claim. The following section discusses the complex ethnic compositions of North-East India. In doing so, it tries to show how this complex construction of ethnic compositions apace with illegal immigration and other factors (intentional segregation, neglect) have led to the emergence of 'identity politics.'

Background

Also known commonly as the 'Land of Seven Sisters' – a land-locked region connected to mainstream India by a narrow corridor (Siliguri Corridor or 'chicken's neck') 33 kilometres wide on the eastern side and 21 kilometres wide on the western side. It covers approximately 7 per cent (or 25,5036 sqare kilometres) of the total geographical area of the country.[21] At the time of India's independence in 1947, the political map of North-East India embraced undivided Assam including the North-East Frontier Agency (NEFA) and the princely states of Manipur and Tripura, which were balkanised several times following geopolitical unrest over demands for ethnocentric identity/belonging and independence (which I will discuss). Currently, the region is home to 44.8 million people (Table 6.1),[22] covering approximately 3 per cent of the population of the country. Ninety-six per cent of its border comprises international boundaries. To the north lie Bhutan and Tibetan China; to the east is Myanmar; to the

Table 6.1 Statewise Area, Population, Growth Rate, Density, Sex Ratio and Literacy Rate in NE Region

State	*Area in Sq. Km.*	*Population (Person)*	*Growth Rate*	*Density per sq. Km.*	*Sex Ratio (females per 1000 males)*	*Literacy (%)*
Arunachal Pradesh	83743	1383727	26.03	17	938	65.38
Assam	78438	31205576	17.07	398	958	72.19
Manipur	22327	2570390	12.05	115	992	79.21
Meghalaya	22429	2966889	27.95	132	989	74.43
Mizoram	21081	1097206	23.48	52	976	91.33
Nagaland	16579	1978502	−0.58	119	931	79.55
Tripura	10486	3673917	14.84	350	960	87.22
All India	**3287240**	**1210193422**	**17.64**	**382**	**940**	**74.04**

Source: Census of India 2011 http://censusindia.gov.in/

south, the Arakan Yoma of Myanmar and Chittagong and Tippera Hills and the Surma Plain of Bangladesh while to the west lies West Bengal and Bangladesh.

North-East India: the Melting Pot of diverse ethnic communities

It is well known that the physical appearance of the majority of North-East Indians except for the caste Hindus is different from the mainstream. Eleven major 'streams' and varied 'waves' of immigration[23] from different directions and at different times[24] have contributed to a complex peopling process – they have created a home for 357 constitutional communities that embraces 32 scheduled castes and 182 scheduled tribe communities, which in turn makes the region unique to the rest of the country.[25] The majority of the tribal communities follow their animistic religion and fall outside the four caste hierarchies (*jati/varna system*) of India – *Brahmins* – priests and teachers; *Kshatryas* – warriors and rulers; *Vaishyas* – farmers, traders and merchants and *Shudras* – labourers.[26]

There is a consensus that the first group of people to reach this region were the *Khasis* and the *Jaintias*. Both of them are descendants of the Mon Khmer speaking *Austro-Asiatics* from the east. A second racial group[27] (bearing distinct epicanthic eyes folds and oblique palpebral fissures and sinodonty) followed *Khasis* and the *Jaintias*. This group entered the region from the north-east and belonged to the Sino-Tibetan family speaking Tibeto-Burman dialects/language. This Sino-Tibetan family can be further divided into two types – Arunachal and Assam-Burmese. The Arunachal branch subsumes the tribes *Hrusso, Sherdukpens, Khowas, Apatanies, Nissis, Adis, Mishimis, Khamptis, Noctes, Wanchos* and many more, while the Assamese-Burmese group embraces the *Bodos, Nagas* and the *Kuki-Chin* speakers. The epics and ancient literature – the *Mahabharata*, the *Vedas* and the *Puranas* refer to this Sino-Tibetan family as *Kiratas*. It is interesting to note that Babruvahana, Arjuna's son (as mentioned in the *Mahabharata*) was born to a princess from Manipur; and now the Meiteis, one of the indigenous groups of Manipur claims that they are the descendants of Babruvahana. All of this evidence signals that ancient Bharat was well connected to the north-east. It is also important to note that between the fourth and twelfth centuries AD, ancient Assam, also known as Pragjyotishpura or Kamarupa, was ruled by very powerful Barman, Salastambha and Pala dynasties.

Then came the different types and sub-types of the major racial group, Caucasoids or Indo-Aryans from the West, who brought with them Sanskrit, 'Vedic culture, Hindu religion and a higher technology of sedentary agriculture' (page 232).[28] In a way, the key lures of immigration to the region are the fertile Brahmaputra and Surma river systems that eventually gave rise to a compound agricultural society. Historical evidence also suggests that during the early thirteenth century, another group of Indo-Aryans practising Islam entered the region and settled in the plains. They were followed by the Tai-Ahom migrant group that hails originally from the Shan plateau and belongs to the Siamese-Chinese linguistic group. They entered the region through the routes of the north-east in AD 1228 under Sukapha's leadership. This group established a powerful kingdom in upper Assam (the Brahmaputra valley) that survived until 1826. Another five small Tai groups (Khamti, Khamyang, Aiton, Phake and Turung) of the Siamese-Chinese linguistic group entered the region in the seventeenth and eighteenth centuries and settled in Arunachal Pradesh and the eastern parts of Assam.

In the aftermath of the British takeover of the region in 1826 following the Treaty of Yandaboo,[29] the British brought Assam under the provincial administration of Bengal and made Bengali the official language. As a result, the educated Bengali employees from outside the geographical boundary of the region were employed in the administrative and law and order departments. In the wake of the construction of railways, roads and development of tea gardens in Upper Assam, new employment avenues, crafts, trade and commerce in this newly occupied British territory attracted large groups of people from Rajputana, Punjab, Bombay (to take up trade and business) and Nepal (mainly as dairy herders).[30] Following the establishment of the first English tea garden at Chabua in Upper Assam in 1837, the tea business gradually began to flourish and proliferate. Initially, the tea gardeners and the companies employed the local *Bodo-Kachari* people. However, due to the very low wages combined with over-exploitation and reluctance on the part of the employers to pay additional wages, the local labourers demonstrated resistance and withdrew themselves from these gardens. With the growth of the tea gardens across the region followed by acute shortages of human labour power in the tea gardens and the onset of severe famine in the 1850s in most parts of North-West Province and the Oudh regions (Chotanagpur plateau, Kalahandi and Ganjam of Orissa, Baster, Jabalpur and Bilaspur of Madhya Pradesh, Deoria, Balia, Basti, Gazipur, Azamgarh and Gorakhpur of Uttar Pradesh, Guntur and Visakhapatnam of Andhra Pradesh and Midnapur, Purulia, Bankura and Burdwan of Bengal), the British tea companies started orchestrating the situation through large-scale recruitment of famine victims using false promises that they would be able to 'pluck money from the tea in Assam and return back with bags full of money' (page 91).[31] These communities belong to the Mundari speaking group of the Austro-Asiatic linguistic family; their immigration continued until the 1940s. In the nineteenth century, another stream of migrants belonging to Kuki-Chin hills, Naga and Kachin entered the region from upper Myanmar and settled themselves in Mizoram, Manipur, Nagaland and the eastern districts of Arunachal Pradesh.

In fact, the whole region is a unique cultural medley – 'a melting pot of different ethnic groups' (60)[32] – all of which brought with them not only their qualities but also the varied cultural and sub-cultural traits, making the region rich in 'diversity.' Ostensibly, there remains a huge cultural affinity between the communities of India's North Eastern Region (NER) with those of its neighbouring countries regarding food, cultural values, dress codes and even dialects. Apparently, despite anthropological homogeneity among many tribes, because of the geographical inaccessibility of the hilly terrains, most of the ethnic communities remained isolated from each other and developed their unique dialects/languages, lifestyles, faiths and practices. This diversity amidst affinity must be capitalised, mobilised and even eulogised for the benefits of the individuals, society and the region as a whole.

Notwithstanding, the migrations of Muslims from erstwhile East Pakistan (now Bangladesh) to Assam is rooted in colonial history. With the creation of Shillong as the capital of Assam on 6 February 1874, Assam was separated from Bengal and re-amalgamated with East Bengal in 1905 due to the partition of Bengal into the west and east by the then British Viceroy of India Lord Curzon. Nawab Saleemullah Khan, the fourth Nawab of Dhaka and the architect of All India Muslim League, made Dhaka, the capital of the new Muslim majority province. It was he who persuaded the peasantry Muslims of the densely populated districts of Mymensingh, Dhaka and Pabna to migrate to Assam and settle in the fertile char areas of Goalpara, Kamrup, Darrang, Nowgaong, Sibasagar and Lakhimpur.[33] This migration continued until Sir Muhammed Saahdullah's government (1939–1942) allocated 16,055.85 hectares of Assam's land for the resettlement of the Bengali Muslims under the 'grow more food' programme, which was reflected in the Census of India 1931, Volume III, Assam, Part I-Report by CS Mullan (Table 6.2; Figure 6.1). As CS Mullan (1931: 50) put it:

> Probably the most important event in the province during the last twenty-five years – an event, moreover, which seems likely to alter permanently the whole future of Assam and to destroy more surely than did the Burmese invaders of 1820; the whole structure of Assamese culture and civilization – has been the invasion of a vast horde of land-hungry Bengali immigrants, mostly Muslims, from the districts of Eastern Bengal and in particular from Mymensingh. This invasion began sometime before 1911, and the census report of that year is the first-report which makes mention of the advancing host. But, as we now know, the Bengali immigrants censused for the first time on the *char* lands of Goalpara in 1911 were merely the advance guard-or rather the scouts-of a huge army following closely at their heels. By 1921 the first army corps had passed into Assam and had practically conquered the district of Goalpara.

Table 6.2 Number of Persons Born in Bengal in Each District of Assam, 1911–1931 (Ms=Mymensing and Population in 000's)

Year	*Goalpara*	*Kamrup*	*Darrang*	*Nowgong*	*Sibsagar*	*Lakhimpur*
1911	77(Ms.34)	4(Ms.1)	7(Ms.1)	4(Ms.1)	14(Ms.Nil)	14(Ms.Nil)
1921	151(Ms.78)	44(Ms.30)	20(Ms.12)	58(Ms.52)	14(Ms.Nil)	14(Ms.Nil)
1931	170(Ms.80)	134(Ms.91)	41(Ms.30)	120(Ms.108)	12(Ms.Nil)	19(Ms.2)

Source: Census of India 1931, Volume III, Assam, Part I-Report by CS Mullan

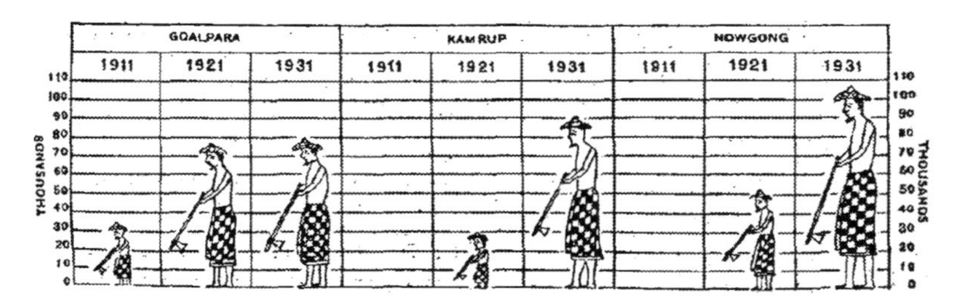

Figure 6.1 Increase in the Number of Persons Born in Mymensingh in Goalpara, Kamrup and Nowgong districts in Assam, 1911–1931

Source: Census of India 1931, Volume III, Assam, Part I-Report by CS Mullan

The ever burgeoning of large-scale Bengali Muslim migrants alongside the British government's 'separation-merger' geopolitics made the native Assamese perceive the situation as a cauldron of threat towards linguistic and ethnic identities,[34] which triggered widespread consternation. Consequently, in their efforts to prevent trespassing into the lands of the indigenous population of Assam and curb the flow of immigrants from East Bengal, the British government drew a 'line system' (modified in 1939). The Muslim League, however, urged the British Government to revoke the line system and replace it with a more liberal immigration policy.[35] In 1947, with the withdrawal of the British from Indian soil, East Bengal became East Pakistan until 1971, when it was renamed Bangladesh. However, in 1946, on the eve of India's independence, Assam was regrouped with East Pakistan via the Cabinet Mission's proposal.[36] But fervent dissension from the Assam Congress Committee, supported prodigiously by Mahatma Gandhi, prevented Assam from being included within the pockets of East Pakistan. Hence, at the time of India's independence in 1947, the political map of North-East India embraced undivided Assam, including North-East Frontier Agency (NEFA) and the princely states of Manipur and Tripura. However, following a referendum from the Muslim majority district of Sylhet (which used to be a part of Assam) excluding four thanas – Badarpur, Patharkandi, Karimganj and Ratabari – Assam had to surrender approximately 18,969 square kilometres of land to East Pakistan.[37]

Subsequently, following Partition, a large number of Hindus fled from Pakistan. The new Indian Constitution made provisions to grant citizenship to these refugees for nearly two decades (until 1 January 1966), but those refugees who entered India after this date were required to go through the legal process of naturalisation to gain citizenship. Most refugees failed to follow the legal course for various reasons and consequently became illegal migrants.[38] Notwithstanding, the rhetoric of rising illegal population from Bangladesh apace with high fertility rates has not only altered the demographic make-up of the region but is also considered one of the key reasons for the slow growth of North-East India.[39] This is because the problems of illegal migrants living in extreme forms of 'multi-dimensional' poverty[40] have exerted excessive pressure not only on the economy of the states but also on its internal security.[41] The problems have taken multiple forms – reducing the myriad ethnic composition to a group of minorities has heightened the identity crisis. And the issue of belonging looms large amongst the diverse ethnic communities exacerbating severe identity oriented and secessionist movements, increased insurgency, militarisation, the rise in unemployment, the shrinking of available land and resources and a rise in crime (including human-, arms- and drug trafficking).[42] Alongside, historical tensions arising from colonialism, inter-state border disputes stemming from balkanisation of the states during the post-independent period, the complex relations with the central government and hegemonic mainstream attitudes and power structures have further aggravated segregations and complexities. Indeed, this highly contested space, which is home to 44.8 million shelters approximately 157 insurgent outfits (Table 6.3), the majority of which are either in proscribed or active modes. The demands of these outfits range from sovereignty to the movement against migrants to creating independent nation(s) or homeland(s) to demanding better lives and political empowerment for the ethnic communities.[43] The Naga movement under the leadership of

Angami Zapu Phizo demanding sovereignty for Nagaland was one of the first secessionist movements of the region. The following section discusses the Naga insurgency, primarily rooted in the Coupland Plan of British colonialism.

The quagmire: The Naga insurgency

The word *Naga* is a umbrella term referring to at least 66 sub-tribes[44] dwelling not only in the current state of Nagaland but also in the hilly areas of Manipur, Assam, Arunachal Pradesh and Northwestern (Sagaing Region) and Northern (Kachin) Myanmar. They speak various Tibeto-Burman dialects/language such as Sumi, Lotha, Sangtam, Angami, Pochuri, Phom, Ao, Mao (Emela), Rongmei (Ruangmei), Poumai, Tangkhul, Thangal, Maram, Zeme and Liangmai. However, they communicate amongst the different sub-tribes using a common dialect called Nagamese Creole, similar to yet different from Assamese. As stated before, each sub-tribe has its own customs, traditional values and dress codes; they practiced head-hunting but engaged in internal fighting amongst the sub-tribes and often attacked the people dwelling in the plains.[45] In 1832, the British occupied the Naga-inhabited regions of the hills and Tuensang. And in 1866, the British formed the Naga Hills district of Assam. Alongside the Naga hills, the other hilly areas occupied by the tribes were transformed into protected areas by promulgations of the Inner Line Regulations (also known as Bengal-Eastern Frontier Regulation) and in 1873 were approved by the then governor general of British India, who considered these areas as backward tracts. This regulation imposed entry restrictions to outsiders (including the people of the plains) except for the American Baptist Missionaries that propounded and preached Christianity, education and English mainly amongst the Nagas[46] through the establishment of government-aided schools. A majority of the Nagas embraced Christianity and did not engage in activities for the Indian Independence movement (except for the Zeme, a Naga tribe residing in North Cachar Hills). Hence, the British too followed least intervention strategies in these hilly areas using lax administrative measures, thereby allowing the Nagas the freedom to move within the region and practice their way of life. However, with increased education, their traditional activities such as head-hunting were reduced. There is also another perspective on this Bengal Eastern Frontier Regulation, 1873 (this act is also known as

Regulation 5 of 1873). The act also aimed at protecting tea, oil and elephant trade from competing agents. This act, however, alienated the Nagas not only from mainstream India but also from the people of the plains and other tribes dwelling in NER. Taking further interest in this strategic tri-junctional peripheral hilly location between India, China and Burma during the inter–World War period (1919–1939), then Deputy Commissioner of Naga Hills District Mr J.H. Hunton, along with the British governors of Assam (Robert Neil Reid and later Andrew Claw) and Burma, germinated the seed to clandestinely contrive a plan known as the Coupland Plan/Protectorate (or British Crown Colony, named after Reginald Coupland, who buttressed the plan). The plan aimed at carving out a fresh political British colony, separate from India and Burma.[47] This colony would have acted as a 'springboard'[48] against India, China and Myanmar. Though it had failed to bear fruit following the Quit India movement,[49] however, this plan and the Cabinet Mission proposal are responsible for the gradual emergence of whole NER as a dialectical space of exclusion from the mainstream. Slowly, NER evolved as multiple spaces of contestation arising from the notions of ethnic 'identity' and 'belonging' incorporated in the slogan mentioned earlier: *Jati, Mati and Bheti*.

Seemingly, increased education amongst the Nagas infused them with a broader sense of identity and belonging. In 1918, the Naga officials formed the Naga Club to foster a shared platform for all the sub-Naga tribes, wherein they first ushered in their ideas for a sovereign nation. In 1929, when the Simon Commission[50] visited the Naga Hills to review the constitutional reforms, a delegate of 20 individuals representing all the sub-Naga tribes submitted a memorandum to the Commission demanding their exclusion from the reforms scheme on the ground that India and the Nagas shared no commonalities and that, hence, they should be given independent status.[51] Accordingly, the Simon Commission recommended the exclusion of the Naga Hills under the Government of India Act 1935[52] and the Naga Hills came under the governance of the government of Assam. The Naga Club was reorganised into the Naga National Council (NNC) in April 1946 under the architect of C.R. Pawsey, the last Deputy Commissioner of the Naga Hills, and Angami Naga Phizo, a former British Indian Army Officer took the leadership of NNC. It can be argued that the Nagas gained inspiration and took advantage of both World Wars I and II. Evidently, the Naga labour corps brought back outfits and money from their recruitment during World War I, whereas Nagaland was one of the locations whence World War II was fought. And the Nagas naturally learnt the modern skills of guerrilla fighting and benefitted from the arms and ammunition from the retreating Japanese army. Phizo not only contacted Subhas Chandra Bose, who revived Azad Hind Fauj or Indian National Army in Burma but also met Gandhiji in early 1947 and argued for an independent Naga country, albeit, the initial demand of the NNC was to create a Naga Hills Autonomy within Assam province. It should be noted here that these incidents occurred simultaneously with the Cabinet Mission proposal where Assam was grouped under the Northeastern Pakistan zone, to which there was large-scale resistance. Phizo was able to exploit this resistance, which paved the way to the Hydari Agreement on 27–28 June 1947, which read: '[t]hat the right of the Nagas to develop themselves according to their freely expressed wishes is recognized.'[53] Akbar Hydari, the then Governor of Assam and NNC, signed this agreement. However, clause IX of this agreement appeared dubious and continued to be a cause of disagreement between the NNC members and the Indian government. Clause IX reads as follows:

> Period of Agreement – The Governor of Assam as the Agent of the Government of the Indian Union will have a special responsibility for a period of 10 years to ensure the observance of the agreement, at the end of this period the Naga Council will be asked whether they require the above agreement to be extended for a further period or a new agreement regarding the future of Naga people arrived at.

While NNC construed this clause as the attainment of sovereignty, the Indian government read it as the signing of a new arrangement within the Indian Union. Consequently, on the eve of India's independence, that is, on 14 August 1947, NNC declared Naga independence and informed the UN Headquarters in New York. On 1 May 1951, Phizo conducted a plebiscite where 99 per cent of Nagas voted in favour of independence. This referendum yielded NNC the strength to boycott the first general election of independent India in 1952. Simultaneously, they launched a violent secessionist movement, although, for the first 9 years (from 2 February 1946 to 25 March 1955), NNC maintained a policy of non-violence. In retaliation for the plebiscite, the Assam government enacted the

Assam Maintenance of Public Order (Autonomous District) Act in the Naga Hills in 1953 and strengthened the police force in the Hills. However, the situation continued to deteriorate and, therefore, on 21 December 1955, the Assam Disturbed Areas Act was promulgated in then undivided Assam [including the North-East Frontier Agency (NEFA) and Manipur] to tackle the Naga uprising, but NNC formed a federal government on 23 March 1956. Simultaneously, NNC activists launched an underground Naga Federal Government (NFG) known as *Tatar Hoho* and a Naga Federal Army (NFA). On 22 May 1958, President Dr Rajendra Prasad promulgated the Armed Forces (Assam and Manipur) Special Powers Ordinance 1958, which was replaced by the Armed Forces (Assam and Manipur) Special Powers Act 1958 (AFSPA) on 11 September 1958.[54] Under the legal framework of AFSPA, the Indian Army and 35 battalions of the Assam Rifles and Assam Police vehemently attacked the Naga rebellion. And by the late 1950s, in 645 Naga villages, over one hundred thousand people lost their lives.[55] Witnessing such volatility, where people were being reduced to 'bare life' embedded in situations of continual and protracted adversity, Phizo planned his escape route via the Angami and Zeliangrong regions through East Pakistan to reach London on 16 June 1960 and addressed the world press on 26 July 1960. Having learnt of Phizo's intention, the Indian government was successful in bringing a 19-member team from various parts of the Naga Hills to Delhi under the banner of the Naga People's Convention. This convention signed a 16-point agreement[56] on the same day with the government, after which Nagaland was granted statehood on 1 December 1963 under the State of Nagaland Act 1962. The agreement added the Tuensang tract, which was a part of NEFA, to Nagaland comprising 16,527 square kilometres, though the majority of the Naga-inhabited areas fell outside this geographical boundary of Nagaland.

On 1 January 1964, the Nagaland Peace Mission was formed by Jai Prakash Narayan, B.P. Chaliha and Rev. Michael Scott, and an Agreement for Suspension of Operation was signed with Phizo's NNC/NFG/NFA, which lasted only until 1968. And their demand for Greater Nagalim continued for Naga-inhabited areas spanning Nagaland and several districts of Assam (adjacent to Nagaland), Tirap, Longding and Changlang districts of Arunachal Pradesh, hill districts of Manipur and parts of Myanmar, covering approximately 1,20,000 square kilometres (Figure 6.2).[57] This area is approximately

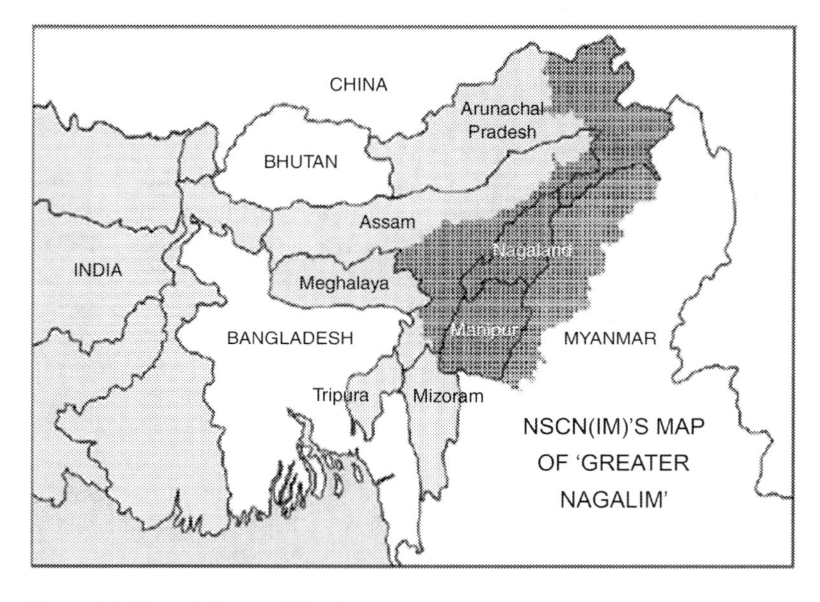

Figure 6.2 Map of Greater Nagalim

Source: Kashyap, Samudra Gupta (29 March 2017). Why Thuingaleng Muivah's new statement has dug up old fears, anger. Indian Express, Retrieved from, http://indianexpress.com/article/explained/why-thuingaleng-muivahs-new-statement-has-dug-up-old-fears-anger-assam-manipur-protest-4590030/

seven times larger than the area within current geographical boundary of Nagaland.[58] Of course, for this impractical demand, there have occasionally been strong voices of protest from Assam, Manipur and Arunachal Pradesh regarding any territorial divisions.

Earlier, on 11 November 1975, a group of NNC/NFG/NFA members agreed to accept the Constitution of India by relinquishing arms and ammunition and signed the Shillong Accord. However, this accord created factions amongst NNC/NFG/NFA. One hundred and forty members under Thuingaleng Muivah declined the Shillong Accord and launched the National Socialist Council of Nagaland (NSCN) in 1980 along with Isak Chisi Swu and S.S. Khaplang, only to split on 1 January 1988 into the NSCN (Isak and Muivah; (IM) and the NSCN (Khole Konyak and Khaplang; K). In 1991, with the death of Phizo in London, NNC too gradually dwindled but gave rise to some splinter outfits. Nonetheless, NSCN(IM) emerged as the strongest outfit. NSCN (K) further fragmented – in 2011, Khole and Kitovi formed NSCN (Khole-Kitovi). On 27 March 2015, following another cacophony and removal from NSCN(K), emanating from the repeal of the 1997 ceasefire, senior leaders Wangting Naga and P. Tikhak formed the NSCN Reformation.

Notwithstanding, even the Nagaland Assembly has always maintained its support for the 'Greater Nagalim' demands through its endorsements in December 1964, August 1970, September 1994, December 2003 and 27 July 2015 – aimed at the consolidation of contiguous tracts of Naga-inhabited regions within one administrative unit.[59]

During the early 1990s, the lead leaders of NSCN(IM) including Muivah and Swu fled to Thailand and subsequently over 80 rounds of diplomatic talks were held between NSCN-IM and various hierarchies of government officials. Then Governor of Assam, Dr M.M. Thomas (1919–1996) was the first to gain consent from NSCN(IM) for diplomatic talks. On 15 June 1995, Prime Minister P.V. Narasimha Rao met Muivah, Swu and others in Paris. Following this, the group was met by the then Ministry of State for Home Rajesh Pilot in November 1995. On 3 February 1997, Prime Minister H.D. Deve Gowda met NSCN(IM) in Zurich. Thereupon followed meetings with officers in Geneva and Bangkok. After that, on 30 September 1998, Prime Minister Atal Bihari Vajpayee and Principal Secretary to the Prime Minister and National Security Adviser (1998–2004) Brajesh Mishra met them in Paris, even though a ceasefire was signed between both the parties on 25 July 1997, which came into effect on 1 August 1997. Again, from 9–11 January 2003, diplomatic talks were held between Muivah and Isak and Vajpayee and Advani in Delhi.

Hereafter, with the change of power at the centre and formation of the United Progressive Alliance (UPA) government after the 2004 general election, on 7 Dec 2004, NSCN(IM) leaders met Dr Manmohan Singh. The meeting triggered an extension of indefinite ceasefire between NSCN(IM) and the government.

Evidently, over the decades, NSCN(IM), factions of NSCN(K) and NNC's splinter outfits have been operating parallel underground governments with their headquarters located in remote areas of Sagaing Division, Myanmar. These outfits extort large amounts of illegal taxes from businesspersons, government officials, contractors, etc. Nonetheless, the Nagas have witnessed 'massive fragmentation' from within the Naga community;[60] perhaps, NSCN(IM) too realised their utopian, unrealistic and rigid claim for a Greater Nagalim.

In November 2014, Prime Minister Narendra Modi, an icon of good governance[61] visited Nagaland where he promised to restore peace with NSCN(IM). There are several stakeholders to this peace process bearing multiple interests – NSCM(IM), NNC's splinter groups and factions of NSCN(K) along with civil society groups like Forum for Naga Reconciliation, Naga Hoho, Eastern Naga Peoples' Organisation, Naga Mothers' Association and Naga Students' Federation and the Government of India. Hence, there has to be a common solution to the peace process. In the interim, NSCN(K) orchestrated an ambush on 4 June 2015 in Manipur, which killed 18 armed personnel and for which the organisation has been facing a blanket ban for 5 years under the Unlawful Activities and Prevention Act. NSCN(IM) automatically emerged as the key outfit to sign the Peace Accord on 3 August 2015 with the government known as a 'Framework Agreement.' The signing of the Peace Accord also meant a shift in the earlier demands of complete sovereignty and the notion of Greater Nagalim to the acceptance of greater autonomy of the areas inhabited by the Nagas outside the geographical boundary of Nagaland without territorial divisions but through the establishments of Autonomous District Councils.[62] The details of the Peace Accord and the plans to execute the same have not yet been made public. While the proof of the pudding is in the eating, only time will tell to what extent the solution to the Naga issue could be accomplished.

Other insurgencies and reorganisation of North-East India

Indeed, over the last six decades, NER has witnessed a series of structural violence, producing widows, orphans, destitution and rape survivors of killings, looting, losses of property and livelihood and the burning of villages. Also, the region testifies the irony of cultures of impunity enjoyed by armed officials under the umbrella of AFSPA and other legislation such as CrPC 144, Sections 141–60 (under Chapter VIII, Indian Penal Code). Naga insurgency has paved the way for other violent secessionist movements arising from the notions of ethnic identity and territorial belonging over land and natural resources.

In 1979, the All Assam Students Union (ASSU) and All Assam Gana Sangram Parishad (AAGSP) jointly launched the Assam Agitation – a movement against illegal migrants from Bangladesh. Myron Weiner has compared the large-scale civil conflict and violence that occurred because of this agitation to the breakdowns of Northern Ireland, Malaysia, Cyprus and Lebanon.[63] The Assam Agitation was called off in 1985 through an agreement with the government of India stating that new migrants arriving since 25 March 1971, the day on which Bangladesh gained independence, would be deported to Bangladesh. More than three decades have passed since then, and the accord has not yet been implemented. On 25 April 2017, tripartite talks were held between AASU, the Central Government and Assam Government; they agreed to enact the clauses of the Accord with no dilution and within a stipulated period,[64] which might reduce the illegal migrant problem, though NER continues to be a conflicting insurgency terrain. The breakdown of the number of insurgency outfits in different states of NER is illustrated in Table 6.3.

In April 1946, Mizo union was formed in the Lushai Hills and subsequently launched a guerrilla movement demanding a separate Mizo state. In October 1949, the princely states of Manipur and Tripura were merged with India as union territories. NEFA

Table 6.3 Insurgency Outfits in North-East India

States	*Proscribed Terrorist/ Extremist Groups*	*Active Terrorist/ Insurgent Groups*	*Inactive Terrorist/ Insurgent Groups*	*In Peace Talks/ ceasefire (groups/ congrolamates)*
Arunachal Pradesh		2	4	
Assam	3	4	36	14
Manipur	6	6	25	5
Mizoram			1	1
Meghalaya	1	7	5	
Nagaland	1	4	2	3
Tripura	2		25	1
Total	13	23	98	23

Source: India – Terrorist, insurgent and extremist groups, Retrieved 20 June 2017 from www.satp.org/satporgtp/countries/india/terroristoutfits/index.html

was created in 1954. On 21 January 1972, the political map was reorganised under the Northeastern Region (Re-organisation) Act 1971, when Manipur, Tripura and the Meghalaya section of Assam were granted full statehood. Mizoram (carved out of Lushai Hills) and Arunachal Pradesh (carved out of NEFA) were granted union territories in 1972. But in the late 1970s, under the leadership of Laldenga, Mizo National Army launched a massive movement. On 20 February 1987 along with Arunachal Pradesh, Mizoram was raised to the status of full-fledged state, and Laldenga became the first chief minister of Mizoram.

Perceived as 'other' in mainstream

A volatile environment alongside lack of higher educational infrastructure and poor employment opportunities drives youths and students of the region to migrate to metropolitan and other megacities of India for further studies, jobs in the private and public sector(s) and various other forms of livelihood. Currently, an estimated 20 million students and youths from North-East India are pursuing their careers in different megacities of India. Evidently, largely perceived as 'other,' North-East Indians as a 'class' (regardless of gender) often become victims of racial and ethnic slurs manifested in the form of rude nicknames (i.e. backwards, head-hunter, sexy, chinky), harassments, molestations, rape and even murder.[65] The gruesome high-profile murder of a 19-year-old boy – Nido Tania from Arunachal Pradesh – by a group of local men in the south of New Delhi on 29 January 2014 further demonstrates the plight of the community; it is a continuing symptom of pervasive racial discrimination. Arguably, North-East Indians suffer from a sense of dis(belonging) in the public spaces of mainstream India. This observation reinforces previous research on street violence against women, which remains rampant in the public spaces of India.[66] On average, the degree of suffering for women of North-East India is greater when compared to local women from other parts of India. Written by Ritesh Shah and directed and produced respectively by Aniruddha Roy Chowdhury and Rashmi Sharma Telefilms, the 2016 film *Pink* is a nuanced portrayal of the pandemic prevalence of rape culture showcasing in a robust statement that North-East Indian women suffer from the prejudice of being 'available.' It is ironic to note that the horrific incidents of violence and discrimination continue considering that in 1968 India ratified the United

Nation's International Convention on the Elimination of All Forms of Racial Discrimination, which had been adopted on 21 December 1965 and came into force on 4 January 1969.

In the wake of the brutal Nido Tania incident, a writ petition was filed between Karma Dorjee and Others Versus Union of India and Others at the Honourable Apex Court.[67] On 5 February 2014, the Government of India constituted the Bezbaruah Committee,[68] headed by M.P. Bezbaruah, Member, Northeastern Council, who prepared a 78-page report to probe into the problems that North-East Indians face while dwelling in different parts of the country. The Committee submitted its report on 11 July 2014. It awaits implementation.

Another dimension of discrimination that has surfaced is in the increased cases of trafficking/kidnapping of children from the conflict-ridden areas of NER. The data on kidnapping/trafficking of children is hard to retrieve, but Pranjal Baruah[69] argues that children (especially young girls and women) are either kidnapped or trafficked and sold in metropolitan cities for fixed prices into middle class/affluent houses as bonded labourers and forced into marriages or brothels.[70] Further research is required to examine the problem in-depth, though Mr. Kailash Satyarthi, the 2014 Nobel Peace Laureate of Bachpan Bachao Andolan (BBA; Save the Childhood Movement) has also supported efforts to examine this proliferating menace.

Way forward

Clearly, while Salim Dada's 'sense of belonging' can be described by his nuanced feelings and sentiments about and attachments to his homeland in Sylhet (linked to the then undivided Assam), the genesis of ethnocentric identity, territorial belonging and increased political awareness amongst various insurgent groups could be ascribed to the segregation of the NER rooted in colonialism. Arguably, this could be attributed to all the three forms of belonging as identified by Yuval-Davis: social location, identification and emotional sentiments and ethical and political values.[71]

For the region that has witnessed over six decades of insurgencies, only integration with the mainstream, a peace process, economic development and tourism are the answers to uplift it from the grips of underdevelopment. In 1991, then Prime Minister of India Mr. P.V. Narasimha Rao, as a part of its foreign policies, launched the Look East Policy (LEP). LEP envisioned blending the architecture of foreign policies and regional development of the NER via promotion of the region to the rank of economic eminence, while making a foray into cooperation with the Association of Southeast Asian Nations (ASEAN) and its member-countries, particularly, Malaysia, Singapore, Thailand, Indonesia and Myanmar, by strengthening the issues of trade, transit and infrastructure investment.[72] The underlying perception of LEP is that increased trade relations with the economies of these nations would not only boost economic development but also restore peace and stability in the region, and act as a 'natural bridge between India and Southeast Asia'(page 9)[73] to enhance connectivity and encourage trade and investment in human resource development, tourism, health, pharmaceuticals and cultural exchanges. It was only after the Department of Development of Northeastern Region (DoNER) was set up in 2001, that the LEP began to make its presence felt in the NER – on 22 November 2004, then Prime Minister Dr Manmohan Singh from Guwahati flagged off the India-ASEAN car rally, which was held in eight countries, covered over 8,000 kilometres and included 240 participants with 60 vehicles, and which finally ended at Vientiane, LAO PDR on 30 November 2004. Under Prime Minister Modi's regime, this policy has been renamed as Act East Policy. However, this policy is yet to show proper signs of development in the NER.

Notwithstanding, with numerous stakeholders, the integration process with the mainstream India that bears a distinct and different yardstick when compared to NER is not going to be an easy process. However, it does not mean that the possibility of restoring peace and mainstream integration is impossible.

Except for Arunachal Pradesh, the literacy rates of other states (Table 6.1) are about or above the national average, which signals that NER is a good space to exploit its educated human resources for developmental opportunities. Besides, there are large amounts of English-speaking literates. In his 2014 election rally in Guwahati, Prime Minister Modi (then Chief Minister of Gujarat) announced that Gujarat was looking to recruit English-speaking police officers from the NER for communicating with foreign tourists in his state.[74] He had developed a model to recruit 200 female police officers from each of the eight states on deputation for two years, which would strengthen assimilation between families of these police officials and the Gujaratis through their visits to each other's states. He, however, regretted that the respective state governments of the NER have failed to translate this proposal into reality. I argue that Mr. Modi can now translate this model into a policy on a larger scale, perhaps beyond Gujarat, and roll it out across the Hindi-speaking belt including the metropolitan cities not only to help the tourists but also to safeguard North-East Indians living in different cities.

Festivals like that of Namami Brahmaputra, celebrated from 31 March to 4 April 2017,[75] are perhaps a road to strengthening the integration of North-East India with the mainstream and beyond. This festival might lead to flow of tourism, entrepreneurs and developmental activities in the long run. Perhaps each state needs to organise similar festivals. However, only time will tell to what extent such festival will make actual gains.

Notes

1 Bhattacharyya, Narendra Nath (2005) *North East India-A Systematic Geography*. New Delhi: Rajesh Publications, Bhattacharjee; Nabanipa (2013) '"We Are with Culture but without Geography": Locating Sylheti Identity in Contemporary India.' In Tanveer Fazal (ed.). *Minority Nationalisms in South Asia, South Asian History and Culture*. Oxon: Routledge, 53–73; Dasgupta, Anindita (2008) Remembering Sylhet: A Forgotten Story of India's 1947 Partition. *Economic and Political Weekly*, 43 (31), 18–22.

2 Antonsich, Marco (2010) Searching for Belonging: An Analytical Framework. *Geography Compass*, 4 (6), 644–659, DOI: 10.1111/j.1749-8198.2009.00317.x; Yuval-Davis, Nira (2006) Belonging and the Politics of Belonging. *Patterns of Prejudice*, 40 (3), 197–214, http://dx.doi.org/10.1080/00313220600769331; Yuval-Davis, Nira (2011) *Power, Intersectionality and the Politics of Belonging*. Aalborg: Institut for Kultur og Globale Studier, Aalborg Universitet (FREIA's tekstserie; No. 75). DOI: 10.5278/freia.58024502.

3 Fernandes, Walter (1999) The Conflict in the NorthEast: A Historical Perspective. *Economic and Political Weekly*, 34, 3579–82; Singh, Amritjit, Iyer, Nalini and Gairola, Rahul K. (eds.) (2016) *Revisiting India's Partition: New Essays on Memory, Culture and Politics*. London: Lexington Books; Haokip, Thongkholal (2012) Political Integration of Northeast India: A Historical Analysis. *Strategic Analysis*, 36 (2), 304–14, http://dx.doi.org/10.1080/09700161.2012.646508.

4 Op. cit. (Marco, 2010; Yuval-Davis, 2006; 2011)

5 Dutta, Akhil Ranjan (2017) BJP's Electoral Victory in Assam, 2016: Co-Opting the Khilonjiyas. *Social Change*, 47 (1), 108–124, DOI: 10.1177/0049085716683114.

6 Pile, Steve and Nigel Thrift (1995) *Mapping the Subject: Geographies of Cultural Transformation*. London: Routledge.

7 Kwame Anthony Appiah: Mistaken Identities Episodes, the Reith Lectures. *BBC iPlayer Radio*. Retrieved from www.bbc.co.uk/programmes/b080twcz/episodes/player.
8 op. cit. Yuval-Davis, 2006, 2011.
9 ibid. Yuval-Davis, 2006, 2011.
10 ibid. Yuval-Davis, 2006, 2011.
11 de Certeau, Michel (1984) *The Practice of Everyday Life*, Trans. Steven Rendall. Berkeley: University of California Press.
12 Bhattacharyya, Rituparna (2018) Living with Armed Forces Special Powers Act (AFSPA) as Everyday Life. *GeoJournal*, 83 (1), 31–48, DOI: 10.1007/s10708-016-9752-9; Bhattacharyya, Rituparna (2016) Street Violence against Women in India: Mapping Prevention Strategies. *Asian Social Work and Policy Review*, 10 (3), 311–325, DOI: 10.1111/aswp.12099; Bhattacharyya, Rituparna (2015) Understanding the Spatialities of Sexual Assault against Indian Women in India. *Journal Gender, Place and Culture*, 22 (9), 1340–1356, DOI:10.1080/0966369X.2014.969684; Bhattacharyya, Rituparna (2013) *Are We Empowered? Stories of Young Indian Working Women*. Saarbrücken, Germany: Lap Lambert Academic Publishing; Bhattacharyya, Rituparna (2009) *Examining the Changing Status and Role of Middle Class Assamese Women: Lessons from the Lives of University Students*, PhD thesis, Newcastle University, Newcastle, UK.
13 ibid. (Bhattacharyya, 2015; 2016).
14 Ranjan, Amit (2015) A Gender Critique of AFSPA: Security for Whom? *Social Change*, 45 (3), 440–457, DOI: 10.1177/0049085715589471.
15 Srikanth, H. (2000) Militancy and Identity Politics in Assam. *Economic and Political Weekly*, 35 (47), 4117–4124.
16 Barooah, Vani Kant (2013) The Killing Fields of Assam: Myth and Reality of Its Muslim Immigration. *Economic and Political Weekly*, 48 (4), 43–52.
17 op. cit. Yuval-Davis, 2006, 2011.
18 Martel, Yann (2003) *Life of Pi*. Edingburgh: Cannongate Books Limited.
19 op. cit. Bhattacharyya, 2018; Ranjan, 2015; Srikanth, 2000.
20 op. cit. Dutta, 2017.
21 op. cit. Bhattacharyya, 2018, 2005; Taher, M. and Ahmed, P. (2001) *Geography of North-East India*. Guwahati: Mani Manik Prakash.
22 Since 2002, Sikkim was integrated as the eighth state of Northeastern Council (NEC, setup by an act of Parliament in 1971) which is operated under the Ministry of Development of Northeastern Region (MDoNER).
23 'The term "wave" is used to mean a migration that occurred once at a particular point of time and the term "stream" is used to depict a migration of a group of people that continues for long time' (12), see, Taher, Mohammad (2001) Assam: An Introduction. In A.K. Bhagawati, B. Kar and B. Bora (eds.). *Geography of Assam*. New Delhi: Rajesh, 1–17.
24 op. cit. Taher, 2001.
25 Fernandes, Walter and Barbora, Sanjay (eds.) (2002a) *Changing Women's Status in India: Focus in the North-East*. Guwahati: North Eastern Social Research Centre; Fernandes, Walter and Barbora, Sanjay (eds.) (2002b) *Modernisation and Women's Status in North Eastern India:*

A Comparative Study of Six Tribes. Guwahati: North Eastern Social Research Centre.

26 Bhattacharyya, Rituparna and Singh, Suman (2017) Exclusion (and Seclusion): Geographies of Disowned Widows of India. *GeoJournal*, 82 (4), 1–18, DOI: 10.1007/s10708-017-9800-0, and op. cit. (Bhattacharyya, 2009).

27 This racial group is known as Mongoloid. However, the term Mongoloid is highly contested. Hence, for the purpose of this chapter, I refer to them as Sino-Tibetan group; Orr, Gillian (2014, 23 November) Why Are the Words 'Mongol,' 'Mongoloid' and 'Mongy' Still Bandied About as Insults? *Independent*. Retrieved 20 June 2017, from www.independent.co.uk/arts-entertainment/tv/features/why-are-the-words-mongol-mongoloid-and-mongy-still-bandied-about-as-insults-9878557.html.

28 op. cit. Bhattacharyya, 2005.

29 Prior to annexation by the British, Assam was ruled by the Ahom King for nearly 600 years (1228–1826). However, the kingdom was attacked and ravaged by the Burmese who entered Assam through the eastern borders of the Brahmaputra Valley, subsequently in 1816, 1817 and 1821 and declaring it as the First Burmese War. In order to put an end to this War, a Treaty of Peace known as the 'Treaty of Yandaboo' was signed in between the Honourable East India Company and His Majesty the Ahom King of Ava on 24 February 1826; Baruah, Sanjib (1999) *India against Itself: Assam and the Politics of Nationality*. Pennsylvania: University of Pennsylvania.

30 *Census of India 1931*, Volume III, Assam, Part I – Report by CS Mullan.

31 Athparia, R.P. (2009) Settlement and Socio-Economic Life of Tea Garden Labourers in Cachar District of Assam: An Overview. In Sarthak Sengupta (ed.). *The Tea Labourers of North East India: An Anthropo-Historical Perspective*. New Delhi: Mittal Publications, 81–88.

32 op. cit. Bhattacharyya, 2005.

33 Borkakoti, Jitendralal (2013) Demographic Invasion, Assamese Identity and Geopolitics. *Journal Space and Culture, India*, 1 (1), 28–42, http://dx.doi.org/10.20896/saci.v1i1.12.

34 Nath, Hiranya and Kumar, Nath Suresh (2010) *Illegal Migration into Assam: Magnitude, Causes, and Economic Consequences*, Sam Houston State University, Department of Economics and International Business, Working Paper No. 10-06. Retrieved from http://papers.ssrn.com/sol3/papers.cfm?abstract_id=1750383.

35 ibid.

36 With its three members – Stafford Cripps, A.V. Alexander and Pethick Lawrence, on 19 March 1946, the Cabinet Mission arrived in Delhi and divided India into three groups: Group A – the Hindu Majority provinces that incorporated Madras (now Chennai), Bombay (now Mumbai), Orissa and the United and the Central Provinces; Group B – the northwestern Muslim majority province, the Sind and the Punjab and Group C comprised the northeastern Pakistan Zone (including Bengal and Assam), where the balance of religions were in favour of the Muslims (see, James, Lawrence [1997] *Raj: The Making and Unmaking of British India*. London: Abacus.

37 op. cit. Bhattacharyya, 2005.
38 op. cit. Nath and Nath, 2010.
39 Bareh, Hamlet M. (2001) *Encyclopaedia of North-East India*, Vol. 2. New Delhi: Mittal.
40 Multidimensional poverty refers to the burden of income poverty that entail varied interconnected fronts – health (increased nutrition and reduction in child mortality), education (school attendance, years of schooling) and standard of living (asset ownership, cooking fuel, flooring, access to safe drinking water and electricity and sanitation {see, Alkire, Sabina, Foster, James E., Seth, Suman, Santos, Maria Emma, Roche, Jose M. and Ballon, Paola (2015) *Multidimensional Poverty Measurement and Analysis*. Oxford: Oxford University Press, ch. 2, Alkire, Sabina and Sumner, Andy (2013) *Multidimensional Poverty and the Post-2015 MDGs*. Oxford: Poverty & Human Development Initiative. Retrieved from www.ophi.org.uk/wp-content/uploads/MPI-post-2015-MDGs-FINAL.pdf, also, Bhattacharyya, Rituparna and Vauquline, Polly (2013) A Mirage or a Rural Life Line? Analysing the Impact of Mahatma Gandhi Rural Employment Guarantee Act on Women Beneficiaries of Assam. *Space and Culture, India*, 1 (1), 83–101, http://dx.doi.org/10.20896/saci.v1i1.10.
41 McDuie-Ra, Duncan (2012a) Tribals, Migrants and Insurgents: Security and Insecurity Along the India: Bangladesh Border. *Global Change, Peace & Security: Formerly Pacifica Review: Peace, Security & Global Change*, 24 (1), 165–182; op. cit. Nath and Nath, 2010.
42 op. cit. (Bhattacharyya, 2018) & Longkumer, Arkotong (2010) *Reform, Identity and Narratives of Belonging: The Heraka Movement in North-east India*. London: Continuum.
43 ibid. and op. cit. (Bhattacharyya, 2018; Longkumer, 2010; McDuie-Ra, 2012a).
44 Tohring, S.R. (2010) *Violence and Identity in North-East India: Naga-Kuki Conflict*. New Delhi: Mittal Publications.
45 Kotwal, Dinesh (2000) The Naga Insurgency: The Past and the Future. *Journal Strategic Analysis*, 24 (4), 751–772, http://dx.doi.org/10.1080/09700160008455245.
46 ibid. (Kotwal, 2000) & Hardgrave, Robert L., Jr. and Kochanek, Stanley A. (2000) *Government and Politics in a Developing Nation*. Toronto: Harcourt College Publishers.
47 Syiemlieh, David R.(ed.) (2014) *On the Edge of Empire: Four British Plans for North East India, 1941–1947*. New Delhi: Sage Publishers; op. cit. Kotwal, 2000.
48 Ibid. (Kotwal, 2000).
49 Gandhiji launched this movement on 8 August 1942 from the Bombay session of the All-India Congress Committee, which is also known as Civil Disobedience movement or *August Kranti*. Contemporaneous with World War II (1939–1945), this non-violent mass rebellion from all over India demanded the end of British-raj in India (see, op. cit. James, 1997). This movement triggered the process for India's independence, which started after the end of the World War II.
50 Sir John Allsebrook Simon, the chairperson of the Indian Statutory Commission assisted by Clement Attlee and five other British Members

of Parliament of the United Kingdom arrived in India in 1928 to examine the constitutional progress so that new reforms could be introduced. This was against the backdrop of the Government of India Act, 1919 (that introduced the diarchy system to rule British India provinces), which were coming to close in 1929 (see, op. cit. James, 1997).

51 Goswami, Namrata (2015, 07 August) *The Naga Peace Accord: Why Now?* IDSA Comment, Institute for Defence Studies and Analyses. Retrieved from www.idsa.in/idsacomments/TheNagaPeaceAccordWhyNow_NamrataGoswami_070815, see also, op. cit. (Hardgrave and Kochanek, 2000; Kotwal, 2000).

52 The Act classified Assam's hilly areas into two categories – (a) excluded areas comprised of the Balipara and Sadia Frontier tracts, the Naga Hills District, the Lushai Hills district. These areas were denied political participation and remained unrepresented in the legislature. (b). Partially excluded areas included Garo Hills District, the Khasi-Jaintia Hills district (excluding Shillong) and Mikir Hills and were allowed to franchise to elect members to the legislature {see Reid, Robert (1944) The Excluded Areas of Assam. *The Geographical Journal*, 103 (1/2), 18–29, DOI: 10.2307/1789063}.

53 Naga-Akbar Hydari Accord (Nine Point Agreement) Kohima, 26–28 June 1947. Retrieved from http://peacemaker.un.org/sites/peacemaker.un.org/files/IN_470628_Naga-Akbar%20Hydari%20Accord.pdf

54 AFSPA is a draconian statute bearing colonial contents, which allows even a Sergeant to shoot at the site on mere suspicion (see, op. cit. Bhattacharyya, 2018; Ranjan, 2015). Initially, it was enacted in undivided Assam, but over the decades, it was extended to various parts of North-East India. In November 2000, Ms Irom Chanu Sharmila started her hunger strike against AFSPA following the Malom massacre, where 10 people were shot at while waiting at a bus-stand in Malom, Manipur. After nearly 16 years, Ms Sharmila withdrew her protest on 09 August 2016 to contest the 2017 Assembly elections of Manipur, through which she aspired to repeal AFSPA. However, she received massive defeat in this election, and AFSPA continues to be a living reality amongst the majority of the North-East Indians (see, op. cit. Bhattacharyya, 2018); also see, The Armed Forces (Assam and Manipur) Special Powers Act, 1958 (No 28 of 1958). Retrieved from http://artassam.nic.in/Political%20Dept/Armed%20forced%20Assam%20&%20Manipur%20Special%20Power%201958%20.pdf.

55 Kaka, D. Iralu (2000) *Nagaland and India: The Blood and the Tears-Autographed*. Privately Published.

56 The 16 Point Agreement between the Government of India and the Naga People's Convention, 26 July 1960. Retrieved from http://peacemaker.un.org/sites/peacemaker.un.org/files/IN_600726_The%20sixteen%20point%20Agreement_0.pdf

57 Kashyap, Samudra Gupta (2017, 29 March) Why Thuingaleng Muivah's New Statement Has Dug Up Old Fears, Anger. *Indian Express*. Retrieved from http://indianexpress.com/article/explained/why-thuingaleng-muivahs-new-statement-has-dug-up-old-fears-anger-assam-manipur-protest-4590030/

58 Ibid. (Kashyap, 2017).
59 ibid.
60 Dutta, Akhil Ranjan (2015) The Naga National Struggle, 'Framework Agreement' and the Peace Prospects. *Journal Space and Culture, India*, 3 (2), 5–14, http://dx.doi.org/10.20896/saci.v3i2.151.
61 Bhattacharyya, Rituparna (2014) Good Governance and Development Mandate. *Journal Space and Culture, India*, 2 (1), 1–3, DOI: 10.20896/saci.v2i1.65.
62 op. cit. (Dutta, 2015; Goswami, 2015).
63 Weiner, Myron (1983) The Political Demography of Assam's Anti-Immigrant Movement. *Population and Development Review*, 9 (2), 279–292.
64 Tripartite talks on Assam Accord today (2017, 25 April) *The Assam Tribune*. Retrieved from www.assamtribune.com/scripts/detailsnew.asp?id=apr2617/at050.
65 McDuie-Ra, Duncan (2012b) *Northeast Migrants in Delhi: Race, Refuge and Retail*. Amsterdam University Press/IIAS Monograph Series, Amsterdam/Leiden; op. cit. (Ranjan, 2015).
66 op. cit. (Bhattacharyya, 2009; 2015; 2016).
67 Writ Petition (Civil) No. 103 of 2014. Retrieved from www.wbja.nic.in/wbja_adm/files/Title-3%20sc_2.pdf.
68 Report of the Committee Under the Chairmanship of Shri MP Bezbaruah to Look into the Concerns of the People of the North East Living in Other Parts of the Country. Retrieved from http://itanagar.nic.in/documents/Bezbaruah.PDF.
69 Baruah, Pranjal (2012, 23 December) Traffickers Target Northeast Indian Women, Sell Them Like Cattle. *Times of India*. Retrieved from http://timesofindia.indiatimes.com/india/Traffickers-target-northeast-Indian-women-sell-them-like-cattle/articleshow/17725299.cms.
70 Bhattacharyya, Rituparna (2017) Sociologies of India's Missing Children. *Asian Social Work and Policy Review*, 11 (1), 90–101, DOI: 10.1111/aswp.12116
71 op. cit. Yuval-Davis, 2006.
72 Nath, P. and Kumar, S. (2017) India's Look/Act East Policy and the Northeast Region: A Critical Perspective. *Space and Culture, India*, 5 (2), 7–20. DOI: 10.20896/saci.v5i2.265.
73 Haokip, Thongkholal (2011) India's Look East Policy. *Third Concept: An International Journal of Ideas*, 24 (291), 7–11.
74 Narendra Modi Says He Wants 1,600 Policewomen from North East for Gujarat. Retrieved from http://economictimes.indiatimes.com/articleshow/30067476.cms?utm_source=contentofinterest&utm_medium=text&utm_campaign=cppst.
75 Loiwal, Manogya (2017, 2 April) Namami Brahmaputra: A Festival Like Never before in Assam. *India Today*. Retrieved from http://indiatoday.intoday.in/story/pranab-mukherjee-namami-brahmaputra-river-festival/1/919016.html.

Chapter 7

Balochistan: from British rule to a province of Pakistan

Nizam Rahim Baloch

Balochistan strategically lies at the cultural centre of South Asia, Middle East and Central Asia. Balochistan is located on the northern side of the Strait of Ormuz. The latter leads into the Persian Gulf and is an important channel from a global perspective. The British arrival in South Asia brought changes in the political, economic and social dynamics, however one looks at it. The prime objective of British penetration into Balochistan was to station troops to find a way into Central Asia. At that time the Khan of Kalat ruled Balochistan and was unwilling to help the British in their ambitions, as the former had been in a treaty of non-interference with Afghanistan. Additionally, the British authorities were fully aware of the geostrategic location of Balochistan; their supply lines into Afghanistan could not be safe without having control of Balochistan. Therefore, an army detachment of British forces invaded Kalat on 13 November 1839. Mir Mehrab Khan, the then Khan of Kalat, fought bravely and was killed alongside hundreds of his fighters. The British, after defeating them, handed over the region to Shah Nawaz, a 14-year-old relative of Mir Mehrab. Lieutenant Lovely was given the charge to divide the conquered state. He gave Quetta and Mastung to Afghanistan, and Kach was annexed by Sindh. As the British forces left, Baloch tribes initiated a rebellion and Nasir Khan Second, the son of Mehrab Khan, was made the new Khan.

Khan of Kalat Mir Ahmed Yar Khan in his autobiography *Inside Balochistan* writes:

> the socio-political complex of Balochistan was in a disgraceful shape when I ascended to my throne in Kalat in 1933. The British government had totally ignored their promises and the

> treaties which were signed in mutual agreement between them and the government of Kalat. The agent to the Governor General in Balochistan was now the administrative head of Kalat. The Khan-e-Baloch worked merely as a figurehead with no powers at all. He was, as it were, a mechanical contraption which could function as an instrument by putting his signature on the dotted line on orders issued by the political agent who also functioned as the prime minister.[1]

In order to aggrandise its grip over Balochistan, the British introduced the '*Sandeman System*' in which they brought in some tribesmen loyal to British central authorities and installed '*Shahi Jirga*' as the court of law. These steps were mainly taken to mitigate the legitimacy of the Khan of Kalat. The colonisers were most of the time busy with the resistance from Baloch tribes. In 1847, the Bugti tribe fought against the British, in 1867 Bugti, Marri and Khetran started a revolt, in 1893 the Zehri tribe also fought against colonial masters, in 1898 there was an uprising in Makran region and in 1917 the Mengal tribe fought for liberation. These events ostensibly show that the people of Balochistan were never happy with the British policies.

During World War II, some Baloch leaders brought up the idea of a sovereign state of Balochistan. Mir Yusuf Aziz Magsi, who published newspapers from Delhi, Lahore and Karachi and his publications gave impetus to the anti-British sentiments among Baloches. In the early 1920s, with the help of his friends, Yusuf Magsi established '*Anjuman-e-Etihad-e-Balochan*' it was the first political organisation of the Baloch nation. Anjuman's goal was to achieve unity among the Baloch people and to start a movement to create an independent Balochistan. Anjuman started a weekly newspaper *Al-Baloch*. *Al-Baloch* published an article 'An unfulfilled dream,' written by Ghulam Mohammed Baloch in its 25 December 1932 issue, in which the author gave a map of Greater Balochistan showing Western Balochistan, Kalat confederacy, leased area under British control and Baloch land in Punjab and Sindh united.[2]

In 1937, the National Party was established under the leadership of prominent politician Ghous Bukhsh. The sole purpose of his political struggle was to work on the ultimate goal of an independent Balochistan. Interestingly, after seeing the rapid popularity of this newly established political party, British authorities banned the National Party in 1939 when it went against the Sardars loyal to British masters. This party spread awareness among the masses regarding the true face of those Sardars who had compromised Balochistan's interests for their personal benefits and were receiving enormous incentives for their allegiance to the British. This party had a clear policy and even it did not agree to the accession of Balochistan into Pakistan. It was in 1947 when Mir Ghous Bukhsh delivered his famous speech in which he said,

> We have a distinct civilization. We have a separate culture like that of Iran and Afghanistan. We are Muslims but it is not necessary that by virtue of our Muslims we should lose our freedom and merge with others. If the only fact that we are Muslims requires us to join Pakistan, then Afghanistan and Iran, both Muslim countries also amalgamate with Pakistan. We can survive without Pakistan, but the question is what Pakistan would be without us?[3]

The first direct battle over Balochistan between the All India National Congress and Muslim League took place in July 1946. Three constitutional assemblies were proposed under the Cabinet Mission Plan. There were a total of 36 seats for the Assembly group B and amongst them 23 were reserved for the Muslims. One of these seats was reserved for Balochistan. Shahi Jirga and members of Quetta Municipality formed an Electoral College to decide this seat. Furthermore, Congress leadership of Balochistan was united and there was no disagreement over its president, Samad Khan Achakzai. On the other hand, Qazi Isa was the president of the League in Balochistan. Surprisingly, he was neither a Baloch nor a Sardar. Consequently, all Sardars except Jaffar Khan Jamali, were against Qazi Isa for contesting this seat. Therefore, Qazi Isa was in in a quagmire. As a result he met the then Khan of Kalat and requested that he remove the members of the Electoral College belonging to Kalat. He argued that this seat was for British Balochistan in lieu of a Kalat state. Consequently, Sardars from Kalat were taken out of the Electoral College. Additionally, Qazi Isa's next demand was to exclude non-Muslim members in the municipal committee. This demand was rejected, which disappointed Qazi Isa, and he withdrew from race and left for Delhi.

A.B. Awan explainss in his book that

> Mir Jaffar Khan Jamali persuaded Nawab Muhammad Jogezai to stand to contest this seat unofficially for Muslim League, with all his backing. The Congress candidate was Achakzai. Jamali's gamble worked and Nawab Jogezai, standing on behalf

> of the Muslim League, won a thundering victory over the Congress nominee. The first thing Jogezai was to give assurance to Jinnah that he stood for everything the League stood for and from now onwards he placed himself totally under the mandate of the Quaid. This was a great victory for the League but the seeds of discord between the Pathan intelligentsia and Baloch feudalism had sown by Qazi Isa.[4]

The Khan of Kalat, in a memorandum to the Cabinet Mission Plan of 1946 categorically put it that after the withdrawal of British, they would revert to their original pre-1839 shape.

Kalat state and the question of merger with Pakistan

Balochistan consisted of four territorial entities: Kalat, Makran, Lasbela and Kharan, and these were ruled by the Khan of Kalat. It is here important to mention that the events of political awakening in the Indian subcontinent impacted the politics of all states in the region that were being ruled by the same master (Great Britain). Muhammad Ali Jinnah, the leader of the All India Muslim League, understood the significance of Balochistan. Congress also underscored Balochistan while forming its constitutional demands to bring to the British government. It is this very reason that in the Nehru Report (1928) reforms in Balochistan were demanded. In Jinnah's fourteen points of 1929 the same demand was mentioned. It shows that both leading political parties of India were giving considerable attention to that part of subcontinent. However, both these parties had fragile political structures in Balochistan; the prevailing political culture and preponderance of tribal customs impeded the process of organising their respective parties on the soil of Balochistan. But their rhetoric proved their keen interest in Balochistan. Jinnah and the Khan of Kalat had a cordial relationship during British rule, and the former was a staunch supporter of a free Balochistan. The Khan of Kalat in his autobiography illustrates his relationship with Jinnah well, stating that having

> chosen Mr. Jinnah to advise me on constitutional matters and the impediments which the British were creating in my way, I had an open-hearted talk with him on the subject. I gave him a full picture of the historical background of the region; its

> ethological aspects; its evolution through the ages; its past rulers; its present prospects and potentials; and how I had to a certain extent succeeded in preparing a reasonably sound set-up for future development aiming at the betterment of the people and the state.[5]

The respect of the Khan of Kalat for Jinnah can be measured well by the outstanding reception that was given to him whenever he came to Balochistan. The state of Kalat even financially helped Jinnah in his broader cause of attaining an independent Muslim state in India:

> the Quaid-e-Azam had by now come to be loved and respected so much that the people weighed him in pure gold publicly on the scale; and the balancing quantity of solid gold was handed over to him as the contribution of the Baloches towards the efforts of the All India Muslim League. In addition to this, I had the personal satisfaction of presenting a necklace to Miss Fatima Jinnah (the sister of Muhammad Ali Jinnah), the sentimental value which, needless to say, exceeded by far the paltry amount of Rs.1 00000 which it really cost. The Quaid and his sister were both surprised at this; but this was only a humble token of our deep love and Baloch tradition.[6]

Several meetings were held between Jinnah and the Khan of Kalat and British authorities to comprehensively discuss the future of Balochistan. Jinnah always vowed to keep good ties with Balochistan after the independence of both the states. As a result, a communiqué was issued on 11 August 11 1947 after the huddle of Lord Mountbatten, the viceroy of India, Jinnah and the Khan of Kalat. This communiqué included the following points:

- a the government of Pakistan recognizes Kalat as an independent sovereign state in treaty relation with British government with a status different from that of Indian states.
- b Legal opinion will be sought as to whether or not agreements of leases will be inherited by the government of Pakistan.
- c Meanwhile, standstill agreement has been made between Pakistan and kalat.
- d Discussion will take place between Pakistan and Kalat at Karachi at any early date with a view to reaching decision on Defense, external affairs and communication.[7]

This communiqué was obviously part of a deal to establish future ties between these two states. But Jinnah after accepting these terms changed his mind on the future of Balochistan and asked the the Khan of Kalat in October 1947 to sign the accession with Pakistan as other states did before joining Pakistan:

> Following the preliminary talks between the nominees of the kalat government and the government of Pakistan, the Quaid-e-Azam invited me to visit Karachi, the capital of the new state. Accordingly, I called on him in October, 1947. 'As an elder brother and friend,' spoke the Jinnah after the usual exchange of formalities, 'I would sincerely advise you to merge your state with Pakistan. Both the states will be benefited by this measure. As far as the demands and other problems of Kalat are concerned, these will be finally decided in a spirit of friendship.'
>
> 'I have great respect for your advice,' I replied, 'and it is my considered opinion that Kalat's merger is necessary in order to make Pakistan stronger. In this connection, I would suggest that Balochistan being a land of numerous tribes, the people there must be consulted in the matter prior to any decision I take; for, according to the prevalent tribal convention, no decision can be binding upon them unless they are taken into confidence beforehand of their khan.'[8]

The Khan of Kalat, who was running his state with absolute freedom and bringing constitutional and administrative reforms, was unwilling to give away the independent status of Balochistan at any cost. However, due to the changing circumstances he agreed to discuss on defence, foreign affairs and communication with Pakistan. There were two chambers of Balochistan legislature: Dar-ul-Awam (lower house) and Dar-ul-Uma (Upper House). By February 1948, the Khan of Kalat consulted both the houses. Dar-ul-Awan did not accept Jinnah's offer for accession while discussion was going on in Dar-ul-Uma. During this period, different rumours were spreading about the future of Balochistan. Some religious leaders, who were against the Muslim League before the partition of India, now were actively campaigning at the behest of same Muslim League to convince the people to support the scheme of merging Balochistan into Pakistan. They argued that for the greater interest of Muslim Umaah, the Baloch people should be with Pakistan. Though these religious Ulemas strived day and night to delineate Pakistan's narrative, the common people of Balochistan did not take them seriously. Unlike the Muslims of Punjab and other parts of Pakistan, the Muslims living in Balochistan were least concerned with religious identity; rather, they preferred Baloch national identity and were always ready to offer any sacrifice for the Baloch cause.

According to Martin Axmann,

> by 1946 there was little doubt that British Balochistan was an integral part of British India. By now not only the Muslim league but most British officials held this view. Accordingly, the future state of Pakistan claimed to be the legal successor to the British Indian government in these areas. Concerning the future of British Balochistan, the politics of 1946–47 witnessed a tussle between the Muslim League and Indian National Congress. The British could not do more than to play the role of arbitration between the two contestants, while the Khan of Kalat ceased to play any role at all.[9]

With similar activities happening in Balochistan, in March 1948 th Khan of Kalat was informed by the US ambassador to Pakistan in Karachi that his three fiduciary states, Makran, kharan and Lasbela, had acceded to Pakistan. The Khan of Kalat rejected the accession as it was against the agreement with Pakistan and the British government according to the communiqué of 1947. The Khan of kalat returned to Kalat and started mobilisation and consultation programmes. In March 1948, Pakistani military entered coastal areas of Balochistan and a helpless Khan of Kalat was forced to merge Balochistan with Pakistan.

Jinnah was against a referendum in Balochistan because he knew that the people of Balochistan would not abandon their sovereign Balochistan's ambition. He was informed about the failure of using Islam to convince people of Balochistan to merge into Pakistan. So, he accepted the help of Jaffar Khan Jamali and Nawab Jogezi, both of whom represented Balochistan in the Indian Constitutional Assembly; they followed Jinnah's instructions and played their role as the followers of Jinnah. They bypassed the prevailing public opinion that was repugnant to the very idea of accession. One must bear in mind that Balochistan's accession to Pakistan did not solve the political and constitutional enigma inherited from British legacy. In his address to Sibi Darbar in February 1948, Jinnah declared that he considered it vital to enable the people of Balochistan to share the responsibilities of their government and give them advice in the administration.

There is a dichotomy regarding the Khan of Kalat's signing of the accession. For nationalists, it was done through force, but Pakistan's state narrative is that the Khan of Kalat did it without being forced. In his autobiography, the Khan of Kalat states:

> without obtaining the formal sanction from tribal Sardars, I signed the merger documents in my capacity as the khan-e-Azam on 30th March, 1948. I confess I knew I was exceeding the scope of my mandate; yet, I am grateful to my people and the tribal Sardars that, despite this, they did not raise a single voice of any nature of protest against my decision on their behalf. And I am pleased to be able to say that I still enjoy their full support, their confidence and trust today as I had in the past.[10]

The wounds of Balochistan's accession into Pakistan are deep for Baloch nationalists who commemorate it as a black day. The subsequent events that took place in Balochistan were directly impacted by the controversial modus operandi of accession. Since then, five armed insurgences have taken place against state of Pakistan from within Balochistan.

The first insurgency (1948)

Prince Abdul Karim was the first to initiate a rebellion against the state of Pakistan in 1948. Later he was arrested and imprisoned for the charge of sedition against the state. He remained in jail for 10 years and in 1955 was released. He later became a prominent nationalist politician in Pakistan. The rebellion of 1948 was the first insurgency in Balochistan in which a large number of people from both sides were killed. There was conflict between then Governor General of Pakistan Ghulam Mohammad and the constituent assembly of Pakistan. Almost all political parties in West Pakistan were staunch supporters of a unified province; however the dismissal of the constituent assembly by the governor general on 24 October 1954 altered the political scenario of Pakistan. One unit formula nudged the nationalists of Balochistan to reorganise them for another struggle. Field Marshall Ayub Khan took strident measures against the nationalists, and the subsequent events paved the path for Khair Bakhsh Marri, Akbar khan Bugti and Sardar

Attuallh Mengal to join the political movement with zeal. Sheikh Aziz wrote about the attitude of rulers towards Balochistan: 'Ironically, every party that came to power branded the Baloch people as seditious when in reality the Baloch had genuine complaints of being denied their legitimate rights, similarly, natural resources were exploited in the name of homogeneity.'[11]

The second insurgency (1958–1959)

The constitution of 1956 could not earn the favour of Baloch in general and Baloch nationalists in particular. Nawab Noroz Khan, a famous Baloch nationalist leader initially demanded constitutional rights for Balochistan; when his demand was not met, he then led the second insurgency against Pakistan. It deteriorated the situation of Balochistan. Many people were displaced due to war, and harsh actions were taken against rebel sympathisers. When both sides became fed up with war, a peace deal was signed. Surprisingly, the holy Quran, the sacred book of Islam, was used by the Pakistani military to bring Nawab Noroz Khan and his men to the table. It was decided that after the surrender, Nawab and his men would be set free. Contrary to the promise, they were arrested and five followers of Nawab, including his sons, were executed. Nawab Noroz Khan took his last breath in jail. Since then, the Baloch nationalists always refer to this betrayal when they are asked to negotiate.

The third insurgency (1963–1969)

Natural gas was discovered in Sui (Balochistan) in 1952. The provincial leadership was not fully briefed about the quantity and future distribution of gas. However, the constitution of 1956 and one unit formula also aggrandised the sense of deprivation among the people of Balochistan. As a result, the third armed conflict started in 1963 and ended in 1969 with a ceasefire between the rebels and Pakistan army. In 1970, with one unit finally annulled by General Yahya Khan, Balochistan became the fourth province of West Pakistan.

Emergence of NAP and the Bhutto regime

The civil war in East Pakistan resulted in the division of Pakistan. East Pakistan won independence on 16 December 1971 as Bangladesh; West Pakistan became the only territory of Pakistan, with Zulfiqar

Ali Bhutto as leader. There were great expectations for Bhutto, as his slogans were pro-people. However, the dominance of the elites soon took over. The power structure in Pakistan emerged more powerful and Zulifqar Ali Bhutto had to walk back some of his key promises. Undoubtedly, Bhutto was a visionary leader and his policies strengthened the state after losing East Pakistan, but he could not handle the politics of Balochistan holistically. His political party, the Pakistan People's Party (PPP), was defeated by the National Awami party (NAP). The latter was a Pashtun-Baloch nationalist's party struggling for decentralisation of power and provincial autonomy. Bhutto's unilateral decisions on Balochistan enhanced the sentiments of provincialism. Bhutto advocated three distinct models: Islam, democracy and socialism, which ultimately resulted in disillusionment among the masses. Bhutto's policies, particularly those dealing with dissents were authoritarian. As a result, first Chief Minister of Balochistan Attaullah Mengal, who belonged to NAP, was pressured to accept the decrees of federal government. He refused, and the provincial government was dismissed by Bhutto in 1973.

The fourth insurgency (1973–1977)

After the dismissal of Mengal's government, the fourth insurgency started in Balochistan. Thousands of Baloch fighters went to the mountains to take on the military. The insurgency lasted for 5 years and nearly nine thousand people from both sides were killed. The leadership of guerrilla fighters found sanctuaries in Afghanistan. Hence, the government of Bhutto was toppled by General Zia ul Haq and military operations in Balochistan were halted. The fourth insurgency was different from the previous insurgencies in many ways. First, nationalists who stood triumphant in the electoral process were at odds with the centre from the beginning. Second, political participation expanded in this period, but dismissing the provincial government and using coercive measures to tackle nationalists widened the centre-province differences. Balochistan witnessed a comparatively calm situation during the regime of Zia. All political prisoners were immediately freed.

The fifth insurgency (2006–present)

General Pervez Musharraf toppled the government of Nawaz Sharif on 12 October 1999 through a military coup. The 9/11 attacks altered the global economic, political and strategic dynamics.

Balochistan was impacted because its northern region is a porous border with Afghanistan. People from both sides are Pashtuns/Pakhtuns. A large number of war-hit Afghans came to Balochistan as refugees. The killing of Nawab Akbar Khan Bugti, former chief minister and head of the Bugti tribe resulted in the fifth insurgency. Moreover, this insurgency was omnipotent as the nationalist assemblies resigned and their leaders such as Akhtar Mengal were arrested. Attacks on Punjabis living in Baloch areas commenced; many were killed and the rest had to leave Balochistan. Military operations started and, in western Balochistan where theSardari system does not exist, middle class youth took up arms and went to the mountains. Baloch's missing person's tragedy attracted the world's attention. According to the International Voice for Baloch Missing Persons (IVBMP) organization, the number of missing persons is more than 35 thousand, though the military establishment considers that an exaggerated number.

The election of 2008 brought democracy back to Pakistan. With the PPP formed at the centre, Sindh also formed a coalition government in Balochistan. The government of the PPP emphasized constitutional development. As a result, the eighteenth amendment gave powers to provinces. The Aghaz e Huquoq Balochistan Package was announced by Prime Minister Yousaf Raza Gillani to mitigate the wounds of Balochistan. In this package, more than five thousand jobs were provided, and scholarships for indigenous and overseas for Balochs were also initiated, but the core demand of full provincial autonomy, determining the whereabouts of missing persons, was not addressed. The China Pakistan Economic Corridor (CPEC) is a multibillion agreement between China and Pakistan. Gwadar, a coastal city of Balochistan, is the epicentre of this project. Since the initiation of this mega project, development works particularly on infrastructure have benefitted the people of Balochistan; however, there are still many things that are unclear aboutthis project. It is high time for Pakistan to heal the wounds of Balochistan, as these wounds appeared after Partition.

Partition and Balochi literature

Balochi literature is rich with multiple characteristics. The war has always impacted literature. In Balochistan, the epistemology of every period can be gauged well by going through the literature of the people of this part of the world. Taj Muhammad Bresseg is a prolific writer on Balochistan's culture, politics and literature. He writes:

> The Balochs' consciousness of their common language and cultural heritage constitutes another significant foundation of their nationalism. it is manifested in a set of shared social norm, value system, traditions and folklore. The Balochi culture; values, together with the cultural environment is the focus of its nationalist appeals for broader popular support for their autonomy overall demands of which culture is one.[12]

During the Partition period, some religious leaders had started a comprehensive campaign supporting the Pakistan cause and merging with Pakistan. They argued that Pakistan would implement Islamic law in its true spirit. On the other hand, Inayatullah Baloch explained that 'the Baloch have many interesting characteristics in their culture. They have a different perception about religion than other nations in the Middle East. They are not fundamentalist and do not believe in mixing religion with politics.'[13]

After the partition of India, a small number of Baloch who were in India did not come to Balochistan because they were told by Indian media that Balochistan has been occupied by Pakistan and that the Khan of Kalat had written to Nehru to make Balochistan as part of India. The Khan of Kalat later clarified that no such thing had been discussed. Even Nehru wrote a letter to the Khan of Kalat and apologised on behalf of the Indian press. In Balochistan, Balochi literature plays a role in shaping many aspects of life. Bresseg writes that throughout 'the centuries, the Balochi oral literature has been an important vehicle of for transmitting Balochi language and national feelings occupying an important place in their life.'[14] However, postcolonial Balochistan literature got a boost. Balochi and Pashto both found new avenues by which to develop as the guardians of their respective nations: 'since 1948, as Balochistan became a part of Pakistan, a more favourable environment led to the growth of such cultural institutions as the Balochi Literary Society and the Balochi Language Association which have successfully functioned ever since.'

Here one cannot forget the contribution of Balochs living in Karachi for their undeniable contributions to Balochi literature. However, later Quetta replaced Karachi as the epicentre of Balochi literature: 'Being the capital city and the major Baloch residence in

Pakistan, in the early fifties Karachi became the focus of intellectual activities in Balochi. The Balochi Academy and The Fazol Academy were all established in Karachi after 1947.'[15]

As Bresseg writes,

> Stories about the wars against the Persians, Afghans, Indians, Turks and Europeans also form the salient features of the Baloch poetry of later centuries. Among the Baloch, the memory of poet such as Gul Khan Nasir, Syed Zahur Shah Hashomi and Atta shad arouses deep feelings. They depict Baloch as a free, autonomous people resisting Iranian, Afghan, Indians (i.e. Mughals), and Pakistani domination.
>
> As far as Ayub's government, it too had cause for satisfaction. By partial patronage of linguistic and literary activities the bureaucracy could mollify the Baloch intelligentsia and control it. Thus it could prevent the intelligentsia from becoming as alienated from the centre as the militant nationalists were. By contrast, no such institutions have ever been allowed to function in Iranian Balochistan.[16]

Conclusion

It is an undeniable fact that Balochistan, due to its strategic location and enormous natural resources, had to face multi-faceted challenges and still, 70 years after of the partition of India, the impact of this partition can be felt when one visits Balochistan, particularly Baloch dominated areas. It is a bitter reality that the grievances of the people of Balochistan were never addressed shrewdly and that, rather, force has been used to silence the indigenous people of Balochistan. The five armed insurgencies are connected by the controversial modus operandi of merging Balochistan with Pakistan. As it has been comprehensively discussed, during the chaos some powerful tribal heads either sided with the state or anti-state actors in order to augment their power in their respective territories. It is a palpable reality that one brother fights for freedom while the other either works in parliament or at the behest of the civil or military establishment. Moreover, when an ordinary Baloch is asked about Balochistan, their first reply the partition of India or the merger of Balochistan with Pakistan inevitably comes up. In this way, it is clear that the events of Partition of the subcontinent altered the dynamics of princely states in particular. Since the initiation of

CPEC, it has been argued that the wounds of Balochistan would be healed, but history will decide whether this project can bring such a massive change or it is, in the end, just another project of exploitation.

Notes

1 Khan, Mir Ahmed Yar (1975) *Inside Balochistan: Political Autobiography of His Highness Barglan Baigi: khan-e-Azam XII*. Karachi: Royal Book Company, p. 123.
2 Mohammad, Ghulam (1932, 25 December) "An Unfulfilled Dream," *Al-Baloch*.
3 Mahmad, Jan (1989) *Essays on Baloch National Struggle in Pakistan: Emergence, Dimensions, Repercussions*. Quetta: Gosha-e-Adab, p. 174.
4 Awan, A.B. (1985) *Balochistan: Historical and Political Processes*. London: New Century Publishers, p. 168.
5 Khan, Mir Ahmed Yar (1975) *Inside Balochistan: Political Autobiography of His Highness Barglan Baigi: khan-e-Azam XII*. Karachi: Royal Book Company, p. 133.
6 Ibid., 133.
7 Veena, Yogeena (2015, 5 December) "How Balochistan Became a Part of Pakistan: A Historical Perspective," *The Nation*.
8 Khan, Mir Ahmed Yar (1975) *Inside Balochistan: Political Autobiography of His Highness Barglan Baigi: khan-e-Azam XII*. Karachi: Royal Book Company, p. 153.
9 Axmann, Martin (2009) *Back to the Future*. New York: Oxford Press, p. 195.
10 Khan, Mir Ahmed Yar (1975) *Inside Balochistan: Political Autobiography of His Highness Barglan Baigi: khan-e-Azam XII*. Karachi: Royal Book Company, p. 162.
11 Aziz, Sheikh (2014, October 5) "A Leaf from History," *Dawn*.
12 Breseeg, Taj Mohammad (2004) *Baloch Nationalism: Its Origin and Development*. Karachi: Royal Book Company, p. 70.
13 Baloch, Inyatullah (1987) *The Problem of Greater of Balochistan: A Study of Baluch Nationalism*. Stuttgart: Steiner Verlag Wiesbaden, p. 75.
14 Breseeg, Taj Mohammad Breseeg (2004) *Baloch Nationalism: Its Origin and Development*. Karachi: Royal Book Company, p. 78.
15 Hashmi, Sayyid (1973, 9 January) "Balochi zuban aur us ka Rasmulkhat," *Daily Jung*.
16 Breseeg, Taj Mohammad (2004) *Baloch Nationalism: Its Origin and Development*. Karachi: Royal Book Company, p. 81.

Part II

Migration and displacement

Chapter 8

Unwanted refugees

Sindhi Hindus in India and Muhajirs in Sindhi[1]

Nandita Bhavnani

It is now well known that various categories of Partition refugees came into conflict with local governments and communities in their adoptive countries, whether India or Pakistan.[2] To be sure, the scale of population exchange was both vast and unforeseen. It created a huge strain on nascent governments that were still attempting to come to grips with independence and governance, to setup a brand-new capital from scratch (in the case of Pakistan), and to cope with large-scale communal violence, that too with scant resources, barely 2 years after the end of World War II, which had a far-reaching impact on the Indian economy.

In India, the Congress had resisted the notion of 'population exchange' and had actively discouraged migration of minorities well before August 1947. In Pakistan too, once the influx of Muhajirs turned into a flood, this was perceived by the Muslim League high command as a 'demographic assault' on India's part, although, ironically, several among this elite were Muhajirs themselves, notably Pakistan's first governor general, M.A. Jinnah, and its first prime minister, Liaquat Ali Khan.

As Yasmin Khan has pointed out, the swiftness with which Partition was executed, and the ensuing bloodbath, left both dominions with no time to formulate a well-thought-out policy regarding migration and refugees.[3] The initial policy of both India and Pakistan was to discourage mass migration, and on the Indian side, the policy was moreover to encourage refugees to return to their homes.

The brutal carnage in Punjab, however, created much popular sympathy for the victims of this violence. Initially, Hindu and Sikh refugees were welcomed in India, as were Punjabi Muslims in Pakistan. The governments of both India and Pakistan had no choice but to arrange for the organised evacuation of these refugees, as well as their immediate relief and housing and, subsequently, their long-term rehabilitation.

In both dominions, government policy regarding refugees was largely driven by the Punjab experience. In India, this meant that refugees from other areas, such as Sindh and Bengal,[4] where there had been relatively less violence (as compared to Punjab), were viewed, both by the government and the general public, as cowards who had migrated unnecessarily.[5] The fact that these minorities had fled their homes owing to numerous instances of oppression, harassment and intimidation – what Gandhi termed as 'killing by inches'[6] – did not make as great an impact on public or government perceptions as communal bloodshed did. On the other hand, in Pakistan, while Punjabi refugees from East Punjab were accommodated in West Punjab, non-Punjabi refugees were often 'shunted down' to Sindh regardless of their personal wishes. It has become a Muhajir legend that, during the difficult months of 1947–1948, non-Punjabi Muslim refugees who attempted to disembark from trains at stations in West Punjab were told that Pakistan was further on.

Thus, refugees from Punjab were privileged over other refugees, in terms of popular sympathy, government willingness to accept and accommodate them and the quantity and quality of resources allocated towards their rehabilitation.[7](However, it should also be remembered that even Punjabi refugees, on both sides of the border, found that their welcome was short-lived, especially when they came into conflict with local populations over jobs, business and property.[8]) Across the subcontinent, Partition refugees became unwanted, at the level of both central and provincial governments, not to mention of host populations. In Yasmin Khan's words:

> Overstretched provincial ministries across India and Pakistan dug in their heels and tried to resist taking responsibility for refugees. Across South Asia the provincial governments panicked at the prospect of absorbing trainloads of refugees, especially at a time of endemic food shortages and fragile social peace. They had to be cajoled, bribed and ordered to take responsibility for quotas of displaced. The [United Provinces] government steadfastly resisted the arrival of refugees in 1947 and attempted to seal the state borders. In Gujarat, the government announced that it would not be giving any aid to itinerant Gujarati traders coming 'home' from areas that now lay in Pakistan, although many of them had been away from Gujarat for generations.[9]

In this essay, I seek to explore the instances of refugees from and to Sindh – Sindhi Hindus in India and Muhajirs in Sindh – both of whom faced a considerable degree of unpopularity and/or hostility in their adoptive countries. I will compare these two instances, and attempt to show how, despite certain superficial similarities, these two groups of refugees were faced with diametrically opposite circumstances, and so employed differing strategies to create a new sense of identity for themselves. In this context, the cultural perceptions of the refugees –both of themselves and of the local communities – played a significant role, as we shall see here.

Sindhi Hindus in India

Sindhi refugees begin to migrate

At the time of Partition, there was a Hindu population of approximately 1.4 million in Sindh, forming a minority of approximately 27 per cent, in addition to a tiny population of Sikhs,[10] and a relatively small number of Christians, Jews, Parsis and other minorities.[11] There was no large-scale violence against these minorities in Sindh until December 1947.[12] Consequently, there was no large-scale migration of Sindhi Hindus in 1947.

Some Sindhi Hindus had begun to migrate to India even before August 1947, mainly owing to fear of communal discrimination and oppression, and also a fear of loss of social status in Muslim majority Pakistan. While not many in number, these early emigrants were partly able to plan their departure and their stay in India (as opposed to numerous Sindhi Hindus who fled at short notice in 1948). Most of these Sindhi Hindus were relatively affluent and could afford to rent or buy their own accommodation, or they had family or friends in India, at whose homes they could take shelter.

However, the first Sindhi Hindus to come to India *as refugees* were those who were affected by the anti-Hindu and anti-Sikh pogrom that occurred in Quetta in Balochistan on 20 and 21 August 1947. In early September 1947 they were evacuated, first to Sindh, and subsequently by steamer to Bombay city, where they received a warm welcome. In those early days there was a high degree of sympathy in India for the Hindus and Sikhs who had survived the Quetta violence. (This was against a larger, nation-wide backdrop of sympathy for the survivors of the carnage in Punjab.) These refugees were housed in camps setup on the outskirts of the city, and were given free rations.

The exodus intensifies

On 17 December 1947, there was an anti-Hindu pogrom in the Sindhi city of Hyderabad, which was followed by a much more severe pogrom in Karachi, when Sikhs and Hindus were killed and their properties looted and burnt. These two pogroms, especially the second, more brutal, one, engendered much fear and panic among Sindhi Hindus all over Sindh. Subsequently, the Indian government was persuaded by senior members of the Sindh Congress to arrange for an organised evacuation of Hindus and Sikhs from Sindh. From 9 January onwards, steamships were chartered to ferry Hindus and Sikhs to India, while 'refugee special' trains were run from Hyderabad and Mirpur Khas in Sindh to Pali and Marwar Junction in present-day Rajasthan. By the beginning of May 1948, though, the bulk of Sindh's minorities had migrated to India. Initially, most of these refugees were brought by ship to Bombay. However by the end of 1947, the city's refugee camps were already full, and so refugees from Sindh were taken to more distant refugee camps, such as Kalyan (present-day Ulhasnagar). Some refugees, who preferred to be in the city, even camped at Alexandra Dock in Bombay for several months at a stretch. Furthermore, ships from Karachi were diverted to ports in present-day Gujarat such as Okha and Porbandar.

Ultimately, most Sindhi Hindus settled in western India in the present-day states of Maharashtra, Gujarat, Rajasthan, Madhya Pradesh and Chhatisgarh, and even today the bulk of Sindhi Hindus are still found in these states.

Hostility towards Sindhi Hindus

The sympathetic welcome extended by the government and local populations to Sindhi Hindu refugees soon began to sour for a number of reasons. Their consequent unpopularity was reflected in the local press. Newspapers like *The Times of India* and the *Free Press Journal*, which had earlier displayed great sympathy for the difficulties faced by Sindhi Hindus in Pakistan, now began to refer to refugees 'invading Bombay' and the 'refugee problem.'[13] This unpopularity prevailed at the level of both the government as well as the general public.

A large proportion of the Sindhi Hindu refugees came to areas that were then part of the Bombay state (i.e. present-day Maharashtra and Gujarat). In early October 1947, it was expected that a total of about 30 thousand Sindhi Hindu refugees would be absorbed in Bombay.[14] By mid January 1948, however, there were already about 250 thousand Sindhi refugees in Bombay state, and Sindhi Hindus were still arriving daily by boat and train. The Bombay government was clearly not prepared for such a large influx of refugees.

Moreover, as mentioned above, there had not been as much violence in Sindh as compared to Punjab, and various echelons of the Bombay government viewed the Sindhi Hindu migration as cowardly and therefore unwarranted. In the early months of 1948, senior ministers in the Bombay government encouraged Sindhi Hindus to return to their homes in Pakistan.[15] This view went hand in glove with their unwillingness to shoulder the gargantuan task and costs of refugee relief and rehabilitation.

In the autocratic opinion of the government, Sindhi Hindus were classic refugees, who had thrown themselves on the mercy of the state, and so were not justified in voicing or acting on their preferences in matters pertaining to their lives and their future. (This was in stark contrast to the parallel, official homecoming narrative of the Indian state regarding the migration of Hindus and Sikhs to India.)[16] After the Bombay government decided that Bombay city was 'saturated' and could not accommodate more refugees, Sindhi Hindus disembarking at Bombay were not allowed to enter the city. They were given train tickets and transported to refugee camps in the hinterland, to places such as Daund and Deolali.

Illegalities on the part of the Sindhi Hindus also contributed greatly to the deterioration of their relationship with the local government. Sindhi Hindus were found to be illegally 'squatting' at various public properties, such as Alexandra Dock or the Sion Hospital's barracks.[17] Moreover, similar to Partition refugees across the northern subcontinent, Sindhi Hindus also began to illegally occupy property belonging to Muslims. Finally, in the years soon after Partition, Sindhis also participated in communal violence against Muslims in towns such as Godhra, Udaipur, Rajkot and Ajmer.

For their part, Sindhi Hindus resented that they were not permitted to enter the city of Bombay, or forced to go to refugee camps distant from the city. Some refugees were not consulted about where they wanted to resettle, and only discovered their final destination after they were taken there. Sindhi Hindus also resented the enactment of the Bombay Refugees Act in 1948, which they perceived as a humiliating piece of legislation designed to treat them as quasi-criminals, and therefore as deeply stigmatising.[18]

The poor quality of the refugee camps was another sore point with the refugees. To start with, these camps were located in far-flung outside cities, ensuring a long commute for those Sindhis who needed to visit the city daily to earn a living or obtain education. Often, there were inadequate or no facilities for transport. Further, these camps – often military camps used by the British during World War II, which had not been maintained for the following 2 years – were in a sorry state of repair: broken or damaged walls, doors and windows; roofs without tiles; decrepit bathrooms and toilets, sometimes without doors. Accommodation was in the barracks – generally large, long halls – which afforded scant privacy to the families who were obliged to live there. Supply of utilities like water and electricity was erratic. Rations were adulterated, or sold on the black market; occasionally, supposedly free rations were sold to refugees.

Local populations also resented the influx of Sindhi refugees. A community of traders and merchants, Sindhi Hindus worked extremely hard to rehabilitate themselves, like refugees all over the world. This meant that they were willing to hawk goods in trains, or peddle goods on pavements, at dirt cheap prices with wafer-thin margins. Consequently, they ended up undercutting local prices, which created much resentment from local traders, leading to conflict in various cities across India, such as Agra, Gwalior and Daund.

Moreover, in the more Sanskritised Hindu cultures of Gujarat and Rajasthan, various aspects of Sindhi culture – the common belief in Sufi saints and Sufism, the consumption of non-vegetarian food, the Perso-Arabic alphabet, the women's traditional dress,[19] to name just a few – were perceived as quasi-Muslim.[20] Non-vegetarianism in particular was much despised and perceived as 'dirty.' Sindhi Hindus who settled in Gujarat after Partition recall that they were not able to rent apartments or, as children, other children would not play with them for this reason.[21]

There were various other causes for the unpopularity of the Sindhi Hindus as well. For example, some residents of Bombay city resented that certain affluent Sindhi Hindus were willing to pay astronomical rates to acquire apartments in the city. They felt that Sindhi Hindus, especially those living in refugee camps, were simply lapping up the free rations given to them without bothering to earn a living. This was compounded when Sindhi Hindus refused offers of agricultural or manual labour, both of which were deeply disdained in their mercantile culture.

In popular perception, Sindhi Hindus were perceived as cowards who had run away from Pakistan. They were – and still are – seen in many sections of Indian society as loud and flashy, money-minded and materialistic. Their propensity for taking short cuts in business earned them a reputation for being untrustworthy cheats, hence the derogatory saying: 'If you see a Sindhi and a snake on the road, kill the Sindhi first.'

Sindhi Hindus' unpopularity varied from region to region. It occurred more in northerly regions like Gujarat and Rajasthan which possessed not only a more Sanskritised Hindu culture, but also a considerable population of traders with a strong local mercantile tradition who were then obliged to compete with arriving Sindhi Hindu traders. However this unpopularity was comparatively less prevalent in a cosmopolitan city like Mumbai; it also waned as Sindhi Hindus climbed the class ladder.

Sindhi response

By and large, Sindhi Hindus responded in several ways to this sense of hostility and unpopularity. Firstly, they deeply resented the very term 'refugee,' or various local equivalents such as *sharanarthi*, *nirvasit* and *panaahgir*. These were interpreted by them as pejorative terms which implied weakness (especially financial weakness), helplessness and dependency. All these attributes were viewed very negatively by members of a mercantile community that laid great store by wealth and self-reliance. Moreover, Sindhi Hindus subscribed to the 'homecoming' narrative of the Indian state, and so did not consider themselves as 'outsiders' or as 'refugees.' Sindhi Hindus had internalised the nationalist narrative and thought of themselves as rightful citizens of an independent India. They had always considered themselves as belonging to India, although this sense of belonging was temporarily under a cloud for a few months with the creation of Pakistan, in other words, from 15 August 1947 to the date of their migration to India. Consequently, once they arrived in India, Sindhi Hindus worked hard to improve their financial standing so as to avoid the stigma of being perceived as 'helpless and dependent,' and also to gain a higher socio-economic status.

Secondly, in order to gain a higher degree of acceptance in local societies, Sindhi Hindus also chose to adapt to local cultures. This included learning the local language – whether Gujarati, Hindi or Marathi – and participating actively in local festivals such as Ganesh

Chaturthi or Navratri. More and more Sindhi women dropped their traditional dress of *suthan-cholo* and took to wearing the sari or *salwar-kameez*. Some Sindhi Hindus living in Gujarat and Rajasthan also turned vegetarian in order to gain social acceptance. (Indeed, in the early years after Partition, Sindhi Congress leaders, inspired by Nehruvian notions of pan-Indianism, told Sindhis that they should not cling to their ethnicity, but should assimilate to the local culture wherever they resettled.)

Thirdly, their adaptation to local cultures also meant that Sindhi Hindus actively downplayed or jettisoned elements of their own Sindhi ethnic culture and identity, especially those which had 'Muslim' overtones. The Perso-Arabic alphabet, which had been widely used by Sindhi Hindus for the Sindhi language over the preceding century, was one of the first casualties of this move.[22] This was followed by a similar decline in the written use of the Sindhi language in India, and to a lesser extent in the usage of the spoken language.

Furthermore, Sindhi Hindus had become strongly disillusioned with the Congress (which was then in power, both at the centre as well as in Bombay state) for agreeing to Partition, and for not making adequate arrangements for the evacuation of Sindhi Hindus, or their subsequent rehabilitation. This translated into disrespect for the government, and by extension, for law and authority. Moreover, Sindhi Hindu voting patterns began to change, shifting from the Congress, first to other parties, and ultimately to the BJP in more recent years. This occurred in tandem with Sindhi Hindus increasingly turning towards the Hindu Right in terms of embracing a more Sanskritised form of Hinduism as well as a strong belief in India as a 'Hindu state.'

After their migration from Pakistan, Sindhi Hindus ceased to be a religious minority in Hindu majority India. However, they found that their specific practices of Hinduism were perceived as quasi-Islamic, particularly in more Sanskritised Hindu societies. These factors have contributed to the fact that the Sindhi Hindus' religious identity – the main cause of their migration – has become strengthened, and their shift towards the Hindu Right, while diluting those elements of their religio-cultural traditions that are construed as Islamic, such as faith in a Muslim *pir* or saint.

Unlike other migrant communities who have constructed themselves as diasporas, such as Jews or Tibetans, Sindhi Hindus do not perceive Sindh (since it is now overwhelmingly Muslim) as a 'sacred homeland,' a place to which they would wish to ultimately 'return,' either as a physical homeland or as an imaginary construct. If Sindhi Hindus were attached to their holy shrines in Sindh, they arranged to 'transplant' most of these to India.[23] Moreover, there was little or no sense of an overarching Sindhi provincial identity that transcended religious differences, so after Partition this has translated into little or no attachment to the land of Sindh beyond personal nostalgia, limited to one's home, one's neighbourhood or one's city. On the contrary, for many Sindhi Hindus, Partition and the creation of Pakistan transformed Sindh into a 'Muslim,' and therefore alien, country, with former Hindu homes and properties occupied by Muslim 'outsiders' i.e. Muhajirs. More often than not, this construction of Sindh is one to be largely turned away from for many Sindhi Hindus. This turning away from Sindh, coupled with the fact that certain elements of Sindhi culture were perceived as 'Muslim,' have greatly fuelled the process of the dilution of Sindhi Hindu ethnic identity in India.

However, in a multi-ethnic society like India, ethnic identity can never be erased since it is reinforced from the outside. Sindhis in India will remain Sindhis, but their strategies of adaptation and acculturation in the post-Partition era have given rise to subsequent generations of Sindhis who have grown up, not only with a sense of a cultural vacuum, but also with having internalised the negative stereotype of Sindhis; consequently, they are embarrassed about being Sindhi. This sense of a cultural vacuum is often compensated for by identifying with the Hindu Right.

Muhajirs in Sindh

The first Muhajirs arrive in Sindh

The first Muhajirs to come to Sindh came as early as the end of 1946. These were Muslim victims of the communal violence that had broken out in Bihar in October and November 1946. While some of their compatriots migrated to East Bengal, about 1,500 made their way to Sindh where they were welcomed with open arms by the Muslim League government. During the early days of Muhajir immigration, Sindhi Muslims, viewing themselves as *ansaars*,[24] gave enthusiastic help to them, welcoming them at railway stations, and arranging for food (sometimes home-cooked) to be served to them as soon as they arrived, as well as in refugee camps. In smaller Sindhi towns, Muhajirs were taken by the local Sindhi Muslims to the homes of Hindus who had migrated to India; they were also given surplus pieces of furniture, quilts and other household goods to help them settle.

The first Muhajirs to come to Karachi were accommodated in the Haji Camp, as well as in schools and hospitals controlled by the Karachi Municipal Corporation. There was a proposal to settle them permanently on a large plot of land at Bunder Road Extension, but since this was a residential area dominated by affluent and influential Hindus, the government was swayed into shifting the proposed resettlement site to Lyari. Through the first few months of 1947, Muhajirs continued to trickle into Sindh, and in early July, Yusuf Haroon, the then president of the Sind Provincial Muslim League, publicly announced that he expected a total of 23 thousand Muhajirs to come to Sindh over the next six months; and further, that the Sindh government would have a problem accommodating them.[25]

Muhajirs flood into Pakistan

By mid September 1947, given the communal carnage that raged in Delhi and other parts of northern India, by one estimate Muhajirs were pouring into Karachi at the rate of about five hundred per day;[26] there were already about 11 thousand Muhajirs in the city.[27] It is estimated that at least7 million Muslims ultimately migrated to Pakistan from India.[28] Of these, the bulk were Punjabi Muslims from East Punjab, most of whom resettled in West Punjab. A large proportion of the remaining Muslims – mostly from the present-day states of Uttar Pradesh, Bihar, Rajasthan, Gujarat, Maharashtra, Madhya Pradesh, Andhra Pradesh and Telengana – were sent to Sindh. Since Karachi was then the capital of the new nation, numerous Muhajirs were attracted to the city and its prospects for employment.

However, with Muhajirs pouring into the city, including the administrative staff of the new Pakistan government, accommodation in the city became increasingly difficult. It had been only 2 years since the end of World War II, and the subcontinent was still living in an era of shortages and rationing of necessities. The Sindh provincial government, and by extension, the Pakistan central government, found that they simply did not have the resources to accommodate and rehabilitate all the Muhajirs who were flooding into Sindh. In Punjab too, refugee camps were already full, while new refugees arrived from India daily.

Overwhelmed by the refugee crisis, Liaquat Ali Khan, Pakistan's first prime minister, made a public statement in early October 1947, in which he stated that Pakistan was willing to accept refugees only from East Punjab, and from its princely states such as Patiala, Nabha, Jind and Faridkot.[29] In the months before and after Partition there was a perception in Pakistan that there was a plot on the part of the Indian government to destabilise the infant state of Pakistan by flooding it with refugees. Liaquat Ali Khan's statement was made in this context, but was immediately met with much criticism from Muslims in both India and Pakistan; he was obliged to claim that he had been 'misquoted' and to clarify what he meant: 'While Pakistan would not refuse shelter to any Muslim settler, it must refuse in any way to facilitate abandonment by Muslims of their homes and properties in India outside East Punjab.' He also stated that Pakistan would resist any attempt on India's part to 'create conditions' leading to the mass exodus of Muslims other than from East Punjab.[30] Clearly, the Pakistan government was apprehensive about accepting more refugees from India, yet, given that Pakistan had been created as a homeland for the Muslims of South Asia, it could not refuse them entry.

Refugees from East Punjab preferred to resettle in West Punjab, and the common language and culture enabled them to do so with relatively greater ease. The West Punjab government, under the impression that it could not accommodate additional refugees from outside Punjab, sent these refugees further south to Sindh.[31] Consequently, by the end of 1947, the Sindh government also found it difficult to accommodate and provide relief to the large numbers of non-Punjabi refugees that were still arriving in Sindh. In early January 1948, the Pakistan central government requested Sindh to accept two hundred thousand more refugees. When Mohammed Ayub Khuhro, then the premier of Sindh, agreed to accept only one hundred thousand, not only did it create a controversy between the central and provincial governments, but it also sparked resentment among the Muhajirs who felt that the Sindh provincial government was being parochial and inhospitable, not to mention unappreciative of the sacrifices made by Muhajirs to achieve the creation of Pakistan.[32]

Initial causes of conflict between Muhajirs and Sindhis

One of the most significant aspects of the Muhajir immigration into, and subsequent conflicts in, Sindh was the quantum of the demographics involved. By the end of May 1948, seven hundred thousand Muhajirs had arrived in Sindh;[33] this number would eventually climb to three million.[34] The sheer number of migrants overwhelmed the Sindh government and deterred it from accepting more Muhajirs. This in turn created much resentment not only in the upper echelons of the Pakistan central government, staffed mostly by Muhajirs, but also among the general Muhajir public.

There were several other causes contributing to the gulf between Sindhi Muslims and Muhajirs. Firstly, in its attempt to maintain law and order in Sindh, and to encourage Sindhi Hindus to remain in the province in a bid to prop up Sindh's economy, the Sindh government had moved harshly against Muhajirs who had forcibly occupied Hindu property, or had participated in the Hyderabad and Karachi pogroms of December 1947 and January 1948, respectively. Muhajirs found breaking the law were arrested, and sometimes even flogged. This went down rather poorly with the Muhajirs, including with Prime Minister Liaquat Ali Khan who supposedly reprimanded Khuhro privately: 'What sort of Muslim are you that you protect Hindus here when Muslims are being killed in India. Aren't you ashamed of yourself? You have even killed some Muslims [in the police firing during the Karachi pogrom].'[35]

Secondly, after the emigration of the Sindhi Hindus, Sindhi Muslims had expected to takeover their landed property. Indeed, a considerable portion of the property owned by Hindus in Sindh had been obtained by them due to foreclosures on mortgages held by Sindhi Muslims. However the Sindh government treated this property as evacuee property and used it to accommodate incoming refugees (as it was in India too). Evacuee property was seen as a crucial element in refugee rehabilitation. The competition for real estate created much conflict and resentment between Muhajirs and Sindhi Muslims.[36]

Sindhi Muslims were also deeply unhappy about other developments. With Karachi as the capital of the new country, and with Sindh as a champion and constituent of the Pakistan movement, Sindhi Muslims had anticipated having a considerable stake in the new Pakistani government. However despite all their efforts, they found that they had negligible representation in the central government which was instead dominated by Muhajirs and Punjabis, leaving Sindhis increasingly sidelined.

A major bone of contention between Sindhis and Muhajirs then became the separation of Karachi from Sindh. Unlike India, Pakistan was burdened with the responsibility of setting up a capital and administrative machinery from scratch. The Sindh provincial government initially bent over backwards in its enthusiasm for nation- and capital-building. It vacated its Assembly building for the Pakistan Constituent Assembly; Government House, the official residence of the governor of Sindh, was vacated for Jinnah. Various other ministers, including Mohammed Ayub Khuhro, then the premier of Sindh, vacated their own homes to accommodate ministers of the new Pakistan government, most of whom had migrated from India. It also managed to swiftly construct several buildings for the use of the central government, while shifting the Sindh government offices to military barracks on the outskirts of the city.

By the end of 1947, with Khuhro and Liaquat Ali Khan at loggerheads over a variety of issues, the central government began calling for Hyderabad to be made the capital of Sindh, and for the separation of Karachi from Sindh for administrative purposes. This was deeply resented by almost all Sindhi Muslims, including Khuhro and most members of the Sind Provincial Muslim League, especially in light of all their efforts and sacrifices to help build Karachi as the new capital. Ultimately, however, the central government succeeded: it had Khuhro dismissed on charges of corruption and maladministration, and then got his successor, Pir Ilahi Baksh, to accede to the separation of Karachi. The rifts between the Sindh government and the Muhajir-dominated Pakistan central government were mirrored in rifts between the Sindhi Muslim public and the Muhajir public.

Cultural differences between Sindhis and Muhajirs

Because Pakistan was founded as the homeland of the Muslims of South Asia, religious concepts and ideals played a significant role in the early years of the nation. Although the term 'Muhajir,' with its references to the Prophet Muhammad and his flight to Medina, initially inspired a sense of religious hospitality among would-be *ansaar* communities in Pakistan, the construction of Pakistan as a Muslim homeland had other, long-term ramifications.

Given the deterioration in communal relations in the period surrounding Partition, and given that Pakistan was supposedly intended for Muslims, Pakistan's minorities – mainly Hindus and Sikhs – migrated or were driven out very soon after its creation. Consequently, in a virtually homogenous Muslim society, there was hardly any competition for jobs and resources between Muslims and non-Muslims.[37] However as various groups of citizens competed for jobs and resources in a nation that was still in the process of building itself, ethnic identity came to the fore. In Pakistan, ethnic identity has been of greater significance than in India because there are so few ethnicities, and two ethnic/political groupings – Punjabis and Muhajirs[38] – have had a history of socio-economic domination of the other groups.

As a religious minority in India, Muhajirs had been keenly aware of their Muslim identity in the years leading up to Partition. Now in Pakistan, where 98 per cent of the population was Muslim, Muhajirs stressed their pan-Pakistani identity. They decried 'narrow-minded' provincialism, especially on the part of the Sindhis, as being detrimental to the important task of nation-building. Perhaps the Muhajirs had naively expected ethnicity to cease to matter, and that only a pan-Pakistani identity would prevail across the nation.

However, in this clash of cultures between Muhajirs and local populations, especially in Sindh, Muhajirs perceived themselves as superior to Sindhis for at least three reasons. Firstly, since the groundswell of support for the Pakistan movement had mostly emerged from those provinces in India where Muslims were in a minority – i.e. the original homes of the Muhajirs – they saw themselves as the original creators of Pakistan. Indeed, they perceived themselves as guests who must be welcomed, as well as nation-builders who were there by right, not by invitation. This was buttressed by the fact that there were a significant number of Muhajirs occupying senior posts in the central government, including Jinnah and Liaquat Ali Khan. Secondly, having suffering communal violence and left their homes, properties and towns to migrate to Pakistan, they saw themselves as having made the ultimate 'sacrifice' for Pakistan; accordingly, they felt that they were entitled to special status and treatment. Finally, while Muslims from East Punjab shared a language and culture with Muslims from West Punjab, most Muhajirs believed that their language – Urdu – and their mostly urban culture was vastly superior to any other in Pakistan.[39] Many urban Muhajirs were unable to appreciate Sindhi culture, which they viewed as rustic and backward.

Moreover, most Muhajirs believed in a more scriptural form of Islam as compared to Sindh, where Islam was strongly influenced by Sufism. Although Sufism was also widespread in United Provinces and other parts of India, its practice in Sindh was quite different, in the sense that it was linked to specifically local Sufi saints and their tombs, and Sufi music was sung in the Sindhi language accompanied by Sindhi musical instruments. Sindh possessed its own distinctive culture of Sufi *pirs*, which although similar to that of Punjab, was quite different from other parts of India. Consequently, Muhajirs tended to look down on Islam as practised by Sindhi Muslims, believing it to be a 'Hinduised' version of Islam.

For their part, Sindhi Muslims had had a history of awareness of domination by outsiders. This awareness had preceded Partition and the arrival of the Muhajirs in Sindh, but it became particularly sharpened after 1932 following the completion of the Sukkur Barrage on the Indus, when thousands of acres of newly irrigated land were distributed by the colonial administration to peasants from Punjab, instead of to local Sindhis. As well the considerable number of Punjabi Muslims in the Sindh provincial civil service, who often gave preferential treatment to their fellow Punjabis, had already engendered resentment on the part of the Sindhi Muslims even before the creation of Pakistan. Wary of being dominated, Sindhi Muslims now found that one urban elite (the Sindhi Hindus) had been replaced by another (the Muhajirs). This and the other causes mentioned earlier only deepened the Sindhi Muslim hostility and resentment towards the Muhajirs.

Muhajir response

Although initially the Pakistan government had clashed with the Sindh government over accepting more refugees, ultimately the continuing influx of large numbers of Muslim refugees from India brought about a change in the central government's position. It too sought to stem the torrent of Muhajirs that continued to enter Pakistan in the late 1940s. Trying to regulate the refugee influx, the government instituted a permit system in 1948, followed by the introduction of passports in 1952.[40] This changed government stance also led to the Nehru-Liaquat Pact of 1950, which sought to reassure minorities of equality of citizenship and of opportunity in public life, as well as freedom of cross-border movement in a bid to reduce refugee inflows.

In the first decade after Partition, Muhajirs dominated the central government, and because they were the majority in the major cities of Sindh, they also dominated Sindh's urban life. However General Ayub Khan's 1958 coup brought about a rise in the power of the military, and the diminishment of the Muhajirs' power and status, which was intensified 2 years later with the shift of the federal capital (and its accompanying jobs) from Karachi to Islamabad. In the 1970s, language riots between Sindhis and Muhajirs (after the imposition of Sindhi as the sole official language of Sindh), and the institution of a quota system for government jobs, further sharpened the Muhajirs' sense of being discriminated against. Unrest was particularly high among Muhajir students, and the founding of the All Pakistan Muhajir Students' Organisation by Altaf Hussain and his associates in 1978 paved the way for his subsequent founding of the Muhajir Qaumi Movement (MQM) in 1984. Although the MQM subsequently split into three factions, and later changed its name to 'Muttahida' in a bid to garner support from non-Muhajir Pakistanis, the rallying of Muhajirs under this political banner only contributed to the sharpening and politicising of the divide between Sindhi Muslims and Muhajirs.

In recent years, both Muhajirs and Sindhi Muslims have come to the belated realisation that neither community can be wished away, and limited efforts have been made to arrive at a rapprochement. Simultaneously, there has been a recognition that it is the Punjabis who truly dominate Pakistan today at the cost of the other ethnic groups. However, conflict and resentment between Muhajirs and Sindhi Muslims still continue.

Conclusion

Sindhi Hindus in India and Muhajirs in Pakistan were both groups of refugees that were initially welcomed in their adoptive countries, but later faced resentment and hostility from both the state and the local populations. Unlike Bengali and Punjabi refugees, neither of these groups had a claim to a province or state in their adoptive countries. The prevailing culture in both groups of refugees possessed or identified with its own distinctive language (Sindhi or Urdu) and culture, but neither group looked back to the land where they had come from, where their language and culture had originated. However, Sindhi Hindus and Muhajirs were almost diametrically opposite in their strategies of resettling and identity formation in their lands of migration.

In the case of the Sindhi Hindus, many perceived themselves to be on the periphery of Sanskritised Hindu culture and so chose to adapt to more dominant local cultures. They also chose to shift towards the Hindu Right in order to gain a degree of acceptance from local communities. Since they were few in number compared to their host populations, they were greatly influenced by the host cultures, and so felt more compelled to make efforts to adapt. Over the decades, they have succeeded admirably in rehabilitating themselves socio-economically, as well as having attained a relatively conflict-free relationship with local communities. But there has been a cost: Sindhi language and culture are on the decline in India, while Sindhi Hindu ethnic identity has narrowed.

Muhajirs, on the other hand, arrived in Sindh believing that their language and culture were superior to those of the Sindhi Muslims. Given their vast numbers, few Muhajirs considered adapting to the local culture or assimilating into the local population. Their sense of cultural superiority, combined with their sense of entitlement as 'creators' of Pakistan, combined with a sense of being discriminated against, have brought about a marked degree of alienation from other ethnic groups in Pakistan. While many Muhajirs have succeeded in rehabilitating themselves socio-economically, they continue to construct themselves as a community of migrants – even subsequent generations who were born in Pakistan – without necessarily referring to their province or country of origin. Given that Pakistan has only a small number of ethnic groups, Muhajir identity has strengthened over the decades, especially with the formation of the MQM in 1984. This strong sense of identity has, however, come at a steep cost: the Muhajirs have experienced tremendous conflict, mainly with the local Sindhis, but also with other ethnic groups such as the Pathans in Karachi. We can see that a sense of belonging to an inferior culture – as happened with the Sindhi Hindus – encouraged the process of cultural adaptation, and so diluted Sindhi Hindu identity. Conversely, a sense of cultural superiority greatly reinforced Muhajir identity, and inhibited cultural adaptation to local cultures, and subsequently contributed to decades of severe conflict.

It is no coincidence that Sindhi Hindus felt inferior when faced with Sanskritised Hindu culture and Muhajirs felt that their Urdu-dominated urban culture was superior to Sindhi rustic culture with its emphasis on 'little traditions,' given that Sindhis were a predominantly rural community. For both Hindus and Muslims, the evolution of Sindhi culture over the centuries was more syncretic than scriptural. For both religious communities, Sindh was distant from their centres of religious orthodoxy. Moreover, it was a region marked by a high degree of fluidity, engendered by trade and invasion which encouraged syncretism and Sufism and discouraged orthodoxy. Thus, it is not surprising that Sindhis were looked down upon by adherents of mainstream scriptural religious ideologies, both Hindu and Muslim, in India as well as in Pakistan. In India, Sindhi Hindus have internalised this sense of inferiority and have reacted by moving more to the Hindu Right. In Pakistan, since contempt for Sindhi culture is coupled with the socio-economic domination of Sindhis by Punjabis and Muhajirs, it has only fuelled Sindhi Muslim anger and has helped to foster Sindhi Muslim nationalism and identity.

The unwillingness on the part of the Indian and Pakistani governments to accept additional numbers of refugees remains. The migration of Sindhi Hindus has continued – albeit in fewer numbers – from Partition to the present. However Sindhi Hindus who migrate to India today have great difficulty in obtaining Indian citizenship, a process that often takes several years to complete and leaves the individuals concerned devoid of citizenship, where they are unable to leave India until they become Indian citizens and obtain passports. As demonstrated by the ongoing conflict between Muhajirs and Sindhi Muslims, the reverberations of Partition continue even today.

Notes

1 This paper was published as 'Unwanted Refugees: Sindhi Hindus in India and Muhajirs in Sindh,' in *South Asia: Journal of South Asian Studies*, Vol. 39, no. 4, Dec. 2016, pp. 790–804. The editor acknowledges the editor of the journal and publisher Routledge, Tylor & Francis group for giving permission to re-publish the paper in this edited book. The link is www.tandfonline.com/doi/full/10.1080/00856401.2016.1230691

2 There are various works describing conflicts between Partition refugees and local governments and communities. For the experience of the Muhajirs in Sindh, see Ansari, Sarah (2005) *Life after Partition: Community and Strife in Sindh 1947–1962*. Karachi: Oxford University Press, pp. 60–68, 86–95, 132–138; Zamindar, Vazira Fazila-Yacoobali (2007) *The Long Partition and the Making of Modern South Asia: Refugees, Boundaries, Histories*. New Delhi: Viking, pp. 54–55, 60–67; Raza, Syed Hashim (1991) *Hamari Manzil*. Karachi: Mustafain and Murtazain, pp. 110, 117. For that of Bengali Hindus in India, see Yong, Tan Tai and Gyanesh Kudaisya (2000) *The Aftermath of Partition in South Asia*. London/New York: Routledge, p. 150; Chatterji, Joya (2007) *The Spoils of Partition: India and Bengal, 1947–1967*. Cambridge: Cambridge University Press, pp. 124–141, *passim*. The

case of West Bengal was complicated by the fact that there were significant cultural differences between the East Bengali refugees (Bangals) and the native West Bengalis (Ghotis). For that of Punjabi Hindus and Sikhs in India, see Saksena, R.N. (1961) *Refugees: A Study in Changing Attitudes*. Bombay: Asia Publishing House, pp. 23–24; Kidwai, Anis (2011) (trans. Ayesha Kidwai) *In Freedom's Shade*. New Delhi: Penguin, *passim*. For the experience of Sindhi Hindu refugees in India, see Bhavnani, Nandita (2014), *The Making of Exile: Sindhi Hindus and the partition of India*. New Delhi: Westland Tranquebar, pp. 170–173, 199, 225–235, 249, 287–289; Kothari, Rita (2007) *The Burden of Refuge: The Sindhi Hindus of Gujarat*. Hyderabad: Orient Longman, pp. 116, 124, 130–131, 147–161; Anand, Subhadra (1996) *National Integration of Sindhis*. New Delhi: Vikas, pp. 71–72, 78, 83–88, 93; and Barnouw, Victor (1954) 'The Social Structure of a Sindhi Refugee Community,' in *Social Forces*, Vol. 33, no. 2, Dec., pp. 142–152.

3 Khan, Yasmin (2007) *The Great Partition*. New Haven/London: Yale University Press, pp. 3–5.

4 Although there had been severe communal violence in Bengal, most notably in Kolkata, Noakhali and Tippera in 1946, the province subsequently remained relatively free of physical violence until 1949–1950, when there were renewed bouts of communal violence in Khulna, Jessore, Barisal and Faridpur. See Joya Chatterji (2007) *The Spoils of Partition: India and Bengal, 1947–1967*. Cambridge: Cambridge University Press, p. 118.

5 Interviews took place in Mumbai, Ulhasnagar, Pune, Ajmer and Gandhidham, India; UAE; and Sindh, Pakistan, between 1997 and 2014. For example, in 1948 Morarji Desai, then the home minister of Bombay Province, reportedly told Sindhi refugees: 'You Sindhi Hindus have no reason to leave your homeland and come as refugees [to] India. We have full assurances [from] Jinnah that the minorities will be well treated in Sindh. There may have been provocations but you should have had the courage to resist these attacks. You must all go back. There is no place for you here.' See Bhavnani, Nandita (2011) *I Will & I Can: The Story of Jai Hind College*. New Delhi: Roli, pp. 18–19.

6 Speech by Gandhi at a prayer meeting on 9 December 1947, as quoted in Jotwani, Motilal (ed.) (1998) *Gandhiji on Sindh and the Sindhis*. New Delhi: Sindhi Academy, p. 536.

7 See Guha, Ramachandra (2007) *India after Gandhi: The History of the World's Largest Democracy*. London: Picador, p. 94.

8 See Saksena, *Refugees: A Study in Changing Attitudes*; and Kidwai, *In Freedom's Shade*.

9 Khan, *The Great Partition*, p. 169.

10 According to the 1941 census, there were approximately 32,627 Sikhs in Sindh. See Lambrick, Hugh Trevor (1942) *The Census of India, 1941, Volume XII, Sind*. New Delhi: Manager of Publications, pp. 25–26. It is unlikely that this number would have been substantially different in 1947.

11 According to the 1941 census, Christians, Jains, Parsis, Buddhists, Jews and Scheduled Tribes amounted to approximately 66,623 persons. *Ibid*.

12 There had been only one incident, near the central town of Nawabshah, when a train carrying Hindus and Sikhs travelling to India was attacked. Between 15 and 20 Sikhs were killed and about 17 were injured. See Bhavnani, *The Making of Exile*, p. 30.
13 *The Times of India* (Bombay) (19 Jan. 1948 and 28 Feb. 1948).
14 *Free Press Journal* (Bombay) (2 Oct. 1947), p. 3.
15 Bhavnani, *The Making of Exile*, pp. 226–228.
16 According to Willem van Schendel, the nationalist framework of the historiographies of both India and Pakistan produced a homecoming narrative in which 'immigrants . . . were seen as sons and daughters of the nation coming home. . . . They were citizens [of the nation across the border] by proxy and their trek across the boundary line – the spatial delimitation of the nation – was a homecoming.' Schendel, Willem van (2005), *The Bengal Borderland: Beyond State and Nation in South Asia*. London: Anthem Press, p. 193. This homecoming narrative was undoubtedly very strong in the case of the Muhajirs, since they believed that Pakistan had been created as a homeland for the Muslims of South Asia, but it was equally strong among Hindus and Sikhs migrating from Pakistan, who believed that they had no place in Pakistan for the exact same reason, and who had also identified with India before Independence.
17 Bhavnani, *The Making of Exile*, pp. 231–235.
18 *Ibid*. The Bombay Refugees Act, 1948, was a piece of legislation designed to enable the government of Bombay Province to 'regulate' the movement of refugees. It became compulsory for Partition refugees to register at registration centres. The Bombay Refugees Act also gave the Bombay government the right to control the location of residence, and movement, of refugees. It was struck down in 1952.
19 This consisted of loose pants and a short tunic, known as *suthan-cholo*, worn with a small waistcoat and a *dupatta* (scarf).
20 Balasubrahmanyan, Suchitra (2011) 'Partition and Gujarat: The Tangled Web of Religion, Caste, Community and Gender Identities,' in *South Asia: Journal of South Asian Studies*, Vol. 34, no. 3, pp. 460–484.
21 Kothari, *The Burden of Refuge: The Sindhi Hindus of Gujarat*, p. 116. Also see the narratives of Javhar Advani and Sundri Uttamchandani, as quoted in Jagtiani, Lata (2006) *Sindhi Reflections: 140 Lives and the Indian Partition*. Mumbai: Jharna Books, pp. 430, 154–155.
22 Some Sindhi Hindus protested against the change of the Sindhi script from Perso-Arabic to Devanagari, which had been put into effect by a small number of Sindhis, mainly from the Congress. This controversy resulted in the recognition of both scripts as official in 1951, but unfortunately this in turn gave rise to a great deal of confusion, and only contributed to the decline of the language.
23 See Bhavnani, *The Making of Exile*, pp. 258–260.
24 When the Prophet Muhammad left Mecca and journeyed to Medina in AD 622, his journey became known as the *hijrat*. Those followers who accompanied him were known as *muhajirs*, while the people of Medina who welcomed and helped them were known as *ansaars*.
25 *The Times of India* (Bombay) (2 July 1947).

26 *The Times of India* (Bombay) (14 Sept. 1947).
27 *The Times of India* (Bombay) (15 Sept. 1947).
28 Das, Suranjan (2001) *Kashmir & Sindh: Nation-Building, Ethnicity and Regional Politics in South Asia*. London: Anthem Press, p. 105; and Ahmed, Feroz (1989) 'The Rise of Muhajir Separatism in Pakistan,' in *Journal of Asian and African Affairs*, Vol. 1, no. 2, Dec., pp. 97–129.
29 *The Times of India* (Bombay) (12 Oct. 1947).
30 Liaquat Ali Khan, quoted in *The Times of India* (Bombay) (15 Oct. 1947).
31 Zamindar, *The Long Partition and the Making of Modern South Asia*, p. 68.
32 *Dawn* (Karachi) (24 Jan. 1948), p. 1.
33 Ansari, *Life after Partition*, p. 64.
34 Das, *Kashmir & Sindh*, p. 105.
35 Khuro, Hamida (1998) *Mohammed Ayub Khuhro: A Life of Courage in Politics*. Lahore: Ferozsons, p. 327.
36 It should also be remembered that there was simultaneously competition and conflict between Muhajirs, and similarly between Sindhis, especially between landlords and peasants, for evacuee property. See Bhavnani, *The Making of Exile*, pp. 330–334.
37 However, it is also important to note that religious schisms amongst Muslims came to the fore, with Ahmadiyyas being legally deemed heretics, and the Shia – Sunni conflict on the boil in various parts of Pakistan, even today.
38 It is worth remembering that Muhajirs came from different parts of India, and so had varied ethnicities and languages. Their perception of themselves as a marginalised refugee community led them (especially non-Punjabis in Sindh) to coalesce as a political group in 1984, but this was a process that took several decades.
39 This sentiment helped to give rise to the Bengali language movement and ultimately contributed significantly to the creation of Bangladesh.
40 See Haimanti Roy (2016) 'Paper Rights: The Emergence of Documentary Identities in Post-Colonial India, 1950–67,' in *South Asia: Journal of South Asian Studies*, Vol. 39, no. 2, June, pp. 329–349.

Chapter 9

1950 riots and fractured social spaces

Minority displacement and dispossession in Calcutta and its neighbouring areas[1]

Subhasri Ghosh

In the annals of 1947 Partition historiography, communal riots occupy a pivotal position. On the Bengal side, the corpus of works (Pravas Chandra Lahiri, *Pak Bharater Ruprekha;* Tathagata Roy, *My People, Uprooted: A Saga of Hindus of Eastern Bengal;* Prafulla K. Chakrabarti, *The Marginal Men: The Refugees and Left Political Syndrome in West Bengal*; Dinesh Chandra Sinha, *1950: Raktaranjito Dhaka, Barisal Ebong;* Sandip Bandyopadhyay, *Itihaasher Dikey Firey: Chhechollisher Danga*) essentially focuses on how the mayhem triggered by the 1946 Great Calcutta Killing spurred a whole train of communal frenzy in eastern India prior to independence and how the 'riots, which preceded partition gradually petered out after the Proclamation of Independence.'[2] As Suranjan Das contends, 'While other regions of India continued to be struck by periodic bouts of Hindu-Muslim violence, West Bengal remained relatively free of the communal virus.'[3] However, such statements deny the historical truth.

To negate such argument, this chapter attempts to explore a somewhat 'sporadic localised' riots in Calcutta and its twin city across the river – Howrah – in February–March 1950. The aim is not only to show that West Bengal was not 'free of the communal virus' but also to analyse what sparked the riots and their hidden implications. In comparison to tomes of literature on the Hindu migrants thronging eastern India, scholarly work on the plight of the Muslim minorities is surprisingly thin. It is left to the erudition of scholars like Joya Chatterji[4], Sekhar Bandyopadhyay[5] and Anwesha Sengupta[6], who have highlighted the predilection of the Muslims in the newly independent and newly carved out state of West Bengal. Belonging to the same genre, this study throws light on the pivotal role played by the riot of 1950, which fractured the urban social space of Calcutta beyond repair. Culling information from personal memoirs, newspaper reports and government records, the chapter brings to the fore the broad implication lurking behind this communal violence and contextualises the issue in the larger framework of the rehabilitation policy of the West Bengal government, saddled with an unending stream of refugees from across the border.

The backdrop

As the clock struck midnight on 14 August 1947, India began her tryst with destiny after shedding almost 200 years of colonial yoke. She awoke to a new dawn – a dawn of freedom. Frenzied enthusiasm was witnessed throughout the country. But at the same time 'it was the best of times, it was the worst of times . . . it was the season of light, it was the season of darkness.' It was also a time of mourning for thousands who could not partake in the joys of independence and freedom. The other side of Independence, was Partition – the creation of two nation-states, India and Pakistan. For many, freedom thus came with a price – a heavy price of losing one's homeland, being torn asunder from the natal setup for good, to lose near and dear ones. The actual announcement of the Partition plan was put on hold until 17 August, keeping the people of the border areas on tenterhooks. Mountbatten's logic was, 'it had been obvious all along that the later we postponed publication (of the new border), the less would the inevitable odium react upon the British,' thus leaving the two nascent states to bear the brunt of Partition. As streams of minorities, that is the Hindus and Sikhs, trekked across the border to find refuge amongst their fellow brethren, the government struggled to cope with the crisis of unending influx.

Migration patterns in the eastern and the northern sectors of India followed different trajectories. While northern India was somewhat blessed with an exchange of population in the sense that an immigration of 4.9 million from West Punjab and the adjoining areas in Pakistan, was matched by an outflow of 5.5 million from East Punjab and the adjoining areas in India; in the Bengal case the movement was essentially unidirectional, the tide of migration flowing from the Pakistan province of East Bengal (East Pakistan from 1956 and Bangladesh from 1971) to West Bengal.[7] No accurate estimate of the exact magnitude of migration exists, since

Table 9.1 Quantum of Migration in West Bengal from 1947 to 1950

Period	*Number of Fresh Arrivals*
1947	4,63,474
1948	4,90,555
1949	3,26,211
1950	11,72,928

Source: Committee for Review of Rehabilitation Work in West Bengal; Report of the Working Group on the Residual Problem of Rehabilitation in West Bengal

there was no exactly defined period of migration, as people started migrating to India even before Partition was actually effected and continued to do so for many years after 1947. The official norms that apply to a 'border' took some time to come into operation in the case of East and West Bengal. Parliamentary debates show that as late as September 1950 (i.e. 3 years after Independence and Partition) finality could not be reached with respect to boundary demarcation. Hence, the boundary line being fluid, it was difficult to keep track of migration. Moreover, many refugees crossed on foot at countless unmanned points. Thus rigorous accounts of those crossing over could not always be maintained.

As per government estimate, the quantum of migration, in the period of study, was to the extent shown in Table 9.1.

As can be gauged, 1950 was the single-most significant year in terms of migration. The Barisal riots of February 1950 opened the floodgates of of migratory influx.

The riots

Gory details of East Bengal riots abound in the form of memoirs and testimonies of the Hindu migrants. But while East Bengal was burning, West Bengal, too, did not remain immune from communal flare-ups. However, the nature of violence varied in the sense that while large parts of East Bengal was up in flames with butchering, physical assaults and torching of houses, the situation in West Bengal was, on a comparative scale, more localised and sporadic with specific pockets being affected. Thus, while East Bengal was being engulfed by sectarian fire, West Bengal, on the face of it, remained peaceful. But beneath this façade of apparent peace lurked sinister designs. The

Varshney-Wilkinson data set comes up with a statistics of eight riots for the year 1950 in West Bengal.[8] The scourge that engulfed Calcutta and Howrah from the beginning of 1950 was one of the most potent of these and thus merits meticulous study. Detailed reports of the riots in Calcutta and the suburbs are difficult to come by, with the government gagging press reportage with prohibitory orders 'not to publish records of events which are likely to excite people and submit them to Government for censorship. . . .'[9] Only the official briefings were to be reported on a daily basis and no independent investigations were to be carried out. What can be pieced together is that on 8 and 9 February 1950 processions with incriminating slogans were carried out in 'certain areas, exciting people to violence.'[10] This prompted the government to promulgate Section 144 Cr. Pc throughout Calcutta, banning all processions and meetings. A curfew was imposed in certain sensitive pockets and the military was summoned to patrol those areas. Under special surveillance was the Maniktala area where a dusk-to-dawn curfew from 6 PM to 6 AM was imposed. But that such measures were not adequate enough to quell the tension was evident from the subsequent government reports. The northern part of the city was in flames on the midnight of 9–10 February with 24 persons receiving injuries, towhich two later succumbed. The tension did not subside – 56 persons were injured on February 10 itself, with one receiving fatal wounds. The deserted shops and slums were set on fire. The radius of violence spread with the areas adjacent to Maniktala, namely Beliaghata and Amherst Street being engulfed by the communal fire. In view of the mounting tension, fresh areas were brought under the purview of a dusk-to-dawn curfew: under Maniktala and Beliaghata police stations, the area bounded by Ultadanga Main Road on the north, Gas Street on the south, the railway bridge on the east and Upper Circular Road on the west, and under the Amherst Street police station, the area encompassing Keshub Sen Street on the north, Mirzapur Street on the south, Upper Circular Road on the east and Amherst Street on the west. The situation seemed to have improved by 11 February, though as a precautionary measure curfew continued to be imposed between 9 AM and 6 PM until 14 February. Though as per the official communiqué no fresh incidents of violence were reported, the 9 AM to 6 PM curfew continued to be imposed on 16 and 17 February. By 18 February, curfew was lifted from all areas in Calcutta.

Fresh outbreaks were again reported from the night of 6 March. Troubles were reported from Panbagan Bustee on Ismail Street under the Entally police station in central Calcutta which continued unabated until 8 March. The ground was prepared when on 4 March, two live bombs were found in the mosque, adjacent to the bustee. Scared, the panicked residents fled the area, only to return on the morning of 6 March, when they came to be attacked in a more concerted manner. The area remained out of bounds for two days. The bustee was completely ravaged – there were blood stains and bullet marks on the wall. Two persons (Muslims) were reported missing, according to the police.[11]

Calcutta's sister city Howrah, too, did not remain immune from the communal violence. Although the chief minister declared in the Assembly as early as 9 February, when trouble first broke out in Calcutta, that they were 'also watching events in Howrah district, particularly Howrah town' that preventive measures failed to dampen the raging fire of communalism is evident from the fact that Howrah was literally drawn into the flames when a slum in Bellillious Road and a shop in Panchanantala Road were set on fire on 12 February. Asok Mitra felt that the crisis did not come as a total surprise: 'The warnings have been gaining intensity for five months.'[12] Bombs and crackers were seized by the police from several areas of the town. The press note of 12 February painted a grim picture: 'There have been a few more cases of arson in Howrah . . . section 144 has been imposed and curfew has been ordered . . . there have been five casualties.'[13] Curfew was declared in Golabari and Malipanchghora areas in Howrah town on 14 February. Peace prevailed, but that it was an uneasy one and that the town was sitting on a tinderbox became evident when the situation flared up to such an extent that the army was called in on 27 March to aid the civil administration in maintaining law and order. This was necessitated when, on 24 March, Hindus and Muslims, both wielding crude, home-made guns, clashed in Howrah town, leading to the death of a few Muslims.[14] Pitched battles were fought on Panchanantala, Sadar Bakshi Lane, Beniapara, Sibpore, Pilkhana and Lillooah.[15] The jute belt along the bank of the river Hooghly was the worst affected. The then Additional District Magistrate of Howrah Asok Mitra recounts that on 24 March a few Muslims were killed. The situation worsened to reach its peak on 25–26 March when around 16 Muslims were killed, following which the military was summoned to control the situation on 28 March. On 26 March, a mob of around three to four hundred attacked a Muslim bustee at Malipanchghora. Between the evening of 27 March and the early morning of 30 March, from the lanes and bylanes of Ghusuri locality of the town, the mutilated bodies of around 60 Muslims were recovered by the district administration. Taya Zinkin, a noted British journalist, pens a spine-chilling account of the bestiality of the carnage:

> the bodies were sprawling . . . the wounds on those corpses were terrible – huge gashes cut into red flesh gaping out of brown skins and blood caked all over the ground. Women, young and old, children, men, infants . . . The dead were mixed up with the living. In front of me a woman squatted, immobile. She had lost an arm, severed from the shoulder which dipped from a huge blood clot. On her lap lay an infant cut into two at the waist. But she the mother was alive. Shivers ran through her mutilated torso as she stared into space . . . we found some 20 survivors amidst 342 dead, in a street barely 300 feet long.[16]

The town was taken over by the military and martial law was promulgated in the police stations of Sibpore, Bantra, Bally and portions of Howrah GRP station. The government press note of 27 March noted with regret, 'In spite of the police and military opening fire in many places in Howrah area, the disturbances have not been brought under control and tension persists. It has been found necessary to hand over the disturbed section of Howrah town to the military to be administered under martial law.'[17] The situation calmed down by 30 March with no further reports of casualties.[18] After a lull of a few days when no major incidents were reported, a few cases of arson took place on 3 April in two villages within the jurisdication of the Amta and Bagnan police stations of the district.[19] The worst-affected area in this phase was Amta, especially the village of Basantapur. Most of the Muslim houses were completely burnt or destroyed and the displaced and uprooted Muslims took shelter in the neighbouring villages of Munshirhat and Jalalshi.[20]

Post-mortem and analysis

Such events were termed in the government discourse 'sporadic outbreaks of violent activities.'[21] What actually caused the riots and who were the culprits responsible? From the government end, various agencies were blamed. In his budget speech on the floor of the Legislative Assembly, Prafulla Chandra Sen put the onus on the restless spirit of the migrants, asserting that the 'vast refugee population floating despairingly mostly in urban areas provide the delicate fuse of explosion.'[22] The Premier Dr Bidhan Chandra Roy was eloquent on the role of the communal situation in East Bengal and the incendiary role of organisations like the Hindu Mahasabha, being directly responsible. The timing of the outbreak in Calcutta and Howrah, coinciding with the riot in East Bengal, led to the linear cause and effect explanation where minority persecution on one side mirrored that of the other.

As per the reports available, violence broke out in Dacca on Friday, 10 February 1950, after the Jumma Namaz. On 12 February, a crowd of Hindu passengers was attacked at the Karimtolla airport near Dacca by an armed mob and a large number of boarding passengers, including women and children, were killed or seriously wounded. This tragedy took place within a stone's throw of the Karimtolla military headquarters and in the presence of Pakistan armed guards.[23]

Reports of massacres flooded in from other parts of East Bengal. In Mymensingh, trains to and from Comilla and Chittagong were stopped on a railway bridge – the Anderson Bridge on the river Meghna. Hindus were singled out from among the passengers and hacked to death in cold blood. Their bodies were thrown into the Meghna. In the Santahar Station in Rajshahi, a similar gory drama was enacted. Large-scale violence against the Hindus was reported from Bianibazar and Barlekh police station of Sylhet district, Putia in Rajshahi, Bhandaria in Barisal, Bagerhat in Khulna, Kalashkathi in Barisal, Nachole in Rajshahi, Habibganj in Sylhet, Comilla in Tipperah and Feni in Noakhali. Perhaps the worst-affected was the district of Barisal. As per the estimate of Mr. Mandal, the casualty list touched nearly 2,500.[24] Total causalities in the East Bengal riots were estimated in the neighbourhood of 10,000 killed.[25] Sukumar Mukhopadhyay of Rajpur village, Barisal, lost his uncle and niece, along with nine others of the neighbouring family. In his own words: 'My uncle was burnt to death, while my niece and the neighbours were mercilessly slaughtered and the severed heads placed on each step of the staircase. . . .'[26]

Parallels can be drawn since specific areas in Calcutta erupted in flames from 10 February – the same day as that of Dacca. No less significant were the role of organisations like the Hindu Mahasabha, R.S.S. and East Bengal Minorities Protection Board. Sekhar

Bandyopadhyay's study explicates the complex role played by the Hindu Mahasabha.[27] While the Mahasabha General Secretary Ashutosh Lahiry spewed venom on the minorities in his speeches, the party, following the backlash it faced after the assassination of Mahatma Gandhi, decided to, as Bandyopadhyay shows, withdraw from active politics and concentrate primarily on philanthropy. But covertly, it carried on its agenda of mobilising the anti-Muslim stand.[28] R.S.S. chief M.S. Golwalkar visited Calcutta on 15 and 16 February 1950 and distributed inflammatory leaflets and handbills urging 'Blood for Blood.' He also held a closed door meeting at Digambar Jain Hall in Burra Bazar.[29] The Bengal chapter of the Hindu Mahasabha held its meeting on 2 March at Bowbazar Street, where after a four-hour prolonged debate, not only was the 'appalling situation in East Bengal' condemned in the harshest words, but also a resolution was adopted whereby the wholesale transfer of Hindu population from East Bengal was demanded and to this end a Council of Action was created consisting of Mahasabha leaders, namely Ashutosh Lahiry, Narendra Nath Das and Sudhir Kumar Mitra. An ultimatum was issued to Nehru to take heed of their resolution by 7 March, failing which the Mahasabha would create a situation where the central government would be forced to take appropriate action.[30]

Thus incriminatory activities of the Mahasabha and the R.S.S played no less a role in inciting passion. The worst-affected were the pockets under Ward nos. 29, 30 and 31.[31] From the census of 1941, which gives a police stationwise break up of communal composition, if the Muslim majority localities of Calcutta could be identified, it would help us to decipher why specifically these areas fell prey to the frenzy. A distinct pattern emerges if one looks at the demographic contours of the affected areas.

Tables 9.2 and 9.3 identify the areas within the city with significant Muslim population. Understandably, since in any communal tension, it is the minorities who receive the barb, it is commonsense that the Muslim majority areas and areas with sizeable Muslim population of Calcutta would be marked out. The Muslim-dominated pockets situated east of the Circular Road running practically for the entire length of Calcutta from North to South was thus targeted to be purged.

But what went on behind the scenes? Who was to blame for the calamity that befell the minorities in Calcutta and Howrah? Was it solely an expression of refugee ire and the incriminating role

Table 9.2 Muslim Majority Police Stations of Calcutta, 1941

Police Stations	*Total Population 1941*	*Muslim Population 1941*	*Hindu Population 1941*	*Pct of Muslims to Total Population*	*Pct of Hindus to Total Population*
Coloootala	90087	48934	36342	54.31	40.34
Taltala	70143	39367	23934	56.12	34.12
Beniapukur	76462	54609	17517	71.41	22.90
Ekbalpore	58966	34432	22577	58.39	38.28
Kalinga	19348	8506	8154	43.96	42.14

Source: R.A. Dutch, *Census of India, 1941, Volume IV: Bengal* (Delhi, 1942)

Table 9.3 Police Stations of Calcutta with Sizeable Muslim Populations (35% and Above), 1941

Police Stations	*Total Population 1941*	*Muslim Population 1941*	*Hindu Population 1941*	*Pct of Muslims to Total Population*	*Pct of Hindus to Total Population*
Fenwick Bazar	52106	20689	25966	39.70	49.83
Maniktala	86480	32153	54092	37.17	62.54
Canal	1784	838	946	46.97	53.02
Port	31783	12494	17071	39.31	53.71

Source: R.A. Dutch, *Census of India, 1941, Volume IV: Bengal* (Delhi, 1942)

of certain organisations in whipping up communal passion? Was the communal atmosphere, with the scars of 1946 not completely healed, already charged up and the refugees and the Mahasabha took advantage of it? Communal skirmishes in Calcutta post-1947 were not altogether a rarity. In November 1948, a Muharram procession was attacked at Maniktala with brickbats and acid bulbs. Anwesha Sengupta's study reveals that the recently arrived East Bengali migrants vented their pent-up anger by assaulting the processionists.[32] It is true that even in 1950, the refugees, as evident from the depositions before the West Bengal Disturbances Enquiry Commission set as per Part C, Clause VI of the Indo-Pakistan agreement signed between Jawaharlal Nehru and Liaquat Ali Khan on 8 April 1950, were an active component among the trouble-mongers. Deposing before the Commission on 15 June, Serajuddin, a poor Muslim grocer of Dattabagan bustee, under the Paikpara police station, narrated how the coming of the immigrants from across the border vitiated the atmosphere, 'the friendly feelings maintained by their Hindu neighbours had changed for the worse due to the presence of the refugees in the area.'[33] It is these immigrants, according to the deposer, who wreaked havoc in the area.

But after all is said and done, one cannot exonerate the state administration of its obligation to protect minorities and envelope them within the new structure and make them feel at home. The gap between preaching and praxis becomes all the more glaring when one recalls Nehru's letter to the Bengal Premier dated 25 August 1948:

> The fact that a man is a Muslim, does not make him a non-national. He may have evil designs in his heart. If so, as an individual we can deal with him. But to say of a group of Indian nationals that we shall push them out because some people elsewhere are not behaving as they should is something which has no justification in law or equity. It strikes at the root of the secular state that we claim to be. We just can't do it whatever the consequences.[34]

But reality had a different story to narrate. The government's failure to fathom the gravity and consequent inaction and the passivity and sometimes partisan attitude of the keepers of law worsened the situation. On 11 February, Serajuddin's shop was barged into by between four and five hundred Hindu rioters armed with lathis. Forcing him out, the goons ransacked the shop. His home, located nearby, too, was not spared. A desperate Serajuddin ran to the police picket on the main road, reporting the incident. But the policemen refused to intervene, citing the reason that since they were posted on the main road, they had no right to enter into the interiors. The estimated cost of loss, according to Serajuddin, was Rs 10,000.[35] Reports to top-ranking officials and police officers on the worsening of the situation and reports of day-to-day happenings in the city could not be communicated over telephone as the operator, in most cases, curtly replied, 'No connection will be given to you.' Frantic telephone calls to the Lalbazar control room went unanswered.[36] In the case of the Panbagan bustee, the very day when the inhabitants returned to their homes, on the morning of 6 March, the area was raided by a huge police force led by the Assistant Commissioner, Central Calcutta with the consequence that the residents once again fled fearing persecution, leaving the entire area unprotected, giving hooligans a free hand to indulge in looting and plundering.[37] Paradoxically, the administration arrested 109 Muslims from the area for inciting trouble.[38] Kalimuddin Choudhury, a Councillor of the Calcutta Municipal Corporation, testifying before the Enquiry Commission, alleged that on 8 February, after the retaliatory killings of a Hindu boy and a Muslim boy in the Ultadanga area, when the Assistant Commissioner and the Deputy Commissioner visited the spot, 'they did not make any enquiries regarding the killing of the Muslim boy and were busy making enquiries regarding the killing of the Hindu boy.'[39] Sheikh Muhammad Rafiq, an MLA from Calcutta North constituency, blamed police inaction for escalating tension, 'it takes time for the police to arrive. The police arrive not only one or two but sometimes three or four hours after the occurrence.'[40] Often, the junior level or the locally stationed officers were involved in abetting communalist forces. Ms Mridula Sarabhai very eloquently, in the context of the Howrah riots, pointed out,

> Personal experience of the Howrah episode confirmed my doubt . . . the flaring up in the industrial areas was a planned affair abetted by the local authorities. Those who were behind it appeared to be confident of support from the higher quarters. This was substantiated by the Government's action in not taking steps against those . . . the manner in which the officers behaved left no doubt that they were involved in it.[41]

Asok Mitra's account, too, corroborates Sarabhai's conviction. Mitra, too feels, that precautionary proactive measures in Howrah could have quelled the tension: 'The local police might have been more alert by resorting to arrests of those persons who in their records are always marked as "bad characters," who have traditionally made the most of civil disorders.'[42] However, not always could the local administration be blamed for the escalation of tension. They, too, had to work under certain pressing compulsions and were powerless to act independently. The testimony of the Superintendent of Police of Howrah district, in front of the Enquiry Commission, laid bare the brutal truth. While he frantically called Writers' Buildings for additional forces to control the situation, and also asked for permission to open fire, not only was his plea for extra contingent denied, but the S.P. was instructed by Writers' Buildings not to take any action to combat the rioters and 'let things take its own course.'[43] In the context of 1946, Das opines: 'What most clearly distinguishes the 1946 violence from earlier outbreaks was its highly organized nature and direct links with institutional politics.'[44] Of course, it was not to that extent and scale, but the dubious role of the administration in 1950, is hard to ignore.

Thus, ironically, while Prime Minister Jawaharlal Nehru was crying hoarse in the Parliament about the persecution of the minorities in East Bengal, in West Bengal, too, the minorities suffered from insecurity: 'How we feel? We feel insecure, we feel unsafe. We want security, guarantees for protection. . . .'[45] Nehru was categorical, commenting, 'there is no sense of security in the minds of the minority community in East Bengal,'[46] while the government remained oblivious to the plight of a section of its own minorities. On 2 April, a delegation of three Muslim MLAs from West Bengal headed by Syed Badruddoja met the Prime Minister during the latter's visit to Calcutta and urged him to take appropriate steps to curb the menace in Calcutta and the industrial areas of Howrah. Nehru assured them that 'his government was fully alive to the situation and would do everything possible to see that law and order is maintained.'[47] The denial mode of the government becomes all the more evident when on the floor of the West Bengal Legislative Assembly, in the inaugural address of the respected Governor in 1950, the plight of the minorities did not find any reference. Thus, while Nehru exhorted the 'assimilating and absorbing nature of India's glorious and ancient culture'[48] and Dr B.C. Roy declared with conviction on the floor of the Assembly, 'As long as I have anything to do with the West Bengal Government, every citizen will be protected to the best of the Government's ability,'[49] the Muslims in the heart of the city and its neighbouring industrial belt continued to suffer, with the tacit support of the very government that assured them of their safety and security, time and again.

One cannot absolve the government of its role in worsening the situation in Calcutta and Howrah, especially the state government, since as per the newly promulgated Constitution, 'Police' and 'Public Order' are included within the State List. Joya Chatterji opines, in the context of the border areas of West Bengal, 'state authority was thinly spread and deeply compromised and the police gave Muslims little protection.'[50] But if one looks at the heartland of West Bengal, the scenario does not differ much. Protection of minorities often remained rhetoric, confined to lofty statements. When it came to actually reading the situation and acting accordingly, the government attitude was lackadaisical and appropriate action was, in many cases, found to be severely wanting.

The question is what did the government stand to gain from this arson and looting? These 'localised' riots were pregnant with consequences of great depth. At the macro level, the riot, carried out at times with the covert support of the government, was meant to act as a pressure tactic to force the Prime Minister of Pakistan Liaquat Khan to come down to Delhi for peace talks. Moved by the plight of the Muslims at Howrah, Liaquat Khan declared on 29 March that he would reach Delhi on 2 April for peace talks. The very day rioting, stopped. Asok Mitra laments, 'it is a tragedy that in order to bring Liaquat Khan to Delhi, it was necessary to instigate riot in Howrah.'[51] Sarabhai's statement corroborates this: 'On the eve of the Inter-Dominion talks . . . the policy of the Government seemed to have changed overnight . . . everywhere the District Officers were busy provoking the Muslims . . . to migrate to Pakistan.'[52]

At the micro level, the ulterior motive of the state government was to rehabilitate the Hindu migrants by evicting the Muslims and instilling fear psychosis so as to prevent their return for good. The migrants from East Bengal between 1947 and 1950 were essentially what can be termed as 'the middle classes and they generally are from amongst the lawyers, government servants and other such persons.'[53] Calcutta was their preferred destination because of the opportunities it offered in terms of employment – 'we see the scene that while cities like Calcutta have been invaded by a large number of refugees, the rural areas have not been equally invaded. . . .'[54] However, for the nascent state of West Bengal, accommodating this burgeoning stream of migrants proved to be a daunting task. Partition had reduced West Bengal to one-third of its previous size or 36.4 per cent of the area of the parent province, and at the same time saddled it with a huge population.[55] The average density of the city of Calcutta, in 1951 (area 32.33 square miles) was around 88,953 persons per square mile or 139 persons per acre[56] – a whopping increase from 751.2 persons per square mile in undivided Bengal.[57] Given the differing trajectory of migration in the eastern and the western sector, while the properties left in East Punjab amounted to 1,10,732 houses, 17,542 shops and 1,495 factories,[58] in the case of West Bengal, the land left was an insignificant 500 bighas.[59] On top of that, the step-motherly treatment of the central government with regard to funds under the banner of rehabilitation further compounded the problem. That the stress was mainly on ad hoc assistance is evident from the information in Table 9.4:

Table 9.4 Central Government's Assistance for Relief and Rehabilitation in West Bengal

Year	*Relief (in Rs.)*	*Rehabilitation (in Rs.)*
1947–1948	4,08,929	0
1948–1949	1,94,19,452	11,12,453
1949–1950	1,61,87,750	31,13,535
Total	3,60,16,131	42,25,988

Source: Government of West Bengal, *Five Years of Independence, August 1947–August 1952* (1953) Calcutta: Government of West Bengal, p. 70

While the migrants demanded to be settled on a permanent basis, that rehabilitation under the circumstances would pose a herculean task, thus, is a foregone conclusion. In the given situation, the abandoned properties of the Muslims in the heart of Calcutta and Howrah would go a long way in resolving the crisis.

If one looks at the pre-riot and post-riot population growth rate of most of these affected Muslim majority wards, especially those with a significant Muslim population in Calcutta, one would be able to gauge the implications. The riot-affected areas witnessed a negative growth rate in the inter-census decade. Unfortunately, the census of 1951 in the case of Calcutta did not record the communitywise split-up of population in each police station. One can question, why did the Census Commission not come up with such statistics? The question becomes all the more significant in light of the fact that a religionwise break up of police stations of all the other districts of West Bengal is readily available in the respective district census handbooks. Why does one not find such data sets in Volume VI, Part III titled Calcutta City or in Volume VI, Part IC where one finds the tables pertaining to West Bengal? Was the government trying to shield some crucial facts by not publishing such statistics? No explanation was offered and the questions remain unanswered. In the absence of police station split-up of the communal composition, to specifically pin-point and prove the scaling down of the Muslim growth rate would be difficult. But, if the available data is correlated, one can conclude that the negative growth rate in the overall population of the Muslim majority wards that were affected in 1950, at a time when the city registered an overall population growth of +20.6 per cent, is an indicator of the deep-seated sense of insecurity pervading the minority mind.

Table 9.5 Inter-Census Growth Rate (1941–1951) of Muslim Majority Wards Affected in 1950

Police Station	*Total Population 1941*	*Total Population 1951*	*Rate of Growth of Population (1941–1951)*
Colootala	90087	90203	−1.39
Bowbazar	37199	40794	−0.31
Taltola	70143	69254	−1.73
Kalinga	19348	25107	−1.28
Port	31783	17481	−53.52

Source: R.A. Dutch, *Census of India, 1941,Volume IV: Bengal* (Delhi, 1942); Asok Mitra *Census of India, 1951: Vol.VI, Part III: Calcutta City* (1954)

However, the area with the maximum concentration of Muslim population in 1941, Beniapukur (71.41 per cent), located in the Park Circus area and remaining more or less unaffected in 1950, did not record any negative growth rate in terms of total population. In fact, there was a positive growth rate of +31.33 per cent. With a paltry 14.42 per cent of the total population of Beniapukur being returned as displaced as per the 1951 census, one cannot account for this population growth by the resettlement of the migrant population. It can be assumed that the growth was directly proportional to a redistribution of minority population of Calcutta. Being hemmed in by wards which traditionally housed Muslims and which were targeted in 1950, Beniapukur became a safe haven for the minority population who, evicted in the early months of 1950, found it safe to huddle with their co-religionists. The localities of lower class, poor Muslims, who eke out a hand to mouth living, were specifically targeted by the rioteers. The Park Circus area, as shown by McPherson was peopled by middle class educated Muslims and by 1947, as Chatterji shows, the heterogeneity and hierarchy within the Muslim fold became marked with distinct living spaces, where Park Circus was the preferred destination of the upper class educated Muslims who distanced themselves from their rustic, poor co-religionists.[60] As Bose points out, the 'Moslem population, although it is not fractioned by caste, is quite explicitly stratified by class.'[61] 1950 jumbled up this setup by obliterating the boundaries between the rich and the poor, where the latter fled from their dinghy shanties, which were burnt down, to take shelter amongst their relatively affluent brethren. The state administration, too, acknowledged, 'There has been a concentration of evacuees in certain areas, particularly in Park Circus.'[62] There was thus reconfiguration of the living pattern of the minority population within the city, following the conflagration.[63]

Recasting urban residential patterns was not the only fallout of the 1950 violence. It somewhat achieved its end in injecting fear into the Muslim psyche so much so that a government estimate shows a fall in the total population of Muslims of the city. Had there been only a reorientation of living space, the case of 'missing' Muslims could not be explained. Thus an efflux from Calcutta could not be ruled out. As per the 1951 census, Muslims in Calcutta should have numbered approximately 437,000. With an actual population of 305,932, there was a deficit of around 131,000. Of these, a paltry 15,000 had migrated to East Bengal.[64] The rest left Calcutta to seek refuge either amongst their co-religionists within the state or outside. One can draw a parallel with the urban scenario of Howrah, which, too, registered a negative growth rate of the city-based Muslim population.

Thus, the core area of West Bengal saw an exodus of Muslims from their traditional habitat. On the other hand, if one looks at the growth rate of Muslim population in some of the districts of West Bengal, one can note an unusually high rate. The border district of Murshidabad registered a Muslim growth of 105 per cent between 1941 and 1951, while Birbhum located on the far western corner of Bengal had a growth of 49.7 per cent. Nahid Kamal points out that this growth rate cannot be attributed to influx of Muslims from across the border but, rather, to redistribution of the Muslims of West Bengal or from other neighbouring states, who found succour amongst their fellow brethren.[65] Juxtaposing the two, what emerges

Table 9.6 Growth Rate of the City-Based Muslim Population (1941–1951)

Police Station	*Muslim Population 1941 (Percentage to Total Population)*	*Muslim Population 1951 (Percentage to Total Population)*	*Rate of Growth (1941–1951)*
Howrah City	65198 (17.18)	41274 (9.51)	−36.69
Bally (Urban)	11887 (23.56)	6446 (10.20)	−45.72

Source: R.A. Dutch, *Census of India, 1941, Volume IV: Bengal* (Delhi, 1942); Asok Mitra *Census of India, 1951: District Census Handbook: Howrah* (1953)

is that the Muslims, especially the poor labouring class with limited resources, uprooted from their setup found it safe to relocate either amongst their more affluent co-religionists who were more or less untouched by the riots or migrate to the districts bordering East Bengal which would provide them with an escape route in case of extreme brutality. Thus the riot of 1950 redrew the communal maps of Calcutta and Howrah, and West Bengal, for that matter, in terms of number and physical space. Ironically, even after the mayhem of 1946, not all was lost in terms of cordiality between the two communities – Abdul Majid, a resident of the Muralibagan bustee recounted that friendly feelings existed between the Hindus and the Muslims of the locality prior to 1950.[66]

Another trend that becomes evident from the census data is that in some of these Muslim majority pockets, the vacuum was filled by the immigrants. As the Census Commissioner notes, 'During the riots most of the bustees were deserted. . . . Between December 1950 and March 1951 almost all these deserted areas were rehabilitated and filled up by large settlements of displaced Hindus from East Bengal.'[67] Take the example of Maniktala, which was one of the worst-affected areas of the riot. Being stalked by fear and insecurity, people started fleeing from Maniktala, taking shelter amongst their co-religionists in the contiguous areas of Park Circus, Beniapakur, or Kidderpore. But even then Maniktala recorded a growth rate of 37.17 per cent. When one looks at the percentage of displaced population settled there, a somewhat linear conclusion can be drawn, since 44.66 per cent of the total population in 1951 fell within the 'displaced' category. N.K. Bose, surveying the social scene of Calcutta in the 1960s noted that the refugees had settled in large numbers mostly in the northern and northeastern wards, many of which 'were formally inhabited by Muslim labourers and artisans. The latter have been largely replaced by displaced Hindus from East Pakistan.'[68] Serajuddin's shanty came to be occupied by the East Bengali immigrants. So was the house of Nazrul Huq of Belgachia. Deven Sen, Secretary, Bengal Provincial National Trade Union Congress, in his written memorandum submitted to the Enquiry Commission, listed among other things the causes of the riot as an 'acute shortage of housing accommodation.'[69] The then Relief and Rehabilitation Commissioner, Government of West Bengal, Hiranmoy Bandyopadhyay opines, 'If the refugees had not occupied these abandoned plots and houses, I shudder to think how the Government would have shouldered the burden of accommodating thousands of refugees in the relief camps.'[70] Many of the plots were forcibly squatted on by the immigrants in the fringe areas of the city, like that of Bijoygarh, after elbowing out the local Muslim residents.[71] Thus Hindu rehabilitation at times became co-terminous with minority persecution, eviction and displacement, and the minorities became pawns in the political power play.

Conclusion

In 1950 the Constitution of India was adopted, where Articles 5–8 outlined the clauses for acquiring citizenship. By virtue of Article 6 of the Constitution, those migrating before 19 July 1948 and those on or after that date were bestowed citizenship of India. Ironically, while the government was keen to grant citizenship to the Hindu migrants, it remained silent on the plight of another set of its citizens. As one sitting member of the minority community lamented on the floor of the Legislative Assembly, 'though we are citizens of free India, we are held here as hostages.'[72]

To a large extent, the cleavage waged between the two communities by the riots of 1950 resulted in a reconfiguration of the living patterns of the Muslims who were squeezed, marginalised and cornered to coop themselves up in what Chatterji terms 'ghettos.' Pre-1950 Calcutta, notwithstanding the 1946 carnage, could still boast of mixed localities. As one witness from Kankurgachi Road testified, prior to the riot the bustee contained a mixed population and there was complete harmony between neighbours of the two communities.[73] But spatial segregation became exacerbated and more watertight post-1950. Cross-border dislocation was complemented by intra-city dislocation. Calcutta, thus, emerged in a new mould – a potpourri, where the social space came to be contoured along communal, ethnic and linguistic lines. While no less marked was the animosity and distrust between the people of East Bengal and the local inhabitants, the Bangal and the Ghati in local parlance, who were often at loggerheads, the communal cauldron continued to boil only to spill over in 1964 with another surge of violence.

Notes

1 Subhasri Ghosh has earlier published a paper on the issue of migration but the case study was different district of West Bengal. This chapter has taken certain facts and contents from that paper. See Ghosh, Subhasri (2014) 'Population Movement in West Bengal: A Case Study of Nadia District,

1947–1951,' in *South Asia Research Sage*, Vol. 34, no. 2, July. Web Link http://journals.sagepub.com/doi/abs/10.1177/0262728014533850?journal Code=sara.

2 Chakrabarti, Prafulla K. (1999) *The Marginal Men: The Refugees and the Left Political Syndrome in West Bengal*, Calcutta: Naya Udyog, p. 6.

3 Das, Suranjan (2000) 'The 1992 Calcutta Riot in Historical Continuum: A Relapse into "Communal Fury"?,' in *Modern Asian Studies*, Vol. 34, no. 2, Cambridge: Cambridge University Press, p. 281.

4 'Of Graveyard and Ghettos: Muslims in Partitioned West Bengal, 1947–1967' in Mushirul Hasan and Asim Roy (2006) ed. Living Together Separately: Cultural India in History and Politics, Delhi: Oxford University Press; Joya Chatterji (2007) *The Spoils of Partition: Bengal and India*, 1947–1967, New York: Cambridge University Press.

5 'Communal Riots and the Minorities' in Sekhar Bandyopadhyay (2009), *Decolonization in South Asia: Meaning of Freedom in Post-Independence West Bengal*, 1947–1952, New York: Routledge; 'The Minorities in Post-Partition West Bengal: The Riots of 1950' in Abhijit Dasgupta, Masahiko Togawa, Abul Barkat (2011), ed. *Minorities and the State: Changing Social and Political Landscape of Bengal*, New Delhi: Sage Publications

6 'Becoming a Minority Community: Calcutta's Muslims after Partition' in Tanika Sarkar and Sekhar Bandyopadhyay (2015) ed. *The Stormy Decades: Calcutta*, New Delhi: Social Science Press.

7 *Jugantar*, 10 May 1955.

8 Varshney, Ashutosh and Steven Wilkinson (2004) *Varshney-Wilkinson Dataset on Hindu-Muslim Violence in India, 1950–1995, Version 2*, Ann Arbor, Michigan: Inter-University Consortium for Political and Social Research, p. 24.

9 *Proceedings of the West Bengal Legislative Assembly* (hereafter referred to as *WBLA*), 9 February 1950, pp. 96–97.

10 *The Statesman*, 10 February 1950.

11 *Short Report of the Serious Development of Communal Frenzy in Calcutta*, Home (Political) Department, No File No. 1950, West Bengal State Archives (Hereafter referred to as WBSA), p. 24.

12 Mitra, Asok (1991) *The New India, 1948–1955: Memoirs of an Indian Civil Servant*, Calcutta: Popular Prakashan, p. 71.

13 *The Statesman*, 13 February 1950.

14 Mitra, *The New India*, p. 72.

15 *WBLA*, 27 September 1950, p. 46.

16 Zinkin, Taya (1962) *Reporting India*, London: Chatto & Windus, pp. 37–38.

17 *The Statesman*, 28 March 1950.

18 Mitra, Asok (1997) *Tin Kuri Dash*, Vol. 3, Kolkata: Dey's Publishing.

19 *The Times of India*, 5 April 1950.

20 *WBLA*, 27 September 1950, p. 42.

21 *WBLA*, 'Budget for 1950–51,' 10 February 1950, p. 184.

22 Ibid.

23 Lahiri, Pravas Chandra (1980) *Pak Bharater Ruparekha*, Nadia: Shyama Prakashani.

24 Chatterji, Kedarnath ed. (1950, December) *The Modern Review, July-December 1950*, Vol. 88, Calcutta: Modern Review Office, p. 345.

25 Ibid.
26 Bandyopadhyay, Sandip (1999) *Deshbhag: Smriti aar Sattwa*, Calcutta: Progressive Publishers, p. 18 (translation mine).
27 op. cit. Bandyopadhyay, 2005.
28 For details refer to Bandyopadhyay, *Decolonization*.
29 WBSA, *Short Report*, p. 17.
30 Ibid., p. 12.
31 Ward No. 29 comprised Beliaghata and Entally Thanas encircled on the north by Narkeldanga Main Road, on the south by Christopher Road, on the west by Circular Road and on the East by Canal and Railway line. A part of Maniktalala thana too falls within this ward encircled by Ultadanga Main Road on the north, Narkeldanga Main Road on the south, Circular Road on the west and Railway line on the east. The rest of Maniktala thana falls in Ward no. 30 comprising of Belgachhia Road on the north, Ultadanga main road on the south, Circular Road on the west and Railway Line on the east. Chitpur thana falls under Ward no. 31 surrounded by Dum Dum Road on the north, Belgachhia Road on the south, Grand Trunk Road on the west and Railway Line on the east.
32 Sengupta, *The Tea Labourers of North East India*.
33 *Amrita Bazar Patrika*, 16 June 1950.
34 Quoted in Saroj Chakrabarty (1974) *With Dr. B.C. Roy and Other Chief Ministers: A Record Up to 1962*, Calcutta: Benson's, p. 109.
35 Ibid.
36 WBSA, *Short Report*, p. 31.
37 Ibid., p. 29.
38 Ibid.
39 *Amrita Bazar Patrika*, 22 June 1950.
40 *WBLA*, 6 February 1950.
41 WBSA, *Short Report*, "Statement of Smt Mridula Sarabhai."
42 Mitra, *The New India*, p. 72.
43 WBSA, *Short Report*, "Evidence of the S.P. before the Commission of Enquiry, 4 August 1950."
44 Das, 'The 1992 Calcutta Riot in Historical Continuum,' p. 176.
45 *WBLA*, 6 February 1950, p. 18.
46 *The Statesman*, 8 March 1950.
47 *Amrita Bazar Patrika*, 2 April 1950.
48 *The Statesman*, 1 January 1950.
49 *WBLA*, 8 February 1950, p. 74.
50 Chatterji, Joya (2006) 'Of Graveyards and Ghettos: Muslims in Partitioned West Bengal, 1947–67,' in Asim Roy and Mushirul Hasan ed. *Living Together Separately: Cultural India in History and Politics*, Delhi: Oxford University Press.
51 Mitra, *Tin Kuri Dash*, p. 122.
52 WBSA, *Short Report*, "Statement of Smt Mridula Sarabhai before the Commission of Enquiry."
53 *Constituent Assembly of India (Legislative) Debates, Part I: Questions and Answers, Starred Questions and Answers, Oral Answers, 24 February 1949*, New Delhi: Government of India, 1950, p. 1099.
54 *WBLA*, 8 February 1950, p. 72.
55 *WBLA*, 17 February 1948, p. 18.

56 Asok, Mitra, ed. (1951) *Census of India*, 1951, Vol. VI, Part III: Calcutta City Delhi: Government of India, p. VII.
57 Government of India, *Constituent Assembly of India (Legislative) Debates, Part I: Questions and Answers, Starred Question and Answers, Oral Answers, 8 March 1948*, New Delhi: Government of India, 1949, p. 1738.
58 Government of India, *Constituent Assembly of India, Part I: Questions and Answers, Starred Questions and Answers, Oral Answers, 24 February 1949*, New Delhi: Government of India, 1950, p. 1012.
59 Ibid.
60 For details, see op. cit. Joya Chatterji, 2007.
61 Bose, Nirmal Kumar (1968) *Calcutta, 1964: A Social Survey*, Bombay: Lalvani Publishing House, p. 102.
62 *The Statesman*, 13 February 1950.
63 For a more recent study of the Muslim localities of Kolkata like Beniapukur, refer to Seabrook, Jeremy and Imran Ahmed Siddiqui (2011) *People without History: India's Muslim Ghettos*, London: Pluto Press.
64 Mitra, *Census*, p. xvi.
65 Kamal, Nahid (2009) *The Population Trajectories of Bangladesh and West Bengal during the Twentieth Century: A Comparative Study*, Phd dissertation, London School of Economics, pp. 107–108.
66 *Amrita Bazar Patrika*, 17 June 1950.
67 Mitra, *Census*, p. xiv.
68 Bose, *Calcutta, 1964*, p. 33.
69 *Amrita Bazar Patrika*, 1 July 1950.
70 Bandyopadhyay, Hiranmoy (1970) *Udbastu*, Calcutta: Sahitya Samsad, p. 73.
71 For details, see Sanyal, Romola (2014) 'Hindu Space: Urban Dislocations in Post-Partition Calcutta,' in *Transactions of the Institute of British Geographers*, 39 (1), pp. 38–49.
72 *WBLA*, 6 February 1950, p. 13.
73 *Amrita Bazar Patrika*, 24 June 1950.

Part III

Personal history, interpretation and (re)presentation

Chapter 10

Kashmir as Partition's 'unfinished business'

Farooq Sulehria

In academic discourses on India and Pakistan as well as journalistic narratives – emerging out of the Orient as well as the Occident – Kashmir is usually delineated as the nuclear 'flashpoint.' That Kashmir constitutes a disputed *territory* between India and Pakistan is a commonsensical understanding in and beyond South Asia. This understanding is reinforced by an unending war of words between New Delhi and Islamabad.

These oral and diplomatic duels notwithstanding, in this chapter I argue that Kashmir remains unfinished business of the Partition for two reasons. Firstly, because India and Pakistan mutually want to maintain a status quo on the Kashmir dispute for strategic reasons. They are not interested in any settlement compromising the present stalemate. Secondly, the Indo-Pak policy of maintaining status quo, hence Kashmir's continual Partition, has been abetted by the political failure of the Kashmir liberation project in building a secular unity capable of overcoming ethnic and sectarian divisions. This chapter, besides relying on secondary sources, largely draws upon my interaction with activists and leaders from Kashmir, on both sides. However, I will begin with my own experiences.

My family home in the countryside stood in marked contrast to the one in which I was born, in Sargodha (Punjab province). I was born in a two-room military quarter. My father was an airman in the air force. It was funny: air force officers, often having only two kids, were allotted fancy bungalows with many rooms, while airmen fathering seven or eight kids were given two-room quarters. It was therefore lots of fun visiting our big family home in the countryside. It was a spacious, mud-and-brick house with a courtyard so large that my brothers and I could play cricket in it. My cousins would look on with surprise while we played this strange game. Cricket fever had not yet reached the countryside.

Though this was the biggest house in the village, it was not the best. The old *Haveli* (old-style brick house) in the middle of the village was definitely the best. Situated at one corner of the village, my family home had a door opening towards the north with another to the south. If the door on the north was open, and often it was wide open during the daytime, one could see the hills of Jammu while sitting in our courtyard.

One day, I found out that it was these distant, dark hills that made my grandfather and his brother leave that fancy *Haveli.*

'Your great grandmother was old and sick. She would go upstairs every morning to catch a glimpse of those hills. But it was tiring to climb the stairs every morning for your ailing great grandmother. She wanted to leave that house and move outside of the village where she did not need to climb stairs to look at the hills. Therefore, your *Lala Ji* (grandpa) decided to move to this house,' *Choti Bobo* told me one day.

I had three *bobos. Bari Bobo* was my grandfather's first wife, *Bobo* was my grandmother, and most talkative of all, *Choti Bobo* was the wife of my grandfather's brother. All lived in the same house.

I was agitated to hear what *Choti Bobo* told me. It was a cousin of my father, a colonel in the army, who was living in the *Haveli.* I used to think Colonel *Saab* owned the *Haveli* due to his higher social status.

'Come on! The old woman was crazy and *Lala Ji* was even crazier! How come you could leave the *Haveli* for these stupid hills,' I would often agitate. Or sometimes I would tease *Lala Ji.*

My family occupied the *Haveli* in this border village of Channi, Narowal district, in early 1949. Hindus and Sikhs must have inhabited the village before the Partition. It was deserted when my *Lala Ji* along with his family and relatives moved here from *Panagir* (refugee) camps. He was not alone in moving here. There were other *Panagirs* from Jammu who were allotted houses and a piece of agricultural land in this village. Channi, comprised of almost two hundred households, is now inhibited by *Panagirs*, a term used for immigrants from Jammu.

Those who migrated to Pakistan from India were *Mohajirs* (immigrants). The Channi residents were *Panagirs*. The *Mohajirs* had moved to Pakistan permanently. *Panagirs* were supposed to go back as soon as the Kashmir problem was solved. The houses and farms they were allotted were a temporary arrangement. They did not own them. But *Panagirs* knew that their land and property 'back home' still belonged to them. After all, the Kashmir war was just a temporary uproar. Things had gone wrong due to trouble in neighbouring Punjab. 'Maharaja had decreed that the land and property of *Panagirs* should belong to them for next 100 years,' *Lala Ji* used to tell us.

My brothers and I had read about kings only in storybooks. We had only seen military dictators in Pakistan. No kings. No queens or princesses either. It was therefore fun to hear about our Maharaja. His name was Hari Singh. I had learnt it since I learnt other names: *Lala Ji*'s name was Abdur Rehman, *Abba Ji*'s (father's) name was Dilawar, Maharaja's name was Hari Singh.

Lala Ji held Maharaja in high esteem. He used to hate Jinnah. He was fond of listening to the BBC Urdu on radio while he was in our countryside home. And he would never miss watching the TV news at 21:00 when he would visit us in town. He would sit in front of the television the whole evening waiting for the news. The news would start with a saying of the Prophet Muhammad, followed by a saying of 'Quad-e-Azam' Muhammad Ali Jinnah. As soon as Jinnah's picture would appear on screen, *Lala Ji* would start swearing at him. 'I hate to see this moustacheless. It was him who caused bloodshed on the border.' He would say and swear at him in a way typical of him.

I and my brothers would laugh at his outrage. 'He was a great politician. Without him, we would have been Hindu slaves,' one of us would repeat the phrases we had learnt at school. Learnt is perhaps the wrong word. The correct term would be *indoctrinated*. He would get even more agitated. 'You kids know nothing.' That was his routine answer.

Sometimes he would narrate our family history. It was always a source of pride for us to know about the big feudal estate my ancestors owned in Jammu. It was an escape from the harsh realities and deprivations we suffered everyday as working-class kids. (Later I found out we did not have that of a big feudal estate, it was bit of an exaggeration.) Ramgarh, our ancestral village in Jammu, had become a kind of wonderland for us. *Lala Ji* would narrate stories of his Hindu and Sikh friends. He would miss them. He would praise the Maharaja. 'Maharaja used to say Muslims are my right moustache and Hindus my left,' he would tell us. Moustache had a special meaning for him. It was symbol of honour, manhood, bravery. That was why he would call Jinnah 'moustacheless.'

All he would tell us was in stark contrast with the state indoctrination I was going through at my school. It also was in strong contrast with what the newspapers, television, radio, mosque and all the other institutions of indoctrination used to shamelessly convey day in and day out.

My schooling occurred at an air force school: Airbase Intermediate College, Sargodha. I was taught: Hindus are enemies; Kashmir is Pakistan's jugular vein; The soldier is the epitome of humanity; *Shahadat* (martyrdom) is the supreme act. As a kid, I wanted to join the Pakistan Air Force, and sacrifice my life in Jihad against India to take back Kashmir.

At Friday prayers, the *mullah* (priest) would pray for the liberation of Palestine and Kashmir. Bosnia and Chechnya were words he perhaps even did not know. He would lament the youth who were more after girls, Indian films and cricket than launching Jihad for Kashmir. My blood would start boiling while listening to fiery speeches by our mullah. I would become even more determined to join the air force to liberate Kashmir.

It was *Lala Ji* who would confuse me. 'We do not belong to Pakistan. *Riasat* itself was a country.' He would always refer to Jammu and Kashmir (J&K onwards) as *Riasat* (state). He did not agree that Hindus were bad. For him, caste was more important than religion. Though a Muslim, as a proud Rajput he held a Hindu Maharaja in high esteem merely because Maharaja was a Rajput[1] too.

Later on I found out it was not just Rajput fraternity. It had economic reasons as well. Caste carried certain privileges. Hence, Dogra dynasty's social base among Rajputs.

By the time I finished my secondary school, my enthusiasm for Jihad had subsided. The mullahs delivering fiery speeches did not send their own children to Jihad. Military officers were busy smuggling heroin on the Western front (Afghanistan) instead of liberating Kashmir on the east. I was disillusioned.

But more than that, it was the writings of Krishan Chandar, the great Urdu short story writer, that had introduced me to new ideas: secularism, socialism, internationalism. In the Indian subcontinent, it has been writers and poets who won over more youth to the ideas of socialism than the propaganda sheets of communist parties. Reading Sadat Hassan Manto[2] further helped in understanding the partition of India. Kashmir was just a byproduct of this Partition, I concluded on reading Manto.

By the time I moved to Lahore in 1990 for further studies, a lot had happened both nationally and internationally. The Soviet Union had collapsed. With it collapsed the old left in Pakistan. The khaki hawks had sent the first Benazir Bhutto government home. It was not the end of her regime; it was rather her miserable performance that had disillusioned me like millions of other Pakistanis. Most importantly, Kashmir had broken its decades of silence. A militant armed struggle had paralysed Indian Jammu Kashmir (IJK). But I had lost interest in Kashmir.

I was more interested in finding out the answers to 'big' questions: 'Is socialism dead? Is there a God?' Like the rest of my friends at the Government College Lahore (elevated now as Government College Lahore University), I would spend hours and hours arguing about these questions.

It was not until 1993 when I met Massod Kashmiri that I earnestly started discovering my lost country: J&K. Masood was my class fellow at the Punjab University, Lahore. Apparently, a simpleton, dressed in *shalwar kameez*, isolated from rest of the class, Massod hardly attracted me until one day he took part in a discussion in a political science class. Kashmir was the topic under discussion. All he said was exactly what *Lala Ji* used to say. After the lecture, I went to him. He was chairperson of JKSLF, I found out. JKSLF, the Jammu Kashmir Students Liberation Front, was the student wing of the nationalist JKLF, the Jammu Kashmir Liberation Front.

The JKLF had become a household name since the movement in 1988 had flared up. It had emerged as the leading political force both in IJK and Pakistani Jammu Kashmir (PJK). I started going to JKLF meetings. Masood himself and many of his friends had been active in the movement. Many had been to Afghanistan for training. On their way back, they went *par*(other side of the Kashmir) to be part of guerrilla action. I was sceptical of JKLF's Afghan connection. Meeting these freedom fighters, holding nightlong discussions, travelling to different parts of PJK helped improve my understanding of J&K. I had for the first time started discovering my real homeland. But the JKLF comrades never impressed me. Not even JKLF chairman Aman Ullah Khan. I met him a few times. It was with Khan I conducted my first ever interview as a journalist. The JKLF's ideas and leadership disillusioned me. But the exposure to the JKLF had reinforced many of my ideas about J&K: I was taught lies in the textbooks, I was told lies by newspapers and television, I was misguided by mullahs and politicians. I had now found out Kashmir was not a disputed territory between India and Pakistan. But the truth? Well, truth requires a look into India's Partition in 1947.

Section 1: J&K partitioned

Stretching over 222,236 square kilometres, J&K consists of four regions: Jammu, Kashmir, Laddakh and Gilgit Baltistan (GB). In 1941, the population of Jammu was 1,561,580 (Hindu majority), Kashmir 1,728,600 (90 per cent Muslims) while GB (almost 100 per cent Muslim) and Laddakh (slight Buddhist majority) had a total population of 200,000 (with only 40,000 in Laddakh).[3] Out of 4,000,000 J&K state-subjects (residents), Muslims constituted 80 per cent. A nearly similar religious configuration holds today when the population has swelled to 14 million. With almost a dozen languages and dialects, and a variety of religions and cultures, J&K was in no way a monolith. It, however, had a proud tradition of religious harmony.

The state of J&K was created in the first half of the nineteenth-century by a Dogra Rajput chieftain Gulab Singh. Under the colonial rule, J&K was one of the largest princely states. In 1947, there were over 560 'Princely States.' These states were not part of British India, which consisted of 11 provinces and Tribal Areas. However, rulers of these states, princes, were part of the Indian Empire by virtue of having acknowledged the British Paramountcy. On the cusp of Partition, princes were given the right to choose accession either to India or Pakistan, or they could choose independence. Maharaja Hari Singh decided to stay independent. His decision bewildered both India and Pakistan. India expected the Hindu maharaja to accede with India. Pakistan, taking into account the Muslim majority, expected a revolt against Hari Singh's decision. Both were mistaken. Instead of accession, the Maharaja entered into a standstill agreement with Pakistan while India kept evading the question.[4]

Key political parties – the National Conference (NC), led by Sheikh Abdullah and sympathetic to Gandhi's Indian National Congress, Muslim Conference (MC), allied with Jinnah's Muslim League, and J&K Rajya Hindu Sabha, with a strong base among Jammu Hindus – also lent support to the idea of an independent Kashmir (Snedden, 2013: 25).[5] That the major political parties and the Maharaja were acting in unison is a fact non-Kashmiri historians often tend to ignore.

When Kashmiri leadership frustrated Pakistani hopes, tribal mercenaries backed by Pakistani regulars entered J&K on 21 October 1947 to 'liberate' it from Hindu rule. Why mercenaries? Because Pakistani and Indian militaries were still under the joint command of the British commander-in-chief Field Marshal Auchinleck. Also, a large proportion of military officers were British. Auchinleck had made it clear to Jinnah that any use of force in Kashmir would lead to termination of British support. Hence, the mercenaries were used.[6]

On 22 October, mercenaries had reached Baramola, within one hundredmiles of Srinagar. Panicked, the Maharaja asked Delhi for help. Help was available but at a high price: J&K accession to India. India claims that he opted for that. However, J&K nationalists claim that Maharaja never signed any Instrument of Accession (IoA). Researchers such as Lamb (1991) and Whitehead (2015) have also contradicted the Indian claim.[7]

On 27 October, Indian soldiers were airlifted to Srinagar. Within a few days, 35,000 Indian troops drove the mercenaries out from parts of Kashmir. To end further skirmishes, the issue was brought to the UNO by India. Through UN intervention, a ceasefire was agreed by India and Pakistan on 1 January 1949. On 27 July 1949 representatives from these countries met in Karachi and a ceasefire line (renamed as Line of Control, or LoC, in the Simla Agreement) was agreed upon between the two countries. The LoC ever since has divided J&K into PJK and IJK. A solution to Kashmir has been the subject of UN resolutions calling for a plebiscite, under UN supervision. Meantime, the areas captured by Pakistan through the proxy-militia of mercenaries were declared Azad (Independent) Kashmir. A provisional government headed by an MC leader, Sardar Ibrahim, was put in place.

In IJK, Abdullah was appointed as the prime minister while IJK was granted a 'special status' under the Article 370 of the Indian constitution. Jawaharlal Nehru, India's first prime minister, promised Abdullah a plebiscite to decide Kashmir's future. When Nehru dragged his feet, Abdullah agitated. Hence, Delhi removed him from power and incarcerated him, accusing him of collaboration with the USA and Pakistan. His arrest in August 1953 triggered a twenty-day agitation paralysing the Valley. Abdullah was released in 1958. Kashmir broke out again. This time to welcome him. In a few months time, he was again jailed for another 6 years. On his release, the 'Lion of Kashmir' was again welcomed by a 'million man rally.'

Nehru had realised the Kashmir problem could not be solved by coercion and dispatched Abdullah to Pakistan for negotiations. While Abdullah was in PJK, Nehru died. With Nehru's death Abdullah's hope for a peaceful settlement to the Kashmir issue also died. The desperate Abdullah, in order to muster international support for his cause, toured many capitals. In Beijing he was received by Zhou En Lai. This created uproar in India. Memories of the Indo-China war were still fresh. On reaching home, Abdullah again landed in jail. Kashmir broke out yet again: strikes and demonstrations were met by repression.

Pakistan, enthused by the agitation, decided to dispatch paratroopers to Kashmir in September 1965, hoping to ignite a widespread uprising. Pakistan had miscalculated yet again. The protests did not symbolise pro-Pakistan feelings. The misadventure led to 1965 Indo-Pak War which culminated in Tashkent Accord (discussed later in this chapter).

Meantime, impressed by Che, a group of Kashmiri nationalists, led by Maqbool Butt, took to guerrilla struggle. Two of its members, Ashraf Qureshi and Hashim Qureshi, highjacked an Indian plane in 1971 (known as the Ganga Highjacking case) and emerged as a resistance symbol overnight. The plane was brought to Lahore, its passengers set free and the plane set on fire while Hashim and Ashraf served long terms in Pakistani jails, suffering torture at the notorious torture cells in Lahore.

By the mid-1970s, when Abdullah was released from jail, he made peace with Delhi. By 1977, he was again running IJK as chief minister until his death in 1982. His huge funeral was also the swan song of civil resistance in IJK. Two years later, Butt was hanged in Delhi on the charge of murdering a policeman. He had been languishing in Indian jails since 1976.

Abdullah was replaced by his son Farooq Abdullah. The NC under Farooq simply capitulated to the Centre. Consequently, oppositional space in the Valley was occupied by a miscellany alliance of diverse groups. This alliance, Muslim United Council (MUC) contested election in 1987 against NC-Congress alliance. Rigging, real and imagined, denied the election results any credibility, on the one hand, and isolated a new generation of activists, on the other. Out of the MUC-experience emerged an armed uprising – initially led by JKLF – accompanied by a mass uprising, paralysing the Valley.

The JKLF leadership committed a blunder by allying with Pakistan's Inter Services Intelligence (ISI). The ISI was happy to engage India in a proxy war in Kashmir. However, JKLF was not acceptable to Pakistan for long. As soon as the Mujahideen were no longer needed in Afghanistan, they were reorganised for launching Jihad afresh in Kashmir.[8]

The first victims of bearded Jihad were intellectuals and secular, pro-independence political activists, including JKLF sympathisers. The JKLF itself split into many factions, courtesy of ISI money. In 1994, JKLF's Aman Ullah Khan told me there were over 30 militant Kashmiri groups fighting each other. What had started in 1988 as a powerful mass movement had by the mid-1990s turned into a fiasco.

Kashmir buried between 60 to 80,000 dead bodies of its youth in the 1990s.[9] Another wave of militancy, struggle and sacrifice had passed, apparently fruitlessly. In 1999, yet another small-scale war was fought between India and Pakistan in the Kargil sector of Kashmir. The dispute led to the fourth coup in Pakistan which coincided with 9/11. Post-9/11, owing to renewed US interest in the region Islamabad had to de-escalate LoC activity.

Meantime, a period of calm – punctuated by waves of agitation in 2010 and 2013 – in the Valley culminated in yet another breakdown of literally everything in the Valley in the autumn of 2016 and the situation remains out of Indian control despite increased repression. While there is no let up in Indian state violence in Valley, resistance is also re-embracing militant ideas. At the time of writing these lines (April 2017), Valley remains under curfew-as-usual while networking sites are abuzz with messages for violent resistance. It remains to be seen if these messages translate into practice. However, one conclusion can also be drawn. The present chaos in the Valley is bound to continue also because Kashmiris' declared enemy (India) and their perceived friend (Pakistan) have an unwritten consensus to maintain a stalemate on the LoC.

Section 2: Division as status quo

In this section, I will refer to the Tashkent Accord, the Simla Agreement and the Lahore Declaration[10] to argue that India and Pakistan have preferred a strategic status quo *ante bellum* on the question of Kashmir. Neither India nor Pakistan, public and diplomatic narratives notwithstanding, wants to incorporate J&K in its entirety. But before answering why, I will show an unspoken Indo-Pak elite consensus on respecting the LoC and an attempt to avoid plebiscite.

Arguably, this consensus emerged over time even if the status quo has practically been in place ever since 1947. While India – after initially dilly-dallying under Nehru's long stint at the helm as shown earlier – has fanatically pursued the status quo, Pakistan was cowered into this position from misadventures initiated by its rulers. For the first time, it was the 1965 War that steeled the Indian stance to defend the status quo, on the one hand, and convinced Pakistani leadership to prefer a stalemate, on the other. Let us begin with Indian side of the story.

Firstly, in 1947 the Indian policy on the accession of princely states was topsy-turvy. Ideally, New Delhi wanted the subjects of princely states to exercise their right to self-determination as in the case of the diminutive Junagarh where the Muslim ruler of a Hindu majority state acceded to Pakistan. In the case of much larger Hyderabad with a similar problem, the dispute was settled through a military action. The case of Kashmir has been stated earlier.

Once the Kashmir dispute gained an international and bilateral dimension, wavering marked Nehru's policy on Kashmir. For instance, in June 1953 Pakistani Prime Minister Muhammad Ali Bogra and Nehru discussed Kashmir in London at the Queen's coronation. Later, Bogra visited New Delhi. They discussed the naming of the Plebiscite Commissioner for a plebiscite across the state. However, Pakistan refused to accept anyone except US Admiral Nimitz as the Plebiscite Commissioner, and the process was derailed.[11] 'Such an opportunity never arose again,' says Schofield.[12] That just before his death, as highlighted earlier, Nehru dispatched Abdullah to Pakistan is yet more evidence of Nehru's irresolute stance on Kashmir. However, neither the bogus existence of IOA nor Nehru's ideological/personal persuasions were the reason behind India's wavering over Kashmir. The actual reason: the Valley would erupt, repeatedly, demanding the right to self-determination. Nehru's inability to pacify Kashmir explains his wavering. Post-Nehru, it all changed and the 1965 War proved the catalyst.

The war was not merely a military folly encouraged by events in the Valley (described in Section 1). It was equally an outcome of an exaggerated self-image Pakistani generals had nurtured following the Run of Kutch episode, a minor border dispute that was viewed as a military victory by Pakistan. This military victory crystalised into a belief if not a military doctrine that 'the Hindu has no stomach for a fight.'[13] The better quality US weapons available to Pakistan further nurtured this grandiose stance.[14] Once these delusions were punctured by Indian reality, the then military ruler General Ayub told his cabinet, 'I know of people who want to risk Pakistan for the sake of Kashmir.'[15]

'This appears to show the shift in Ayub's thinking, as he had now seemingly been persuaded by the line that Pakistan was not worth sacrificing for the sake of Kashmir and was using this justification for not continuing the war,' comments Bajwa (2013: 344). On the other side of the border, Indian prime minister Lal Bahadur Shastri was claiming that the United States would support the status quo in Kashmir provided that India could establish a popular government there (*ibid*: 345). Finally, the two sides met at Tashkent and signed an accord on January 10, 1966. The nine-point Tashkent Accord, only once discusses the actual cause of war: Kashmir.

In five years' time, Pakistan had unwittingly locked horns with India yet again. However, the military defeat in 1971 was accompanied by a huge strategic, political and psychological loss for Pakistan. Not only did Islamabad lose East Pakistan (now Bangladesh), over 90,000 military and civilian personnel were now prisoners of war in Indian jails. Prime Minister Ali Bhutto's government was under huge pressure domestically to bring back prisoners of war.[16] Yet again, Kashmir was conveniently ignored when Bhutto travelled to India and inked the Simla Accord with his counterpart, Indira Gandhi. Signed on 2 July 1972, the Simla Accord solidified the mutual policy of maintaining the status quo on LoC while the Kashmir dispute was de-internationalised by declaring it a bilateral issue. Snedden (2013: 101), in fact, goes as far to claim that there was a secret agreement at Simla between the two countries that they would settle the Kashmir dispute by incorporating their respective parts.

While the Kargil War in 1999 was an apparent breach, both countries quickly returned to the status quo. For instance, even during the war India did not breach the LoC,[17] while in the 'Washington Accord,' signed by President Clinton and Prime Minister Nawaz Sharif on 4 July 1999, Pakistan promised to stick by the Simla Accord.[18]

Arguably, the Kargil War was an attempt by the Pakistan military to derail the peace process initiated by the Lahore Declaration, signed in 1999, when Indian Prime Minister Atal Bihari Vajpayee travelled to hold peace talks with his counterpart, Nawaz Sharif.

While the Kashmir dispute was mentioned three times in the Lahore Declaration, the reference to Kashmir was ambiguous. Resolving to solve it, the Lahore Declaration did not specify if the dispute would be resolved under the UN mandate or through mutual cooperation.

Fact of the matter is this: neither India nor Pakistan wants a plebiscite simply because neither party is sure to win. Secondly, the puritanical nature of Pakistan and the troubled relationship of the Hindu majority Indian ruling class with a sizeable Muslim population dissuades both countries from occupying/integrating the entirety of J&K.

In the meantime, the Indo-Pak strategy to maintain a status quo is reinforced by a failure of the J&K liberation movement to present a convincing case that they constitute a nation with a right to self-determination. But are they a 'nation'? Informed by a Marxist analysis, the next section is an attempt to answer this question.

Section 3: Nation as desire

In academic discourses, nation is characterised in two ways. The primordialist schools emphasises objective criteria – common language, history, ethnicity and culture – as the defining characteristics of the nation. In contrast, in the modernist approach, subjective criteria (denoted by such psychological factors as joint identity, mutual recognition and shared sympathies) are flagged.

The latter approach has generated a fashionable but highly flawed open-and-shut definition, coined by its most fashionable theoretician: Benedict Anderson. In his view, nation is: 'an imagined political community – and imagined as both inherently limited and sovereign.'[19] While imagination is a constituting element in any project of nationbuilding, in the absence of tangible commonalities (such as language, geography, common memory of, persecution, exclusion, or race/ethnicity), it will be impossible to arbitrarily imagine a community no matter how hard academics like Anderson try. In the absence of a commonality as a starting point, imagination will not be set in motion.[20]

In the Marxist tradition, Stalin's definition of the nation was mainstreamed owing to the centrality assumed by the Soviet Union. Stalin's rigid definition is the exact opposite of Anderson's elusiveness. Stalin defined nation as 'a historically constituted, stable, community of people' on the basis of common language, territory, economic life and 'psychic formation.'[21]

While Anderson's definition is being imported into the Indian subcontinent by the middle class graduates from Western universities, the latter holds sway over leftist discourses in South Asia, including Kashmir. One can point out dozens of examples negating the restrictive definition Stalin coined in 1913. Israel, notably, defies any such restrictive definition. Similarly, one can point out Kurds in this regard. While Lenin sympathised with Stalin's charaterisation without much inquiry into the definition of a nation, he unapologetically advocated oppressed nations' rights to self-determination. He viewed the right to secede as the basic tenet for a volunteer association or union of nations. He praised the peaceful dissolution of union between Norway and Sweden.

Sympathetic to principled Leninist positions on the question of Kashmir, I will draw on Basque Marxist Jose Iriarte Bikila to define nation as a consensus community organised by way of a political project whereby consensus overrides other factors such as class, gender, clan, caste, sect and so forth (Bikila, 1992).[22] In other words, it is a consciousness as well as a desire triggered by either one or an ensemble of tangible commonalities such as religion, geography, language, economy and even perhaps ideology.

With this definition in mind, we will be better placed to appreciate the gigantic challenges facing the Kashmir national struggle as well as its utter failure. In the first place, a commonality that may become a starting point for Kashmir nationalism is still missing. The factor of religion does not help owing to geographical division along religious lines. Similarly, with over a dozen languages and dialects, this project cannot be rallied around the language question. History equally vitiates against this project. The 1947 pogroms and expulsion of Hindu Pandits from Kashmir Valley in the late 1990s invoke bitter memories. The geographical factor could possibly cement and nationalists often invoke this factor. However, the actual division into two parts has further complicated the matter. One may explore other factors such as culture. It will, however, be difficult to imagine a unifying element.

It is obvious, therefore, that only a secular and progressive ideology can transcend the dividing forces. Socialism or communism also did not provide that alternative because the Indian left, in particular, and the Pakistani left in the initial years of conflict, subscribed to an antagonistic attitude towards the 'nationalistic' solution to Kashmir question (Ahmed [1967] briefly touches on the role of the Pakistani left in 1947). Nationalism as an ideology was the other secular and progressive alternative. The nationalists have invoked the existence of the pre-October 1947 state as the basis for their project. Can this provide the spur?

The history of the last 70 years negates this possibility. From Abdullah's NC to JKLF, no political project has assembled convincingly majoritarian sections of all the four regions. In fact, a strong nationalist current in Galgit Baltistan, visible in recent years, is emerging as yet another challenge to a unity project. Unity is the oxygen of a nationalistic project. The growing Islamification of the Kashmir valley further complicates the situation. Freedom-loving forces will have to patiently build and wait for this unity to emerge.

My grandfather, *Lala Ji*, could not wait, however. His five-decades-long wait to return to Jammu ended 10 years ago when he breathed his last. I could not join his funeral prayer as I was in Sweden. I went to his grave six months after his death. I did not pray 'May his soul rest in peace.' Partly because I do not pray. Partly because I know his soul will not rest in peace away from his *pind* (village) Ramgarh and *watan* (homeland) Jammu. He lays buried in our village graveyard. A tear ran down my eyes as I was standing by his graveside overlooking Jammu hills. Another *Panagir* buried away from Jammu.

Notes

1 A so-called 'martial race' in the Vedic caste system.
2 Manto (1912–1955) considered the most gifted Urdu-language fictionist, was traumatised by the Partition. He moved to Pakistan, drank himself to death but could never understand the illogical Partition.
3 Lamb, A. (1991) *Kashmir: A Disputed Legacy 1846–1990*. Karachi: Oxford University Press, p. 10.
4 Schofield, V. (2000) *Kashmir in Conflict: India, Pakistan and the Unending War*. New Delhi: Viva Books, pp. 41–43.
5 Though MC was wavering every now and then. Snedden, C. (2013) *Kashmir: The Unwritten History*. Noida: Harper Collins India.
6 Ahmed, G. (1967) *Pakistan Meets Indian Challenge*. Rawalpindi: Al Mukhtar Publishers; Amin, A. H. (1999) *The Pakistan Army Till 1965*. Arlington, VA: Strategicus and Tacticus, p. 89; Jalal, A. (1990) *The State of Martial Law: The Origins of Pakistan's Political Economy of Defence*. Cambridge: Cambridge University Press, pp. 58–59.
7 In 2003, BBC correspondent, Owen Bennett Jones, found IoA in his email box. For details, Whitehead, A. (2015) *A Mission in Kashmir*. Srinagar: Gulshan Books, pp. 338–339.
8 The first batch of Af-Pak militants, sponsored by notorious warlord Gulbadin Hikmatyar, arrived in Kashmir from Jalalabad in the early

1990s and joined the Hizb-ul-Mujahideen. Khan, Z. (1999) 'Inside the Mind of Holy Warrior.' *Herald*, July, p. 43.

9 Estimates vary. Webb (2012), for instance, has quoted a figure of 40,000 deaths since 1989. Webb, M. (2012) *Kashmir's Right to Secede: A Critical Examination of Contemporary Theories of Secession*. New York: Routledge.

10 The text of all three is available on the website of India's Ministry of External Affairs.

11 Rizvi, G. (1995) 'Nehru and the Indo-Pakistan Rivalry Over Kashmir, 1947–1963.' *Contemporary South Asia*, Vol. 4, No. 1, March.

12 Schofield, V. (2000) *Kashmir in Conflict: India, Pakistan and the Unending War*. New Delhi: Viva Books, p. 85.

13 Gauhar, A. (1993) *Ayub Khan: Pakistan's First Military Ruler*. Lahore: Sang-e-Meel Publications, p. 312.

14 Bajwa, F. (2013) *From Kutch to Tashkent: The Indo-Pakistan War of 1965*. London: Hurst & Company, p. 99.

15 Gauhar, A. (1993) *Ayub Khan: Pakistan's First Military Ruler*. Lahore: Sang-e-Meel Publications, pp. 378–379.

16 See Ayesha Jalal, (2014) *The Struggle for Pakistan: A Muslim Homeland and Global Politics*. Harvard Business Publishing, Cambridge, Massachusetts, London; Ahmed, Ishtiaq (2014) *The Pakistan Military in Politics: Origins, Evolution, Consequence*. New Delhi, Amaryllis Publication; and Ali, Rao Farman (2017) *How Pakistan Got Divided*. Karachi: Oxford University Press.

17 Behera, N. C. (2006) *Demystifying Kashmir*. Washington, DC: Brookings Institution Press, p. 68.

18 Riaz, S. (2016) Sino-US Relations: Implications for Pakistan. University of Quaid-e-Azam. PhD Thesis. Unpublished, p. 329.

19 Anderson, B. (2006) *Imagined Communities*. London: Verso, pp. 5–6.

20 For a Marxist critique of Anderson's work, see Davidson, N. (2007) 'Reimagined Communities.' *International Socialism*, No. 117. Accessed on 20.04.2017: http://isj.org.uk/reimagined-communities/. Also, for a Marxist conceptualisation of 'nation-state,' see, Davidson, N. (2016) *Nation-States: Consciousness and Competition*. Chicago: Haymarket.

21 Stalin, J. (1973) *The Essential Stalin, Major Theoretical Writings 1905–52*. Ed. Bruce Franklin. London: Croom Helm, p. 60.

22 Bikila, J. I. (1992) *Do the Workers Have a Country?* Amsterdam: IIRE.

References

Ahmed, G. (1967) *Pakistan Meets Indian Challenge*. Rawalpindi: Al Mukhtar Publishers.

Amin, A. H. (1999) *The Pakistan Army Till 1965*. Arlington, VA: Strategicus and Tacticus.

Anderson, B. (2006) *Imagined Communities*. London: Verso.

Bajwa, F. (2013) *From Kutch to Tashkent: The Indo-Pakistan War of 1965*. London: Hurst & Company.

Behera, N. C. (2006) *Demystifying Kashmir*. Washington, DC: Brookings Institution Press.

Bikila, J. I. (1992) *Do the Workers Have a Country?* Amsterdam: IIRE.
Davidson, N. (2007) 'Reimagined Communities.' *International Socialism*, No. 117. Accessed on 20.04.2017: http://isj.org.uk/reimagined-communities/
———. (2016) *Nation-States: Consciousness and Competition*. Chicago: Haymarket.
Gauhar, A. (1993) *Ayub Khan: Pakistan's First Military Ruler*. Lahore. Sang-e-Meel Publications.
Jalal, A. (1990) *The State of Martial Law: The Origins of Pakistan's Political Economy of Defence*. Cambridge: Cambridge University Press.
Khan, Z. (1999) 'Inside the Mind of Holy Warrior.' *Herald*, July, p. 43.
Lamb, A. (1991) *Kashmir: A Disputed Legacy 1846–1990*. Hertfordshire: Roxford Books.
Riaz, S. (2016) Sino-US Relations: Implications for Pakistan. University of Quaid-e-Azam. PhD Thesis. Unpublished.
Rizvi, G. (1995) 'Nehru and the Indo-Pakistan Rivalry Over Kashmir, 1947–1963.'*Contemporary South Asia*, Vol. 4, No. 1, March.
Schofield, V. (2000) *Kashmir in Conflict: India, Pakistan and the Unending War*. New Delhi: Viva Books.
Snedden, C. (2013) *Kashmir: The Unwritten History*. Noida: Harper Collins India.
Stalin, J. (1973) *The Essential Stalin, Major Theoretical Writings 1905–52*. Ed. Bruce Franklin. London: Croom Helm.
Webb, M. (2012) *Kashmir's Right to Secede: A Critical Examination of Contemporary Theories of Secession*. New York: Routledge.
Whitehead, A. (2015) *A Mission in Kashmir*. Srinagar: Gulshan Books.

Chapter 11

Lucknow

A personal history

Mehru Jaffer

My maternal grandmother's older and only sister migrated to Pakistan from Lucknow in the early 1960s. This was more than a decade after India was partitioned in 1947 to make room for a new homeland for Indian Muslims.

My maternal grandmother was called Badki Amma, or older mother, by many of us. Her sister went to live in Pakistan not because there was a shortage of living space in India. She did not believe in any two-nation theory either. She was not thinking of the move to Pakistan as *hijrat*, similar to the flight of Muhammad, the Prophet of Islam and his followers from Mecca to Medina in AD 622 to practice peace and egalitarianism.

She went from Lucknow to live in Karachi because her husband had retired as a senior official in the government of India and two of their four children had already made a home across the border before Partition.

After having spent a lifetime all over Uttar Pradesh on official assignments, the couple chose to live in Lucknow after retirement. This was only natural as they knew the city well and it was full of countless relatives.

Badki Amma's sister's husband was a nephew of Sir Syed Wazir Hasan. He was a jurist and politician originally from Kalanpur that is still a predominantly *shia* Muslim village in district Jaunpur.

Hasan championed rapprochement between the Indian National Congress and the Muslim League. In 1912, he had replaced Aziz Mirza as secretary of the Muslim League after its headquarters shifted from Aligarh to a bungalow on Lucknow's Lal Bagh Road. He drafted a new constitution for the Muslim League allowing it to work with other concerned citizens for a system of self-government suitable to all Indians.

He transformed Muslim League politics by bringing it close to the Congress. A leading lawyer of his generation, Hasan was admired by a group of young lawyers, journalists and political aspirants mainly from small landowning backgrounds. His Young Party within the League differentiated itself from the Old Party of large landholders and successful men whose interests were often tied to the British.

Nearly all members of the Young Party lived or worked in Lucknow and for some, the then Raja of Mahmudabad was an important patron. This group was not anti-Hindu. For that reason a critic called the Raja the source of all evil and positively dangerous and ruinous to the cause of Islam. Hasan and his followers were famous as the Lucknow Gang that made the pact between the Congress and the Muslim League possible in 1916. After the Lucknow Pact was signed, the focus of Indian politics moved away from the coastal cities of Bombay and Calcutta towards the Hindustani heartland.

Hasan was an influential figure. He was the first Indian chief justice of the Avadh Court and later president of the Muslim League. Later the religious politics of Chaudhry Khaliquzzaman and Maulana Abdul Bari Firangi Mahali of Lucknow replaced Hasan's progressive ideas of Hindu-Muslim unity. His presidential address in 1936 was filled with promises of unity but it was like a cry in the wilderness as demands by the League for a separate homeland became even more shrill. That broke his heart and Hasan passed away at the age of 73 in the same month and year that India won independence from the British and Pakistan was born, in August 1947.

Despite momentous changes taking place around them, Badki Amma's older sister and her husband settled down to a leisurely life in Lucknow in the midst of old friends and close relatives. Their youngest child finished dental studies at the King George Medical College in early 1960 and left for London. Soon the elderly couple began to miss their children, even though the children visited them often.

Their younger daughter had found a teachering job in Kuwait after graduating from the Aligarh Muslim University. When she decided to return home from Kuwait she chose to settle down in Karachi as her older sister had already been living there since before Partition. The teacher daughter was separated from her husband because he had wanted to live in India, and not in Pakistan.

Once she built a home in Karachi, this daughter wanted her elderly parents left alone in Lucknow, to live with her. The elderly couple did go to Karachi but soon after Badki Amma's sister had a nervous breakdown. Everyday she begged anyone to take her to the then Indian Prime Minister Indira Gandhi.

'I want to say sorry to the Prime Minister. I want Indira Gandhi to allow me return home to Lucknow,' she died pleading ad nauseam to anyone who bothered to listen to her.

This is what Partition did to Badki Amma. Partition robbed Badki Amma of many of her six siblings, and other relatives she had loved while she seemed to have little use of all the landed property left in her possession without her asking for it.

Badki Amma was the youngest child of an affluent landlord in Chakesar, a medium-sized village in the district of Jaunpur. In a Persian document called the *Jaunpurnama* it is written that Mughal Emperor Shah Jahan travelled through Jaunpur on his way back to Delhi after a battle in Bengal in the seventeenth century. He was impressed by the grand architecture of the city that was home to thousands of authors, poets, thinkers and philosophers. Before he left, he gave Jaunpur the title of Shiraz-e-Hind after Shiraz (that glorious city in southern Iran so famous to this day for its flowers, gardens, nightingales, wines and poets). Jaunpur was founded in the fourteenth century by Firoz Shah Tughlaq, Sultan of Delhi, and named after his first cousin and predecessor Muhammad bin Tughlaq also known as Jauna Khan. The city rose to prominence as a glittering capital between 1394 and 1479 of the independent kingdom of the Sharqi, or rulers of the East. Emperor Akbar, grandfather of Shah Jahan overthrew the Sharqis in the sixteenth century and brought it under Mughal rule.

Today Jaunpur is just another dusty city in eastern Uttar Pradesh but some of the former glitter seems to have rubbed off on its modern day citizens and on populations residing in surrounding areas as well.

Badki Amma's swagger and her feisty temperament revealed many a faded glimpse of that lost glamour of bygone days. After all, her ancestors had once owned several villages and endless fields of fertile agricultural land in the heartland of the area. She married into a family in Bhadi, a village about seven kilometres from Chakesar and with many *shia* Muslim homes. This family did not possess as much land as her father did but to a youthful Badki Amma that had mattered less than love and security provided to her by an army of older family members.

Word of the immense wealth of this agriculturally rich region peaked in the early eighteenth century as the sun began to slowly set on the Mughal court in Delhi:

> Well it is known to all the peoples of the earth that the city of Nakhlau (which the vulgar and rough-tongued call Lakhnau, or One Hundred Thousand Boats) stands without equal for the beauty of its gateways, and the majesty of its walls, the grace of its towers, the sheen of its domes, the lustre of its meanest dwellings washed with lime and shimmering under an indigo sky. Who has not heard of Chowk, with its heaven-embracing markets loaded with silks and incense, sugar and mangoes, its colonnades festooned with peacocks, its fragrant stairs washed hourly with crimson juices? Here veiled pass heart-expanding women with chaplets of flowers and comely boys with languid gait. Here are bejeweled elephants and haughty eunuchs, there frolic charioteers and vegetable lambs. Here are pannikins of crushed pearls, trays heavy with sweetmeats, the mouth-rejoicing gulab jamun, the tongue delighting jalebi, the tooth vibrating kulfi, the universe-arresting Sandila laddu; there are philtres, a thousand roses distilled in a vial; here again are gossamer bodices, chikan-worked, of which a courtesan may put on twelve and still not be modestly clad . . . have not visitors from Constantinople and St. Petersburg, Toledo and Tashkent, Peiping and Aleppo, Bokhara, Kon and Mandalay stood speechless on the top of Lakshman Tila? And do they not then burst into tears and coming down disband their retinues, paying off their assherds and muleteers, their cooks and compote factors, their masalchis, sutlers, food tasters, scullions, guides, guards, unguent-mixers, herbelots, mustard-oil-pressers and masseurs, because after this can there be more travel?[1]

It is believed that the first ancestors of Badki Amma's family of feudal lords came to South Asia from Khorasan, an area that is now part of modern day Afghanistan and Iran. Some other members of this *shia* Muslim family came from southern Iraq. The scholarly amongst these economic migrants were employed as teachers in different parts of South Asia while the more adventurous had preferred jobs in the army of Muslim rulers of Delhi.

On winning battles, some soldiers were rewarded with a higher post in the army and sometimes with agricultural land. They found employment as revenue collectors and other brave hearts settled down as cultivators. They built lavish homes in the countryside where the crockery used came from China, chandeliers from Europe and paintings and books from all over the world. The family library was often panelled with wood from the neighbouring forest. A flock of villagers did the dirty work in these homes from cleaning to cooking to ploughing fields while the landlord and his family members spent the money earned from hectic agricultural activities to travel, to entertain and to indulge in passions like horse riding and trinket collecting.

Later the British East India Company enriched the landlord further by buying endless amounts of sugarcane, rice wheat and indigo from local cultivators to be sold in Europe.

Mir Ali Sajjad, my maternal great grandfather made himself wealthy with the cultivation and sale of indigo. Before his sudden death sometime in early 1940, he had lorded over nearly 52 big and small villages around Chakesar.

But being a woman and the youngest child, Badki Amma was not meant to inherit anything in this world except love and security from her elders. After Partition she watched helplessly as one by one relatives from her close-knit family left the land of their birth to live in Pakistan. Without her asking she became the owner of all the family property left behind by her siblings.

Badki Amma was already a widow by the time Partition happened and no one told her how the abolition of *zamindari* or landlordism would affect the life of people like her. The large landholdings came to this *purdah*-observing female tutored in Arabic and Urdu at home, because the brother who had inherited the family property left in a huff for Pakistan after a misunderstanding with a sibling. What he left behind were relatives who loved him and numerous cases of unsettled disputes over property in Indian courts.

Another brother who had taken up a job in Hyderabad never returned. The two brothers who stayed back in the village died before Badki Amma. All these events took place in her very sheltered life around the time that landlordism was eventually abolished in India in 1951, and that remained a cause of life-long anxiety for her.

Badki Amma died at the age of 89 but without witnessing any closure to the endless disputes and legal battles over the ancestral property that continue to this day. But my maternal grandmother is not the only Muslim in North India taken by surprise at the almost sudden birth of Pakistan, and to face problems she never imagined would cross her path.

Take the curious case of Mohammad Amir Mohammad Khan, 73. The current Raja of Mahmudabad is Suleiman Bhai. He returned to Lucknow after his studies and travels abroad. Ever since the death of his father in 1973, he has been engaged in a fight with Indian authorities for the return of his ancestral property confiscated under the Enemy Property Act enforced after the 1965 India–Pakistan War.

Under the Act, all that belonged to Indians who migrated to Pakistan after Independence was declared evacuee property and brought under the custody of the government. However, Suleiman Bhai is Indian. It was his father who took Pakistani citizenship in 1957. It was the father who migrated to Pakistan and not him.

'We all make existential choices. My father made his and I made mine,' admits Suleiman Bhai.

Suleiman Bhai was elated when a judgement by the Bombay High Court and by the Supreme Court finally concluded in 2005 that a claimant could inherit property if the person was an Indian citizen and a natural legal heir. Naturally, he felt vindicated but before he could say yes, an Enemy Property Ordinance annulled the Supreme Court judgement. Now a fresh law threatens to give the government, and not the courts the power to decide who is the owner of property left by those who migrated to Pakistan.

Today Suleiman Bhai lives with his family in the midst of ruins but he is determined to fight. Some estimate that the property claimed by the family may be worth more than Rs 200 crore. When Suleiman Bhai's father joined the Muslim League he was only following in the footsteps of his father. Soon he became deeply involved with the Muslim League founded in 1906 to safeguard the commercial and landed interests of Muslims. The idea was conceived during the height of the popularity of a literary movement at the Aligarh Muslim University (AMU). Even before that Sir Syed Ahmed Khan, founder AMU had been suspicious about the Indian National Congress. Ever since the late nineteenth century there has been a dream to have a separate organisation to the Congress, to better safeguard the interest of professional Muslims and Muslim landlords in India.

In early twentieth century, the then Raja of Mahmudabad was the youngest member of the working committee of the Muslim League. Around 1931 Mahmudabad was one of the richest estates in Avadh and the Raja was treasurer of the Muslim League. Later when the Muslim League voiced a need for Pakistan, he supported the idea. He was surely responsible for the 26 seats won by the Muslim League in Avadh in the 1937 elections. The Muslim League got only one seat in the North-West Frontier Province, Punjab and Sind. What irony, that it is mostly this territory that makes up Pakistan.

It was Suleiman Bhai's paternal grandfather who hosted the signing of the Lucknow Pact in 1916 between the Indian National Congress and the Muslim League. It was agreed by members of both organisations to pressure the British government unitedly to adopt a more liberal approach to India and to give Indians more authority to run the country. At this time Muhammad Ali Jinnah was a member of both the Congress and the Muslim League and had enjoyed the reputation of being the best ambassador of Hindu-Muslim unity.

The 1916 Lucknow Pact was signed at Mahmudabad House, once a part of Lucknow's last ruler Wajid Ali Shah's fairy tale imperial city of Kaiserbagh. The Raja was gifted the palace by the British. This is when the colonial powers had looked to befriend local people of influence to help them settle down in Avadh after being nearly booted out by freedom fighters during the 1857 war, not just from Avadh but perhaps from the country as well.

Since provisions of the Lucknow Pact did not legally bind the Congress and the Muslim League to always remain united in the struggle against the British, there came a time when members of both organisations stopped to see a common future. Later when demand for Pakistan by the Muslim League rent the air, the then Raja heard nothing else. He abandoned not only Mahmudabad, Lucknow, Avadh, India but also his wife and son in Lucknow. He crossed the border after Independence in 1947 to live in Pakistan. But after 4 years he left for London. He travelled to Iraq to the city of Karbala that is considered sacred by *shia* Muslims. He spent the rest of his life disappointed in Pakistan and as Director of London's Islamic Culture Centreuntil his death in 1973.

To face Suleiman Bhai today against the decaying splendour of Mahmudabad House is to want to burst into tears. For Suleiman Bhai is not just an individual tragedy in flesh and blood but a mirror of the fate of millions of Indian Muslims, many of whom continue to lead half lives after they or their elders were wrenched away from their place of birth and from their loved ones.

Avadh is repeatedly described as Gods' own country with the Ganga, Jamuna, Sarayu and Gomti flowing through it. Lucknow had experienced a Renaissance of sorts in the eighteenth and the nineteenth centuries of the last great flowering of an Indo-Islamic culture. The rulers were liberal and civilised. Wajid Ali Shah, the last ruler, is the author of one hundred books, a great poet and dancer. The culture of Lucknow was not limited to the elite. Even common prostitutes had quoted Persian poets. Even horse carriage drivers and tradesmen in the bazaar spoke in a chaste language and were famous for exquisite manners. No wonder the British saw Avadh as the cherry on the cake and wanted to have it by hook or by crook. Once Avadh was theirs, the lush fields and booming markets here became the jewel in the crown of the ruler of England.

But in the second half of the nineteenth century the city saw a steady decline in its economic and political fortunes. Now Avadh was in the grip of brute British power. After a near defeat at the hands of Indian freedom fighters, the colonial army went on a rampage in 1858 to bleed Avadh, to destroy Avadh. A catalogue in the Government of India Archives simply called *Loot* lists items taken by the British but ten times as much wealth was looted in Lucknow than was acknowledged by the East India Company. Sikh soldiers hired from the Punjab joined their British counterparts in the pillage to loot fabulous riches and jewels from the royal residences in Lucknow. These exquisite trophies were dispatched to England to bedeck Queen Victoria and the royal family there.

The British tried to subordinate Lucknow further and moved the administrative headquarters to Allahabad. The old lands of Avadh were meshed into territory in the northwestern part of the region in 1877 and Allahabad was made the capital. However, by early 1920s the fortunes of Lucknow revived. As the freedom struggle against the British gained momentum, Lucknow was chosen as headquarters of both the Indian National Congress and the Muslim League. Now all the powers of the colonial masters could not take away from Lucknow its position as the most favoured city of the region's powerful landlords.

Lucknow was a great centre of landed power and it was home and office of landholders who had rights of ownership and revenue collection. The strength of the landlords was acknowledged by the larger than life existence of the British Indian Association and by the shared love of the elite for the culture and climate of Lucknow. Most landlords went to school in Lucknow to the Colvin Taluqdars College. It is in Lucknow that many had apartments in the old Kaiserbagh palace complex and where they socialised at the Kaiserbagh Baradari.

In 1900 the large landholders who controlled two-thirds of the territory in Avadh had numbered over two hundred. Together they had collected one sixth of the total revenue in the region. The landlords were important when it came to raise money whether it was for political purposes or for the further development of Lucknow. The political importance of landlords was acknowledged by the British who were careful when the matter concerned the interest of landlords. During the peak of the freedom movement, it was discovered that the landlords wanted Lucknow, and not Allahabad as the capital of Avadh.

In Lucknow there was an amazing concentration of Muslim landlords and professional government employees. The Kidwai families of Gadia and Bara Gaon, the family of Chaudhury Kaliquzzaman and that of Firangi Mahal lived in the city. Lucknow was a natural meeting place for these people and it was only natural for their political life to also begin and blossom in the same city.

The city was also modern and urbane. By the early twentieth century two English language newspapers *The Advocate* and *The Indian Daily Telegraph* took to the stands. It was Newal Kishore who made Lucknow a publishing hub. However, insecurity plagued Muslims throughout the twentieth century even as Muslim leaders remained in the forefront of the mass struggle to get the British to quit India. Who would lord over whom after the British left? was a question that niggled at the collective consciousness of all Indians. It was difficult for some Muslim leaders to imagine a future in a majority Hindu country.

And crucial to the rise of Lucknow as a major political centre was the emergence of Muslim political activism. Up to the turn of the century North Indian Muslims had followed policies laid down by Sir Syed Ahmad Khan. Nationalist politics was not the preoccupation. The goal was educational development and trust in the colonial government.

Later when Persian was removed from the curriculum of Allahabad University, Muslims took to real politics and protested in public more frequently. This was a new development and it drew increasingly on the large concentration of Muslim talent and wealth that lay in and around Lucknow. Ever since the annual sessions of the Congress were held here for the first time in 1899, Lucknow emerged as an important centre of all India politics.

The primary objective of the Congress was to promote by constitutional means the interests and the well-being of the people of the Indian empire. But some Muslims suspected that the Congress wanted to shift the whole basis of government support in Avadh more towards the Hindus.

In 1901 Viqar ul mulk Kamboh one of the founders of All India Muslim League organised a meeting to discuss political organisation in the house of barrister Hamid Ali Khan in Lucknow. Delegates were invited here in 1902 from Bihar, Punjab and Avadh to form a Central Mohammadan Political Association. The Congress always had a presence in Lucknow. Now the Muslim League was here and the Hindu Mahasabha and both were active with the support of Lucknow based landlords. The Muslim League was patronised by the Raja of Mahumudabad and Raja Maheshwar Dayal Seth fed the Mahasabha. The interest of Hindu nationalists in Lucknow was strong as well and landlord politicians like Raja Sir Rampal Singh of Kurri Sidhauli were never far from the centre of Hindu political activity.

However, nightmares of an uncertain future continued to occupy Muslims in varying degrees. This was the state of mind of Muslims ever since 1857, leading to the partition of South Asia in 1947 when Pakistan was born with the active support of the elite Muslim population of Avadh and Bihar. Apart from riches, Avadh lost many people to Partition.

Lucknow lost Chaudhry Khaliquzzaman. From the Mirzapur district of Uttar Pradesh, Zaman was an elected leader of the Muslim League in the Indian parliament. After the birth of Pakistan, MK Gandhi had sent Zaman to prevent the migration of Sind's Hindu population to India. In Karachi he met Acharya Kirplani, local Congress president who helped Hindus to cross the border. Zaman found little support for his mission and was so depressed at his helplessness that he did not return to India and went on to become the first president of the Pakistan Muslim League.

As for the family feud in Badki Amma's home, it was unpleasant but nobody saw it as a tragedy. For none had imagined at that time that the two sulking siblings would never see each other again.

A somewhat similar situation occurred in his family and is best described by Saeed Naqvi in *Being the Other: The Muslim In India*, his latest book.

Saeed's ancestral home in Mustafabad is in the same region of eastern Uttar Pradesh as Chakesar and Bhadi. He writes in *Being the Other: The Muslim in India:*

> Up to her dying day Naani Ammi had great difficulty understanding the document called the passport. She had grown up with the knowledge that to travel from one place to another

> all one needed was a railway ticket. This made immense sense because all her earlier journeys were confined to Avadh in UP. She was born in Barabanki, married in Bilgram and visited my parents either in Mustafabad or Lucknow. Then Partition came, followed by the abolition of zamindari and the death of her husband, a minor aristocrat. The houses in Barabanki and Bilgram were in ruins. Naani Ammi moved in with us, commuting between Mustafabad and Lucknow.
>
> After the marriage of her daughters to men in Lahore the same aunt could not understand how passports were needed to go to a place that was closer to home than Mumbai or far away Chennai.[2]

The permanent separation of Indians and Pakistanis is the most tragic and divisive aspect of Partition.

In 1981, Badki Amma got herself a visa to visit Karachi for the first, and last, time in her life. She had married her only surviving daughter to a grand nephew of Wazir Hasan and together they looked forward to meeting members of the various clans from Bhadi, Chakesar and Kalanpur who had migrated to Pakistan.

Being the only survivor amongst seven siblings, she was feted and pampered by many nieces and nephews and members of their respective extended families, some of whom remembered her from childhood and others who were eager to see a character emerge before them alive, out of the numerous tales told to them by their elders who were still nostalgic for that faraway but wondrous place called Chakesar.

She did not meet her only sister or the brothers who had left Chakesar after an argument in the family. They were already dead. While visiting the grave of her favourite brother in Karachi, I heard my grandmother whisper in between copious tears, 'Brother you did not keep your promise to me. Why did you promise to take care of me and then leave me alone in this world . . . ?'

Totally apolitical, Badki Amma was surprised that all those relatives who had settled in Karachi from her village were called *muhajir* or refugees. She did not connect that the bloodshed during Partition may have taken place on the border between India and Pakistan in Punjab and in Bengal but the largest number of people who populated Karachi went mainly from Urdu-speaking Uttar Pradesh and Bihar. The Muslim population of both states was considerable and had traditionally wielded significant power. There was no great exodus of Muslims from Uttar Pradesh in 1947. Most went voluntarily throughout the two decades of the 1950s and 1960s from cities around north India. The not so affluent Muslims from rural areas stayed back mostly due to ignorance of a country that was created in their name and also due to a lack of funds to undertake any journey.

In Karachi Badki Amma wondered why all the children of the family had given up their names so typical in Muslim homes in the Avadh countryside? Like the very affectionate Abban was called Raza in Karachi, Babu was Anwar in Lahore and Bibban something equally formal. To add further salt to wounds, some friends of her relatives on being introduced to her exclaimed, 'So you are the one taking care of the ancestral property in India for your family in Karachi?'

One member from the *muhajir* community she had met randomly in Karachi told her that he finally made it to the fabled city of Lucknow only to find it depressing, in utter decay, and stinking. He had heard so much about Lucknow's Prince of Wales Zoological Gardens so he went there to spot tigers he mistook for cats! Badki Amma who had never visited the zoo in Lucknow did not know what the stranger was talking about. She tried to get the joke but did not know whether to laugh or to be annoyed when she was told that in the 1971 war with India and during a regular blackout in Karachi, an erstwhile member of the Avadh royal family made sure that he carried his silver casket of betel leaves and a traditional *lota* filled with water for use in personal hygiene, to the pitch dark trenches dug up around the city for the safety of citizens.

She did not know what to say when a nephew asked her why no one from the family had tried to find him when he was brought to India as one of the 90,000 prisoners after the 1971 war between India and Pakistan? He was arrested in Bangladesh as he filmed the war for Pakistan television and was confined to an Indian prison. He was heartbroken that his relatives in Chakesar did not respond to the many letters he wrote to them. All that he had wanted from them at that time were magazines and newspapers to read in prison.

It is true that no one from the family answered his letters. It is suspected that this was done on the advice of my father, a grand nephew of Syed Wazir Hasan who was a freedom fighter, well-known journalist and politician in Lucknow. He may have wanted his relatives here to keep a distance from a Pakistani prisoner of war as well.

In Pakistan, Badki Amma met relatives who were compensated property in desert cities of Sind like Sukkur where it was difficult to till the land unlike the naturally fertile fields left behind in the Indo Gangetic plains of Uttar Pradesh. Many of the children born to these relatives in the bowels of Sind were not interested in agriculture or in a sound education and had moved to cities like Karachi even to drive taxis for a living. Badki Amma felt rather distressed in her relative's home in the middle of the desert in Sind. Her maiden visit to Karachi had overwhelmed her. Towards the end of a month-long stay in Pakistan her emotions were drained and she was ready to return home.

I had accompanied her to Pakistan as well and throughout the flight back from Karachi I found her very quiet. As the plane began to lower over Delhi we looked outside the window and gasped at the sight below. We saw a carpet of lights as the city was lit up with millions of lamps in celebration of Diwali. Badki Amma could not take her eyes away from the twinkle laid out before her. She turned to me with a big smile, as if grateful for the experience so high above the sky from where she could just enjoy the earth and not be forced into participating in plans and plots to either possess, or to conquer any part of it.

The ancestral home still stands in Chakesar and continues to be called *the court* as villagers have been going there for decades expecting justice from the reigning landlord. The owner of *the court* has changed hands though. Now a Yadav, a local politician from the Samajwadi Party, owns the place. This Yadav recently bought *the court*, the lush fields, orchards and sandalwood forests around it for a pittance from my octogenarian mother who lives in Lucknow and who did not know what else to do with the family property in Chakesar.

Notes

1 Sealy, I. Allan (1988) *The Trotter-Nama*. New York: Knopf.
2 Naqvi, Saeed (2016) *Being the Other: Muslim in India*. New Delhi: Aleph Book Company.

Further Reading

Cohen, Stephen. *The Idea of Pakistan*. Washington, DC: Brookings Institution Press, 2006.

Gandhi, Rajmohan. *Understanding the Muslim Mind*. New Delhi: Penguin India, 2000.

Khan, Yasmin. *The Great Partition*. London: Yale University Press, 2007.

Pemble, John. *The Raj, the Indian Mutiny and the Kingdom of Oudh 1801–1859*. New Delhi. Oxford University Press, 1977.

Chapter 12

Bacha Khan

The legacy of hope and perseverance

Altaf Khan

Khan Abdul Ghaffar Khan is introduced in the Pakistani textbooks in the following words: 'This movement was led by Khan Abdul Ghaffar. This movement was against the formation of Pakistan. After Pakistan's established Khan Abdul Ghaffar through his movement did a lot to adversely affect Pakistan.' This is the segment under the title *Khudai Khidmatgar Movement* in the FSc (intermediate level) Pakistan Studies book. Jamat e Islami Pakistan's present Amir Siraj ul Haq who also hails from Dir in Khyber Pakhtunkhwa (KP), in an interview on 3 May 2014, responded to a question regarding Bacha Khan (Abdul Ghaffar Khan) saying, 'Honestly, the person didn't impress me at all. I only know that God had given him a long life, he was tall, and had long arms. He spent most of his life visiting people's Hujras (men's meeting place).'[1] In the same interview he praised Zulfiqar Ali Bhutto as a national leader with an attractive style. He spoke very highly of Nelson Mandela. He showed the same scornful disrespect for Bacha Khan's son, Abdul Wali Khan, whose jokes, according to Siraj Ul Haq, he used to enjoy as a school goer. 'Although I never understood his confused politics,' he added. These were the only two political figures who were mentioned by the Jamaat Chief from KP with contempt.

But why is Bacha Khan treated so adversarially in the textbooks and in political discourse? 'The great leader is remarkably absent from many Pakistani history books – or, worse, referred to in passing.'[2] The reference in passing is also never positive. Better not to say anything than malign him. Is there anything wrong with his movement or his person? But why is the world so awed by the rugged Pashtoon? Why do people revere the non-violent soldier of Islam? Is it because he is non-violent? This would be a strange thing in our modern world, in a country that espouses democracy as its guiding principle. Is it because he is respected in India? But Gandhi is not disrespected in Pakistan. He is mentioned in many contexts in the textbooks and all of these are not negative. Bacha Khan, on the other hand, is either conspicuously absent or given a passing negative remark. Ignoring someone in the social narrative is annihilating the legacy of the person, movement or any social artefact. But the question still remains. Why?

Bacha Khan was never welcomed in the mainstream Pakistani narrative. Despite being the 'nonviolent soldier of Islam'[3] and the Frontier Gandhi,[4] the Khan never got any place in Pakistani sociopolitical history. The man who 'dedicated the majority of his life teaching his fellow Pukhtuns the value of tolerance. His main exertion often centred on their education, mannerism, self-respect, well-being and self-reliance.'[5]

Although often compared with Gandhi due to the similarity in the choice of non-violence as their method to change the destiny of their fellow men, Bacha Khan remains 'his own unique person and should never have to be referred to or viewed in someone else's shadow (or name, in this case).' Despite the similarities 'they were undoubtedly two quite distinct individuals.'[6]

Despite his life long 'passion towards education, for both girls and boys, and the creation of schools in villages especially created quite a melee; his work was not seen as positive reinforcement but taken instead as "rebellion" – an opposition.'[7]

The reasons for this rebellion are not sentimental, as many might presume. This was a calculated move in a struggle for power. Liaqat Ali Khan was the most powerful leader in Pakistan after Jinnah. But in a democratic polity the nawab of Meerut did not have a constituency. Meerut was left behind in India. The Khan, on the other hand, was the beloved leader in among his own people. A stronger contender to power at the highest level, though never a Muslim League supporter. He was, in contrast, a Congress ally. The Red Shirt identity (wearing the red colour and the non-violent Khudai Khidmatgar Movement) were used to name Bacha Khan as traitor. Muslim League was declared as synonymous to Islam. All this was done to get a constituency for himself and other elite immigrants from India. There was no other way to do this than to discredit the sons of the soil. Bacha Khan being one of the prominent ones got the bear the worst brunt. The Red Shirt was made a symbol of communism, the then enemy of Islam, while the Servants of God (Khudai Khidmatgar) an Indian puddle due to the non-violent nature of both Gandhi and Bacha Khan's approach to politics. All this farce was built to ensure one thing: wrenching power from the legitimate power centres within the different ethnic groups of the country and concentrating it in the urban, immigrant elite in the newly born nation. 'By declaring the entire country as one constituency and setting ones perceived Islamic credentials as the only qualification, Liaqat Ali Khan tried to create a constituency for his class – the politically insecure Muslim elite that had migrated from the Muslim minority provinces of India.'[8]

The above narration gives the impression that the legacy of the sons of the soil was annihilated to create room for a group of people who did not have their roots in the soil. Though the government and the mainstream politics never recognised him as a leader there are many people outside his native Pashtoon ethnic group who consider him a real reformer. Prominent religious scholar, Javed Ahmad Ghamedi praises him as the only political reformer/leader who went to the people in villages for the very purpose of educating them about their civic rights and duties. 'You have to change the people to bring change in the society. Most of the politicians remain seated in their drawing rooms. I don't know many leaders in Pakistan who approached the common people to educate them. The only one I know is Bacha Khan who went to the villages to educated people,' says Ghamedi in his television show on Dunya News (Urdu).[9]

But the question we have is whether it was a simple case of prejudice or if there is something deeper in the unpopularity of the man in his own country of birth. First, this was not the country he chose to be in. Yes, it was his motherland, the place where he was born. This was also the land where his ideology and social reformation took place. The country changed its identity. Bacha Khan and mainstream Pakistan lived in two different countries. As Stuart Hall puts it, a national identity is a 'system of cultural representation.'[10] The symbolic community is formed by a sense of belonging to the idea of a national ideal. It is not sufficient to be a legal citizen of a nation state. Participation in the idea of a nation state that is represented in the 'national culture' is also important.[11] Since national identity is seen as an all-encompassing, monolithically present phenomenon, there is no room for a traditional concept of identity: The holistic idea of identity of something that is always there. The primordially present, continuous bonding element that has a mystical presence. A national character that remains there, 'unchanged through the vicissitudes of history.'[12]

The conflict between Bacha Khan and the Pakistani state might have started as a clash of egos and that of different ethnicities, but even if this was not the case, it was destined to happen. He was clearly a man for his own people. And he did it without any prejudice against the other ethnic groups in Pakistan, or undivided India, for that matter. As he has repeatedly said, he worked for the betterment of Pashtoons because he felt responsible for them. And also because he could understand them. He did not have any knowledge about any other ethnic group in the Subcontinent. They could have their own leaders from within them. And yes, like all the Pashtoons he was very outspoken. A man who never liked mincing his words. This also made him hugely unpopular in the Punjabi-Muhajir (immigrants from India at the time of Partition) dominated country. The Punjabis were, and are, the dominant ethnic group, while the Muhajirs control the civil and military bureaucracy, and other ruling institutions (like the media). This numerical dominance combined with the power dynamics of the country has really given dominance to these two ethnic groups in the country, giving them the ultimate right to decide the national narrative. These groups and their narrative became what could be seen as 'Pakistaniness.' Since Pakistaniness is based on the abstract meshing of religion with geography, rather than the assimilation of all the existing cultural identities in within the geographical boundaries of the country, the question of a holistic Pakistani identity to become a basis of system of cultural representation became obsolete. And this is the point where the whole problem begins. The vilification of leaders from different ethnic groups in the country started from the very onset. Since the dominant narrative was formed in exclusion of the existing cultural contexts, symbolic annihilation was practiced to build a Pakistani identity. Despite the need to present Bacha Khan's non-violence to vindicate Pakistan of the charges of 'inherent terrorists,' none accepts his importance in the country. 'For everyone who thinks Islam and the Pashtuns are best represented by the Taliban, there is no clearer rebuke than the name Bacha Khan,' says Kamila Shamsi in her article *Why Pakistan must never forget Bacha Khan, its great unsung hero.*[13] She answers the question of the risks and dangers of not owning the non-violent soldier of Islam: 'It's no wonder that a commemoration of his death anniversary, at a university bearing his name, should have drawn the attention of a man best known for sending his followers to slaughter children.'[14]

It is assumed that in such conditions any alternative to violence would be used to pacify the destructive tendencies within society and salvage the image of the country in the comity of nations. Seen as an alternative to extremism, because 'every young person attracted to Sufism is one less attending a Wahabi imam's sermon, preaching incitement *to violence.*' [Italics added by author.] As traditional Islam is not recognisable in the rigid doctrines, predominantly Wahabi, 'Today, Muslims face two options: either the historical Islam, resting on art, music, the aesthetic, the communal form that was joyous . . . or the modern, highly politicised form,' Sarah Feuer writes in her 2015 article *Sufism: an alternative to extremism?*[15] The utility of Sufi Islam is constantly debated in the struggle against extremism in Muslim societies that the idea of 'harnessing' it against radicalism. The pros and cons of this unique brand of faith are seldom discussed, only to reach the two following conclusions, both of these being impractical. First, that the Sufis might have begun with the idea of an alternative to radicalism and a quest to eradicate the ills within Muslim societies but they have long forgotten it. And second, the fallacy of Sufism being a bulwark against extremism, which derives its strength from the very Shariah, is a very wrong assumption. Sufism, no matter how ecstatic, esoteric and other worldly it seems, functions within the confines of Shariah.[16] It will never confront any verdicts of the Shariah. And as the title of the article suggests, Sufis in Pakistan have become the great expectations of the West. These expectations are seriously wrong, says Sameer Arshad. Whatever the final outcome of the discourse is, Sufism is seen as one alternative to extremism.

The flirtation with all ideas that could somehow tame the monster of extremism, if not altogether annihilate it, shows the importance of all these in the mainstream narrative. But one fails to understand why Khudai Khidmatgari, the role of Bacha Khan, and the active, successful presence of non-violent soldiers of Islam, never caught anyone's imagination. Even the Pashtun youth are not aware of the presence and importance of such a great movement, if not personalities, in their very lives. Symbolic annihilation is the reason behind it. The simple statement by George Gerbner sums up symbolic annihilation, 'Representation in the fictional world signifies social existence; absence means symbolic annihilation.'[17] The aversion to Bacha Khan and his non-violent ideology has caused a systematic process of annihilation. A process that conforms with Tuchman's 1978 theory of '*omission, trivialization and condemnation*.' And as Coleman and Yochim argue in the *The Symbolic Annihilation of Race: A Review of the 'Blackness' Literature*, 'those racial groups who are not presented as fully developed in media, be it through absence, trivialisation, or condemnation, may see their social status diminished.'[18] Symbolic annihilation is based in the theoretical concepts of Pierre Bourdieu, who considers 'symbolic capital' as the real source of power. Since Bourdieu's 'philosophical anthropology is not based on interest, but on recognition,' in the quest for identity 'social existence means difference and difference implies hierarchy, which, in its turn, implies the infinite dialectic between distinction and claim, recognition and non-recognition, arbitrariness and necessity.'[19]

The reason for being locked out of the mainstream narrative and steadily relegated into oblivion, in social anonymity, even within its own home, is nothing emotional. It is not as simple as some elder brother, the Punjab, getting angry with the younger insolent hothead, the Pashtun. In fact, this oversimplification of the issue over many decades has complicated and confused our knowledge of the dynamics of symbolic annihilation. Of a process of systemic demonisation, accompanied by structured omission and shameless trivialisation. It is no coincidence. It is nothing emotional. It is rather a cold-blooded murder of a cultural construct, a nation that had the heritage of service of God, of selfless social reformation, of education for all, of a sense of hygiene that could lead to a better and modern dispensation. Instead, the people were thrown into the dark recesses of oblivion through constant demonisation. Name calling, ridicule combined with omission and trivialisation has wrenched the very identity of the Pashtuns. It is not simply about Bacha Khan or his Khudai Khidmatgars, it is about the heritage of a people, whose only 'fault was their sense of selfless service,' borrowing the words of Bacha Khan himself.

If we get into the controversy of proving his worth or that of his ideas and the movement, it won't lead us anywhere. There is a lot of material available on the topic. It is nothing but beating the rotten path. The question that is more important to answer is that who was Bacha Khan? What was the Khudai Khidmatgar movement. It could also be said that this topic has also been discussed threadbare. But I think there is still a lot of room for discussion. We know Bacha Khan the politician. Bacha Khan the person who is known as Frontier Gandhi. Or Bacha Khan who reached the masses. But what did he do among the masses? What were his immediate local aims? And how did people around him, his native environment, see him? It is not about how close he was to Gandhi or Jawaharlal Nehru, or whether his ideas preceded those of Gandhi, or whether Gandhi appreciated his efforts to bring non-violence home to a people who live by the sword.

Bacha Khan, as anybody interested in him knows, was born in to a Pashtoon family in the Pashtoon heartland, Utmanzai, in district Charsadda. His movement was a local social reformation movement. He never had purely political dreams, though in his own words the British forced them into politics by persecuting the Khudai Khidmatgars. 'Khudai Khidmatgar was not, like other movements, purely political. It was political, social, reformative, and spiritual. Khudai Khidmatgars served their country and their people for the sake of God.'[20] The reformation was based on the analysis of the ills that were hindering the social growth and the achievement potential of Pashtoons. The worst thing among Pashtoons was revenge. Bacha Khan focused on the elimination of this vice and had a plan for it. It was not simply a preaching plan. It was a total strategy, starting with a pledge to non-violence and encompassing human activity from education to cleaning the streets.

Each Khudai Khidmatgar had to take a solemn oath with specific points to focus on:

- Serving the people of God in His name, since He did not need any service.
- The vow to refrain from violence and revenge. And also that of forgiveness for those who even suppress the Khidmatgar.
- Refraining from anti social customs.
- Refraining from taking part in feuds.
- Doing at least two hours' community service every day.

The agenda was very clear. Pashtoon had to work on their own selves to be better human beings. This sense of service was supported by a vigorous educational plan.

Now the question is whether the Khudai Khidmatgars stood by the oath and made these changes in themselves and the immediate environment. This is a very ambitious reform agenda. Some individual impressions would help us understand the impact of the movement, if not ensure the authenticity of the person.

During the first Gulf War the old barber in my village Tangi used to sit outside his son's shop. Gul's father was known as Gandhi in the village. I went there for a haircut and heard the old man analysing the situation in the Gulf. 'We have learned during our youth (meaning the Khudai Khidmatgari days) that the imperialist powers blame the countries they decide to invade for their own benefit. After these nations are blamed they are isolated and nobody in world sympathizes with them. Once this is done, it is easy to invade them and exploit their national resources.' I was very impressed. As a young man I thought myself a very informed person, reading newspapers and discussing things in the university. But how did Gandhi get it. Gul Mama (his son, the barber) did not know anything about world affairs. He even did not know anything about local affairs! I asked Gul about his father's sense of internationality. 'This is the Surposhi (Red Shirt) thing. Baba talks this stuff all the time,' Gul replied nonchalantly. So, Gandhi (the barber) is evidence of the success of the educational reforms Bacha Khan carried out. The educational effort was very much hated by the British. Bacha Khan refers to the success of the school at many instances. The schools were also sustainable. These ran even when Bacha Khan was in prison.[21]

When it comes to social reformation, Dr Shamshad Ali has an inspiring story to tell. Dr. Ali is a medical doctor and lives in Agra, a village near the Kabul river. I asked him why he revers Bacha Khan so much? 'I even heard that you have a picture of Bacha Khan, framed in gold. Is it true? You are even critical of Gandhi and think he was not a Mahatma,' I asked. 'Well, reverence for Bacha Khan has nothing to do with his political stature. Neither does the picture in my home convey my whole feelings for Baba (Bacha Khan. Pashtoons use to call him Baba, father). He came to our village when I was a child. Our elders, the khans, asked him to stay. Bacha Khan used to stay for months among his followers and the whole villages were so happy. But Bacha Khan had a condition during that visit. He would stay only if the landowners, instead of their peasants, tilled the land. Our elders were not ready to do this. But they agreed and started working in their own fields, growing vegetables for the summer season. Once these were ripe, Bacha Khan asked them to bring the vegetable in baskets and sell these in their streets. This was so humiliating for the khans. How could a khan sell vegetables to his peasants, the people whose every breath was in their control? But they did it for Baba and brought the sales to him. Baba returned the money and told them to disburse it among the needy. "There is a lesson in it for you," baba told them. "Now you know how hard it is to toil for someone else. You do not even know it yet, because it was only once. The peasants are going through it for generations." '

'This is the man I revere,' Shamshad Ali told me. 'This is the reason why I think there is no mahatma but if there is any, it should be Bacha Khan,' Dr Saheb told me, looking deeply into my eyes. 'And I always look for examples. To find any other movement that has contributed so much to the immediate needs of the human beings. Honestly, I find none,' he added, with a sense of pride.

When it comes to equality and brotherhood, I have an example in my own house. My grandfather, Maaz Ullah Khan, was a landlord and a close follower of Bacha Khan. My grandfather took pride in the fact that Baba called him his son. My grandfather fell, but he was very unhappy to know that Bacha Khan had come to meet one cobbler in our village, but did not come to see his son, my grandfather. Bacha Khan came one fine afternoon. He sat with my grandfather in our veranda. They talked. We stood at a distance and watched them in awe. My grandfather complained about the earlier visit and told Baba that he expected him and that it saddened him a lot when he knew that Baba was here but did not come to see him. 'You are my son,' Bacha Khan said in a voice full of authority and love. 'But he was too sick and he is poor. I must go to see him. I was sick too and couldn't visit two places in one day. You must understand. I am old now.' And my grandfather was happy. He agreed. This is a simple lesson in human dignity. No books, no lectures.

He used to visit Pahtuns everywhere. Staying with the Chai Wala in Karachi in the back of his shop. It was the role in the movement and the commitment to the cause that Bacha Khan valued, not the financial or political standing. And the Khan was also a law abiding citizen. In his last days he was brought to Charsadda hospital in the back of a van in a charpoy. He refused to break the lane, although both doctors and patients insisted. After the treatment in a government hospital he was on his way back. The young men halted for a moment in Charsadda to buy the medicine the doctor had prescribed. Baba asked them to wait and insisted that they should bring the receipt, and cash memo, with the medicine. Otherwise he would not take it. When the young guys brought the medicine with the cash memo, Baba told them that this receipt was very important. 'Otherwise the shopkeeper won't pay taxes to the government,' Baba told the weary young men.

There are myriads of such examples where one can see how someone can stay committed to the path of humanity, justice and amelioration of the common people for such a long time. It is really unfortunate that in a country rife with conflict, all experiments are carried out to bring peace, but only one is left out of our collective consciousness. And ironically this is the one that has really worked. It is a working indigenous model. Bacha Khan has lived his life. He is beyond our love and reproach. He might be sitting in heaven, looking down at the world he tried so hard to be better. He cannot do it anymore. But we can. We should know it for sure that it is not Bacha Khan who is going to benefit if we follow in his footsteps. It is we who will benefit; it is in our own best interest to follow the man who matched his mountains. He was even taller than all Alps and Himalayas together.

Notes

1 Safi, Saleem. *Jirga, Talk Show on Geo TV, Interview with Sirajul Haq*. 03.05.2014. Retrieved from www.unewstv.com/18914/jirga-with-saleem-safi-jamat-e-islami-chief-siraj-ul-haq-exclusive-interview-3rd-may-2014. Accessed on 26 May 2017.
2 Esapzai, Sameer. The Expresse Tribune, Blog. *The Well Remembered Gandhi But the Oft Forgotten Bacha Khan*. 21.01.2015. Retrieved from http://blogs.tribune.com.pk/story/25847/the-well-remembered-gandhi-but-the-oft-forgotten-bacha-khan/. Accessed on 26 May 2017.
3 Easwaren, Eknath. Non Violent Soldier of Islam: Bacha Khan, a Man to Match his Mountains. *Nilgiri Press*. 1999. Retrieved from www.librarything.com/publisher/1016/Nilgiri-Press/
4 Korejo, Muhammad Soaleh. *The Frontier Gandhi: His Place in History*. Karachi: Oxford University Press, 1994.
5 Ibid.
6 Ibid.
7 Ibid.
8 Mehdi, Tahir. Daily Dawn. *The Two-Muslim Theory*. 14.08.2012. Retrieved from www.dawn.com/news/742169 Accessed on 25 May 2017.
9 Ghamdi, Javed Ahmed. *Ilm O Hikmat (TV Show)*. 26.08.2016. Retrieved from www.youtube.com/watch?v=cuBhMgKGYYI. Accessed on 25 May 2017.
10 Hall, Stuart. The question of cultural identity. In Hall, Stuart, et al., eds., *Modernity: An Introduction to Modern Societies*. Meldon, MA: Wiley Blackwell, 1996, pp. 596–632.
11 Ibid.
12 Ibid.
13 Shamsi, Kamila. *Why Pakistan Should Never Forget Bacha Khan, Its Great Unsung Hero*. 20.01.2016. Retrieved from www.theguardian.com/commentisfree/2016/jan/20/bacha-khan-pakistan-terror-attacks-education-institutions. Accessed on 24 May 2017.

14 Ibid.
15 Feuer, Sarah. *Sufism: An Alternative to extremism?* N.d. Retrieved from www.religionandgeopolitics.org/islam/sufism-alternative-extremism. Accessed on 20 May 2017.
16 Arshad, Sameer. Pak Sufis become Victims of West's Great Expectations. *The Times of India*. 11.04.2011. Retrieved from http://epaper.timesofindia.com/Repository/getFiles.asp?Style=OliveXLib:LowLevelEntityToPrint_TOINEW&Type=text/html&Locale=english-skin-custom&Path=TOIM/2011/04/11&ID=Ar01701. Accessed on 17 May 2017.
17 Gerbner, George and Gross, Larry. Living with Television: The Violence Profile. *Journal of Communication*, Vol. 26, No. 2, Spring 1976, pp. 172–199.
18 Coleman, Robin R. Means and Yochim, Emily Chivers. The Symbolic Annihilation of Race: A Review of the "Blackness" Literature. *African American Research Perspectives*, Vol. 12, 2008, pp. 1–10.
19 Nicolaescu, Christina. Bourdieu-Habitus, Symbolic Violence, the Gift: "You Give Me/I Give You" Principle. *Euromentor Journal*, Vol. 1, No. 3, September 2010, pp. 1–10.
20 Khan, Abdul Ghaffar. *My Life and Struggle*. Translated in English from Pashto by Bouman, Helen H. New Delhi: Hindi Pocket Book.
21 Ibid.

Chapter 13

Whose history of partition?

Tamil cinema and the negotiation of national identity

Kalathmika Natarajan

> You will not understand (Partition). You are a south Indian.

In an emotional sequence in the Tamil film *Hey Ram*,[1] a Sindhi friend reuniting with the Tamil protagonist makes this point as he recounts his personal trauma of experiencing the partition of India. It is this statement that animates this chapter's discussion of Tamil cinema's response to Partition as a means of understanding the ways in which the southern state of Tamil Nadu negotiated the centrality of Partition to the making of Indian identity.

The diverse and ever-growing academic literature on the partition of India is itself indicative of both the centrality of Partition to understanding 'the making of modern South Asia' and the ways in which the afterlives of Partition continue to shape identity and politics. Scholars have questioned top-down narratives of independence by exploring Partition from the margins in all its administrative and bureaucratic detail,[2] traced its borders and cartographic anxieties,[3] and explored its many manifestations: as nostalgia, as postmemory, as trauma, mourning and silence.[4] Partition, therefore, is not to be understood as a singular 'moment' in the making of nation-states, but as a 'long' Partition[5] that has embedded itself into our collective psyche. The vocabularies of Partition are omnipresent, be it the longing for an invincible joint India–Pakistan cricket team,[6] or the fact that 'Wagah,' 'Lahore-Amritsar,' 'Kolkata-Dhaka' and 'Srinagar-Muzaffarabad' are hardly just names of places.

The very term 'Partition' is synonymous with communal violence: indeed, not just for survivors for whom 'Partition *was* violence, a cataclysm, a world (or worlds) torn apart'[7] but also for generations born long after 1947. As Urvashi Butalia has noted, 'It took 1984 to make me understand how ever-present Partition was in our lives too.'[8] Therefore, it is widely acknowledged that:

> Partition played a central role in the making of new Indian and Pakistani national identities and the apparently irreconcilible differences which continue to exist today. . . . Partition then is more than the sum of its considerable parts . . . it signifies the division of territory, independence and the birth of new states, alongside distressing personal memories and potent collective imaginings of the other.[9]

There is indeed little doubt that life in India and Pakistan has been 're-made by that violence (of Partition) and the curious memory-history we have of it.'[10] In this chapter, I seek to interrogate who exactly this 'we' is and how south India – and in particular, Tamil Nadu – relate to the 'national' 'we' whose lives were irrevocably shaped by the experience of Partition. While it is hardly true that south India was untouched by Partition – violent police action in the princely state of Hyderabad, perhaps, is the most unequivocal rejection of such a statement[11] – it is still the case that the trauma of Partition remains and, more importantly, is perceived for the most part to be a (north) Indian[12] experience.

In discussing the ways in which Partition has shaped Indian identity and sociopolitical life, it is important to recognise the fact that there was no singular 'Indian' experience of Partition. Indeed, Bhaskar Sarkar[13] acknowledges this very aspect and goes on to the extent of noting that a question posed at a conference by a man from Kerala 'pressed me to examine my assumption that Partition was essential to post-1947 identity and my . . . conviction that Indians needed to come to terms with the experience. Was it necessary, or even pragmatic, to accord such a centrality to the event?'

Therefore, if Partition 'has emerged as a national trauma,'[14] it is important to ask how those in most southern states who were not directly touched by this constitutive moment relate to its watershed status in the making of the 'national' subject and the very psyche of Indianness. This chapter makes such an effort by studying Tamil cinema's response to Partition through the case study of two rather different films: *Naam Iruvar (We Two)*,[15] released a few months before Indian independence, and the critically acclaimed and controversial *Hey Ram*, which was selected as India's official entry to the Academy Awards in 2000. Given the incredibly significant role of cinema in the political and cultural landscape of Tamil Nadu, ranging from war-time propaganda films and pre-independence 'nationalist' cinema, to their role as vehicles of Dravidian anti-caste, anti-north Indian politics, this is an especially relevant case study.

Indeed, several scholars have studied post-independence Tamil cinema as a text of Dravidian politics directly resulting in the electoral success of the Dravida Munnetra Kazhagam in 1967.[16] It is an oft-mentioned truism that almost 'all the Chief Ministers of Tamil Nadu since the late 1960s have been involved in the Tamil film industry.'[17] Pre-independence Tamil talkies ranged from mythologies and films on social themes such as caste discrimination to war-time propaganda films and Gandhian, nationalist cinema, exemplified by the films of K. Subrahmanyam.

It was the symbolism and languages of these films that were subverted and contested in the era of the 'DMK film':[18] films scripted by the then rising stalwarts of Dravidian politics such as C.N Annadurai and M. Karunanidhi that questioned the hegemony of religion and caste, and the dominance of north India. Annadurai's *Velaikkari* (Servant Maid)[19] and M. Karunanidhi's *Parasakthi* (The Goddess)[20] are iconic films of this genre, with the latter widely regarded as an 'explicit DMK film'[21] that 'overtly displayed its politics.'[22] While I shall touch upon *Parasakthi*'s evocation of 'Dravidanadu' (the Dravidian nation) as the true, pure nation subservient to hegemonic north India, especially as a contrast to the 'nationalist' films that preceded it, I am most interested in understanding the ways in which one of the most iconic, 'overtly nationalist'[23] films of its time – *Naam Iruvar*, released in January 1947 – viewed the Indian nation and the prospect of Partition.

Naam Iruvar: Anticipating partition and calling for Gandhian unity

Naam Iruvar makes for an especially important case study, given that it is considered to be 'the last of the genre of patriotic films'[24] in Tamil cinema. Based on a play by the NSK Drama Company, the film traces the lives of two brothers, the Gandhian Jayakumaran and the younger Sukumaran, and their estrangement and eventual reunion. This served as a metaphor for a country which would be partitioned unless the two communities realised they were both equals: brothers and sons of the same nation. Indeed, it is not just the usage of songs by the famed Tamil poet Subramania Bharathi – whose copyright was purchased by director A.V. Meiyappan – but the very story of the once-inseparable brothers who were divided due to the impressionable younger brother falling prey to Westernised bad influences, that makes it an 'explicit allegory of the nation in the making' and the prospect of Partition.[25]

The narrative begins with the Gandhian brothers walking out of the house united in protest against their father's corruption, both financial and moral, proclaiming that the youth do not hesitate to call out injustice and that 'brave, Tamil blood' was coursing through their veins. This is a persistent metaphor in the movie – of a younger, more revolutionary nation that is fed up of the backwardness and corruption of the older generations who were often complicit in the sad state of affairs. Indeed, when Sukumaran and his lover Kannamma (named after Bharathi's famous muse) decide to marry despite her father's objections, they would note the need for them, as educated Indians free to make their own choices, to move forward from the superstitions and backwardness of their parents' generation. As part of their wedding celebrations, Kannamma and Sukumaran eventually donate a sum of one lakh rupees for the welfare of 'Harijans.'

However, the film is careful to delineate the corruption in the younger generation too. Sukumaran is depicted as falling prey to the bad influence of a group of Westernised youngsters who remain friends with him only until he is rich. Indeed, they are shown telling him that by drinking and smoking with them, he could become modern/Western. The suit-clad Sukumaran is in stark contrast to the khadi-clad older sibling Jayakumaran, and it is when Sukumaran begins believing the ill-intentioned comments of his friends that he demands to be given his share of the family property right away. Even as he confronts his brother for his share of wealth, he is constantly reminded of the words of his friends: 'Brothers never remain united. One must not believe any sibling who claims to want unity.' In this representation of a gullible brother demanding the division of property and wealth due to the seeds of distrust sown by sly Westernised influences, the film depicts the state of the nation and the flawed beliefs of those that are calling for its Partition. Indeed, the film makes this explicit too when the Gandhian Jayakumaran says in anguish:

> Are you saying you want to go your own way and separate from me? Are you saying you want our united strength to

> shatter? Is it not because of this lack of unity that 40 crore people are enslaved by a small lot? How are you able to ask for such a thing, even after looking at the state of our nation?

Jayakumaran further exclaims that he believes all the wealth is Sukumaran's and is saddened by the fact that his love for his brother has only managed to end up in such a scenario. Sukumaran is unmoved, even arguing that he sees a conspiracy in his brother's hesitation to give him his share. As he hands over the property papers to his younger brother, the camera cuts to a statue of Gandhi in Jayakumaran's house while the soundtrack is set to one of Bharathi's iconic verses that proclaim the need for unity.

Ultimately, the brothers reconcile when Sukumaran realises the folly of his ways and the greatness of his brother when he lands in jail, abandoned by his friends, after running into debt in an attempt to make a movie. Upon his release due to Jayakumaran paying off all his debts, Sukumaran falls at his feet – this is a moment that is framed with the statue of Gandhi behind them, and indeed looking upon them, following which the brothers and their younger sister hold hands together as they bow to the statue. Such a framing makes it all the more obvious that the only hopeful solution for the nation – as depicted in *Naam Iruvar* – is for those that are misguided and want division to realise their errors and reconcile in the Gandhian way.

There is a lone Muslim character – Raheem – in the film, who is part of the group of Westernised friends that influence Sukumaran. Apart from the Muslim *topi* that visually signifies his religion, Raheem is not really defined in terms of his religion. He smokes, drinks and also plays the role of Hanuman in Sukumaran's doomed mythological film. While *Naam Iruvar* functions very much as a call for the nation to prevent Partition, it does not pitch this explicitly in religious terms. Indeed, scholars have argued that 'one major reason for the absence of any wilful demonisation (of Muslims) in the film is that unlike the north, the south did not witness any major Hindu/Muslim riots like those in Calcutta during the Direct Action Day.'[26]

Perhaps the most remarkable aspect of *Naam Iruvar* is its iconography of Indian nationalism. Flags, maps, statues and portraits of national leaders are omnipresent, not just outdoors but very much in every frame of the house in which the brothers live. A statue of Gandhi plays the role an idol or portrait of Gods and Goddesses would: the family fall at its feet and weep in times of sorrow and rejoice by bowing before it in times of joy. They garland, sing and dance before the statue. This statue of Gandhi is therefore in the realm of the divine, to be worshipped, and stands as the anchor around which the happiness and distress of the household – and by extension, every good Indian household, it would seem – takes place.

Maps of an undivided India, embossed with lights, embedded with the tricolour, with the Bharat Mata as a 'bodyscape' – territory embodied by a human, often a woman[27] – take centre stage, especially in the opening song *Aaduvome Pallu Paduvome*, Bharathi's song anticipating and celebrating Indian independence. Flags and the charkha are also icons frequently spotted in a movie where characters greet each other with the phrase '*Jai Hind*.' One of the final sequences of the movie features a montage of portraits of nationalist leaders – Jawaharlal Nehru, Sardar Vallabhbhai Patel, Abul Kalam Azad, Acharya Kripalani, V.O. Chidambaram Pillai, C. Rajagopalachari and Subhash Chandra Bose. The diversity of this lineup is no coincidence. The mainstream Congress leadership is featured alongside a portrait of the revolutionary Bose of the Indian National Army (INA), which comprised of a significant number of Tamil workers who joined the INA, especially in Malaya.[28] Indeed, the role of Tamils who joined Bose's INA has found resonance in several Tamil films as a mark of their valour and patriotism. The most notable example is *Indian*,[29] starring Kamal Haasan, where a former Tamil soldier who fought in the INA sets out to fight for independence again: this time, for freedom from the postcolonial political structure of corruption and dishonesty. Similarly, *Thevar Magan*,[30] also written by and starring Haasan, proclaims the bravery of the Thevar community as reflected in their men joining the INA.

By featuring the 'national' leadership alongside more regional icons like Rajaji, Bharathi and V.O. Chidambaram Pillai, *Naam Iruvar* seeks to not just balance but firmly intertwine the local with the 'national.' Neither is it a coincidence that the film relied heavily on the songs of Bharathi in order to communicate an Indian nationalism that was firmly routed through the Tamil language. Indeed, posters of the film would advertise the movie as a chance to hear 'Bharathi in Talkie! Come hear the national songs of the immortal poet!'[31] *Naam Iruvar* therefore anticipates the birth of Indian independence by celebrating the Gandhian nationalist struggle that lead to the moment and does so by utilising the poetry of an iconic regional poet to mark a national triumph. The film however also acknowledges the divisions in Indian society that have lead to the prospect of Partition, even as it expresses the hope that those misguided by Western influences and fears of conspiracies to take away their rightful share, will realise the folly of their ways and reunite with peaceful Gandhians.

Soon after the release of *Naam Iruvar* began the era of films that strongly contested some of these notions of pan-Indian nationalism to instead stress the weakening of the 'true' nation – Dravidanadu – by the Brahmin, 'national,' religious mainstream as represented by the Congress government in Tamil Nadu headed by C Rajaji. Scholars have delved into these films in detail and I do not seek to analyse them for the purpose of this chapter, but it is essential to understand how these 'DMK films' subverted the existing script of Tamil cinema. Indeed, a vivid example is *Parasakthi*'s opening sequence, which utilises the familiar musical and dance cues of nationalist Tamil films like *Naam Iruvar*, but subverts them by raising the question of which nation is to be celebrated.

Where *Naam Iruvar's* Bharatanatyam dancers pay tribute to Bharat Mata, the tricolour and an array of maps of the undivided Indian nation, the artistes in *Parasakthi* dance to the famed Tamil poet Bharatidasan's paen to the greatness of the Dravidian nation and its languages.[32] Moreover, as Sumathi Ramaswamy has shown, Tamil Nadu has had an ambivalent tryst with the 'bodyscape' of *Bharat Mata*, whose symbolic status has often been subverted and contested by the bodyscape of *Tamilttay*, the Tamil language embodied as the Divine Mother Goddess, transforming 'a goddess of language and learning into a mistress of territory and polity.'[33] Thus to confront the *Naam Iruvar* template of sorts was part of the politics of the DMK film.

Hey Ram: A south Indian trauma of Partition

*Hey Ra*m, directed by and starring Kamal Haasan and made simultaneously in both Tamil and Hindi,[34] is a film that most explicitly and controversially provides a Tamil cinematic response to Partition and thereby makes an essential case study for my analysis. The film depicts the ways in which Partition irrevocably altered the life of Saket Ram, a Tamil Brahmin archaeologist who witnesses the brutal gang rape by Muslims of his Bengali wife Aparna in Calcutta during Direct Action Day. This traumatic experience transforms him into a violent fundamentalist Hindu who seeks to assassinate the man he holds as responsible for the communal carnage in India: Mohandas K Gandhi. A tragic encounter with an old archaeologist friend – the Pashtun Amjad Ali Khan – from their days of excavating Mohenjodaro, forces Ram to confront the religious hatred that has immersed him. The film flits between Partition as a flashback, shot in colour, and a present-day scenario, shot in black and white, set in 1999 where an emaciated, Gandhi-like figure on his death bed – Saket Ram – exclaims 'Even now?' when told of communal violence during the anniversary of the demolition of the Babri Masjid.

There is a considerable amount of critical attention given to *Hey Ram*, particularly for its graphic depiction of the dangerous intertwining of masculinity, sexuality and violence – a 'spectacularisation of Partition violence'[35] – exemplified by a particularly stunning hallucination sequence when the body of Saket Ram's second wife Mythili transforms into a rifle.[36] Moreover, there is also the representation of the justification of Ram's violence as a response to the violation of the Hindu body – not just his wife's, but also the threat of his own sexual violation during Aparna's rape, a 'scene that the film cannot forget.'[37] Another important point of focus has been the fact that *Hey Ram* 'undeniably flirts with Hindutva in a . . . dangerous manner,'[38] engages in a 'troubling romance with Hindu right wing ideology,'[39] fails to 'distance the spectator from an extreme Hindutva perspective'[40] and does not sufficiently make the case for Ram's final transformation from to be assassin to Gandhian.[41] Indeed, film critic Namrata Joshi has described the shocking atmosphere in the cinema where she saw the film: 'Much to your shock and dismay . . . for them (the audience), Gandhi is the villain of the piece and they cheer at each potshot taken at him, while every word in praise of the Mahatma is greeted with either a jeer or with dismissive silence.'[42]

While these are vital points of enquiry, my focus is on the centrality of the south Indian/Tamil subjectivity of the protagonist Saket Ram through which the politics of *Hey Ram* must be understood. While most scholars and film critics have either neglected or paid very brief attention to this aspect, often as a mere mention in the description of the character,[43] I argue that the film must be viewed as a south Indian story of Partition, a south Indian attempt to make the trauma and loss of Partition – a constitutive moment in the making of Indian identity – their own. In an interview with NDTV in 2000, the actor-director Kamal Haasan made this crystal clear:

> It's about a man called Saket Ram . . . (and) his travel through (the) India of that times . . . I chose him from a community which I was born in. . . . I chose that community intentionally so that I will be as honest as possible . . . and that's why I have taken the protagonist of the film . . . is (sic) *a Tamilian Brahmin, even in the Hindi version. It's owning up the country as mine. It's asking the rest of the country to own up the rest of the country.*[44]
>
> (Italics added)

Far from this simply being stated intent, the film itself makes this aspect clear on several counts. First, *Hey Ram* marks an attempt to make the idioms and symbols of the Brahminical south come directly in contact with the idioms and symbols that marked the violence and horror of Partition. This is most evocatively demonstrated in the transition from Calcutta to Srirangam: a shot of a wild elephant that charges past a bloody, riot-torn Calcutta street cuts neatly to a sequence with a chained and seemingly more peaceful and restrained temple elephant of Srirangam. The soundtrack recites verses modelled after the holy Vaishnavite Tamil hymns, describing the madness of one who roams, let loose like a wild elephant. This marks Saket Ram's journey to a peaceful south that seems untouched by Partition violence.

This portrayal of a south India with its apparently gentler Hinduism – marked by a recurring soundtrack of M.S. Subbulakshmi songs – right from the first shot of the film to the flashback – bhajans and temple processions – marks both the distance of the average Tamil or south Indian to Partition and the exceptional status of Saket Ram. He is the only one that has transcended the distance of his south Indian subjectivity by being a direct witness to Direct Action Day – a fact repeated throughout the film, especially by his Tamil film – and yet is forced back 'home' after this trauma.

Moreover, Saket, by marrying Aparna against the wishes of his family, had also in a sense transcended his state and region to claim a more 'national' status, before the violence of Partition made him return home and agree to a traditional marriage arranged by his family. As Ravi Vasudevan has noted, the depiction of the Gandhian Tamil Iyengar family – Ram's in laws are outspoken Gandhians, and his wife's song of choice when Ram meets her for the first time is *Vaishnava Janato*, Gandhi's favourite bhajan – 'is suggestive of the earlier linkage between nationalism, modernity and high caste society emblematised by a leader such as C. Rajagopalachari'[45] The slow domesticity of his life in Tamil Nadu is contrasted with the violent politics of Partition that marked his life in Calcutta. Indeed, Ram makes this especially evident when he notes that even as his wedding was taking place 'in leisure' in Srirangam, what was happening in Delhi was the 'world's biggest political divorce.'

Second, the fact that this is a Tamil protagonist who runs into characters who, by some reason or the other, are able to speak Tamil to some extent and/or have some relationship with the south, should not just be construed as a matter of filmmaking practicality which requires the willing suspension of disbelief. Instead, the 'logic' of these Tamil-speaking characters becomes an exercise in demonstrating the historical and cultural links between Madras presidency/Tamil Nadu and (north) 'India' at the very traumatic moment of Partition when the nation state was being forged.

Indeed, in one of the first sequences set in Karachi, a British official asks Ram how it is that his friends the Pashtun Amjad Ali Khan and the Sindhi Lalwani 'spoke your Dravidian language. You're from Madras, right?' These men establish their connections to the south as through their alma mater, the Madras Christian College. Yet, in Khan's case, there is more: he recounts his father's experience of selling carpets in the south and an even more powerful personal connection, the fact that his wife is a Muslim from Ambur, Tamil Nadu. The Tamilian then – be it Ram or Amjad's wife Nafisa – is thus a 'national' subject, moving from Ambur or Srirangam to Karachi and Calcutta, thereby being tied to the national trauma of Partition. Even the Hindu fundamentalist Shriram Abhayankar speaks in halting Tamil while noting that he is a Thanjavur Maratha. Indeed, in one of the first scenes following the Direct Action Day violence, Abhayankar asks Ram: 'You're not a Bengali, are you? What is your mother tongue?' Ram's unique Tamil subjectivity – a subjectivity that, as we have seen, Haasan retained deliberately even in the Hindi version of the film – both complicates the idea of a 'national' subject by making an 'outsider' both the victim and perpetrator of violence during Partition, even as it enables a south Indian to be part of the trauma and terror of Partition.

Perhaps the most vivid representation of this is the scene described earlier in the chapter when Ram runs into his old Sindhi friend Lalwani in Maharashtra. A tattered Lalwani recounts to Ram the horrors of losing his wife and daughter in Partition violence in Karachi and points out that as a south Indian, Ram 'will not understand.' In tears, Ram replies 'No, I do,' and the two men embrace each other. It is exactly this which *Hey Ram* tries to do. It attempts to make the pain of Partition the south Indian's and seeks to enable the south Indian to mourn for Partition. This mourning would thus serve as a way in which they would be part of a 'national' trauma.

Conclusion

As I have shown, *Naam Iruvar* and *Hey Ram* mark two different responses of Tamil cinema to Partition: the former released a few months before independence and the latter released as late as 2000. *Naam Iruvar* celebrated the forthcoming birth of the Indian nation even as it sought to allay fears of Partition by representing it as a story of two brothers who, despite divisions and misunderstandings brought about by Westernised influences, must reunite by following the Gandhian path. *Hey Ram* remains the most direct Tamil cinematic response to Partition by placing a Tamil Brahmin in the centre of events and depicting him as both a survivor and perpetrator of Partition violence, whose Indian identity is irrevocably shaped by this experience.

Such an analysis that focuses on the depiction of Partition in these films complements the literature on Tamil cinema's ambivalent portrayals of Tamil and/or Indian identity and the ways in which it unsettles the idea of a 'national cinema.'[46] Moreover, it also adds to the literature on 'mourning the nation,'[47] which thus far predominantly focuses on Hindi, Urdu, Punjabi or Bengali cinema, by taking into account the fact that in the case of *Hey Ram*, this serves as a Tamil/south Indian mourning of Partition.

As Nalini Iyer has recently shown in her analysis of the fiction of some writers from south India who have written about Partition, they expressed their 'anxiety about how the experience of Partition was shaping ideas of citizenship and belonging in a new nation. Were those in the South to be perpetual outsiders in the nation?'[48] *Hey Ram*, as I have shown, is an attempt to answer this very question. While scholars are beginning to explore the ways in which south India related to Partition and its central status in identity politics, there is a lot more room for research.

Notes

1 *Hey Ram*, Dir. Kamal Haasan, Raaj Kamal Films, 2000. I will discuss this film in detail later in this chapter.
2 Notable examples are Zamindar, Vazira Fazila-Yacoobali, *The Long Partition and the Making of Modern South Asia: Refugees, Boundaries, Histories*, New York: Columbia University Press, 2007; and Roy, Haimanti, *Partitioned Lives: Migrants, Refugees, Citizens in India and Pakistan, 1947–65*, New Delhi: Oxford University Press, 2012.
3 See Krishna, Sankaran, 'Cartographic Anxiety: Mapping the Body Politic in India,' *Alternatives: Global, Local, Political*, Vol. 19, No. 4, 1994, pp. 507–521; and Kabir, Ananya, 'Cartographic Irresolution and the Line of Control,' *Social Text*, Vol. 27, No. 4, 101, 2009, pp. 45–66.
4 There is a substantial literature on these topics, but for examples see Butalia, Urvashi, *The Other Side of Silence: Voices from the partition of India*. New Delhi: Penguin Books, 1998; Pandey, Gyanendra, *Remembering Partition: Violence, Nationalism, and History in India*, Cambridge: Cambridge University Press, 2001; and Kabir, Ananya, *Partition's Post-Amnesias: 1947, 1971 and Modern South Asia*, New Delhi: Women Unlimited, 2013.
5 Zamindar, *The Long Partition*.
6 Pandey also makes this point in *Remembering Partition*.
7 Ibid., p. 7.
8 Butalia, *The Other Side of Silence*, p. 6.
9 Khan, Yasmin, *The Great Partition: The Making of India and Pakistan*, New Haven: Yale University Press, 2007, p. 9.
10 Pandey, *Remembering Partition*, p. 16.
11 See Sherman, Taylor, *Muslim Belonging in Secular India: Negotiating Citizenship in Postcolonial Hyderabad*, Cambridge: Cambridge University Press, 2015.
12 I use the term 'north Indian' in this context not merely as a geographical signifier but more so as a cultural term often used in the 'southern' states to refer to the dominant region 'north of the Vindhyas.'
13 Sarkar, Bhaskar, *Mourning the Nation: Indian Cinema in the Wake of Partition*, Durham, NC: Duke University Press, 2009, p. 39.
14 Sarkar, *Mourning the Nation*, p. 2.
15 *Naam Iruvar* (We Two), Dir. A.V. Meiyappan, AVM Productions, 1947.
16 Hardgrave, Jr., Robert L. and Neidhart, Anthony C, 'Films and Political Consciousness in Tamil Nadu,' *Economic and Political Weekly*, Vol. 10, No. 1/2, 1975, p. 27.
17 Velayutham, Selvaraj, 'Introduction,' in Velayutham, Selvaraj, ed., *Tamil Cinema: The Cultural Politics of India's Other Film Industry*, New York: Routledge, 2008, p. 7.
18 For usages of this phrase, see Pandian, Mathias Samuel Soundra, 'Parasakthi: Life and Times of a DMK Film,' *Economic and Political Weekly*, Vol. 26, No. 11/12, 1991, pp. 759–770.
19 *Velaikkari* (The Servant Maid), Dir. A.S.A. Sami, Jupiter Pictures, 1949.

20 *Parasakthi* (The Goddess), Dirs. R Krishnan and S Panju, AVM Productions and National Pictures, 1952.
21 Ibid., p. 761.
22 Pandian, Mathias Samuel Soundra, 'Parasakthi: The Goddess,' in Gopalan, Lalitha, ed., *The Cinema of India*, New York: Wallflower Press, 2009, p. 77.
23 Chakravarthy, Pritham K. and Chakravarthy, Venkatesh, 'Naam Iruvar: We Two,' in Gopalan, Lalitha, ed., *The Cinema of India*, New York: Wallflower Press, 2010, p. 47
24 Baskaran, S. Theodore, *The Eye of the Serpent: An Introduction to Tamil Cinema*, Madras: East West Books, 1996, p. 101.
25 Chakravarthy and Chakravarthy, 'Naam Iruvar,' p. 49.
26 Ibid., p. 50.
27 Ramaswamy, Sumathi, 'Maps and Mother Goddesses in Modern India,' *Imago Mundi*, Vol. 53, 2001, p. 109.
28 See Amrith, Sunil S., 'Tamil Diasporas across the Bay of Bengal,' *The American Historical Review*, Vol. 114, No. 3, 2009, p. 570.
29 *Indian*, Dir S. Shankar, Sri Surya Movies, 1996.
30 *Thevar Magan* (Son of Thevar), Dir Bharathan, Raaj Kamal Films International, 1992.
31 See poster in Chakravarthy and Chakravarthy, 'Naam Iruvar,' p. 49.
32 Pillai also makes this point. See Pillai, Swarnavel Eswaran, *Madras Studios: Narrative, Genre, and Ideology in Tamil Cinema*, New Delhi: Sage Publications, 2015, p. 124.
33 Ramaswamy, 'Maps and Mother Goddesses in Modern India,' p. 109.
34 I am analysing the Tamil version of the film in this paper.
35 Sarkar, *Mourning the Nation*, p. 278.
36 Mallot, J. Edward, *Memory, Nationalism and Narrative in Contemporary South Asia*, New York: Palgrave Macmillan, 2012, pp. 76–77.
37 Gopalan, Lalitha, *Cinema of Interruptions: Action Genres in Contemporary Indian Cinema*, London: British Film Institute Publishing, 2002, p. 192. Bhaskar Sarkar also makes this point. See Sarkar, *Mourning the Nation*, pp. 277–278.
38 Dwyer, Rachel, 'The Saffron Screen? Hindu Nationalism and the Hindi Film,' in Meyer, Birgit and Moors, Annelies, eds., *Religion, Media, and the Public Sphere*, Bloomington and Indianapolis: Indiana University Press, 2005, p. 281.
39 Sarkar, *Mourning the Nation*, p. 276.
40 Vasudevan, Ravi, 'Another History Rises to the Surface: "Hey Ram": Melodrama in the Age of Digital Simulation,' *Economic and Political Weekly*, Vol. 37, No. 28, 2002, p. 2917.
41 See Biswas, Ashis K., Joshi, Namrata and Joseph, Manu, 'Hey Ram, Hey Nathuram,' *Outlook Magazine*, 6 March 2000, www.outlookindia.com/magazine/story/hey-ram-hey-nathuram/208996 (Last accessed 4 May 2017).
42 Joshi, Namrata, 'Mahatma Amid the Mob,' *Outlook Magazine*, 6 March 2000, www.outlookindia.com/magazine/story/mahatma-amid-the-mob/208997 (Last accessed 4 May 2017).

43 There are many such examples ranging from Joshi, Biswas and Joseph's review to the critical analyses of Sarkar, Mallot, Dwyer and Gopalan.

44 Haasan, Kamal, *Interview with NDTV Talking Heads*, February 2000, www.ndtv.com/video/shows/talking-heads/talking-heads-in-conversation-with-kamal-haasan-aired-february-2000-288885 (Last accessed 4 May 2017).

45 Vasudevan, Another History Rises to the Surface: "Hey Ram", p. 2919.

46 Velayutham, Selvaraj and Devadas, Vijay, 'Encounters with "India": (Ethno)-Nationalism in Tamil Cinema,' in Velayutham, Selvaraj, ed., *Tamil Cinema: The Cultural Politics of India's Other Film Industry*, New York: Routledge, 2008, pp. 154–171.

47 See for example Sarkar, *Mourning the Nation*.

48 Iyer, Nalini, 'Partition's Others: The View from South India,' in Singh, Amritjit, Iyer, Nalini and Gairola, Rahul K, eds., *Revisiting India's Partition: New Essays on Memory, Culture, and Politics*, London: Lexington Books, 2016, pp. 329–342.

Chapter 14

Re(presenting) refugee women in Bengal's partition narratives[1]

Roshni Sharma

History and historical writings have always been 'His Story,' and often in the process of writing that story, the way 'Her Story' has been represented remains untouched. It is rightly said that 'the invisibility of women in history is due to the fact that men held power and women appeared not to have had the power to write themselves in.'[2] Revealingly, wherever women have appeared, they appear as marginal, secondary and in their affiliations to males as mothers, wives, sisters or mistresses, but not as independent agents. Historians have neglected women's historiography,[3] making it selective which presents a very narrow record of human past in terms of time, space and numbers.[4] Recent feminist historiography argues that 'representative history can only be written if the experience and status of one half of the mankind is an integral part of the story.'[5] With the introduction of gender into the discussion of the history and politics of Partition, a very different kind of story has emerged – different in terms of the understanding of Partition it provides and of what it means to write history and read literature about the period. It does not matter who writes about women's history as such notions might lead to gender bias and minimise the objective of bringing the women back into history. What is important is the perspective from which it is written, the kind of research that has been done in an attempt to present a total picture of history.[6] Therefore, it would not be a misinterpretation to argue that the study of women's history 'implies not only a new history of women, but also a new history.'[7]

This chapter investigates the way in which refugee women have been represented and the way in which they were relocated during and after Partition. It provides a detailed picture of the experiences of women as victims and of those who became the agents of surviving the trauma that Partition led to. Though the nature of Partition on both sides of the border has been different, there is a point of similarity – on the question of violence that women from both sides faced.[8] With the lack of alternative stories on Partition, little emphasis has been made to read and write about the images that have been constructed of refugee women.

Women have been subjected to all sorts of unimaginable atrocities and violence. They were arguably the worst victims of Partition, having to endure not only the destruction of their homes, displacement and violence, but also abduction, prostitution, mutilation and rape as they became symbols through which men communicated with each other. An estimated 75 to 100,000 women were abducted by members of other religious communities to be raped and murdered, sold into prostitution, or forced into marriage.[9] These abduction numbers were considered 'wild figures.'[10] Women's bodies were treated as territory to be conquered, claimed or marked by the assailant.[11] They became the battleground for men of different religious faiths. Atrocities were enacted upon the bodies of women as men of one religious group sought to dishonour the men of another faith, by proving them impotent in their ability to protect their 'women.' Interestingly, the abduction of women (especially Hindu women) gets tied up with the image of the 'weak Hindu' race,[12] which is also connected with a weak Hindu man, who cannot protect his women. Such violence was directed against the minority community leading to impregnation with the seed of the 'superior' or 'pure' race. Killing foetuses, knifing and opening pregnant wombs, constituted offences against the father/husband.

Forced migration became a common feature of the time. The suffering of those women who had to accept their abductors as husbands was tremendous indeed. Partition opened new challenges for women as they came out of their private domains and took up public duties driven by economic motives. Taking up prostitution as victims of economic distress has been looked upon as immoral and seen as a violation of the honour of the community, which challenged the entire 'existing social order.'[13] By engaging in such activities, they were looked down upon and seen as a 'disgrace to the refugee colony.'[14]

The figure of the refugee woman is a doubly marginalised figure; she is marginalised both as a refugee and as a woman. However, throughout the course of this study she is not portrayed as a victim. Rather she is seen as an agent of survival, of 'triumph.' Going beyond depicting women as victims, which they admittedly were, this chapter argues how the willingness to survive combined with determination and courage to discover new roles assigned to them by Partition. The refugee women, driven by circumstance, opened new opportunities for many other middle class Bengali women. This newly formed image of the refugee women as breadwinner destabilised the Bengali middle class value system. 'She changed the woman's role, as an earning member, in the family, albeit not without inherent tensions.'[15] In the process of self-settlement, 'caste rules were bent, traditional occupations were abandoned in the search for employment, families became more nuclear and women came out of the home to work.'[16] The role of women both in the inner and outer spaces (private and public spheres) underwent changes. Refugee women moved from 'victimhood' to 'triumph,' discovering an ability to survive and attain success. Surprisingly, many men became 'extremely proud' of their working wives and daughters in the colony.[17] Several refugee women took up careers in acting in the Calcutta film industry and commercial theatres. For thousands of refugees, like Sabitri Chattopadhyay, it became a necessity to take up acting as profession.[18] A few among them took up more challenging and unconventional jobs, such as hawkers and bar dancers. However, this is not to say that Partition was a liberating experience. It dissolved, though temporarily, strict distinctions between private and public. Many refugee women returned to the domestic world as soon as their families were comfortably situated, both financially and physically.[19]

The image of refugee women has undergone many changes with the change in the discourse and interests of the nation. Emerging from the colonial era, the image of refugee women kept changing through the Swadeshi movement thriving well through Partition and continues till date. The discourse of women's chastity was deployed to counter issues of foreign domination, which was done by making a clear-cut distinction between the material and the spiritual world. This binary corresponded well to the divide between the home and the world outside the home. Women became the symbol of nation and have remained so since the mid-nineteenth century. The chastity of the Hindu wife became the image of national purity. The middle class woman, 'the *bhadramahila,*' became a depository of 'essential cultural identity.'[20] The purity and chastity of women was to be preserved beyond the death of her husband, through an 'indissoluble non-consensual infant marriage, and through her proven capacity for self-immolation.'[21] The hymn 'Vande Matram' captures the icon of the nation, the land as the mother, where women were required to reproduce the nation physically and symbolically while men protected, defended and avenged the nation.[22] Therefore the bodies of women become the embodiment of the nation; the nation became the Mother, and her people became the Sons of the Mother.

With the lack of alternative stories on Partition, little emphasis has been placed on reading and writing about the images that have been constructed of refugee women. This chapter is an attempt to explore and comprehend the experiences of Partition that shaped people, especially women's lives and their identities, with an exclusive focus on Bengali literature. Unlike the Partition narratives of Punjab, where 'the author can find voice only through impersonal narrators, or teller-actors'[23] the narratives of Bengal are painful in the details of dead bodies lying through the streets of Calcutta and Noakhali and what it means to survive a traumatic event. However, cross-border migrations were totally different and complex phenomena in Punjab than in the other side of India. It has been estimated that 73 per cent of migrants were from India in Punjab, whereas only 9 per cent came to East Bengal.[24] There is a surge of novels that are written post-Partition, which revisit Partition. The two texts that this chapter deals are written in Bengali. These two texts – *Epar Ganga, Opar Ganga* (*The River Churning*) and *Swaralipi* (*The Notations*) are written by female authors Jyotirmoyee Devi and Sabitri Ray, respectively. These novels offer the possibility of coping with the loss of household and livelihood, rehabilitation, opening up the possibility of the labour market, new uncertainties in employment, re(structuring) the home and the world, remembrance and trying to explore the gaps and silences that are a part of stories on Partition. I focus on these two texts because both have female authors, and one of the authors remains an outsider to Partition while the other author is very much affected by the Partition, and is a refugee herself. The prospect of analyzing stories on Partition from two different perspectives compelled me to read these texts.

The first text, *Epar Ganga, Opar Ganga*,[25] revolves around the aftermath of Partition, depicting the struggle, trauma and journey of the refugee women to rediscover their new identity within the family and the community. It raises a fundamental question of the chastity of refugee women, the idea of 'honour' that is attached to a particular family/community. Here it is depicted by a Hindu girl, *Sutara*, a victim of Partition, who takes shelter in a known Muslim family headed by *Tamij Saheb*. After tracking down her own family, *Sutara* relocates and comes down to Calcutta, where her chastity is questioned by the women in the family. She is despised because family members and women in particular, feel that she is 'polluted' and 'ritually unclean.'[26] The women in the family do not like *Sutara* and they believe that she must have eaten 'god knows what kind of forbidden food.'[27] She becomes a 'jhonjhat' which literally means 'problem' in Bengali. It depicts the story of a woman who is not accepted within her family and within the community at large because she has brought shame and dishonour to the family by spending a few days with the people of a different community. The author, therefore, focuses on society's repression of women's bodies and its habit of dishonouring and humiliating them everywhere and in all times. It reflects the violence to which women are exposed all over the world because of their gender.

The text, however, remains silent on the trauma and atrocity that *Sutara* witnessed, though there is a brief mention by the narrator that she was completely shattered both physically and psychologically and was unable to get up from bed. The reader is given several details about the physical and psychological torture she has endured. It is assumed that she might have been raped, though the narrator does not give any account. Such silences in women's stories over their own body should not be resolved, accounted for, unveiled or recovered but rather understood as women's inability to subsume their experience.[28] It is well pointed out by the author when she elaborates by saying that 'History is not written by cowards, and there are no female epic poets. Even if there were, they could hardly write stories of their own dishonour and shame. The language for it has yet to be fashioned. . . .' Therefore, it would not be an exaggeration to suggest that such violence finds it difficult to get expressed in language. It becomes difficult to speak about the trauma, especially among women in a patriarchal structure, where the fear of rape itself is enough to marginalise women and to prevent them from being accepted by their own community.[29] The victim is scared of her 'own' family because of the stigma attached with her being 'polluted.' By portraying *Sutara* as a 'polluted' woman within her 'own' family, it then shifts from the community divide of 'us' and 'them' to the gender divide. One gets identified as the 'other' amongst her own family members because of the fact that she does not possess the right (unpolluted) body like other women in her own family. Consequently, the struggle goes on between the image of the 'good woman' and that of the 'bad woman' (Sutara), who confronts the negative aspects as their bodies are treated as shameful, polluted, dirty and impure. Such women then become survivors with nothing to lose. The purity of the body becomes a symbolic marker between good woman and bad woman.

Therefore, the sense of dislocation, disruptions of notions of home, difficulties of feeling in place, divided and forced kinship are common to many women's experiences. For example, the story of *Zainab*, a young Muslim woman, and *Buta Singh*, her Sikh husband, which had wide reverberations, memorialised as it was in newspaper accounts, a memoir, and a Punjabi film, titled *Shahed-e-Mohabbat. Zainab* had been abducted during the relocation of her family from India to Pakistan. She had passed through many hands, and was eventually sold to Buta Singh, an Indian Sikh. Singh married her and 'in time, the two grew to love each other. They had a family, two young girls. Once she was recovered and relocated, she was returned to her family, expecting to return to Singh later. However, they never stayed together thereafter and Singh committed suicide.'[30] The novel *Pinjar* is also a classic on this aspect, where the story is based on the case of the abduction of a Hindu girl *Pooro* (later as Hamida) by a Muslim named *Rashida*. Her bitter experience of the entire episode made her feel and see herself as 'neither *Pooro* nor *Hamida*, but as *pinjar*, a skeleton, which had no shape, no name.'[31]

These stories of *Sutara, Zainab* and *Pooro* and many others demonstrate some of the gender-, sex-, and religion-based complexities of Partition. While some kinds of stories narrate 'honourable' deaths, there are fewer accounts of those women who have survived such trauma.[32] For too many of the abducted women, official recovery meant a second uprooting. Many of them openly protested against the recovery operations and refused to return to their parents or kin folk. They were very well aware of what was waiting for them. For such women it may be said to have occupied a space between two deaths rather than between life and death.[33] For such women, the government of two dominions decided that they should be forcibly evacuated.[34] The recovery was considered an issue of national honour. One of the Members of Parliament argued: 'You will remember Sir, how when Mrs. Ellis was kidnapped by some Pathans, the whole of Britain shook with anger and indignation and until she was returned Englishmen did not come to their senses. Here, where thousands of girls are concerned, we cannot forget this.'[35]

However, the struggle of the refugee women was not confined within the four walls of their homes. The employment of women in jobs outside their homes, as workers in metropolitan space, involves certain metamorphoses of the ideas of space, labour and identity that come out clearly in Sabitri Ray's novel *Swaralipi*.

The novel highlights the changes that women affected by Partition underwent with increasing politicisation and urbanity. Roy is more interested in depicting her characters like Sita, Radha, trying to redefine their lives within the complexities of inner divisions corresponding to personal and political debate – the choices that women make as human beings rather than as victims. The text raises a fundamental question of 'what a nation state does once it has emerged.'[36]

With the formation of a new nation state, at the cost of thousands of lives, the author asks how human beings (especially women) cope with the changing scenario. The building of a new nation state determines their role in both the spaces of home and world. For all the female characters in the novel, both the home and the world blend into each other as they 'come out' of the domestic sphere into the public arena of works and politics by joining the Communist Party or by taking active part in refugee movements across Bengal. The contributions of the refugee women in the *Jabardakhal* movements (land-grabbing movements) are mentioned as worthy, movements in which the refugee women continue a bitter struggle against the police for about four days. It 'gave a new impetus to the founding of colonies with greater determination and planning.'[37] Under the leadership of the Communist Party, the refugee women become political agitators and struggle their way out for survival, still managing their role in the private world. Parmila, whose role had been confined to the domestic until Partition, sets out for the streets of the city along with Kshetramani, an aged woman.

The novel *Swaralipi* is filled with such examples of refugee women who are continuously struggling within the private and public spheres. Each and every woman tries to redefine their lives within the private and the public. Women in this novel are engaged in labour to meet their political ends. They are highly active in their political roles as members of the Communist Party. They serve meals, provide shelter, clean up and nurse wounded comrades. Radha is a Tebhaga fighter in the novel. She is a peasant woman who works and travels from village to village staying and hiding in different peasant households. Sita, who is the main character in the novel, is more active in the public arena than is the character in the earlier novel, *Epar Ganga, Opar Ganga*. She helps in organising her students, raising funds to fight cases for political prisoners. In deep contrast to this side of hers, she feels that her brother Phalgu and Prithvi, whom she loves, does 'not know, cannot even begin to find out the deep ugliness that is hidden in every household of this great city.' Interestingly, in the novel the outer world of politics stays outside and does not affect the private sphere. The underlying assumption is that the labour which is employed in the private sphere is by nature not political. In the later part of the novel, Sita is arrested by the police. She becomes a victim of taking part in politics, for giving shelter to communist fugitives. Her personality in the entire novel is of a courageous political prisoner, equivalent to her male counterparts.

The novel, therefore, breaks the divide between the home and the world – where the women belonged to a *bhadralok* household but challenged the same by 'coming out' actively in politics. Many refugee women in the novel feel that it is important to join the communist-led processions to protest against police firing in refugee colonies. In many processions, a large group of refugee women participated, carrying half naked, skeletal children. Even elderly women came forward shouting slogans. However, this coming out was a failed attempt. As the refugee women did not really move into their public life, but rather the domestic world expanded to include their participation in political, community and economic affairs. This expansion of their role was 'legitimised on the basis of women's domestic roles as wives, mothers and daughters.'[38]

Going back from where it all began women have been portrayed as derivative figures, in their relation to their male counterparts, which gets reflected in the texts. For it is considered that she 'belongs to someone else and therefore to his caste, nationality and religion.'[39] Thus, these fictions on Partition explore the pain, trauma and conflicts of loyalties and raise a need to revisit concepts like chastity and honour.

A close reading of these novels helps in mapping the female psyche. Women being considered as representatives of their family/community had to undergo inhuman treatment, and novels of this kind attempt to portray a picture of the uncertainties that women faced during Partition. I read both of these novels as interventionist tools with which to witness the event of Partition that brought along with it rehabilitation and resettlement. Gender dynamics have become recurrent in the history of independent India, by taking newer forms and shapes in everyday life. They pose the question of silence that Devi's novel imposes with respect to language and that Roy's brings out by assessing how changing women's roles in the public sphere contribute to the formation of a new nation state.

Notes

1 This chapter is part of Roshni's M.Phil. dissertation on Partition Literature and Refugee Woman submitted to University of Delhi in 2012.
2 Shah, Kirti K., ed. (2005) *History and Gender, Some Exploration*. New Delhi: Rawat Publication, p. 5.
3 Lerner, Gerda (1976) 'New Approaches to the Study of Women in American History: Theoretical and Critical Essays,' in *Liberating Women's History: Theoretical and Critical Essays*, ed. Bernice A. Caroll. Chicago: University Of Illinois, p. 350.
4 Shah, ed., *History and Gender*, p. 5.
5 Menon, Ritu and Kamla Bhasin (1998) *Borders and Boundaries: Women's in India's Partition*. New Delhi: Kali for Women, p. 10.
6 Rowthham, Sheila (1971) *Hidden from History: 300 Years of Oppression and Fight Against It* New York: Pantheon Books.
7 Gordon, Ann D., Mari Jo Buhle and Nancy Shrom Dye (1976) 'The Problem of Women's History,' in *Liberating Women's History: Theoretical and Critical Essays*, ed. Bernice A. Caroll. Chicago: University Of Illinois, p. 89.
8 Bagchi, Jasodhara and Subhoranjan Dasgupta, eds. (2003) *The Trauma and Triumph: Gender and Partition*. Kolkata: Stree Publications, p. 3.
9 Scott, Bede (2009) 'Partitioning Bodies: Literature, Abduction and the State,' *Interventions*, Vol. 11, No. 1, p. 35.
10 Major. Andrew, J. (1949, 10 December) "The Chief Sufferers," *The Tribune*.
11 Menon, *Borders and Boundaries*, p. 43.
12 Datta, Pradip Kumar (1999) *Carving Blocs: Communal Ideology in Early Twentieth Century Bengal*. New Delhi: Oxford University Press, pp. 148–151.
13 Chakrabarti, Prafulla K. (1990) *The Marginal Men: The Refugees and the Left Syndrome in West Bengal*. Calcutta: Kalyani, p. 433.
14 Banerjee, Sudeshna (2003) 'Displacement within Displacement: The Crises of Old Age in the Refugee Colonies of Calcutta,' *Studies in History*, Vol. 19, Part 2.
15 Chakravarty, Sudeshna, *The Impact of the Flow of Refugees from East Bengal on West Bengal: Political Economic and Social Aspect* (unpublished) thesis submitted to Calcutta University.
16 Chatterjee, Nilanjana (1990) 'The East Bengali Refugees: A Lesson in Survival,' in *Calcutta: The Living City*, ed. Sukanta Chaudhuri, Vol. II. New Delhi: Oxford.
17 Weber, Rachel (2003) 'Re(Creating) the Home: Women's Role in the Development of Refugee Colonies in South Calcutta,' in *The Trauma*

and Triumph: Gender and Partition, ed. Jasodhara Bagchi and Subhoranjan Dasgupta. Kolkata: Stree Publication. The refugee colony that was studied by Weber was the Bijoygarh colony.

18 Sabitri Chattopadhyay, the famous Bengali actress, who came from East Bengal to Calcutta after Partition.
19 Weber, Rachel (1995) 'Re(Creating) the Home: Women's Role in the Development of Refugee Colonies,' *Indian Journal of Gender Studies*, Vol. 2, No. 2. Sage Publication.
20 Chatterjee, Partha (1993) *Nation and Its Fragments: Colonial and Post Colonial Histories*. Princeton, NJ: Princeton University Press, p. 117.
21 Tankia Sarka, ibid., p. 203.
22 Ivekovic, Rada and Julie Mostor, eds. (2004) *From Gender to Nation*. New Delhi: Zubaan, p. 10.
23 Das, Veena (1991) 'Composition of the Personal Voice: Violence and Migration,' *In Studies in History*, Vol. 7, No. 1, p. 67.
24 Waseem, Mohammed (1999) 'Partition, Migration and Assimilation: A Comparative Study of Pakistani Punjab,' In *Region and Partition: Punjab, Bengal and the Partition of the Subcontinent*, ed. Ian Talbot & Ghauharpal Singh. Karachi: Oxford University Press, p. 203.
25 The novel literally means *This Side of Ganga, That Side of Ganga*, was first published in 1967 in Bengali as *Itihashe Stree Parva* (Women's Chapter in History) in Autumn-Annual volume of the prestigious Bengali periodical *Prabashi*. The book was translated into English by Enakshi Chatterjee in 1995 as *The River Churning*.
26 Devi, Jyotirmoyee (1995) *The River Churning*. Trans. Enakshi Chatterjee. New Delhi: Kali for Women, pp. 34, 42.
27 Devi, *The River Churning*, p. 33.
28 Didur, Jill (2006) *Unsettling Partition: Literature, Gender, Memory*. Toronto, Buffalo, London: University of Toronto Press, p. 11.
29 Bagchi and Dasgupta, eds., *Trauma and Triumph*, p. 4.
30 Butalia, Urvashi (2000) *The Other Side of Silence*. New Delhi: Penguin India, p. 130.
31 Pritam, Amrita (2000) *Pinjar*. New Delhi: Aarsi Publications, p. 31.
32 Menon, *Borders and Boundaries*, p. 59.
33 Das, Veena (1996, Winter) 'Language and Body: Transactions in the Construction of Pain,' *Daedalus*, Vol. 125, No. 1, p. 79.
34 Pandey, Gyanendra (2004) 'Disciplining Difference,' in *Post Colonial Passages: Contemporary History Writing on India*, ed. Saurabh Dube. New Delhi: Oxford University Press, p. 169.
35 Pandey, Gyanendra (2001) *Remembering Partition*. Cambridge: Cambridge University Press, p. 166.
36 Gupta, Dipankar (2006) 'Between Ethnicity and Communalism: The Significance of the Nation-State,' in *Religion, Violence and Political Mobilization in South Asia*, ed. Ravinder Kaur. New Delhi: Sage Publication, p. 85.
37 Chakrabarti, *The Marginal Men*, p. 65.
38 Weber, 'Re(Creating) the Home,' pp. 75–76.
39 Pandey, *Remembering Partition*.

Part IV

Relationships

India–Pakistan–Bangladesh

Chapter 15

Seventy years of India–Pakistan relations

Sajad Padder

India and Pakistan are the two largest countries in South Asia. Ever since their independence in 1947, both countries have had a fraught relationship. They fought three major wars in 1947–1948, 1965 and 1971. Both countries went nuclear in 1998. Thereafter, they engaged in a war on the Kargil heights in 1999. These wars were followed by stints of peace. But the deep rooted mutual distrust and suspicion, conflicting claims over Kashmir and what Stephen Cohen calls the clash of state and national identities[1] have put this relationship on hold. The chances of any breakthrough are minimal unless the policy makers in both countries realise the futility of continued conflict and recognise their overarching common interests.

Jammu and Kashmir: A bone of contention

Jammu and Kashmir emerged as a thorny issue immediately after independence of the two countries from the colonial yoke. As Stephen Cohen rightly puts it, 'Kashmir is the most important single conflict in the subcontinent, not just because its territory and its population are contested, but because larger issues of national identity and regional power balances are imbedded in it.'[2] A cursory look at the events of the last decade would reveal that India, Pakistan and even Kashmiris have reached the *Mutually Hurting Stalemate* (MHS) stage on Kashmir, and that there is no way forward other than reaching an understanding at the political level. It is clear that none of the parties involved in the conflict – India, Pakistan, Kashmiris and militants, can alter the status quo through military means. The status quo, on the other hand, is also not acceptable, as it is hurting all parties concerned. India and Pakistan have failed to alter the status quo in Kashmir, despite the different political and military strategies that they employed in recent years. Before the Islamabad Summit in January 2004, there had been more than 35 occasions in which the Heads of State in India and Pakistan had met. Besides these meetings at the highest levels, there were at least 12 rounds of talks between 1989 and 1998 before the Lahore and Agra Summits. Neither the meetings at the Heads of State level nor at the Foreign Secretary level, could proceed further. All these attempts inevitably broke down due to the failure of both governments to reach an understanding on Kashmir.

During 2004–2007, General Musharraf put forward various proposals for resolving the Kashmir imbroglio. In November 2003, in an interview with the BBC Radio Urdu Service, Musharraf re-introduced his 'four-step' approach to Kashmir, one he had tentatively put across during the Agra talks which offered to eliminate all options unacceptable to India, Pakistan and the people of Kashmir and then evolve a consensual solution. The 'four-steps' envisaged the following:

- i Official talks commence.
- ii Centrality of the Jammu and Kashmir dispute is acknowledged.
- iii Any proposal unacceptable to India, Pakistan or Kashmiris is taken off the table.
- iv The best solution acceptable to India, Pakistan and the Kashmiris is taken.[3]

It is believed that the Musharraf's 'four-step' proposal was discussed amongst the officials of both countries during the course of the Composite Dialogue process. On 24 September 2004, General Musharraf and Indian Prime Minister Dr Manmohan Singh met in New York and signed a joint statement indicating that they would start looking into various options on Kashmir and move the peace process forward. On 5 December 2006, Musharraf further polished his ideas and put forward the 'four-point formula':

- i Softening of LoC for trade and free movement of people.
- ii Self governance/autonomy.
- iii De-militarization of the whole of Jammu and Kashmir.
- iv Joint supervision/management.

While the official process of Composite Dialogue and Musharraf's 'thinking aloud' in the media continued between 2003 and 2007, an unofficial back channel was activated to discuss issues in an informal and more nuanced manner. The two principal envoys were, for Pakistan, a college classmate of Musharraf named Tariq Aziz, and, for India, Satinder Lambah. Their exertions produced a framework solution that was cleared on the Indian side by the Cabinet Committee on security and on the Pakistani side by the Corps Commanders Conference, before domestic political difficulties triggered by his dismissal of the Chief Justice forced Musharraf to back off.[4]

Water sharing and Indus Water Treaty: A critical appraisal

The waters of the Indus basin begin in the Himalayan mountains in the state of Jammu and Kashmir. They flow from the hills through the arid states of Punjab and Sindh, converging in Pakistan and emptying into the Arabian Sea, south of Karachi. Where once there was only a narrow strip of irrigated land along these rivers, developments over the last century have created a large network of canals and storage facilities that provide water for more than 26 million acres – the largest irrigated area of any one river system in the world.[5] Protracted talks in the 1950s mediated by the World Bank enabled India and Pakistan to sign the Indus Water Treaty. The treaty was signed by Jawaharlal Nehru, then Prime Minister of India; Field Marshal Ayub Khan, then President of Pakistan; and W.A.B. Illif, then President of the World Bank, in Karachi in September 1960.[6] India received the three eastern rivers (the Sutlej, Beas and Ravi) or 20 per cent of the basin's waters, and Pakistan received the remaining 80 per cent or the three western rivers (the Chenab, Jhelum and Indus).[7] Under the IWT, India can undertake projects on the western rivers for general conservation, flood control, irrigation and hydropower generation, and duly inform Pakistan of the same. Pakistan's objection would render it a matter of dispute to be settled either by negotiations or by a neutral expert, or by arbitration.[8] Three members, one from India, one from Pakistan and the third member by mutual agreement or an International Court of Justice appointee *in lieu* would be the arbitrators. Any unresolved question between the two parties through the Permanent Indus Commission becomes a 'difference' to be referred to a neutral expert, who is appointed by the two countries, and failing that, the World Bank. If the neutral expert's recommendations are unacceptable to either of the parties, the matter would be treated as a 'dispute' and it would be referred to a Court of Arbitration established by the World Bank, along with other institutions such as the secretary general of the United Nations.[9]

In India, there is a growing demand for revisiting the Indus Water Treaty. After the 18 September 2016 attack on the Indian army in the disputed region of Kashmir at Uri allegedly by a Pak based militant group, Indian Prime Minister Narendra Modi said that 'blood and water can't flow together at the same time.' Since then, India has suspended the Indus Water Commission talks. These talks resumed on 20 March 2017 in Pakistan. A UNDP report highlights that the treaty fails to address two issues: the division of shortages in dry years between India and Pakistan, when flows are almost half as compared to wet years, and the cumulative impact of storages on the flows of the River Chenab into Pakistan.[10] The Indus Water Treaty is one of the most successful water sharing arrangements in the world. With or without the treaty, India is duty bound to release a sufficient amount of water to the lower riparian state of Pakistan. But unilateral abrogation of this treaty will plunge the region into a deep crisis. Practically speaking, India cannot divert the waters of the Indus river or its tributaries. The water flows through deep gorges of the Karakoram and Himalayan mountains. The only way to divert water is to build hundreds of kilometres of tunnels through the toughest mountains.[11] It is financially unviable. India as a founder of the Non-Aligned Movement, aspiring for a permanent seat at the Security Council cannot afford to scrap the Indus Waters Treaty; it would invite international condemnation.

An enduring rivalry

Relations between India and Pakistan deteriorated after the Sino-Indian war of 1962 when the situation in the Indian subcontinent changed completely. The Indo-US relations started improving and the Sino-Pak ties were further strengthened. Pakistan condemned India for attacking China. When the firing was going on, the *Dawn*, Pakistani newspaper wrote: 'China is already teaching them how foolish and costly the dreams of conquest can prove. And this is only the beginning of the story.'[12] It was observed that if there would have been the slightest sympathy from Pakistan for India, then there would have been a wave of goodwill for Pakistan all over India.

After the Sino-India war, negotiations between India and Pakistan started at the ministerial level on the Kashmir issue. There were six rounds of talks from December 1962 to May 1963. In the meanwhile, on 2 March 1963, the Sino-Pak Border Agreement was signed in Peking by the Foreign Ministers of China and Pakistan.[13] The India Government strongly condemned the agreement. It blamed the Government of China for intending to destroy the amity which had been developed between India and Pakistan, as a result of the joint talks between the two countries on Kashmir and other related matters.[14]

The Kutch episode in April-May 1965 worsened the Indo-Pak relations which had cooled down in 1964. A dispute arose over disagreements regarding the border in the Rann of Kutch (a 20,000 sq. km. salt marsh). Limited hostilities took place between India and Pakistan after each side accused the other of crossing what they respectively regarded as the international boundary. The matter was referred to arbitration and the Indo-Pakistani Western Boundary Case Tribunal's Award on February 19, 1968, upheld 90 per cent of India's claim to the entire Rann, conceding small sectors to Pakistan. This still left the boundary of the Sir Creek from its head in the marshy lands of the Rann to its mouth in the Arabian Sea and the maritime boundary between India and Pakistan un-demarcated. India and Pakistan had agreed not to refer this part of the un-demarcated boundary for adjudication to the tribunal. Two joint surveys were conducted in the marshy strip by both countries in 2005 and 2007 respectively. Since it has become a politically sensitive issue no country is willing to concede to the demands of other.

In 1965 India and Pakistan fought a second war over Kashmir. The war ended in a stalemate. It was followed by the Tashkent agreement. This was less an agreement ending the Kashmir dispute, as one allowing it to be pushed to one side so that the two countries could resume relatively normal relations. Its main point was that both sides forces would withdraw to the positions they had held before hostilities began (dated 5 August). Other practical points included repatriation of prisoners-of-war and resumption of diplomatic relations.

In Pakistan, Ayub Khan had been overthrown in a military coup in March 1969. His successor, Yahya Khan, had promised to hold free elections to instal a civilian government. The elections were originally scheduled for October but were held in mid-December.

The results of the National Assembly elections as well as the East Pakistan Provincial Assembly Poll produced a landslide victory for Sheikh Mujibur Rahman's Awami League. However, the West Pakistan establishment and even more so Zulfikar Ali Bhutto (leader of the Pakistan People's Party which won the most votes in West Pakistan) were unwilling to be ruled by a Bengali government. Predictably, the failure to hand over power to the Awami League led to the widespread public protests in East Pakistan. Yahya Khan responded to these protests with a military crackdown, leading in turn to armed resistance by the Bengali Mukti Bahini, a force partly trained and armed by India.[15] As more and more Bengali refugees fled across the border to India, New Delhi sent its forces into East Pakistan to openly assist the Mukti Bahini. Pakistan responded by invading India from the West on 3 December 1971, and later launched attacks into Indian Administered Jammu and Kashmir. The Indians countered by attacking West Pakistan in Sindh and north Punjab, and by also crossing the ceasefire line in Jammu and Kashmir. The war did not go well for Pakistan, especially in the eastern wing were it faced strong local opposition as well as supply and communications problems (increased by the Indian overflight ban). On 17 December, Pakistani forces in Dhaka surrendered unconditionally to Indian forces, ending the third Indo-Pak war after just fourteen days.

The Simla Agreement of 1972 was another attempt to normalise Indo-Pak relations after war. Between 28 June and 3 July 1972, after talks at lower levels had been held since April, and following a great deal of international diplomacy by both sides, Zulfikar Ali Bhutto and Indira Gandhi met in Simla to try to restore some order to Indo-Pak relations.[16] The Simla Agreement affirmed that both sides would settle future problems through bilateral negotiations or 'any other peaceful means' and both sides would respect the ceasefire line, referred to as the line of control; neither would unilaterally seek to alter it. It further stated that the UN Charter would govern relations between the two countries.

Siachen is another major bilateral issue which needs an immediate redressal. Sliding down a valley in the Karakoram Range, the glacier is 76 kilometres long and varies in width between 2 to 8 kilometres. It receives up to 6 to 7 metres of the annual total of 10 metres of snow in the winter months. Blizzards can reach speeds of upto 150 knots (nearly 300 kilometres per hour). The temperature drops routinely to 40 degrees centigrade below zero, and even lower with the wind chill factor. For these reasons, the Siachen Glacier has been called the 'Third Pole.'[17] Neither the 1949 Karachi Agreement nor the 1972 Simla Agreement demarcated the area because of inhospitable terrain. New Delhi first became suspicious in 1983 when an American map showed the Siachen and places like Lyogme and Lagongma as part of Pakistan. Subsequently, the Indian army came to know that a Japanese mountaineering expedition team was seeking Islamabad's permission to scale certain mountains in the area.[18] India launched *Operation Meghdoot* on 13 April 1984,[19] when the Indian Army and the Indian Air Force went into the glacier. Pakistan quickly responded with troop deployments and what followed was literally a race to the top. Within a few days, the Indians were in control of most of the area, as Pakistan was beaten to most of the Saltoro Ridge high ground in about a week. India eventually agreed to negotiate and the two sides managed to reach an agreement after the conclusion of the fifth round of talks. The agreement was announced on 17 June 1989,[20] but this agreement was never implemented because the Indian leadership became apprehensive of the likely reaction in India and decided to put it in cold storage, where it is still languishing.

Nuclear tests and the challenges ahead

The nuclearisation of South Asia forced a rethink in the policy making circles. On 20 February 1999, Indian Prime Minister Vajpayee rode a bus into Pakistan along with a group of eminent Indians for a two day visit. He was warmly and enthusiastically received at the border by his counterpart in Pakistan, Nawaz Sharif. Stepping out of the bus on Pakistani soil the Indian prime minister described his visit as the 'defining moment in the South Asian history.'[21] While the two prime ministers could hardly afford to ignore the negative baggage of the past 52 years, they made efforts to put the relationship on the right track. The two day visit produced the 'Lahore Declaration,' along with a Memorandum of Understanding and a joint statement. Both countries agreed to take immediate steps to reduce the risk of a nuclear conflict between them, sincerely negotiate with each other to resolve all outstanding issues including the Kashmir dispute,[22] introduce more CBM's like agreeing to provide advance notification of ballistic missile tests, and also periodically review the implementation of existing CBMs.

But three months after the historic visit of Vajpayee, fighting flared up on the LoC, particularly Kargil area. Beginning in the fall of 1998, Pakistani light infantry troops, accompanied by mujahidin volunteers, infiltrated undetected across the LoC to establish positions on the Himalayan peaks, which Indian troops regularly abandoned during the harsh winter months. When returning Indian troops discovered the Pakistani emplacements the following May, the ensuing fighting led to 'a short, sharp, war.'[23] India's attempts to dislodge the Pakistani troops led to high casualties and little success until Indian air strikes, coupled with strong American diplomatic pressures, led to a Pakistani withdrawal. Kargil intensified the deep Indian distrust of Pakistan. India's Prime Minister Vajpayee, who expended a good deal of political capital on the Lahore summit, complained that he had been 'stabbed in the back.'[24] The Kargil experience could not help but only reinforced the Indian view that the only way to deal with Pakistan was through the application of force, a perspective reflected in the Kargil Review Committee Report.[25] When the fighting concluded, India announced plans to create a new army corps headquarters in Kashmir (14th Corps, at Leh in Ladakh) as well as to station one of its mountain divisions permanently in the Kargil sector, steps whose financial requirements were bound to be substantial.[26]

Nuclear weapons favour the status quo. The nuclear tests by India and Pakistan have neutralised India's conventional military superiority and thus may have been partly responsible for hobbling India's capacity to react to what it perceives as Pakistan's constant provocations. The Kargil crisis of 1999 clearly demonstrated it. Indian military response during the crisis was limited to dealing with the forces that had already crossed the LoC. There was no intention to attack their support bases across the LoC. The Indian air force was clearly instructed to stay within the Indian territory.

Composite dialogue process

The Kargil episode taking place against the backdrop of the region's move to overt nuclear weaponisation had heightened the urgency of revived official dialogue between India and Pakistan. It had made the most emphatic case possible for a more resolute regional commitment to Kashmir's settlement.[27] It took almost one year after the fighting ended at Kargil before the first major sign surfaced of any softening in the formal positions of either side on Kashmir. It came on 24 July 2000 in the form of a unilateral declaration of a three-month ceasefire by Hizbul-Mujahideen, one of the most powerful as well as the most indigenously rooted of the Kashmiri militant organisations. The ceasefire appeared to have Islamabad's at least tacit approval.[28] It was greeted enthusiastically by New Delhi, which quickly ordered its own security forces to observe a ceasefire while at the same time initiating talks with the Hizbul-Mujahideen commanders. A second and still more momentous sign of possible movement toward more conciliatory government (Indian and Pakistani) postures on Kashmir came about four months later, on 19 November, when Indian Prime Minister Vajpayee announced that Indian security forces in Jammu and Kashmir would observe a month-long unilateral ceasefire of their own.[29] This one was to commence on 28 November with the onset of the Islamic holy month of Ramadan.[30]

On 23 May 2001 Indian government abruptly terminated the ceasefire, by then in its sixth month, coupled with a seemingly incongruous invitation to General Pervez Musharraf, viewed in India as the architect of Kargil, to visit India.[31] Fifty-two days later, on 14 July, the Pakistani president[32] arrived in India for talks. The talks were held at Agra, known as the site of the Mughal architectural gem, the Taj Mahal. The Agra Summit failed ignominiously even without a joint statement.

The failed Agra Summit, attack on Indian Parliament on December 13, 2001 and the subsequent mobilisation of troops on the border led to the difficult phase in the bilateral relations. This phase saw active US and British mediatory efforts to de-escalate the situation. On the sidelines of 12th SAARC summit held in Islamabad in 2004 the Indian Prime Minister Atal Bihari Vajpayee and Pakistan President General Pervez Musharraf agreed to revive the Composite Dialogue process.[33] The dialogue process revolves around eight issues: Peace & Security Confidence Building Measures; Jammu and Kashmir; Siachen; Wullar Barrage Project/Tulbul Navigation Project; Sir Creek; Terrorism and Drug Trafficking; Economic and Commercial Cooperation; and Promotion of Friendly Exchanges in Various Fields.[34] The first two issues were discussed at the level of foreign secretaries and for the remaining six issues relevant ministries were engaged.

Composite Dialogue process failed to resolve any of the eight issues mentioned in it. But the agreements on CBMs were highly helpful in normalising the relationship between the two belligerent states. In November 2003 a ceasefire was operationalised on the LoC and International Border. Bus services were operated on Srinagar-Muzaffarabad and Pooch-Rawlakot routes in 2005 and 2006 respectively. Bus and train services were also resumed across International Border between the two countries. Official trade between India and Pakistan gained momentum with a jump from few million dollars in 2003–2004 to more than 2.7 billion dollars in 2010–2011.[35] Also the trade across LoC commensed in 2008 with both mainstream and separatist leaders in Kashmir welcoming the move. During this phase, active back-channel negotiations were held between the trusted emissaries of Dr. Manmohan Singh and President Musharraf in different parts of the world and a 'non-paper' on Kashmir was ready for discussion at the highest political level.

All this goodwill turned into bitter hostility due to the Mumbai terror attacks of 26 November, 2008. The dialogue process was suspended unilaterally by India under tremendous public pressure. The UPA-II government under the leadership of Dr. Manmohan Singh did try to resume the process after 2011 onwards but to no avail. It was followed by the beheading of Indian soldiers on the border allegedly by Pakistani rangers. The opposition BJP exerted tremendous pressure on the government to sever all ties with Pakistan.

Prime Minister Modi started his tenure on a positive note. He invited all the SAARC heads of state/government to his swearing-in ceremony which was held on 26 May 2014. Against all odds, Pakistan's Prime Minister Nawaz Sharif attended the event. On 25th December 2015, Mr. Modi reciprocated by a drop-in at Lahore and offered birthday wishes to his Pakistani counterpart. But the 2nd January 2016 attack on the Pathankote airbase allegedly by Pakistan based groups gave a setback to the Modi-Nawaz bonhomie. Since then, the two countries have failed to resume the dialogue process. Thereafter, the renewed unrest in Indian Kashmir and the attack on the Indian army camp in Uri on 18 September 2016, killings dozens of soldiers, further plunged the subcontinent into a deeper crisis. After the Uri attack, the Indian Director General of Military Operations declared that the Indian army had conducted surgical strikes across the LoC. Now, if a major terror incident linked to Pakistan based groups happens in India what will be the latter's response? Keeping in mind the post Uri war hysteria, will India undertake a major strike across the LoC or International border? If this happens, where is the guarantee that Pakistan will not consider the option of using the tactical nuclear weapons? The people of both countries must unite to reverse the trend.

Conclusion

A careful study of India–Pakistan relations reveals that the relationship has been and rather remains diabolical. There are limited people-to-people contacts that may contribute to overcoming the negative perceptions that many Indians and Pakistanis have for each other. Most contacts other than family reunions are restricted to members of a small, middle-to-upper class elite prepared to endure the demanding visa and entry regimes. Indians and Pakistanis also have limited and difficult ways of accessing one another, with few flights each week between the two nations and even fewer border crossing points along their long border. There is one road crossing (Wagah-Attari) and two rail crossings (Wagah-Attari and Munabao-Khokrapar). The two nations also have very little direct trade, with Pakistan still refusing to grant India 'Most Favoured Nation' status as Islamabad claims that the balance of trade is heavily tilted in India's favour. Nevertheless, the Composite Dialogue shows that India–Pakistan relations are advancing slowly, although it seems unlikely that there will be any groundbreaking agreements in the short- to medium-term.

As neighbours, India and Pakistan cannot afford to live in a state of enmity forever. Both countries must ease the visa restrictions and allow greater interactions between their people. Trade relations must be improved by removing the tariff and non-tariff barriers by both sides. The potential for bilateral trade is estimated to be around $20 billion. For this, efforts must be made to remove the restricted road-based trade via Wagah which is limited to 137 items only. Further, there is an imperative need for a political engagement to discuss the issue of Kashmir. The unrelenting protests and killings in Kashmir demand a parallel engagement on both tracks, New Delhi-Srinagar and New Delhi-Islamabad. Experience shows us that whenever India–Pakistan relations have improved, peace prevailed in Kashmir. A tension-free relationship with Pakistan will enable India to play its due role in international affairs.

Notes

1 Cohen, Stephen P. (2002) Draft Case Study "The Compound Crisis of 2002," in *South Asia Amid Crisis*, Washington: The Brookings Institution.
2 Ibid., p. 31.
3 The Pakistan Ministry of Foreign Affairs mentioned it in its official brief in 2005. See http://www.mofa.gov.pk/Pages/Brief.htm.
4 Varadarajan, Siddharth (2010, 26 April) "Time to End the Impasse with Pakistan," *The Hindu*.
5 The Henry L. Stimson Center, "The Indus Waters Treaty," *Stimson*, www.stimson.org/southasia/?sn=sa20020116300.
6 Seema, Sridhar (2008) "Kashmir and Water: Conflict and Cooperation," *Program in Arms Control, Disarmament, and International Security (ACDIS)*, Urbana-Champaign: University of Illinois.
7 Alam, Undala Z. (2002, December) "Questioning the Water Wars Rationale: A Case Study of the Indus Waters Treaty," *The Geographical Journal* 168, no. 4: 344.
8 Ibid.
9 Ibid.
10 Hassan, Maheen (2016, December) "Water Security in Pakistan: Issues and Challenges," *Development Advocate Pakistan* 3, no. 4: 8.
11 Zaman, Fahim and Syed Muhammad Abubakar (2016, 13 December) "Assessing India's Water Threat," *Dawn*.
12 Bindra, Sukhawant Singh (1981) *Indo-Pak Relations: Tashkent to Simla Agreement*, New Delhi: Deep and Deep Publications, p. 34.
13 Ibid., 27.
14 Dobell, William M (1964, Atumn) "Ramifications of the China-Pakistan Border Treaty," *Pacific Affairs* 37, no. 3: 287–288.
15 Malik, Iffat (2005) *Kashmir: Ethnic Conflict, International Dispute*, Karachi: Oxford University Press, p. 137.
16 Ibid.
17 Ahmad, Samina and Varun Sahni (1998) "Freezing the Fighting: Military Disengagement on Siachen Glacier," *Cooperative Monitoring Center Occasional Papers*, Albuquerque: Sandia National Laboratories, pp. 9–10.
18 Nayar, Kuldip (2003) *Wall at Wagah: India–Pakistan Relations*, New Delhi: Gyan Publishing House, p. 232.
19 Kumar, Rajesh (2007) *Getting to Rapprochement Over Kashmir: Is Using the 'China Model' a Viable Alternative*, Colombo: RCSS, p. 20.
20 Chari, P.R Pervaiz Iqbal Cheema (2001) *The Simla Agreement 1972: Its Wasted Promise*, New Delhi: Manohar Publishers, p. 164.
21 Baruah, Amit (1999, 12 March) "The Bus to Pakistan," *Frontline*.
22 *The News*, 22 February 1999.
23 Ibid.
24 Sidhu, Harjinder (2002, 11 February) "Ansari Arrest Proves Pak Hand: PM," *Hindustan Times*.
25 For more details, see The Kargil Review Committee Report, 1999.
26 Wirsing, Robert G. (2004) *Kashmir in the Shadow of War: Regional Rivalries in a Nuclear Age*, India: Spring Books, p. 58.

27 Ibid.
28 Ibid.
29 At its inception, the Indian ceasefire was formally described as "non-initiation of combat operations" (NICO).
30 Constable, Pamela (2000, 20 November) "Indian Announces One-Month Cease-Fire in Kashmir; Unilateral Move at Opening Talks With Rebel Groups," *Washington Post*, A 11.
31 Wirsing, *Kashmir in the Shadow of War*, p. 61.
32 Musharraf had dismissed the incumbent president Mohammad Rafiq Tarar and had himself declared president of Pakistan on 20 June, 2001 only weeks prior to the Agra Summit. On his arrival in India, he thus held three top posts – president, chief executive, and chief of army staff.
33 In May 1997, in Male, the capital of the Maldives, on the sidelines of a South Asian Association for Regional Cooperation (SAARC) summit, Indian Prime Minister Inder Kumar Gujral and his Pakistani counterpart Nawaz Sharif mooted the idea of a structured dialogue or the Composite Dialogue Process.
34 Padder, Sajad (2012, February) "The Composite Dialogue between India and Pakistan: Structure, Process and Agency," *Heidelberg Papers in South Asian and Comparative Politics*, Working Paper No. 65: 2.
35 Padder, Sajad (2014, January–March) "India–Pakistan Trade: Challenges and Opportunity," *Journal of Peace Studies*, New Delhi, 21, no. 1, p. 9.

Chapter 16

India, Bangladesh and International Crime Tribunal

Punam Pandey

Seeking safety in their faith, Bengalis fought vigorously and valiantly for a separate independent nation state. Thus, Pakistan was born as a homeland for Muslims. Soon people of East Pakistan (the majority of them Bengalis) realised that common religiosity was not able to mitigate material, administrative and linguistic disadvantages which they experienced daily in comparison to their West Pakistani inhabitants. Gradually, civic and economic inconveniences were overwhelmed by political discrimination when the military administrator refused to call Mujib-ur-Rahman and his political party Awami League to form a government even after they won the majority of seats in the national parliament. This was followed by a nine-month-long bloody fight between military and freedom fighter guerrillas (popularly known as Muktijodhhas). This concluded with the war between India and Pakistan.

The background to the final showdown between Bengalis and the military can be traced to the 1950s when the government declared that Urdu would be the state language despite the fact that the majority of people were Bengalis. A manifestation of serious displeasure against the government's decision was demonstrated by protests spearheaded by students and political leaders of East Bengal. Several students and participants were killed; tens of thousands of them were injured. Following this, a series of incidents took place which further weakened the fabric of trust between the two wings of Pakistan. Soon after the language movement, the elected government of the East Bengal was dismissed on some flimsy grounds. Another tear came in the middle of 60s when Mujib and some other leaders of the Awami League were charged in the Agartala conspiracy case in which these leaders were imprisoned on the suspicion of conspiring with India for secession of East Pakistan.

This really infuriated ordinary Bangladeshis. Though Mujib and other leaders were released, this left a deep scar among the common people in general and political leaders in particular. With tensions running high in East Pakistan, the military government announced that an election would be held in 1970. In the run up to the general election, natural tragedies struck East Pakistan. Devastating floods took place that summer and a severe cyclone destroyed lives and much of the coastal ecosystem in November 1970. Relief supplied by the government was not sufficient to meet people's needs and expectations which accentuated dissatisfaction among the people.

In the election the Awami League emerged as the largest party winning 167 of East Pakistan's 169 National Assembly seats. The second largest party in the National Assembly was Pakistan People's Party (PPP) with 81 seats. Zulfikar Ali Bhutto headed the PPP. Awami League and Pakistan People's Party of West Pakistan could not reach an agreement about the nature of the new government. Though the military tried unsuccessfully to generate consensus among political parties the PPP was not ready to accept a secondary position to the Awami League in the new government. But consensus could not be reached about the nature of future government between elected political leaders of West Pakistan and military on the one hand; and between East and West Pakistan political leaders on the other hand. Observing no further movement, the Awami League intensified the agitation first for autonomy and then for complete independence of East Pakistan as a sovereign independent nation state. The military responded with force to these developments using all its might to crush protests.

Armed military personnel and tanks were deployed to dismantle police and the paramilitary organisation, East Pakistan Rifles. They unleashed havoc on ordinary people as well. Slums were set ablaze and fleeing inhabitants were gunned down. Dhaka University was one of the important targets where students and faculty were brutally killed. Shahid Minar, erected to commemorate the sacrifices of the language movement, was bulldozed to the ground. In the eyes of the military, this monument of cultural assertion was seen as progenitor to the rise of the present Bengali nationalist consciousness. To create a communal schism, Hindus were strategically picked up from homes and were killed gruesomely.

To counter the freedom fighters, the Pakistan army created civilian groups like the Peace Committees and paramilitary groups like Razakar, AL-Shams, Al-Badr under Pakistani command. Pakistan's military also colluded with a number of political parties, particularly the Jamaat-e-Islami and the Muslim League. Members of these political parties became members of paramilitary forces which perpetrated crimes. They are popularly known as collaborators. The Pakistan army supplied arms to these squads, constituted by local Bengali and Bihari. They committed widespread violence against the nationalist Bengalis. Pro-Pakistan Al-Badr militia rounded up writers, professors, artists, doctors and other professionals in Dhaka, blindfolded them and butchered them. Militias acted as death squads and provided counterinsurgency intelligence. They often attacked villages and razed them to the ground. Pakistani attackers murdered the old and the young in villages and raped women. Sexual violence was widespread and according to Bangladesh, some 400,000 were raped.

The unfolding violent situation created panic and shock among the people. Facing strong reprisals from the military, the Awami League leaders fled to India and formed the government in exile in West Bengal province. People fled to India to avoid atrocities committed by the Pakistan army. There were almost seven million refugees from East Pakistan to Assam, Tripura and West Bengal causing massive demographic pressures on these states. Huge Indian resources were diverted for giving shelter to these people.[1] Keeping the large number of refugees in mind, a separate department was setup to deal with East Pakistan refugees.[2] Gradually, a strenuous pressure was being felt on the exchequer because of the influx of such a large number of people. Mrs. Indira Gandhi, the Prime Minister of India made a statement to Parliament 'On present estimates, the cost to the Central Exchequer on relief alone may exceed Rs. 180 crores for a period of six months. All this, as Hon. Members will appreciate, has imposed an unexpected burden on us.'[3] This became one of the important reasons for India to be in the whirlwind of the liberation movement.[4]

India used all its energies to generate positive international opinion for the liberation movement. Military training camps were established with Indian assistance at a number of places in the Indian territory close to the East Pakistan border. It also provided military training and civil supplies to the Muktijoddhas. The Indian army provided firepower to Mukti Bahini which helped it to inflict deep damage on the infrastructure in East Pakistan, including bridges, rail lines, roads, water transportation networks, power stations, communication systems and ships in the Chittagong port. A Radio

Free Bangla was setup near Calcutta. The Indian political authorities sanctioned the establishment of local cells to arm the Bengali Mukti Bahini guerrillas to fight the Pakistanis and their supporters.[5]

Historical trajectory of International Crime Tribunal

According to Bangladesh sources, the nine month of the liberation movement saw 3,000,000 people dead and 400,000 women raped. Soon after independence, the government showed its strong intensions to prosecute the collaborators by promulgating the Bangladesh Collaborators (Special Tribunals) Order by a presidential decree. Sheikh Mujib reiterated the promise to try those who had committed war crimes. The government's initial identification of 1,100 war criminals for persecution was trimmed to 195. But prevailing realities compelled the government not to go-ahead with prosecution.

Bangladesh was yet to be recognised by Muslim-majority West Asian countries; they put pressure on the country not to conduct the trials. Almost 400,000 Bangladeshis were stranded in Pakistan. At least 203 Bengali officials were arrested in 1973, and they were now used for a bargaining chip. Pakistani President Zulfiqar Ali Bhutto threatened to try many of them, particularly those who were working for the Pakistani government at the time of the war. This was confirmed when Bhutto told the Indian Prime Minister's special envoy P.N. Haskar that 'if Bangladesh did proceed with the trials, he would be forced to charge 203 Bengali civilian officials in Pakistan with espionage and high treason.'[6] Previously, China had blocked Bangladesh's entry to the United Nations by using its veto power in August 1972, arguing that it exercised its veto because, 'the country has failed to observe UN resolution calling for prison repatriation.'[7] Another report suggests that the war crime trial issue was dropped by Mujib in exchange for Pakistan's formal recognition in February 1974. A delegation from Islamic Summit Conference consisting of Secretary General and representatives of Kuwait, Somalia, Lebanon, Algeria and Senegal visited Dhaka on 20 February to persuade Mujib to attend the summit at Lahore beginning on 22 February. He agreed to join the summit only provided Bangladesh was recognized by Pakistan. But, he also agreed that the war crimes trial would not be pursued further.[8]

The war crime trial issue, especially of Pakistani military personnel, disappeared completely when the tripartite agreement for repatriation of war criminals between India, Bangladesh and Pakistan was signed on 9 April, 1974. Though the Treaty acknowledged that 'there was universal consensus that persons charged with such crimes as the 195 Pakistani prisoners of war should be held to account and subjected to the dues process of law'; simultaneously the foreign Minister of Bangladesh announced that the Bangladeshi government would not proceed further with the trials as an act of leniency as the Pakistan Prime Minister's appeal 'to the people of Bangladesh to forgive and forget the mistakes of the past.'

Meanwhile, the *International Crimes (Tribunals) Act 1973* was passed by the parliament on 20 July 1973 and was incorporated into the constitution. Under the Collaborators Act, between 1972 and 1974, some 37, 471 people were arrested. Cases against about 11,000 people were filed. Altogether 73 tribunals were established to try these cases. Over the course of these trials 22 people were sentenced to death, 68 to life imprisonment and 752 to imprisonment for various terms. These included senior leaders of the proscribed political parties, such as Khan Abdus Sabur, Fazlul Qauder Chowdhury of the Muslim League and Shah Azizur Rahman of the Pakistan Democratic Party, and Abbas Ali Khan of the Jamaat-e-Islami (JI). Some of the accused were granted amnesty but the general amnesty was not granted to those accused of murder, rape, arson, or genocide.

Mujib and his family was killed in August 1975. The process of the trials of the collaborators was disrupted after the law was repealed in December 1975. Coups and counter-coups led to amnesia about the trial issue from the political landscape. Military rulers and emerging political parties were not interested in pursuing the issue as these groups served critical roles in consolidating their position.

After a decade and a half of military rule, democracy was restored in 1991 and demands for justice began appearing. An important person who played a crucial role in the revival of the memory of the liberation struggle was Jahanara Imam. She published her diary as *Ekkaturer Dinguli* (The Days of '71). Imam kept a meticulous record of the 1971 war, including murder of her 18-year-old son, Rumi, by the Pakistani army. Her diary became an instant bestseller in Bangladesh after its publication in 1982. Imam's personal account played a central role in the transmission of the lived memories of an older generation to a new generation who had not witnessed the 1971 events. Further, an English translation of the book in 1986 helped to extend and deepen public discussion of the atrocities committed during the liberation movement. In 1992, Imam launched a movement for trials of war criminals. Before discussing the movement, the context is underlined here.

An important figure, Golam Azam, an accused war criminal, left the country in 1971 but came back in 1978 and continued to stay in Bangladesh ever since. But, in 1991, Golam Azam was elected 'ameer' of Jamaat-e-Islami for the fourth time and what was different from previous occasions was public announcement of the event. This provoked a group of people who set up a National Coordinating Committee for Realisation of Bangladesh Liberation War Ideals and the Trial of Bangladesh War Criminals of 1971 (in short '*Nirmul*'). The Committee appointed an enquiry committee to look into a number of alleged war criminals, most of whom were the leaders of the JI. Based on the report of the enquiry committee, Imam also organised a mock trial of war criminals at a public park popularly known as 'gano adalat' (people's court), in Dhaka on 26 March 1992. More than two dozen lawyers pronounced that Golam Azam's crimes were punishable by the death sentence. The demand to hold war criminals accountable gained further ground in 1993 when Golam Azam sought full citizenship rights through the High Court. The trial raised questions like the meaning of rights and belonging. This debate refocused discussion on the recollection of the brutality of the war and the state's failure to incorporate accounts of the country's independence struggle in public debate. This also challenged the rewriting of school texts that excluded discussions of the liberation struggle after the imposition of martial law. The BNP government led by Khaleda Zia filed a sedition case against the organisers of 'gano adalat' at the metropolitan magistrate's court, but also got Golam Azam behind bars for staying illegally in Bangladesh.

This was followed by another enquiry committee and another public tribunal in 1993. In spite of government crackdowns, public support for the symbolic trials was immense. The civil society movement continued, even though muted. The issue gained attention again in 2007 as a forum of former commanders of the liberation war began a public campaign. While all political activities were banned during the tenure of the caretaker government between 2007 and 2008, the Sector Commanders Forum (SCF) organised public consultation meetings. While the SCF keep campaigning and demanding trials, the JI Secretary General Ali Ahsan Mojahid asserted that there were no war criminals in Bangladesh. The statement infuriated people and added impetus to the SCF's demand.

Bangladesh's internal political environment and its response to the cause of transitional justice

The Awami League incorporated the demand for the trial of war criminals as one of the chief objectives in its 2008 election manifesto. After coming to power, the government made some changes in the ICT Act in 2009, and set up the tribunal in 2010. A second tribunal was appointed in March 2012 and scrapped 3 years later. The arrest of Delwar Hossain Sayeedi in October 2011 set the motion for the trial process. The BJI contested that the ICT was politically motivated and demanded that it be scrapped. It appealed people to come for demonstrations. In late 2012 the party intensified its pressure on the government to discontinue the trial process by staging violent demonstrations. The BNP also questioned the process on technical grounds that the current tribunal lacked transparency and that the process was inconsistent with international standards.[9]

The tribunal began delivering its verdicts in early 2013. It sentenced Abdul Quader Mollah, a senior Jamaat-e-Islami leader to life imprisonment in Feb 2013, finding him guilty of murder and rape. After the verdict, discontented youths staged a demonstration at Shahbagh public square near Dhaka University, alleging that the court had shown leniency to the accused as part of a secret deal between the government and the JeI. The demonstrators, mostly online bloggers, spearheaded a movement demanding that those convicted of war crimes be awarded with the death penalty. Their demands also included the outlawing of the BJI. The demonstration quickly became the rallying point of secularists and drew unprecedented spontaneous participation from women of all walks of life. Protests in solidarity with those at Shahbagh spread across the country and further afield, fuelled by social media. Confronted by growing demands that the government appeal against the sentence awarded to Abdul Quader Mollah, three amendments to the International Crimes (Tribunals) Act 1973 were approved by parliament in mid-February 2013 (with retrospective effect from 14 July 2009). The amendments enabled the ICT to charge and place on trial organisations for their role in the 1971 war of liberation, allowed the government, a complainant, or informant to appeal an order of acquittal or order of sentencing, and imposed a statutory obligation on the Appellate Division of the Supreme Court to dispose of any appeal filed before it within 60 days.

When JeI was busy fighting for disbanding of the trial process, a new Islamist organisation, Hefazat-e-Islam (HI-Protector of Islam), emerged. This was an umbrella organisation of smaller Islamist organisations and Islamic scholars associated with traditional (qaumi) madrassas (Islamic seminaries). The organisation put certain demands on the government including that of dismantling the Shahbagh movement immediately and arresting the activists. It organised a protest march in April 2013. After negotiations between the HI and the government, it was allowed to organise a mass gathering in the capital. The BNP extended its support to the HI campaign and its local activists provided assistance; General Ershad's Jatiya Party, a member of the ruling coalition, also extended it support. Protests led to massive violence and loss of lives. The ICT has attracted not only internal criticism but international comments as well.

International opinion on the ICT

The trial process has attracted wide international attention and commentaries. The fairness of the trial process has been questioned widely. The US Ambassador-at-Large for War Crimes Issues visited Dhaka four times and expressed reservations about the process. In 2011 Human Rights Watch called upon Sheikh Hasina to amend the International Crimes (Tribunals) Act 1973 to ensure a credible and fair tribunal. Later, a number of amendments regarding rules of procedure were made in 2011. However, critics did not find these amendments adequate. In November 2012 the UN Working Group on Arbitrary Detention requested the government to take steps that conform to the International Covenant on Civil and Political Rights and the Universal Declaration of Human Rights.

A major chink appeared in the trial process in December 2012 when a national daily newspaper published transcripts of internet telephone conversations and emails between ICT-I Chairman Justice Md. Nizamul Huq and Ahmed Ziauddin, an expatriate Bangladeshi expert in international law. A major international publication, *The Economist* also published a report on December 15, 2012 which concluded that the correspondence 'raise(s) profound questions about the trial.' The leaks raised 'questions about conflicts of interest,' as Ziauddin appeared also to have advised members of the prosecution team at the ICT.

European human rights organisations also oppose death sentences since the European Union has abolished the death penalty. The Office of the UN human rights Commissioner also held a press briefing questioning the fairness of the trials and called for abolition of the death penalty.

Examination of India's response to the ICT

Before analysing India's response to the ICT, it is important to understand the nature of bilateral engagement figured in the domestic politics of Bangladesh in the last four decades. India and Bangladesh embarked on a friendly journey with the signing of the Treaty of Friendship, Cooperation and Peace for 25 years in 1972. Thus, India became thickly involved in the Mujib government; the downside of this association was that whatever went wrong with the Mujib government, India was also blamed for the lapses. In the early days of independence, discontentment against the Bangladesh government became visible among common people, likewise, an intense disenchantment appeared between the civilian government and the military. This culminated in the assassination of Mujib and many of his family members by disgruntled members of the army. This domestic turmoil was a setback for the friendly relationship between India and Bangladesh. Since India was invested in Bangladesh's cause and later in its new government, the Indian government did not hide its displeasure at the unfolding situation of military takeovers. This can be illustrated with an example. Pakistan was the first nation to recognise the new regime and promptly made a radio announcement that the new government in Dhaka had changed the name of the country from 'The People's Republic of Bangladesh' to the 'Islamic Republic of Bangladesh.' On the contrary, the Indian government did not communicate with the new government for three days because telephone communications between New Delhi and Dhaka were cut off and the Indian High Commissioner to Bangladesh had come to Delhi for consultations. The friendly charm in the relationship was gone; the military administration reversed the policies of the Mujib regime.

The Indian approach to the military takeover was as expected because it does not support having a military government in the neighbourhood. Mrs. Indira Gandhi had forged an excellent rapport and partnership with Mujibur Rahman and as a matter of principle she did not favour having a military regime in India's neighbourhood and thus, made little effort to evolve even a working relationship with General Ziaur Rahman.[10] A decade and a half of military rule wrecked the friendly bonhomie.

The dawn of democracy in 1991 brought BNP led by Begum Khaleda Zia to power. This also did not really help to strengthen the bilateral relationship because of internal political dynamics where both parties Awami League and Bangladesh Nationalist Party were positioned as pro or anti-India respectively. In 1996, the Awami League returned to power after a two-decade gap; New Delhi was very keen to buttress this regime in Dhaka. This was done through the resolution of one of the persistently irritating issues between the two neighbours – the Ganga water. Both governments showed a strong desire to overcome the impasse over the Ganga waters issue. Finally, the treaty on the sharing of the Ganges waters was signed by India and Bangladesh for 30 years on 12 December 1996. This was a major breakthrough because until now only a five-year agreement with the Zia government and three MoUs (Memoranda of Understanding) with Ershad government for one year each had been concluded. Begum Zia has opposed the Ganges treaty as opposition leader and had promised to ask for review once she came back to power. But when she came back to power, she did not ask for it. Again the Awami League came to power in 2009 on the pledge of setting up a war crime tribunal to meet popular demand of justice.

India has supported the International War Crime process. The spokesperson of the Ministry of External Affairs said, 'India has been supportive of judicial process under the International Crimes Tribunal (ICT) of Bangladesh to address the pending issue of justice for war crimes committed during the movement for the independence of Bangladesh in 1971.' He further added, 'The ICT process to bring the perpetrators of war crimes to justice has wide popular support in Bangladesh. It is also an internal issue of Bangladesh.'[11]

Pakistan, expectedly, has opposed the tribunal and said that the executions of the Jamaat-e-Islami leaders was 'contrary' to a tripartite agreement signed by India, Bangladesh and Pakistan in 1974. The Pakistani Parliament also passed a resolution which condemned ICT trials and urged Islamabad 'to seriously raise at all the International forums the sentencing of political opponents in Bangladesh.'

But India's support to the trial process cannot be understood as a foregone conclusion because of the history of liberation support.

There are certain other imperatives which reinforce India's position on the trial process. As discussed earlier, in the fractured domestic politics of Bangladesh, the Awami League is known as India's friendly party. This assures India that the Sheikh Hasina government takes care of India's security interests better. Bangladesh became a heaven for anti-India operatives and pro-Pakistan terrorists during her regime. Naga underground activists and militants from Manipur operated from Bangladesh.

As alleged by India, Pakistan engaged in anti-Indian activities in India's neighborhood. In Bangladesh, it has tried to use pro-Pakistani elements who are also regarded as stranded Pakistanis in Bangladesh to influence a section of Bangladeshis against India's presence in Bangladesh. Remove the highlighted. It has found Begum Zia's government holds a benign view about its anti-India activities. But since the Hasina government came to power in 2009, their infrastructure has been shaken because of the government's heavy crackdown. This includes her decision to cooperate with India by handing over Indian insurgent leaders using Bangladesh as a sanctuary.

Timing of the trial process is also significant. The bilateral relationship is on an upswing since Awami League came to power in 2009. In almost a decade both countries's head of governments have visited each other on a regular interval. Hasina visited India in 2010. This was a landmark visit because India granted 1 billion US dollars in credit to Bangladesh.[12] This was the largest credit support to any neighbour in South Asia. A number of initiatives were undertaken during the visit. India has given full support to the current government because it is determined to have friendly relations with its eastern neighbour. Unlike the present bilateral visits, Begum Zia visited India in 2006, she made another visit after 6 years in 2012 as leader of opposition at the government of India's invitation. But BNP chief Khaleda Zia refused to give a courtesy call to Indian President Pranab Mukherjee when he was visiting Dhaka in March 2013 because of safety concerns.

The change of government in India has not seen a change of government policies towards Bangladesh. Indian Prime Minister visited Dhaka in 2015. During the visit, 22 agreements were signed. India extended a second Line of Credit of 2 billion US dollars for developing infrastructure projects in Bangladesh. The government of Bangladesh conferred the Bangladesh Liberation War Honour on former Prime Minister of India, Mr. Atal Bihari Vajpayee for his outstanding contribution to the Liberation War of Bangladesh.

Deepening the relationship further, the Bangladesh Prime Minister visited India in April 2017. During this visit, the Bangladesh liberation movement was prominently mentioned. This was reflected in the joint statement issued during the visit. 'The two Prime Ministers condemned the genocide that occurred in Bangladesh in 1971. They solemnly acknowledge the atrocities and called upon the international community to recognize and preserve the memory of those who lost their lives and those suffered during the genocide.'[13] Bangladesh has decided to recognise the Indian soldiers who fought and sacrificed their lives for Bangladesh liberation. Prime Minister Narendra Modi announced a special medical scheme under which 100 Muktijoddhas of Bangladesh will be provided with medical treatment in Indian hospitals every year. He also extended the Mutkijoddhas scholarship scheme for 10,000 heirs of Muktijoddha for another 5 years.

Another issue which India is keen to pursue is to connect North-East India with Southeast Asia that can only be possible through Bangladesh. More importantly, as a friend of Bangladesh, India has to stand behind the Hasina government when it is facing international flak over the trials.

India has a reputation for slow execution of policies. If the same government is in power, visibility of friendship becomes noticeable, and it helps in creating a more positive perception among the people.

Conclusion

India's position in South Asia is already fragile because of visceral anti-India attitudes from their Western neighbour, unstable dynamics of domestic politics in Nepal and the competitive attitude of China to spread its influence with countries of South Asia. In this kind of situation, India has made a political decision. Fairness of the procedure to meet the demand for justice can be debated in terms of whether a more subtle way could have been explored to fulfil the demand for justice, but strategically and historically, the Indian decision to support the Bangladesh government on ICT is salient. Had the decision been otherwise, it would have suggested a tectonic shift in India's foreign policy. Hasina's government has boldly taken care of Indian concerns for security. From Bangladesh's perspective, water is a crucial issue because Bangladesh receives almost 85 per cent of its water through India. The Teesta Transboundary river water sharing interim agreement, which the two countries agreed upon in 2011, will consolidate India's position in Bangladesh. The West has questioned the fairness of the trial process. But for India, pragmatism wins the day. According to experts, the agreement on transit routes is a win-win situation for both countries. As discussed earlier, some landmark solutions to knotty bilateral problems have come about during the Hasina regime.

Notes

1 All these states of India share borders with Bangladesh.
2 Dixit, J.N., "India Gets Involved," in *Liberation and Beyond Indo-Bangladesh Relations*, New Delhi: Konark Publishers, 1999, p. 49.
3 Prime Minister Indira Gandhi's Statement in Lok Sabha on 24 March 1971, "The Refugee Influx," in *Indira Gandhi India and Bangladesh Selected Speeches and Statements March to December 1971*, New Delhi: Orient Longman, 1972, p. 16.
4 Various motives have been attributed to India for supporting Bangladesh cause.
5 Saikia, Yasmin, "Creating the History of 1971," in *Women, War, And the Making of Bangladesh Remembering 1971*, London: Duke University Press, 2011, p. 46.
6 Srinath Raghavan, *1971: A Global History of the Creation of Bangladesh*, Harvard, MA: Harvard University Press, 2013, p. 270.
7 Riaz, Ali, "From Optimism to Retreat of Democracy (1991–2015)," in *Bangladesh: A Political History since Independence*, New York: I.B. Tauris, 2016, p. 92.
8 Ibid., p. 93.
9 Ibid., p. 95.
10 For details see, *Indira Gandhi, Selected Speeches and Writings*, vol. III, September 1972–March 1977, New Delhi: Publications Division, 1984, p. 72 and p. 270. Also see, it is quite true that "we do not favour military dictatorships and things like that," *Indira Gandhi: Select Speeches and Writings*, vol. IV (1980–81), New Delhi: Publications Division, 1985, p. 552; Lawrence Ziring, "Pakistan and India: Politics, Personalities, and Foreign Policy," *Asian Survey*, vol. 18, no. 7 (July, 1978), p. 729.
11 Roche, Elizabeth (2016, 9 September) "India Backs Bangladesh's 1971 War Crimes Trials," *Live Mint*, September 9, 2016, www.livemint.com/Politics/vdDeIq22xToheKxYmNjcFI/India-backs-Bangladeshs-1971-war-crimes-trials.html, accessed at April 24, 2017.
12 'India and Bangladesh Sign 22 Agreements, Discuss Water Sharing' *The Wire* 9 April 2017. https://thewire.in/diplomacy/india-bangladesh-relations-talks.
13 India–Bangladesh Joint Statement during the State Visit of Prime Minister of Bangladesh to India (8 April 2017), www.mea.gov.in/bilateral-documents.htm?dtl/28362/India__Bangladesh_Joint_Statement_during_the_State_Visit_of_Prime_Minister_of_Bangladesh_to_India_April_8_2017, accessed on May 1, 2017. 10:30.

Chapter 17

Bangladesh–Pakistan ties

Future prospects of a troubled relationship

Pallavi Deka

Past: reasons of differences and division

The partition of India in 1947 is a painful chapter in the history of this subcontinent, but little did anyone imagine at that time that one partition would not be enough and that there would soon be a need for another within less than three decades. The state of Pakistan that came into existence after the partition was a strange geopolitical entity divided into two parts – East and West Pakistan, which were separated by a hostile neighbour and a distance of thousands of kilometres. Since the day of its formation, West Pakistani elites, who controlled the nation, had maintained a troubled relationship with its erstwhile eastern part. Initially it was thought that religious bonding would compensate for all these problems, but a systemic neglect of the majority East Pakistani population, ethnic and linguistic differences, regional disparities, and partisan attitudes of the West Pakistani ruling elite continued to exacerbate the problem. The West Pakistan elite refused to acknowledge or let these differences peacefully co-exist. On the contrary, it tried to maintain political control over the nation despite the fact that East Pakistan had a larger population and, hence, a greater say in the nation's destiny. All of this led to the birth of secessionist sentiments in East Pakistan. Surprisingly, these sentiment were emboldened by the famous Lahore Resolution of Muslim League passed in 1940, which is considered the founding stone for the partition of India.

The Lahore Resolution was moved on 23 March 1940 by Maulana Fazlul Huq, the stalwart Muslim leader the undivided Bengal province at the Lahore Session of the All India Muslim League. The resolution, which became the guiding objective of the League called for:

> The establishment of completely Independent States formed by demarcating geographically contiguous units into regions which

> shall be so constituted, with such territorial adjustments as may be necessary, that the areas in which the Mussalmans are numerically in a majority, as in the North-Western and Eastern zones of India, shall be grouped to constitute Independent States as Muslim Free National Homelands in which the constituent units shall be autonomous and sovereign. . . .[1]

The fact that the resolution talked about 'Independent States' and not 'one state' provided enough space for interpretations, and in the face of the future disenchantment, the Awami League leadership used this technicality to assert that the Bengali Muslims had always had the idea of a separate homeland in mind, even during the pre-independence days. However, in 1941, Huq was expelled from the League over differences with M.A. Zinnah and the subsequent leadership of the Muslim League continued to remain the hegemony in East Pakistan until the partition.

The first challenge to the League's leadership came in 1948, when in its attempts to homogenise the Pakistani nation, the Muslim League-led government tried to deny state language status to Bengali while continuing to impose Urdu as a national language on the linguistically rich and proud Bengalis, resulting in student unrest, mass protests and shootings.[2] Sensing an opportunity, the opposition backed this demand, which later became a popular demand of the native Bengali speakers cutting across religion and class lines, uniting the opposition and alienating the Muslim League. Before the first general elections in 1954, the East Pakistan Awami League of Sheikh Mujibur Rahman formed a United Front with Maulana Fazlul Huq and the Muslim League lost badly in the polls, with the UF winning 223 of 237 seats.[3]

This rift between the Muslim League and the West Pakistan-led political establishment and the East Pakistani people, led by the political alliance of Sheikh Mujibur Rahman, continued to widen in the 1950s and 1960s for numerous reasons. The Awami League opposed the joining of the America-led cold war treaty organisations Southeast Asia Treaty Organisation and the Central Treaty Organisation (SEATO and CENTO) by Pakistan.[4] Further, since East Pakistan was cut off from the world for seventeen days in the wake of the 1965 War, as most of the defence forces were concentrated in defending West Pakistan, a sense of helplessness entered the East Pakistani mindset as it became clear that the Pakistani Army would not be able to defend itself in the face of a prolonged war.[5]

As the war 'adversely affected the legitimacy not only of the Ayub government, but of the entire Pakistan Political system in Bengal,' the demand for 'regional autonomy' increased with renewed vigour.[6]

In February 1966, Mujib came up with the six-point 'Charter of Survival Programme' which demanded a democratically elected parliament, a separate currency, control over the accounts and foreign currency earned and its own paramilitary to defend East Pakistan, among other things.[7] As the demands of this programme succeeded in making a connection with the common masses of Bangladesh, Sheikh Mujib's popularity rose, forcing the Ayub Khan-led government to take action. Hence Mujib was put under detention in May 1966, and later charged with 'conspiring against the state' and 'attempting to break up the nation' in the famous *Agartala Conspiracy Case*, along with 34 other people.[8] The trial of the case that began in June 1968 became a rallying point for uniting the Bangladeshi masses against the West Pakistani establishment, leading to student unrest from November 1968 to early 1969, culminating in the unconditional withdrawal of the case and release of Sheikh Mujib, who emerged as the spokesperson of all East Pakistanis from this ordeal.

In March 1969, General Yahya dethroned General Ayub in a military coup in West Pakistan and imposed martial law again, while scheduling fresh national elections for the National Assembly in 1970.[9] The Awami League fought the election on the 'Six Points Charter,' with Mujibur Rahman calling it a 'referendum on regional autonomy on the basis of the six-point program';[10] the call for secession was still not publically declared, which Mujib thought was the last resort once the electoral option was exhausted. The Mujib-led Awami League got an absolute majority in the National Assembly by winning 167 of 313 seats, after which the demands of the programme became non-negotiable.[11] Since accepting them and transferring power to Sheikh Mujib would have meant an end to West Pakistani domination, Zulfikar Ali Bhutto, the leader of the Pakistan People's Party and the strongest politician of West Pakistan, opposed them, giving an opportunity to Yahya Khan to postpone the transfer. As Sheikh Mujib mounted pressure on the regime by total non-cooperation from East Pakistan, that became a de facto power transfer, Yahya arrived in Dacca in March 1971 for talks, but left midway through on 25 March without concluding the negotiations. The same night, the West Pakistani military began its crackdown and repression campaign against East Pakistani politicians and people, a process that culminated in the liberation of Bangladesh on 16 December 1971 after the conclusion of the third India–Pakistan war.

Change in stance: Improving relations between Pakistan and Bangladesh

After the liberation of Bangladesh, the relations between Pakistan and Bangladesh continued to remain sour as Pakistan refused to recognise Bangladesh as a sovereign nation and tried to delay its UN membership through a veto by its ally China. Other issues like an apology for the war crimes committed in 1971, repatriation of Pakistani prisoners of war, repatriation of stranded Bihari Muslims who helped the Pakistani military in the liberation war and were declared stranded Pakistani nationals later, and the division of resources between the two countries also contributed to this tension.[12]

A period of normalcy started in 1974 when Pakistan's PM Zulfiqar Ali Bhutto invited Bangladesh's premier Sheikh Mujib to the Islamic Summit to be held in Lahore and also formally recognised Bangladesh as a sovereign nation. However, the actual process of normalisation started after the assassination of *Bangabandhu* in August 1975. One may wonder at the sudden turn of events when the biggest figure of Bangladesh was assassinated by a small coterie of army majors without any popular resentment but the reasons for the same lie in the increasing unpopularity of the Mujib regime. While increasing factionalism that characterised his regime contributed to that process,[13] rising inflation, inefficient administration, failure to fulfil the heightened expectations of the people and economic suffering, combined with a high degree of nepotism, also helped discredit Sheikh Mujib. His call for a 'Second Revolution' in January 1975, which was aimed at embarking on a strong presidential system and taking control of the nation through Bangladesh Krishak Sramik Awami League (BAKSAL), the renamed Awami League, while undermining multi-party system and other institutions of the democracy, proved to be the last straw that broke the proverbial camel's back.

Subsequent governments in Bangladesh in the late 1970s and 1980s, led by Zia-ur-Rehman and Hossain Mohammad Ershad re-aligned Bangladesh's domestic and foreign policies, distancing itself from old allies like India and brought it closer to Pakistan.

Immediately after Mujibur Rahman's assassination, the regime came in to the hands of cabinet minister Khondkar Mushtaq Ahmad, who brought significant changes to Bangladesh, despite re-iterating commitment to the four principals of the constitution. Though secularism remained a guiding principal of the state, the regime started showing a tilt towards Islamisation, as the state slogan was changed from *Joy Bangla*, which appeared a bit 'Hinduised' to *Bangladesh Zindabad*.[14] Similarly, liberalisation of foreign trade, especially Jute, was done while on the foreign policy front, attempts were made to improve relations with those countries 'who had not been friends before,' resulting in increasing distance from India, Pakistan's recognition of the new regime and diplomatic recognition by Saudi Arabia and China, who had not recognised the new nation until then.[15]

The year 1975 witnessed three military coups in Bangladesh, and after the August coup, on 3 November 1975, Mukti Bahini leader Khaled Musharraf dethroned Mushtaq Ahmed. His regime proved to be short-lived as rumours of it being sponsored by India led to a counter-coup by soldiers on 7 November 1975, which killed Musharraf and established Major General Ziaur Rahman's regime. During the liberation war, Zia, as Major of the East Bengal Regiment (EBR) had declared independence of Bangladesh over radio in Chittagong and later he became a major Mukti Bahini leader, and then the Chief of Staff of Army. During his rule, Zia tried to consolidate his position by balancing the leftists and the radicals through a centrist approach, while also mobilising the support of the Islamists, not only through symbolic gestures but major concessions as well. It was during Zia's regime that the constitution was amended in 1977, doing away with secularism and declaring 'Absolute trust and faith in the Almighty Allah' as the guiding principle.[16] By formally doing away with secularism as a guiding state principle of the constitution, Zia completed the process of Islamisation started by Mushtaq Ahmed's regime (his successor General Ershad declared Islam as the state religion of Bangladesh in 1980s), while also trying to increase proximity to the Islamic world and pursue a foreign policy independent of close relations with India.[17]

The Pakistani media gave immense prominence to these developments, condemning India for its alleged counterproductive role in trying to undermine them.[18] On 5 October 1975, Pakistan and Bangladesh decided to establish diplomatic relations, and in 1976i regular flights to each other's capitals were also resumed. In December 1977, President Ziaur Rahman visited Pakistan, which was the first official visit of Bangladesh's head of state to Pakistan. During the vist, Zia and his Pakistani counterpart Fazal-Ilahi Chaudhry (General Zia ul Haq was the chief martial law administrator), agreed to increase the volume of bilateral trade, and set up a 'Joint Economic Commission' for promoting economic and technical cooperation.[19] On the home front, in an attempt to 'civilianise' his regime to increase its legitimacy and longevity, President Ziaur Rahman started preparations for holding elections and launched Bangladesh Nationalist Party (BNP) in September 1978, with himself as its chairman.[20] Zia's party won the 1979 parliamentary elections by a huge majority.

Amidst the growing closeness of Bangladesh and Pakistan, President Zia was assassinated in May 1981, and after a short period of intermediate democratic government under army supervision, in March 1982, General Ershad came to power in Bangladesh, implementing martial law which lasted until November 1986. Signalling the closeness of both countries, Pakistan's President Ziaul Haq visited Bangladesh in 1985 and paid homage to the liberation war martyrs at Bangladeshi war memorial, saying 'Your heroes are our heroes.'[21] Continuing with the previous government's policies of seeking closer ties with Pakistan and distancing Bangladesh from India, General Ershad (later President after the 1986 elections) visited Pakistan in July 1986 and, other than agreements regarding trade and cultural exchange, signed an MoU for mutual exchange of plots in each other's capital's diplomatic areas, for their respective diplomatic missions; Zia was awarded Nishan-e-Pak, the highest civilian honour of Pakistan, in 1989. The official visits of Head of State of both countries continued in years to come, though the period of Benazir-Sharif led civilian governments in Pakistan failed in giving new heights to relations between both countries. Pakistan PM Benazir Bhutto visited Bangladesh in 1992. Since despite winning elections, Benazir could only become PM after agreeing to a number of terms and conditions put on her regime by the Pakistan military, she could not take sweeping decisions on foreign policy matters[22] and as a result nothing concrete came from her Bangladesh visit. In 1995, Bangladesh PM Khalida Zia visited Pakistan and though her Pakistani counterpart Nawaz Sharif had made some efforts to solve the 'repatriation issue,' domestic pressure prevented him from going ahead with the initial efforts, with the meeting of both head of nations failing to be a landmark in this regard.[23]

All through these years, Bangladesh's relations with India were strained, and the issue of illegal migrants from Bangladesh remained a big bone of contention between both countries. While India alleged that the number of illegal entrants from Bangladesh to India ranged in the millions, Bangladesh's official position was that there were no illegal migrants from Bangladesh into India.[24] It is also the time when the northeastern states of India were witnessing a series of insurgent movement and the Indian security agencies alleged that Bangladesh served as a safe heaven and training ground for these organisations who had established bases in the country and were getting weapons and training from the Bangladeshi intelligence and anti-India elements.[25] The issues of river water sharing, border demarcation, cross-border smuggling and skirmishes between Bangladesh Rifles and the BSF also exacerbated the worsening relations. Things improved briefly in the late 1990s, especially after Sheikh Hasina's coming to power post 1996 elections.[26]

Some of the reasons for increased warmth between Pakistan and Bangladesh are Bangladesh's tilt towards Islam, which it went through in the late 1970s and 1980s (mentioned previously)[27] leading to a closeness with Islamic nations, and the alliance of Zia's Bangladesh Nationalist Party (BNP) first with the pro-Pakistan Muslim League and later with Bangladesh Jamiat-e-Islami, who had opposed the independence of Bangladesh previously.[28] In 1998, Bangladesh's PM Sheikh Hasina visited Pakistan. This trend continued during the time of Khalida Zia also, whose second term witnessed visit of Parvez Musharraf in the capacity of Pakistan's president. It was during Musharraf's period that relations between Pakistan and Bangladesh entered a new phase of cooperation.

During his visit to Bangladesh, Musharraf visited the National Memorial at *Savar* and communicated next day that 'my brothers and sisters in Pakistan share with their fellow brothers and sisters in Bangladesh profound grief over the parameters of the events of 1971,' giving indications of a willingness to cede to the long-term demand of Bangladesh of a formal apology for war crimes committed by Pakistani military during 1971.[29] It is during this time that Pakistan agreed to give Bangladeshi jute and tea duty-free access in its markets, up to 10,000 tonnes a year.[30] In 2006, Zia went to Pakistan on a state visit and signed four MoUs on trade, standardisation and quality control, agriculture and tourism, while also agreeing to finalise a Free Trade Agreement by 30 September 2006.[31] However, Musharraf failed to issue an unconditional apology for the 1971 genocide, keeping the Bangladeshis unsatisfied and attempts to normalise relations came to an end after 2008, when Musharraf had to give up power in Pakistan.[32]

After the increased efforts of Parvez Musharraf the relations between the two countries have soured again since 2009. The biggest reason for this was the establishment of the International Crimes Tribunal in 2009 by the *Awami League* government in Bangladesh led by Sheikh Hasina, to investigate and prosecute those who helped the Pakistan military in suppressing the 1971 liberation movement. Since then, a number of top leaders of *Bangladesh Jamaat-e-Islami*(BJI) including Abdul Quader Molla have been arrested and prosecuted, much to the disdain of Pakistan, who opposed these moves, arguing that the trials should not take place since the war crimes dispute between Pakistan and Bangladesh was settled long back.[33] As expected, the trials rekindled the horrific memories of 1971, and Bangladesh's relations with Pakistan took a downhill turn.

In the 2014 elections, the elimination of the clause of 'caretaker government' by the ruling Awami League led to election boycott by the main opposition BNP, with the Awami League winning the elections under the leadership of PM Sheikh Hasina.[34] The continuation of the Awami League government gave much needed stability to its policies, and while close relations with India and a crackdown on war criminals (which included a large number of leaders from BJI, the alliance partner of main opposition BNP) continued, and relations with Pakistan continued to worsen. This was exacerbated by the allegations of espionage and support for terrorist activities by both countries on each other's diplomats since 2015.[35] The celebration of Genocide Day on 25 March by Bangladesh, with the country's Parliament passing a resolution declaring this date as Genocide Day has further irked the Pakistani establishment.[36]

While Bangladesh's relations with Pakistan worsened, its relations with India kept on improving. The June 2015 visit of Indian PM Narendra Modi's to Dhaka and signing of major agreements, including finalisation of the Land-Boundary agreement, the communication gateway between Bangladesh and Tripura and Indian assistance in construction of Bangabandhu Bridge over Padma (Ganga) to increase connectivity are all significant indicators of this trend.[37]

Trade relations between Bangladesh and Pakistan and the China Pakistan economic corridor: Opportunity or closure

With the past efforts facing severe limitations in taking the bilateral relations of Bangladesh and Pakistan to new heights, economic cooperation and trade seem to be the only other possible way to mend relations. However, despite observing a constant rise in preceding years, the scale of trade between Pakistan and Bangladesh stood at around $340 million in 2009–2010, which was described by the Deputy High Commissioner of Bangladesh, Ruhul Alam Siddique as 'negligible when taking into account the combined population' (of both countries).[38] Further, the trade balance is tilted in favour of Pakistan, which exports more to Bangladesh and imports less. Textiles and energy sectors are two priority sectors where Bangladesh hopes to attract investment from Pakistan, and steps like import of pharmaceuticals and tea have been suggested by Bangladesh officials and ministers to their counterparts in Pakistan to minimise the imbalance of foreign trade.[39] Bangladesh PM Sheikh Hasina has been urging Pakistan to give each other zero-tariff access under the early harvest programme, while also asking Pakistani businessmen to invest in the IT, telecommunications and pharmaceuticals sectors in Bangladesh.[40] However, despite all these efforts of giving priority to trade and having started negotiations for finalising of a Free Trade Agreement (FTA) between both countries way back in 2003, the agreement is yet to come into effect.[41] As of now, the major export partners of Bangladesh are EU and the USA (Bangladesh enjoys duty-free exports to these countries due to its Least Development Country status), with its major exports being low cost, labour intensive products, especially textiles.[42] The table below shows the state of trade between Pakistan and Bangladesh; the total trade between both countries stood at a little more than 550 million US $.[43] To compare it with other neighbours, Bangladesh–India trade stood at more than 6500 US $ in 2015–2016.[44] While the current situation of Bangladesh–Pakistan trade could not be considered as very encouraging, things are expected to get complicated after Pakistan's commitment to the 'China Pakistan Economic Corridor' (CPEC).

The CPEC is a US $ 46 million mega project of China aimed to connect Gwadar port in Pakistan's Balochistan to the trading hub of Kashgar in the Chinese province of Xinjiang by land through the

Table 17.1 Bangladesh–Pakistan Bilateral Trade Statistics (Value in million US$)

Year	*Export*	*Import*	*Trade Ratio*
2009–2010	77.67	323.7	1:4.16
2010–2011	86.79	669.3	1:7.71
2011–2012	73.21	517.1	1:7.06
2012–2013	68.70	488.4	1:7.10
2013–2014	56.04	530.53	1:9.47
2014–2015	57.57	481.82	1:8.39
2015–2016	47.07	507.468	1:10.78

Source: Report of Dhaka Chamber of Commerce and Industries, 2016

China occupied Kashmir and Gilgit-Baltistan.[45] This includes not just highways, but railway lines, oil pipelines and power stations as well, and the official website of the project, run by the Pakistani government, lists all such projects, with the current status of their completion.[46] It is a flagship project of the extremely ambitious 'One Belt One Road,' a transcontinental infrastructure project of China, aimed at making it 'into the logistics hub of Eurasia and, potentially, the centre of the global economy,' which is why some view is as the new great game.[47] The corridor is likely to act as the 'pivot to China's economic and energy security,' as by directly connecting China to Middle East via Gwadar, it would reduce its dependence on the contested south China sea and the Indian ocean, while also reducing its maritime transportation distance from approximately 12 thousand kilometresto approximately three thousand kilometres, by-passing the current trade route via Straits of Malacca.[48]

Because of having such high stakes in the project, China has been investing in the project since as early as 2001–2002, when the construction of the port at Gwader in Baluchistan was started with its help.[49] Apart from the linkage between Kashger and Gwadar and the up-grade of Gwadar port, the project aims to widen the existing Karakoram highway connecting both countries, while also modernising the Peshawar-Karachi railway line.[50] The project is estimated to boost Pakistan's GDP by 15 per cent in the initial phase, while also improving its dismal energy scenario, giving much needed economic fillip to the country; in long-term, Pakistan is likely to gain heavily as a significant transit centre for world trade.[51]

By getting access to the markets of the Central Asian region and the Middle East along with a physical presence in this region, the project is aimed at not just economic, but also geopolitical domination of the whole area.[52] These geopolitical and strategic advantages that China and Pakistan are likely to get through CPEC pose severe challenges to India,[53] surrounding not just India but other South Asian nations in an arc comprising land-routes between Pakistan and China, with the 'string of pearls' of Chinese ports or naval presence in Indian Ocean completing the circle.[54] It is due to these regions that India primarily views this corridor as a geostrategic threat and has been raising serious concerns about it.[55]

With the transportation of a Chinese cargo to Gwadar via road, the CPEC became partly operational in November 2016, but clouds of uncertainty still loom large as since 2014, more than three dozen Pakistanis working on the CPEC projects have been killed by the Baloch militants, who have targeted the Chinese as well.[56] Pakistani establishment and the media has been squarely putting the blame for the same on subversive activities by India. The issue has been further complicated as the British Parliament has passed a resolution on CPEC's illegality, since it passes through the disputed territory of Pak-Occupied Kashmir.

Some analysts are hopeful that CPEC will act as an opportunity to boost trade ties between Pakistan and Bangladesh. The current dismal state of affairs on this front leaves huge possibilities for the future, and if the CPEC boosts slowing economy of Pakistan, it could create a spill over impact on neighbouring economies as well. However, given the lack of any significant initiative on the part of Pakistan or China to bring Bangladesh on board forces one to keep their expectations low.

There is another possibility that the corridor may further worsen Pakistan's relations with neighbouring countries, including Bangladesh. With Pakistan becoming a direct maritime trade centre for China through this project, China's need to engage with Bangladesh for maritime trade through its ports is expected to decrease. Further, the prominence given by Pakistan to CPEC and lack of similar interest in furthering ties or improving relations with other neighbours, not to mention its counterproductive role in forums like SAARC shows that Pakistan is greatly invested mainly towards the north (i.e. China) and the west, at the cost of east or south.[57] Therefore, an alternative grouping in SAARC in the form of Bangladesh-Bhutan-India-Nepal (BBIN) group is taking place, and steps like the Motor Vehicles Agreement (MVA) and electricity grid connectivity, along with other forms of cooperation indicate that in future, this grouping is expected to be the axis of SAARC. In this scenario, with both nations appearing to head in different directions, the CPEC is expected to increase the gulf that exists today between Pakistan and Bangladesh.

Notes

1 Syed Sharifuddin Pirzada (ed.), *Foundations of Pakistan* (Karachi: National Publishing House, 1970), Vol. II, p. 341.
2 Hasan Zaheer, *The Separation of East Pakistan: The Rise and Realization of Bengali Muslim Nationalism* (Dhaka: UPL, 1998), pp. 21–27.
3 Maniruzzaman Talukder, *The Bangladesh Revolution and Its Aftermath* (Dhaka: Bangladesh Books, 1980), p. 30.
4 Vidya Shankar Aiyer, "Bangladesh," in P.R. Chari (ed.), *Perspectives on National Security in South Asia: In Search of a New Paradigm*(New Delhi: Manohar, 1999), p. 35.
5 *Ibid.*, p. 36.
6 Mizanur Rahman Shelley, *Emergence of a New Nation in a Multi-Polar World: Bangladesh* (Dacca: UPL, 1979), p. 37.
7 Sheikh Mujibur Rahman, *Six-Point Formula: Our Right to Live* (Dhaka: East Pakistan Awami League, 1966).
8 Syed Badrul Ahsan, "Agartala Conspiracy Case and Its Ramifications," www.bongobondhuinfocenter.org/political-life/agartala-conspiracy-case-and-its-ramifications.
9 Yahya Khan hoped that no party would be able to get a complete majority in the National Assembly, and hence throw a challenge to his authority, while conducting elections would increase the legitimacy of his regime.
10 *Bangladesh Documents* (New Delhi: Ministry of External Affairs, not dated), p. 101.
11 Before elections, Mujibur Rahman had given indications to Yahya Khan that the six points programme was negotiable, but after elections he took a rigid stand, see Rounaq Jahan, *Bangladesh Politics: Problems and Issues* (Dacca: UPL, 1980), p. 35 and p. 50.
12 For a detailed treatment of issues like repatriation, asset division and war crimes apology, see Sanam Noor, "Outstanding Issues Between India and Pakistan," *Pakistan Horizon*, Vol. 58, No. 1 (January, 2005), pp. 47–60.
13 The main factions of the Bangladesh's establishment, the military, the bureaucracy and the Awami League party would all compete with each other for a greater share and say in allotment of resources and decision-making, thus giving more power to Sheikh Mujib to adjudicate between them, thus leading to greater factionalism. This process has been termed Factionalism's vicious cycle by Rounaq Jahan. For more, see Rounaq Jahan, "Bangladesh in 1973: Management of Factional Politics," *Asian Survey* (February, 1974).

14 Abu Nasar Saied Ahmed, *Fundamentalism in Bangladesh: Its Impact on India* (New Delhi: Akansha Publishing House and OKDISCD, 2008), p. 101.
15 Rounaq Jahan, *Bangladesh Politics: Problems and Issues*, *op. cit.*, p. 138.
16 Kirsten Westergarrd, *State and Rural Society in Bangladesh* (London: Curzon Press, 1986), p. 92.
17 Aminur Rahim, *Politics and National Formation in Bangladesh* (Dhaka: UPL, 1997), pp. 246.
18 For a detailed treatment of the increasing nearness between Pakistan and Bangladesh, based upon coverage in Pakistani media, and its treatment, see Farzana Shakoor, "Pakistan–Bangladesh Relations: A Survey", *Pakistan Horizon*, Vol. 42, No. 2 (1989), pp. 109–133.
19 See, C. M. Shafi Sami, "Pakistan–Bangladesh Relations in the Changing International Environment", *Pakistan Horizon*, Vol. 44, No. 4 (1991), pp. 23–29.
20 Before that in May 1977, Ziaur Rahman had held a 'National Referendum,' winning massive support for continuing as president, amidst allegations of foul play. Later, he contested presidential elections in June 1978, as a candidate of Jatiyabandi Front (JF), which consisted Jatiyabandi Gonotantrik Dal (JAGODAL), floated by Zia in February 1978, NAP (B) of Maulana Bhashani, UPP and the Muslim League. The alliance partners of the new party opposed Indian-Soviet influence in the region, favoured Sino-American in its place and propagated the cause of 'Bangladeshi Nationalism.' The victory in elections emboldened Zia, who later dissolved the JF and formed a new party, BNP. It should be noted that it is around this time that the US establishment and media were increasingly raising questions about Human Rights' violations in Bangladesh, and the elections were meant to ease that pressure as well.
21 "PM to Visit Pakistan to Attend D-8 Summit", www.thedailystar.net/news-details-256936, published on 10 November 2012.
22 For the problems faced by Benazir Bhutto due to opposition of military generals, see Benazir Bhutto, *Daughter of the Destiny* (Noida: Harper Collins, 2009).
23 Ashish Shukla, "Pakistan–Bangladesh Relations", *Himalayan and Central Asian Studies*, Vol. 19, Nos. 1–2 (January–June, 2015), p. 224.
24 Late 1970s and the 1980s also witnessed an aggressive anti-migrant movement in Assam (leading to anti-centre sentiments) with incidences of violent attacks on alleged Bangladeshis happening regularly, the Nelli Massacre of 1983 being the most infamous incidence. For a detailed treatment of this issue, see Sanjoy Hazarika, *Rites of Passage: Border Crossings, Imagined Homelands, India's East and Bangladesh* (New Delhi: Penguin, 2000).
25 For more on this, see Dipankar Sengupta and Sudhir Kumar Singh (eds.), *Insurgency in North-East India: The Role of Bangladesh*(New Delhi: Spandan, 2004).
26 Some call this the period of increasing cooperation, for more on this, see Vidya Shankar Aiyar, "Bangladesh", in P.R. Chari (ed.), *op. cited*. pp. 59–60.

27 For a more detailed treatment of this, see Abu Nasar Saied Ahmed, *op. cited*.
28 For more on the strengthening of radical Islamic elements in Bangladesh since the late 1970s, and their role in terrorist activities within and outside Bangladesh, see Hiranmay Karlekar, *Bangladesh: The Next Afghanistan* (New Delhi: Sage, 2005).
29 "PM to Visit Pakistan to Attend D-8 Summit", *op. cited*.
30 Anand Kumar, "Pakistan Bangladesh Free Trade Agreement", www.ipcs.org/article/bangladesh/pakistan-bangladesh-free-trade-agreement-1237.html, published on 8 December 2003, accessed on December 2016.
31 Sreeradha Dutta, "Khalida's Pakistan Visit Shifts Focus to Economic Synergy", www.idsa.in/idsastrategiccomments/KhaledasPakistanvisitShiftsFocustoEconomicSynergy_SDatta_270206, published 27 February 2006, accessed on December 2016.
32 All through this time, Pakistan's stance on problematic demands of Bangladesh, like the apology issue, was dominated by two approaches. The first one, which was more dominant, was to rely on conspiracy theories and blame everything on India, denying agency to Bangladesh. The other one was a hesitant liberal approach, which acknowledged the problem yet stopped short of doing what was needed. It could be understood from the position of noted Pakistani Urdu Poet Faiz Ahmed Faiz. Faiz was persecuted for his progressive views in Pakistan and had good following in East Pakistan, yet he hesitated in calling the West Pakistan's military actions in East Pakistan genocide, and condemning the West Pakistani establishment for the 1971 war crimes in strictest terms. Further, domestic pressure from various quarters withheld Pakistani establishment, especially the civilian governments to take any decision on the repatriation and apology issues, while the military circles have never been very enthusiastic about them, even refusing to acknowledge them.
33 The National Assembly of Pakistan passed a resolution condemning the execution of Molla. For more on this see, Ashish Shukla, *op. cited*.
34 Since the resuming of democratic government in the 1990s, elections in Bangladesh were being held under a caretaker government to ensure free and fair elections, after the incumbent government's resignation once its turn was over. This arrangement was institutionalised in 1996, after pressure from the Awami League led opposition. However, during 2007–2008, the military led caretaker government extended its tenure and continued to operate, conduction elections only after huge international pressure and opposition. After this, the Awami League led government declared to remove the system in 2011, which attracted strong opposition from other parties. See, "Bangladesh Ends Caretaker Government Arrangement", www.bbc.com/news/world-south-asia-13973576, accessed on December 2016.
35 Mateen Haider, "Pakistan–Bangladesh 'Spy' Row: Expelled Diplomat Leaves for Dhaka", www.dawn.com/news/1231165, updated 7 January 2016.
36 Anam Zakaria, "By Marking Genocide Day, Bangladesh Seeks to Remember What Pakistan Wants to Forget", https://scroll.in/article/832420/

by-marking-genocide-day-bangladesh-seeks-to-remember-what-pakistan-wants-to-forget.

37 Pinak Ranjan Chakravarty, "Bangladesh–India Ties: Pragmatic Transformation", Debate: India Bangladesh Relations: Scaling Newer Heights, *Indian Foreign Affairs Journal*, pp. 211–218.

38 Farhan Zaheer, "Dhaka Offers Pakistani Businessmen Multiple Visas", https://tribune.com.pk/story/55446/dhaka-offers-pakistani-businessmen-multiple-visas/.

39 Irfan Ahmed and Javeria Shabbir, "The Changing Face of Pakistan's Economic Relations with India and Bangladesh: Prospects and Challenges", *The Round Table*,Vol. 103, No. 3 (2014), pp. 311–321.

40 "PM for Reducing Trade Imbalance with Pakistan", https://defence.pk/pdf/threads/bangladesh-pakistan-economic-relations.31088/.

41 Asia Regional Integration Centre, https://aric.adb.org/fta/pakistan-bangladesh-free-trade-agreement.

42 For a detailed analysis of dominant trends in Bangladesh's foreign trade and its limitations, see Jinhwan Oh and Rashedur Rahman Sardar, "Gravity Matters: International Trade of Bangladesh", *Review of Urban and Regional Development Studies*, Vol. 25, No. 1 (March, 2013), pp. 34–46.

43 Report by Dhaka Chamber of Commerce and Industries Research Department, www.dhakachamber.com/Bilateral/Pakistan-Bangladesh%20Bilateral%20Trade%20Statistics.pdf.

44 See Rakesh Dubbudu, "Value of Trade with Pakistan lower than that with Nepal, Bangladesh and Sri Lanka", https://factly.in/value-trade-pakistan-lower-nepal-bangladesh-sri-lanka/.

45 Sudha Ramachandran, "CPEC Takes a Step Forward as Violence Surges in Balochistan", www.atimes.com/cpec-takes-step-forward-violence-surges-balochistan/?platform=hootsuite, accessed on December 2016.

46 See the official website, http://cpec.gov.pk.

47 Opinion, "The China Pakistan Economic Corridor is the Great Game of this Century", www.google.co.in/amp/www.hindustantimes.com/editorials/cpec-is-the-gr eat-game-of-this-century/story-S3tg8DNawU9HYNU5WCoK_amp.html.

48 Akber Ali, "China-Pakistan Economic Corridor: Prospects and Challenges for Regional Integration", *Arts and Social Sciences Journal*, Vol. 7, No. 4 (2016), pp. 1–5.

49 Jafar Riaz Kataria and Anum Naveed, "Pakistan-China Social and Economic Relations", *South Asian Studies*, Vol. 29, No. 2 (July–December, 2014), pp. 395–410, pp. 405–406.

50 Massarrat Abid and Ayesha Ashfaq, "CPEC: Challenges and Opportunities for Pakistan", *Pakistan Vision*, Vol. 16, No. 2 (2015), pp. 142–163, p. 149.

51 *Ibid.*, pp. 157–158.

52 Saima Perveen and Jehanzeb Khalil, "Gwadar-Kashgar Economic Corridor: Challenges and Imperatives for Pakistan and China" *Journal of Political Studies*, Vol. 22, No. 2 (2015), 351–366.

53 Ashok Malik, "Why Is the China-Pakistan Economic Corridor such a Challenge to India", *The Economic Times*, November 17, 2016.

54 Haider Talat, "Five Ways India Is Going to be Affected When CPEC Changes World Trade", www.thequint.com, published and accessed on 23 March 2017.
55 Pakistan acknowledges the dominance of this security perspective approach of India, in its dealings with the CPEC; for more, see Ijaz Khan, Shamaila Farooq and Saima Gull,"China-Pakistan Economic Corridor: News Discourse Analysis of Indian Print Media", *Journal of Political Studies*, Vol. 23, No. 1 (2016), 233–252.
56 Sudha Ramachandran, *op. cited*.
57 Pinak Ranjan Chakravarty, *op. cited*, pp. 213–214.

Index

Note: Page numbers in bold indicate table on the corresponding pages.